1.75

Essay Index

P9-CKX-325

In Search of Wonder

other books by damon knight

Novels

A FOR ANYTHING
BEYOND THE BARRIER
HELL'S PAVEMENT
THE OTHER FOOT
THE RITHIAN TERROR

Collections

FAR OUT
IN DEEP
OFF CENTER
TURNING ON
THREE NOVELS

Anthologies

BEYOND TOMORROW
A CENTURY OF GREAT SHORT SCIENCE FICTION NOVELS
A CENTURY OF SCIENCE FICTION
CITIES OF WONDER
THE DARK SIDE
FIRST FLIGHT
NEBULA AWARD STORIES 1965
ORBIT, Volumes 1 and 2
THE SHAPE OF THINGS
TOMORROW X 4
WORLDS TO COME

Translations

ASHES, ASHES, by René Barjavel
13 FRENCH SCIENCE FICTION STORIES

Essay Index

IN
SEARCH
OF
WONDER

essays on modern science fiction

by damon knight

Introduction by Anthony Boucher

Illustrated by J. L. Patterson

Revised and Enlarged

ADVENT:PUBLISHERS

Chicago: 1967

To CHET and LARRY
For old times' sake

Library of Congress Catalog Card Number 67-4260

SECOND EDITION, March 1967
SECOND CLOTH PRINTING, March 1968
FIRST PAPERBACK PRINTING, March 1968
THIRD CLOTH PRINTING, December 1968

Contents

Introduction, by Anthony Boucher   vi
Author's Notes   xii
1. Critics   1
2. The Classics   9
3. Chuckleheads   22
4. Campbell and his Decade   34
5. Cosmic Jerrybuilder: A. E. van Vogt   47
6. Half-Bad Writers   63
7. One Sane Man: Robert A. Heinlein   76
8. Asimov and Empire   90
9. More Chuckleheads   95
10. When I Was In Kneepants: Ray Bradbury   108
11. The Vorpal Pen: Theodore Sturgeon   114
12. Anthologies   117
13. Half Loaves   134
14. Genius to Order: Kuttner and Moore   139
15. Kornbluth and the Silver Lexicon   146
16. The Jagged Blade: James Blish   150
17. Overalls on Parnassus: Fletcher Pratt   158
18. Microcosmic Moskowitz   160
19. Amphibians   164
20. New Stars   177
21. Curiosa   206
22. B-R-R-R!   220
23. Decadents   228
24. Britons   241
25. Pitfalls and Dead Ends   248
26. Symbolism   265
27. What Next?   277
Acknowledgments   285
Bibliography   287
Index   294

INTRODUCTION TO THE FIRST EDITION

THERE ARE FEW more misused words than *criticism.*
In one false sense, it's used to mean restrictedly *adverse* (what
authors call *destructive*) criticism, as if a favorable (*constructive*)
evaluation could not be the result of critical analysis.
And in another misprision, it's used to mean *reviewing.*
Reviewing is a lesser art, with a more immediate functional
purpose. The reviewer's objective is to express his reactions to
a work in such a way that the readers of a given periodical will
know whether or not they want to read it. The critic attempts
to measure the work by more lasting and more nearly absolute
standards, to determine its place, not for the reader of the
moment, but for the cultivated mind viewing the entire art of
which this work forms a segment.
All of the rest of us—Henry Bott,* Groff Conklin, August Derleth, Floyd C. Gale, Villiers Gerson, H. H. Holmes, J. Francis
McComas, P. Schuyler Miller, Hans Stefan Santesson—are pri-
marily reviewers; damon knight, in most of his published assess-
ments of science fiction and particularly in those gathered here,
is a critic.
Professional criticism is extremely rare in the science fiction
field. God knows criticism of science fiction has been more than
plentiful outside our orbit; but the critical contributions of self-
appointed scholars and intellectuals have been marked by equal
portions of distaste for science fiction and complete ignorance
of it. (It's worth noting that one of America's most esteemed
journals of opinion recently asked Ward Moore to contribute a
critique of science fiction—then canceled the assignment when
an outline showed that the piece would be both informed and
favorable.)

*Forgive me, Dr. Asimov; these names are arranged alphabetically.

INTRODUCTION

Within science fiction, criticism—and frequently of a high order
—has appeared almost solely in amateur publications; indeed the
wealth of material, critical, bibliographical and biographical, that
has appeared in fanzines, from *Fantasy Commentator* to *Inside*,
is such that a university library with a complete fanzine file would
be the Mecca of Ph.D. candidates in the twenty-first century.

But damon knight* has introduced criticism into professional
magazines—partly because he is equipped with the background
and intellect to do so (but then so are most of the reviewers
mentioned above), and largely because his magazine outlets,
if not always the most affluent or the most widely circulated,
have given him free rein and virtually unlimited space.

Most of us have free rein to the extent of being allowed to say
precisely what we think (though at least one of my reviewing colleagues has been subject to arbitrary editorial revision of his
expressed opinions), but we're very tightly restricted in the
matter of space, so that we are forced to present a persuasive
(we hope) statement rather than a closely reasoned analysis.

With all due respect to E. E. Smith, Ph.D., who has expended
a good deal of serious research in statistically tabulating the
percentage of verdicts in which various reviewers and critics are
"right" or "wrong," both reviewing and criticism are matters of
opinion. There is no ultimate, absolute Esthetic Truth; and if you
attempt to judge the rightness or wrongness of others, you simply
set yourself up as a reviewer of reviewers, a critic of critics,
and just as fallible as any of them.

Nevertheless, you tend to rate a man according to the extent
to which his opinions agree with yours; but knight, by virtue of the
analytical, essayistic treatment made possible by his freedom in
space, has an all but unique quality: You can disagree completely
on the book in question, and still admire (and even to some extent
agree with) the critique.

Personally I find myself agreeing with knight to an embarrassingly suspicious degree.** But when I do sharply disagree, I always recognize that knight has read the same book (some reviewers seem to have read a wholly different collection of words
printed and bound under the same title) . . . and that a rereading

*Every time I type that name I have to reassure myself that I have *not* been
reincarnated as a cockroach.

**In this volume knight covers 81 books, of which I've read and reviewed 75.
I'm in unquestioning agreement on 56 of these and have minor reservations—
largely matters of emphasis—on 16, leaving only 3 items for real controversy.

might possibly convert me to his viewpoint. A striking example is Curme Gray's *Murder in Millennium VI,* which originally struck me, in 1952, as one of the most unprintable abortions I had ever read. The knight critique in this volume not only brought the entire book vividly back, after four years, to a mind which thought it had mercifully forgotten the whole thing; it also persuaded me that the novel does indeed possess one rare virtue which I had completely overlooked, and I now find myself tempted to go back and reread the book with knight's analysis in mind.

Successively or simultaneously, damon knight has been a science fiction fan, even an actifan (the uninitiated will have no trouble with that fannish word if they'll simply pronounce it aloud), an editor, a critic and a creative writer.

Science fiction readers are used to the phenomenon of the writer-editor; in this field, unlike most others, almost every successful editor is or has been a successful writer. But the writer-critic is more controversial, if by no means uncommon. The question of whether an arbiter should also be a creator is, as I've written elsewhere,* a tough one: "Either way, the victim of an unfavorable review can make what seems a legitimate complaint. If the reviewer is not a writer, what does he know about the field? He's probably soured and frustrated because he can't sell, and takes out his spite on those who do. If he is a writer, he's jealous of competition, he can understand only his own kind of story, and who's he to talk anyway—look at his own stuff!"

In knight's case, at least, the writer-critic duality seems to work out admirably. There's plentiful evidence in this volume that he loves competition and that he understands intimately many types of stories not remotely related to his own work. And if you "look at his own stuff," you can only be dazed and delighted by such virtually perfect short stories as "To Serve Man" (*Galaxy,* November, 1950) and "Not With a Bang" (*F&SF,* Winter-Spring, 1950) and such an imperfect but brilliantly stimulating novel as *Hell's Pavement* (Lion, 1955).

(*Pavement,* incidentally, is knight's only previous book. The present volume marks an unprecedented event: the publication of a science fiction author's collected critiques before his collected short stories. The latter collection is long overdue—*publishers please note!*)

And the practice of the critical profession has developed in knight-the-writer an unusual and valuable quality of self-criticism. He is able, as is almost no other professional writer of fiction, to

The Mystery Writers Handbook, by the Mystery Writers of America (Harpers, 1956).

stand apart from his completed work and look at it objectively.
While an editor is still brooding over what suggestions to make
for salvaging a flawed but potentially fine knight story, he'll re-
ceive an unsuggested rewrite which solves all the problems.
Knight can be so dazzlingly individual as either critic or writer
(he didn't do badly as an editor either; possibly the most tragic
instance of stupidity in the whole misbegotten science fiction
"boom" was the almost contraceptive killing off of *Worlds Beyond*)
that writers and readers alike have been highly curious as to what
he is like as a person.

The science fiction universe teems with flamboyant outsize
extroverts; surely a man who, in print, manages to stand out as
a personality in such company must be something spectacular in
the flesh.

So came the Thirteenth World Science Fiction Convention in
Cleveland in 1955 (that happiest, warmest, most delightful of
Conventions!), and damon knight, who had been out of direct contact with fandom since before his rise to professional prominence,
decided to attend.

The fans at the convention got ready to bug their eyes; the professionals checked the condition of their body armor. (I don't
know why knight has such an undeserved reputation as a hostile
critic; this volume contains far more praise than attack, and if
the debunking of Austin Hall is as devastating a hatchet job as I've
read, the section on Heinlein is a sheer love letter.)

And damon knight appeared . . . and suddenly one understood the
reason for those minuscule initials. One could not possibly write,
with conventional capitalization, "And Damon Knight appeared";
it would be overstating the facts.

A batch of editors and writers staged for the Convention a
satiric skit on the past, present and future of science fiction—
written, memorized, rehearsed, costumed, lighted and presented
in something under 24 hours. And while we were writing it, there
I was in a room with three men who could out-talk me. This is
not a common event, even in science fiction circles; but Fritz
Leiber has trained Shakespearean articulation and projection,
Randall Garrett has an improbable and even indecent amount of
the Effervescence of Youth, and Sam Moskowitz has a voice which
is obviously the Creator's working model for the Last Trump.

I know when I'm licked. I stretched out on a bed and settled
down to the pleasant task of contemplating fellow-collaborators
Mildred Clingerman and Judith Merril, while creative contention
thundered around me.

And off in a corner of the hotel room, damon knight found a

typewriter, set it up on a desk, found paper and carbon, and wrote the skit.

All of the rest of us had starring parts and chewed them down to the last scrap of hamfat; knight did not appear in it.

I should like to know damon knight well; I hope in time I shall do so (and possibly even discover the existence of Damon Knight). But meanwhile I think of him as the man at the typewriter, quietly getting something done while the rest of us make a great foofaraw about it.

This book is, I think, another example of knight's getting something done.

What kind of book is it? Well, it's easier to start off by defining a few things which it is not.

It is not an earnest endeavor to reach the ultimate implications of science fiction as a form and its place in our culture; if you want that, see Reginald Bretnor's *Modern Science Fiction: Its Meaning and Its Future* (Coward-McCann, 1953).

It is not, except inadvertently, a compendium of useful how-to notes for the writer of science fiction; see L. Sprague de Camp's *Science Fiction Handbook* (Hermitage, 1953).

It is not a gently persuasive lure for the reader who knows nothing of science fiction; see Basil Davenport's *Inquiry Into Science Fiction* (Longmans, Green, 1955).

It is not even, to be strictly accurate, quite a book, any more than loosely assembled series of shorts and novelets, as knight points out, are really novels.

It is a collection of critical notes and essays managing to cover, among them, most of the principal trends and individual authors of modern science fiction — in book form, I should add, since the magazines are considered only indirectly as sources of book material.

It is addressed—though the wit and clarity of the writing should make it readable to anyone—specifically to the regular reader of science fiction . . . a marked advantage in that the writer of critiques for the general literary public must spend much of his time in uncomfortable defensive or evangelistic postures. (And too, among ourselves one can attack faults in science fiction without being misinterpreted as attacking the genre itself.)

And (this is the "getting something done") it provides conclusive proof that, to quote knight's introductory credo, "science fiction is a field of literature worth taking seriously, and that ordinary critical standards can be meaningfully applied to it."

Some of us have been going around, aggressively or piteously, arguing that look, science fiction *is* a part of literature. Others have disregarded the problem; and most astoundingly, John W. Campbell, Jr.—who of all people should know better—has recently* asserted flatly that science fiction is *not* literature and cannot be assessed by normal literary standards or critical values.

Meanwhile damon knight has simply gone ahead, taken science fiction seriously as a field of literature, applied ordinary critical standards, and made the result meaningful.

It's as easy as that if you settle down to your typewriter in a corner away from the foofaraw.

ANTHONY BOUCHER

Berkeley, California

---

* "Science Fiction and the Opinion of the Universe," *Saturday Review*, May 12, 1956.

AUTHOR'S NOTES

To the First Edition:

THIS BOOK CONSISTS mainly of critical pieces written from 1952 to the present. I owe very grateful thanks to people like Jim Blish who said there ought to be a book, as well as to editors Lester del Rey and Robert W. Lowndes, who between them gave me my start in this field, and to Earl Kemp and Sidney Coleman for many invaluable suggestions.

These short essays make up an informal record of the period that will be known to science fiction historians as the Boom of 1950-1955. It was a period that produced some of the best science fiction ever to appear in hard covers, along with a fascinating flood of the worst science fiction ever conceived by the mind of man. Bad and good, I've taken it all for what enjoyment or moral could be squeezed out of it. The flood has now receded, but if science fiction runs true to its cyclical pattern, there'll be another about 1960. And, I trust, I'll be on hand with the same net and gun.

To the Second Edition:

THE FLOOD CAME, but I was not there. I resigned as *F&SF*'s book reviewer in 1960 because the then editor, now my agent and a good friend, declined to publish one of my reviews as written. (The review in question appears here for the first time, on p. 104.) Afterward I had a couple of invitations to review s.f. books for magazines, but there seemed to be good reasons why, having stopped, I should not start again.

This new edition contains a few things written especially for it, along with the reviews I wrote between 1956 and 1960, and a mass of material that was omitted from the first edition for one reason or another. I have taken the opportunity to try to correct the typographical errors, dropped lines and other blemishes of the original edition. I have corrected some errors of my own (such as writing "Isaac" when I meant "Jacob") and have made some minor revisions for style. With one or two exceptions, I've made no effort to update the book; topical references, like the one about L. Ron Hubbard's disappearance into the Middle West, remain as written.

DAMON KNIGHT

Milford, Pennsylvania

In Search of Wonder

1. CRITICS

THIS CREDO APPEARED in my first review column for Lester del Rey's *Science Fiction Adventures* (November, 1952); I have stuck to it ever since, and I think it introduces this book as well as the column.

Some readers (not to mention writers, editors and publishers) may be unpleasantly surprised by the pugnacious tone of the reviews that follow. I won't apologize—not very often, anyhow—but I will explain. As a critic, I operate under certain basic assumptions, all eccentric, to wit:

1. That the term "science fiction" is a misnomer, that trying to get two enthusiasts to agree on a definition of it leads only to bloody knuckles; that better labels have been devised (Heinlein's suggestion, "speculative fiction," is the best, I think), but that we're stuck with this one; and that it will do us no particular harm if we remember that, like "The Saturday Evening Post," it means what we point to when we say it.

2. That a publisher's jacket blurb and a book review are two different things, and should be composed accordingly.

3. That science fiction is a field of literature worth taking seriously, and that ordinary critical standards can be meaningfully applied to it: e.g., originality, sincerity, style, construction, logic, coherence, sanity, garden-variety grammar.

4. That a bad book hurts science fiction more than ten bad notices.

The publishers disclaim all responsibility; angry readers please apply to me.

Nowadays, we like to think, everybody loves science-fantasy, from Artie Shaw to Clifton Fadiman; but occasionally we are re-

minded that not all the world's respectable literary parlors are
yet open to us. Such a reminder is Arthur Koestler's short essay,
"The Boredom of Fantasy," in the August, 1953 issue of *Harper's
Bazaar*.
After a burst of good-humored laughter at the expense of one of
A. E. van Vogt's wilder novels (the hero of which Koestler identifies as "Robert Headrock"), Koestler admits that he is partially
addicted to the stuff himself, deals briefly and penetratingly with
the history of the field, and then gets down to his major point: He
likes it, but it isn't art.

> . . . Swift's *Gulliver*, Huxley's *Brave New World*, Orwell's *Nine-
> teen Eighty-Four* are great works of literature because in them
> the oddities of alien worlds serve merely as a background or pre-
> text for a social message. In other words, they are literature
> precisely to the extent to which they are not science fiction, to
> which they are works of disciplined imagination and not of un-
> limited fantasy.

This criticism is less than we might have expected from one of
the most brilliant of all living novelists. All that Koestler says
here is inarguably true, and perfectly irrelevant.
"A similar rule holds for the detective story," he goes on.
Just so; and for the historical story, the realistic story, the story
of protest, the story of ideas, the story of manners, the story of
adventure; in short, for all fiction. Science-fantasy is a form:
what matters is what you put into it.
Again: "This is why the historical novel is practically dead
today. The life of an Egyptian civil servant under the Eighteenth
Dynasty, or even of a soldier in Cromwell's army, is only imaginable to us in a dim outline; we are unable to identify ourselves
with the strange figure moving in a strange world." Koestler
should have added, "unless the writer has genius"; in science-
fantasy as elsewhere, this is not a true statement of a limitation
but only of an obstacle. We have not been to Mars; neither have
we been to Elsinore, nor to ancient Rome, nor, most of us, to a
Russian prison, to a penthouse, to a sweatshop, to a DP camp.
This obstacle was brilliantly surmounted in Koestler's own first
novel, *The Gladiators*; and what is *Darkness at Noon* but a mas-
terful exercise in speculative imagination?
If science-fantasy has to date failed to produce much great
literature, don't blame the writers who have worked in the field;
blame those who, out of snobbery, haven't.

This question of the respectability of science fiction has vexed a lot of the people who read it. Thousands, I suppose, have torn off the covers of science fiction magazines before taking them home, and many must have felt guiltily doubtful about the contents even then. Science fiction has long had, still has a dubious aura: we read it for a certain special kind of satisfaction, but we are frequently aware that according to ordinary standards of taste we ought not to like it.

Dozens of scholarly articles have been written to demonstrate the special nature of science fiction ("the *genre*") and why it really is (or isn't) a scare literature for adolescents. Most of these have been produced by people with only a superficial acquaintance with the field, but even knowledgeable critics often add to the confusion.

To see what may be at the bottom of all this argument, suppose we try asking two questions:

1. What is reputable fiction?
2. What is special about science fiction?

Reputable fiction—meaning fiction that the critics and the librarians like—has many distinguishing characteristics, but two of them appear to be central: It is fiction laid against familiar backgrounds (familiar, at least, to readers of reputable fiction—as far as the reader's personal experience goes, a Dakota wheat farm may be as exotic as the moons of Mars); and it tries to deal honestly with the tragic and poetic theme of love-and-death.

The disreputable forms, the Western, science fiction, sports story and so on are defined by their backgrounds; but please note that this is a convention. You could define all of fiction in this way, piecemeal—"New York stories," "Dakota wheat farm stories" and so on, but it isn't convenient or necessary to do so. What really distinguishes the disreputable forms is their reduction of love and death to perfunctory gestures, formalized almost like ideographs. (The villain falls over a cliff; the heroine falls into the hero's arms; neither event takes more than a paragraph.)

Detective fiction, a half-reputable form, owes its half-acceptance to its partial honesty with death. The popular forms, the slick short story, TV serial and so on, suppress both love and death (substituting "romance" and "menace"); that's why they are popular.

Now, what is special about science fiction?

It might be more appropriate to ask what is special about "mainstream" fiction. The latter is restricted to a small number of conventional times-and-places. Science fiction includes all these, and all others that a writer of our time-and-place can imagine.

Science fiction is speculative; but so is every work of fiction,

to some degree; historical and exotic fiction particularly so.
These are convenient standards, and it's inevitable that librarians and critics will use them—but there must have been a
time when stories about India or Alaska or the South Seas were
"outlandish," "weird," "unbelievable," "unheard-of" and so on.
Such stories have gained mass acceptance simply by being around
long enough to become familiar; and we may expect that science
fiction will do the same.

What we get from science fiction—what keeps us reading it, in
spite of our doubts and occasional disgust—is not different from
the thing that makes mainstream stories rewarding, but only expressed differently. We live on a minute island of known things.
Our undiminished wonder at the mystery which surrounds us is
what makes us human. In science fiction we can approach that
mystery, not in small, everyday symbols, but in the big ones of
space and time.

That's all—or nearly all.

Science fiction is already moving out of the realm of disreputable forms, just as the Western is, and just as, to a considerable degree, the detective story is moving upward from its
half-reputable status. It can't, I'm afraid, ever become a popular
form—it won't stand the suppression. But it can be wholly respectable, and in such stories as C. L. Moore's "No Woman Born"
(*Astounding*, Dec., 1944), Philip José Farmer's "The Lovers"
(*Startling*, Aug., 1952) and many more, it's already well on the way.

The librarians are already on our side; give the critics time.

Literate and informed criticism of our field is rare, as you
know; even in the s.f. magazines, book reviews are mostly of
the "shopping guide" type, written by men who, in James Blish's
phrase, "like everything, but not very much." In the organs of respectable criticism, we are used to reading awe-inspiring blurts
of ignorance from people like Phil Stong, who once innocently
revealed that he thought a light-year was equivalent to 186,000
"plain years."

This volume, therefore, is a unique treasure: *The Science
Fiction Novel, Imagination and Social Criticism.* Here are three
brilliant and searching essays by Robert A. Heinlein, Robert Bloch
and the late C. M. Kornbluth (plus one dud, by Alfred Bester), and
an equally brilliant introduction by Basil Davenport.

Heinlein's contribution is especially valuable, first, because he
happens to have written so many of the pivotal works in the field
since 1939; second, because he has a seldom-displayed but highly
developed critical talent.

For the first time, in this book, he gives the sources of such stories as "Waldo" and "Blowups Happen"—both frequently cited as examples of prophecy in s.f.—and shows why they were no more prophetic than "for a man to look out a train window, see that another train is coming head-on toward his own on the same track—and predict a train wreck."

He pays a graceful tribute to Edmond Hamilton, whose imaginary spacesuits in a 1931 story influenced Heinlein's in 1939—which in turn influenced the real ones he and L. Sprague de Camp helped develop during the war. And he asks, ". . . is it surprising that the present day space suit (or high-altitude pressure suit, if you prefer) now used by the U. S. Air Force strongly resembles in appearance and behavior the space suit visualized by Edmond Hamilton in 1931?"

In the dispute over the best definition of s.f., Heinlein casts his ballot for Reginald Bretnor's (paraphrased): "(Fiction) in which the author shows awareness of the nature and importance of the human activity known as the scientific method, shows equal aware-ness of the great body of human knowledge already collected through that activity, and takes into account in his stories the effects and possible future effects on human beings of scientific method and scientific fact."

This definition is perhaps at once a little too broad and too limited (it includes *Arrowsmith*, but excludes stories which most informed readers would simply call bad science fiction): but it does have the great virtue of defining good science fiction, and of showing that much of the magazines' current contents is not s.f. at all, but "pseudo-scientific fantasy."

Kornbluth's main point, or at least the one which gives his paper its title, is that science fiction is ineffective as social criticism. Within the narrow terms he chose, the point is made; s.f. has pro-duced no novel which has visibly and inarguably changed the ways of the world, as did *Don Quixote* and *Uncle Tom's Cabin*. (But I wonder if Kornbluth didn't get a negative result merely because he was looking in the wrong place. Heinlein mentions an electronic device he thought up for a 1939 magazine serial; a classmate who read the story was intrigued and put the idea into development; the final version was in use all through World War II.)

The remainder of the paper is given over to Kornbluth's first and only try at the tricky, fascinating field of symbological criti-cism. He warned us he would make mistakes, and I think there is no doubt that he made some: for instance, his calling Swift's Houyhnhnms symbols of primitive virtue is pretty clearly an error (tipped off by his remarking in the next breath that "It is curious that Swift's symbol for primitive virtue should be the horse"). He was mistaken, too, in supposing that there is anything unusual in the womb-image as the symbol of dread and horror; see Erich Neumann's monumental work, *The Great Mother*. But his interpretations of Orwell's "Room 101" in *1984*, the unspeakable Eich of Dr. E. E. Smith's Lensman series, and other matters, are nothing short of spectacular.

Alfred Bester's breezy, rambling monologue is disappointing to me as some of his stories are, and the fact that one throws light on the other does not seem to help matters much. My admiration for Bester as an artist is all but unbounded (and goes back almost twenty-five years, to a story he has probably forgotten himself: "The Unseen Blushers"*). But even in his best, most dazzlingly pyrotechnic work, his carelessness with scientific fact sometimes bothers me; and to hear him say, as he does here, that the essential ingredient in a story is charm, or "personality," and that the science in it is unimportant — even though it perfectly and logically accounts for *The Stars My Destination* — only intensifies the irritation.

When Bester suggests that people don't turn to science fiction for information, of course he's right: but people don't turn to s.f. for misinformation, either.

Robert Bloch, a loyal s.f. fan for many years, begins by describing his childhood, when "stories about Bug-Eyed Monsters were read by bug-eyed boys."

He notes in passing, very perceptively, that most science fiction is symbolic rather than realistic. For the adolescent rebelling against his elders, "There's a vicarious thrill in breaking the law, even if it's the law of gravity."

But he wonders what has happened to the uncompromising social rebelliousness of thirty years ago, when novelists dared to suggest that our Way of Life was not in all details sacrosanct: and he shows, in a devastating attack, that s.f., supposedly the last stronghold of independent thought, actually has been repeating the same safe old ideas for years. Part of the list follows (condensed): "1. A TOTALITARIAN STATE. 2. The UNDERGROUND. 3. FORCIBLE PSYCHOTHERAPEUTIC TECHNIQUES. 4. The assumption that SCIENCE WILL GO ALONG WITH THE GAG and obediently wash brains for Capital, Labor, the Military, the Clergy or whatever . . . ." (This one, incidentally, seems to me to be no assumption but a well-documented fact.)

The full list runs to nine points, all deadly accurate. It may be

---

*Astonishing, June 1942.

true, as Bloch intimates, that if better stuff is not being written, it's because the readers don't want it; but it can hardly do any harm to wake writers up occasionally with such a well-directed battery of pins in the rump.

I've said hardly anything about Basil Davenport's introduction, because it is itself a critical summary, competing with this one (and, I'm afraid, superior in every way). But I can't do better than to quote his closing lines, as the publisher's jacket blurb does:

"This book has given me the pleasure, all too rare since my college days, of being a book that I could argue with. No one can agree with all these papers, since they do not agree with each other; but where you disagree you will find yourself wanting to say exactly how far and why. That is my idea of a really stimulating and enjoyable book."

I now turn to a less authoritative but equally stimulating book: *New Maps of Hell*, by Kingsley Amis.

Amis, the lionized author of *Lucky Jim* and other satirical novels, is a young English lecturer who in 1959 took part in the Christian Gauss Seminars in Criticism at Princeton, and had the temerity to take for his subject, not the early English poets, but science fiction. This book is based on the lectures.

". . . whatever my shortcomings, I am not that peculiarly irritating kind of person, the intellectual who takes a slumming holiday in order to 'place' some 'phenomenon' of 'popular culture'; one recalls with aversion those attempts to 'place' jazz by academic musicians who thought Duke Ellington's band was a kind of minstrel troupe."

Jazz and s.f., for Amis, have a good deal in common. "Both emerged as self-contained entities some time in the second or third decade of the century, and both, far more precisely, underwent rapid internal change around 1940. . . . Both of these fields, again, have thrown up a large number of interesting and competent figures without producing anybody of first-rate importance; both have arrived at a state of anxious and largely naive self-consciousness . . ."

He notes that s.f., like jazz, has an indefinable and incommunicable special interest—you either dig it or don't—and goes on to try his hand at two definitions of the field, of which the second is of interest: s.f. "presents with verisimilitude the human effects of spectacular changes in our environment, changes either deliberately willed or involuntarily suffered."

His tone is self-deprecatingly, and rather self-consciously, ironic; nevertheless, his observations are impressively docu-

mented and shrewd. Inevitably, he slips now and then, as when
he swallows Richard Matheson's puerilities, in *I Am Legend*,
as plausible scientific rationalizations of the vampire story (and
writes "aerophobic" for "anaerobic"); or when he states flatly,
"What will certainly not do is any notion of turning out a science-
fiction love story." *

What particularly fascinates me about the book, however, is its
vivid demonstration of how much any critic is at the mercy of
his own bias. To Amis, although he perceives and respects other
values, the main thing about science fiction is its satiric quality.
This shows conspicuously in his assessment of s.f. writers:
he calls Fred Pohl "The most consistently able writer science
fiction, in the modern sense, has yet produced." ** At the other
end of the scale, he deprecates H. G. Wells' work as being not
"a daring imaginative statement" but "a concretization." By this
ugly word, Amis means the quality which to me is the supreme
achievement not only of the story in question, but of all notable
fantasy writing: the quality which gives a story life, makes it a
thing-in-itself, rather than a shadow or projection of anything else.

Amis' hunger for satire in s.f. is unsatisfied even by Orwell's
savage and bitter *1984*, "which instead of being the remote nightmare it is could have been the savage *short-range* admonitory
satire on political forces that Orwell had it in him to write and
that nobody since has even looked like writing."

Presumably what Amis likes most about *Gulliver's Travels* is
its mockery of the people and institutions of Swift's day, rather
than the story for its own sake. From my own bias over to this
is such a leap that I get a strictly science-fictional jolt out of
sharing Amis' viewpoint.

But certainly his bias is as good as mine; so is the bias of the
technically-minded critic who wants more wiring diagrams, or
the socially-minded critic who wants more lectures. If there is
anything reassuring in all this, it is that s.f. is more fruitful and
various than we generally (in our biased impatience) realize;
it contains all the things Amis praises, as well as all the things
for which he professes to look in vain: short-range satire, sexual
inventiveness, anti-interplanetary-colonialism propaganda, and a
lot more, all except a tithe of it crud, according to Sturgeon's
Rule; yet what are we all but God's sparrows?

*Cf. "The Lovers," by Philip Jose Farmer, "Saucer of Loneliness," by Theo-
dore Sturgeon, and "The Escape," by Don A. Stuart, among many others.

**His evaluations of other writers are odd: he slights Kornbluth, and calls
Mervyn Peake "a bad fantasy writer," which is simply incomprehensible until you
realize that for Amis, this phrase is identical with "a fantasy writer."

2. THE CLASSICS

NOW THAT AMERICAN science fiction, past its majority, is heading for the peaceful middle age of an established form, some of its earliest adherents feel as if they had suddenly grown long gray beards; there is nothing more pathetic, I suppose, than the look on the face of an old-guard fan who's waiting to say something about Stanton A. Coblentz, while all around him people are talking about Heinlein.

With understandable bitterness, some have been driven to the extreme position that no science fiction published later than 1935 is worth reading—while among their younger colleagues it isn't hard to find those who will put the date still later, and argue that everything published before it was trash.

But whether you belong to either group, or to neither, there's almost certain to be something in *The Heads of Cerberus* for you. Those who yearn for the Good Old Days are bound to like it— it was first published in *The Thrill Book* in 1919. Those who insist on the close reasoning and the satirical wit of modern science fiction will find surprising amounts of both here; and if, like myself, you have a foot in both camps, you're sure to be delighted by this connoisseur's blend of the quaint and the ageless.

Terry Trenmore, not the ingenu but the hero of this story anyway, is the sort of big, flamboyant, sentimental stage Irishman that used to turn up all the time in the popular arts until, I guess, about the time Victor McLaglen retired and Brian Ahearne went back to drawing-room comedy. You couldn't write about such a man today, he doesn't exist; but here he is, for those that love him, musclebound and poetic as ever.

For contrast, look at the world into which Trenmore and his friends stumble: Philadelphia in the year 2118, ruled as a pocket oligarchy by "Penn Service" and its glittering court of Superlatives—the Loveliest, the Cleverest and so on—chosen and kept in power by blatantly rigged tests, while the proletarians have no names at all, only numbers which they must wear on Landon-sized lapel buttons. It isn't the best social satire in the world; but it's modern enough, if you like, to have come out of the pages of a 1956 magazine.

P. Schuyler Miller calls this "perhaps the first work of fantasy to envisage the parallel-time-track concept." You can read it that way, to be sure, but it's perversity; the author tells you in plain terms that the story's about something quite different and at least as interesting.

Philadelphia 2118 is a world of might-be, a philosophical spark struck off from the brain of the first traveler to find the way out of our prosaic universe of what-is.

> "Many times have I sought him there. Many times has his name come up in some such fantastic connection as it came to you. I have seen, as it were, the shadow of his thought sketched in the tangible phantasmagoria which surrounded me. But either he evades me purposely, or he is dead, and only his mind endures as an invisible force . . ."

That passage has a dusty taste, and much of the writing is the same or worse, but not all by any means. Let me quote the beginning of Chapter 5:

> When the marvelous oversteps the bounds of known possibility there are three ways of meeting it. Trenmore and his sister, after a grave discussion of certain contingencies connected with the Catholic religion and a dismissal of them on grounds too utterly Celtic and dogmatic for Drayton to follow, took the first way. From that time on they faced every wonder as a fact by itself, to be accepted as such and let go at that.
>
> Drayton . . . compromised on the second way, and accepted with a mental reservation, as "I see you now, but I am not at all sure that you are there or that I really believe in you!"
>
> Fortunately there was not one of the three so lacking in mental elasticity as to discover the third way, which is madness.

Now that, I submit, is not dated writing and is never likely to be; it's lucid, didactic, analytical and above all, zestful: an adjective which describes nearly the whole of the book. "Francis Stevens," we are given to understand, wrote only out of need and stopped at once when the need ended; but she wrote in the only way good writing is ever done: with joy. There is no plot necessity for the interlude in the half-world of Ulithia; it's pure fantasy for the love of it; and there are lines in that chapter that are feather-touches along the cheek.

One of science fiction's few genuine classics, out of print in this country since 1937, is Karel Čapek's wonderful *War With the Newts*.

The publisher's cover blurb for the Bantam paperbound edition ("... a great novelist's electrifying story of what *might happen to our world tomorrow*...") is of course pure space gas, as Tom Corbett would say. This is a satire, one of the great ones. It has enormous charm, human warmth, gaiety, wit—and all the time, gently, patiently, it is flaying human society by inches.

The Newts (a giant species hitherto known only as a fossil) were discovered on the shore of Tanah Masa by gloomy old Captain J. van Toch, who took a paternal liking to them. (" 'What's the use, you ought to be honest even with animals.' ") At first they brought up pearl shells, in exchange for tools to build their dams and breakwaters, and weapons to fight sharks. Later, when it was discovered that they could talk, it was natural for more and more people to seek other uses for them.

With great ingenuity, and in spite of the most disheartening obstacles, people succeeded.

> The flesh of the Newts has also been taken to be unfit for human consumption and even poisonous; if eaten raw, it causes acute pains, vomiting, and mental hallucinations. Dr. Pinkel ascertained after many experiments performed on himself that these harmful effects disappear if the chopped meat is scalded with hot water (as with some toadstools), and after washing thoroughly it is pickled for twenty-four hours in a weak solution of permanganate of potash. Then it can be cooked or stewed, and tastes like inferior beef. In this way we ate a Newt called Hans; he was an able and intelligent animal with a special bent for scientific work; he was employed in Dr. Pinkel's department as his assistant, and even refined chemical analysis could be entrusted to him. We used to have long conversations with him in the evenings, amusing ourselves with his insatiable thirst for knowledge. With deep regret we had to put Hans to death, because my experiments on trepanning had made him blind . . .

Fed, protected, dissected, exploited, armed by every nation against every other, the Newts continued to grow in numbers as well as in knowledge. Not so many years after old Captain van Toch passed away, there were already twenty billion worker and

warrior Newts in the world, or about ten times more Newts than
people.

> . . . The young Newts apparently stood for progress without any
> reservations or restrictions, and declared that below the water
> they ought to assimilate all land culture of every kind, not omit-
> ting even football, fascism, and sexual perversions; . . .

Then one day the world awakened to find an earthquake had sunk
three hundred square miles of Louisiana under shallow water.
A strange croaking radio voice came out of the sea:

> "Hello, you people! Don't get excited . . . There are too many
> of us. There is not space enough for us on your coasts any longer.
> Therefore we must break down your continents . . . ."

Only out of a landlocked and tired little nation could have
come such raw despair, so incredibly blended with gentle, calm
affection. "The Newts," says Egon Hostovsky in his *Note on the
Author*, "are, of course, symbols of nazis and communists."
So they are, fleetingly, at the end of the book, which trails off into
a nightmare much as Mark Twain's *A Connecticut Yankee* does;
but most of the time, I think, the Newts are ourselves as Čapek
saw us—gentle, long-suffering, mute; the natural prey of business-
men, politicians, experimenters, militarists, and all other sharks
of the land.

Under the Triple Suns, by Stanton A. Coblentz, is a wild, heavy-
handed 1930-style adventure story, which I can't honestly recom-
mend to modern readers: but I think science fiction writers ought
to read it.

I'm speaking to you, from Doc Smith on, who have fallen into the
habit of describing an alien city, on another planet, as if it were
Manhattan seen through slightly cockeyed spectacles. There is a
failure of communication, the expected article is not reaching the
customer, when a science fiction hero arrives in the metropolis
of Ub-Gloob, on Sirius XII, to find that the only difference between
it and New York is that the cars move faster.

Looking back, it's easy to see how the gambit began: the slam-
bang science adventure epic whose growth took place in the thirties would have been intolerably slowed down if the writer had felt
obliged to examine every new race and culture in detail. But it's
easy to see, too, that the new convention was a betrayal of science
fiction.

Science fiction exists to provide what Moskowitz and others call "the sense of wonder": some widening of the mind's horizons, no matter in what direction—the landscape of another planet, or a corpuscle's-eye view of an artery, or what it feels like to be in rapport with a cat . . . any new sensory experience, impossible to the reader in his own person, is grist for the mill, and what the activity of science fiction writing is all about.

So: notice, once you have passed (or skipped) the wooden dialogue and stereotyped action of the early chapters, Coblentz's notion of a city on another planet:

> He was peering into an enclosure that hardly seemed an enclosure at all. Far above, at a height of thousands of feet, the gray cobweb ceiling curved like an actual sky. Though from without, it had looked opaque, from within he saw it to be translucent: the subdued and filtered radiance of the three suns penetrated it with a soft, even glow. . . . The walls were ribbed with thousands of strands of some fabric that looked like bamboo and crossed it irregularly, and yet somehow gave the impression of branching supports, which likewise suggested a cobweb, curved and bent and twisted between the floor and the ceiling, with closely woven whorls and patterned spirals and platforms and slim long cables that swung faintly as if in an invisible current.

Coblentz's story unfolds itself steeped in the sunless gloom of this gigantic spiderweb tent — a vivid sensory experience that never was in the world before. Coblentz uses this background for an engaging but primitive satire about "social climbers" (the social status of the Ugwugs, the city's inhabitants, depends on their height above the tent's floor) and similar conceits; but it would have served equally well for a straightforward xenographic story, or puzzle, or mood story, or whatever you like. The point is:

If your alien planet is just like Broadway, or even just like Uganda, what the devil is the use of leaving Earth at all?

John Collier, who must now be getting on towards sixty, was once an impudent young man with a poet's heart and an engagingly apelike countenance, the latter two of which qualities he retains to this day. These traditionally Hibernian attributes have been the making of many a great minstrel, warrior, king or rogue. The combination cannot help but explode into things utterly new and astonishing — into heads carved off with goose-quill nicety, or rhymes chopped out with an axe.

Except he take a club or a dirk in his hand, a man so endowed is doomed to be disappointed in love, tyrannized by relatives, gulled twice a week by the unscrupulous, and mocked at by Philistines: but give him a pen, and he will get his own back twice over.

> There was a young man who was invariably spurned by the girls,
> not because he smelt at all bad, but because he happened to be as
> ugly as a monkey. He had a good heart, but this soured it, and
> though he would grudgingly admit that the female kind were very
> agreeable in shape, size, and texture, he thought in all other re-
> spects they were the most stupid, blind, perverse, and ill-natured
> bitches that had ever infested the earth.

This is the first paragraph of "The Devil George and Rosie,"
one of the fifty stories in Collier's collection *Fancies and Goodnights*, in which ugly, good-natured and gullible persons figure at
length. Clearly enough, all these persons are Collier himself;
very infrequently one of them, like George, is allowed to take the
principal role; but most of them appear as demons.

"Hell," said Percy Bysshe Shelley, "is a city much like London";
Collier has made it as easily reached and very nearly as familiar.

> In Hell, as in other places we know of, conditions are damnably
> disagreeable. Well-adjusted, energetic, and ambitious devils take
> this very much in their stride. They expect to improve their lot
> and ultimately to become fiends* of distinction.

This is an ill-founded hope, however; Collier's demons vary
somewhat in appearance and disposition, but there is nothing
really objectionable about any of them; on the contrary, they are
rather likeable fellows but in their pure state hopelessly incom-
petent to meet the challenges of modern living. The nastiest of
the lot is old Tom Truncheontail of "Fallen Star," from which
story the quotation above is taken; and even he, after psycho-
analysis, becomes well-tailored and taillessly respectable, and
makes a fortune in Wall Street.

Not as much can be said for all the human characters in these
stories, which also abound in spiteful and tight-fisted male relations, fat hennaed sluts, murdered wives and the like; however,
there is a bit of Collier in the worst of them, and whatever they
may be doing—poisoning or disemboweling each other, leaping
from the tops of skyscrapers, posing as specimens of the taxi-
dermist's art—it is sure to be done with the utmost aplomb.

Nearly all these stories belong to one canon: the conventional
romantic fantasy, or domestic tragedy, or sophisticated love
story, with the fur side in. Nothing ever works out even approxi-

---

*This word appears as "friends" in the Doubleday text; printers, as we all
know, are the lily-purest and most angelic of mortals, and I doubt if there is one
of them who knows what a fiend is.

mately as expected; every turn of the plot is a wild (but remorse-lessly logical) tangent; wives become husbands, the innocent are guilty, jinn equals Aladdin.

Collier takes an innocent childish delight in pulling the rug out from under his reader, sometimes before he is fairly on it, as in the opening sentence of "Pictures in the Fire":

> Dreaming of money as I lay half asleep on the Malibu sand . . .

These first lines are an especial preoccupation of Collier's (and the last lines as well); there is nothing like them anywhere else in literature; they are sandbags between the eyes. "Great Possibilities," for example, opens as follows:

> There are certain people who do not come to full flower until they are well over fifty. Among these are all males named Murchison.

Collier, besides, was quick to learn the unpalatable truth that bitterness does not make art until it is transmuted into satire, that tragedy bores us unless it is preventable, that beauty is like pablum without a touch of the ludicrous. Only twice in fifty stories, in "The Lady on the Grey" and "Special Delivery," has he made the error of taking himself too seriously; and these are stories that would shine in other company.

In addition to Hell and its environs, Collier has taken a great interest in the domestic scene. In the same volume there are two stories in which a man kills his wife (the classics "De Mortuis" and "Back for Christmas"); one in which the job is carried out for him by an obliging monster; one in which he does his best, but owing to a regrettable misunderstanding is hoist by his own mush-room; and one in which two soul-mates simultaneously poison each other for the insurance; this without taking any account of slaughtered uncles and nephews. Collier has also done incredible things to the triangle as well as the quadrangle plot, and has turned his attention upon M.D.'s, dentists, psychoanalysts, bo-hemians and other curious fauna in London, Hollywood and New York. Some of these tales have the dramatic simplicity of an anonymous anecdote, and in fact one of them (not included here) appeared as such, condensed and shorn of its author's name, in a jackdaw volume of Bennett Cerf's. Three others demand special mention and a category of their own: three tours de force, con-versation pieces in which the implications are everything, the events visible onstage nothing: "Little Memento," "The Chaser," and the finest short murder mystery ever written, "The Touch of Nutmeg Makes It."

In nearly all the stories here collected, the influences of poet and ape are equally felt, which is to say that these stories are brilliantly balanced on the tension between farce and tragedy.

It is the business of the satirist to make his readers forget that he is a living human being, able to be hurt, able to love or hate singlemindedly and without reserve; but in one story, "The Steel Cat," Collier's art is something more than satire. Here the ape speaks alone; the poet has been temporarily won over, and is present only to contribute the artistry that makes the death of a mouse a more shameful and terrible thing than the death of Desdemona.

Elsewhere, however briefly, the poet also is audible alone; and I think it fit to end with this one last quotation, the opening lines of "Variation on a Theme":

> A young man, with a bowler hat, cane, flaxen mustache, and blue suit, was looking at a gorilla in a zoo. All about him were cages floored with squares of desert. On these yellow flats, like precise false statements of equatorial latitudes, lay the shadows of bars. There were nutshells, banana skins, fading lettuce; there were the cries of birds who believed themselves mewed up because they were mad, the obeisances of giraffes, the yawns of lions. In an imitation of moon crags, mountain goats bore about ignobly eyes that were pieces of moon.

We, by Eugene Zamiatin, is an apocalyptic novel first published by Dutton in 1924. Except for a Russian version issued by an emigre group in Czechoslovakia in the late twenties, the book has never been published in the author's native language, and it is still banned in the Soviet Union.

The novel is written in the form of a diary kept by a citizen of a thousand-year-old autocracy, the United State. Names and other personal identifications have been abolished; male and female Numbers dress in identical uniforms, live in identical transparent cells of great cubical buildings of glass; they rise, eat, work and return to bed at the same moment.

The trouble with this brief description of the book is that every word is true, essential, and misleading. *We* is not a museum specimen, not a crude political satire, but a live and kicking masterpiece.

If he had made this future world only to mock it, Zamiatin's book would have been a failure: but his nightmare is only too real.

> We were down in the street. The avenue was crowded. On days when the weather is so beautiful, the afternoon personal hour is

> usually the hour of the supplementary walk. As always, the big
> Musical Tower was playing the March of the United State with
> all its pipes. The Numbers, hundreds, thousands of Numbers in
> light blue unifs . . . were walking slowly, four abreast, exaltedly
> keeping step . . .
>   Then, as this morning on the dock, again I saw, as if for the
> first time in my life, the impeccably straight streets, the glis-
> tening glass of the pavement, the divine parallelepipeds of the
> transparent dwellings, the square harmony of the grayish-blue
> rows of Numbers. And it seemed to me that not past generations,
> but I myself, had won a victory over the old god and the old life,
> that I myself had created all this. I felt like a tower; I was afraid
> to move my elbow, lest the walls, the cupola, and the machines
> should fall to pieces.

In such passages, and with an exuberant flow of mathematical
analogies, the diarist conjures up the fearful joy of unfreedom.
And yet, sentence by sentence, in the very midst of his hymns of
praise for the United State, this dedicated Number who is building
a spaceship, the *Integral*, to take the blessings of order to distant
planets; this mathematician, this poet of sterility, unmasks himself in a flood of sensual images.

Balanced in this way between two worlds, good-humored, naive,
bubbling with ideas, the diarist can at one moment show you a
glimpse of a 20th-century street, and make you *see* it as an incredible and absurd spectacle of disorder; and at the next, suc-
cumb to an erotic attachment of such extraordinary power that
his betrayal of the world-state becomes perfectly credible.

This is a bouncing, lively, enormously readable book; its characters, O-, the round and pathetically young woman who loves
the diarist; R-, the Negro-lipped poet, with whom they have an
amiably triangular relationship; I-, the mysterious woman rebel
("again a smile, bite, and white sharp teeth"), D- himself, the
diarist, all grow comfortably and affectionately familiar. The
author's prose is deceptively simple, like his city of glass, which
he turns with casual ease into a mirror of symbols.

> . . . The Morning Bell! I got up; everything looked different.
> Through the glass of the ceiling, through the walls, nothing could
> be seen but fog—fog everywhere, strange clouds, becoming heavier
> and nearer; the boundary between earth and sky disappeared.
> Everything seemed to be floating and thawing and falling . . . Not a
> thing to hold on to. No houses to be seen; they were all dissolved
> in the fog like crystals of salt in water. On the sidewalks and in-
> side the houses dark figures, like suspended particles in a strange
> milky solution, were hanging, below, above, up to the tenth floor.
> Everything seemed to be covered with smoke, as though a fire
> were raging somewhere noiselessly.

Although Zamiatin wrote this story in the early twenties, when he could already feel the Soviet monolith hardening around him; although he anticipated prefrontal lobotomy and other modern horrors; although his book shows a striking parallelism with Orwell's *1984*, these are not the important facts about *We*. It's a delightful and profound book, a work of art; a lasting pleasure.

The Coming of Conan, by Robert E. Howard, is of interest to Howard enthusiasts, who will treasure it no matter what anyone says, and to students who may find it, as I do, an intriguing companion piece to L. Sprague de Camp's *The Tritonian Ring*. Howard's tales lack the de Camp verisimilitude—Howard never tried, or never tried intelligently, to give his preposterous saga the ring of truth—but they have something that de Camp's stories lack: a vividness, a color, a dream-dust sparkle, even when they're most insulting to the rational mind.

Howard had the maniac's advantage of believing whatever he wrote; de Camp is too wise to believe wholeheartedly in anything.

This book contains the only fragment of a Conan story that I remember from *Weird Tales* — Conan tippy-toeing along a ledge with a naked girl held by the hair, and then dropping her carefully into a cesspool—which turns out to be neither as isolated nor as insignificant as I had supposed. Another naked lady friend of the hero's, in another episode, winds up hanged to a yardarm with a rope of jewels; and for that matter, hardly anyone, man or woman, squeaks through the Conan saga without some similar punishment, except Conan himself.

All the great fantasies, I suppose, have been written by emotionally crippled men. Howard was a recluse and a man so morbidly attached to his mother that when she died he committed suicide; Lovecraft had enough phobias and eccentricities for nine; Merritt was chinless, bald and shaped like a shmoo. The trouble with Conan is that the human race never has produced and never could produce such a man, and sane writers know it; therefore the sick writers have a monopoly of him.

This volume contains seven stories, of which the first two are pre-Conan episodes and deal with a warrior-king named Kull; the difference, except for the name, is not remarkable. The book has been pieced out with snippets of the Howard-Clark essay, "The Hyborian Age," and of Clark's and Miller's "An Informal Biography of Conan the Cimmerian," as well as with letters written by Howard and Lovecraft, and a bit of doggerel, "The King and the Oak"—not credited, though it appears as part of "The Hyborian Age," so that we don't know whether to curse Howard or Clark.

All this makes a crowded contents page, and a patchwork book; I think it would have been more sensible of Gnome—as well as more honest—to integrate the scholarly notes with the stories and forget them.

I found one passage in "The God in the Bowl" that struck me as unusually fine; since this is one of the two posthumous stories which de Camp edited for publication, I wrote to him to ask if he'd made any changes in the scene that begins with Promero's entrance on page 137, and learned that he had: one word, Promero's last, which to me makes all the difference between climax and anticlimax. It seems a great pity that de Camp and Howard never collaborated while Howard was alive. De Camp has been careful, in this recent work, to edit the stories as little as possible, for fear of making them sound like his rather than Howard's; but if he'd been on hand when they were being written, to put solid ground under Conan's feet and an honest itch on his back—what fantasies might we not have seen then!

Enchanted Beggar, by Norman Matson, originally published, in 1926, as *Flecker's Magic*, offers itself as the gentle, unassuming story of Spike Flecker, a red headed young art student in Paris. Spike is living on irregular checks from his grocer uncle in Ohio, and his talent so far is nothing spectacular; the only extraordinary thing about him is that he is so much aware and alive.

The first thing you notice about this story is its pleasing simplicity, making no demands, no effort to shock or startle. The next thing is that everything in the story is observed with the clearest and most innocent vision. Next, that this vision somehow draws beauty out of the simplest things; for instance, a boarding-house meal eaten by Spike in Chapter 14. If there's magic in this story, it is not brought by the witch who offers Spike a wishing ring; the magic is in the story itself, on every page.

Considered as fantasy, within the narrow definition of our field, this book is an astonishing success. The old problem—if you could have any one wish, what would you choose? —here seems as fresh as if newly invented. Reading of Spike's sleepless agonies, you'll find yourself lacking the usual self-satisfied conviction that *you* would know how to handle this, even if the hero is too stupid.

But this does not give the measure of the book. It isn't an exercise on a familiar theme; nothing in it is perfunctory or artificial. What it is, is almost impossible to convey: it escapes all categories, is uniquely itself.

Nowadays, when the novels we read are concerned, almost as a matter of course, with hatred, violence and misery, it comes as

a shock to realize that this engrossing book is about human goodness and the joy of living.

If this were a fantasy novel of the machine-made variety, when
it turns out that the witch has given Flecker the ring in hopes he
will cause some enormous catastrophe, the hero ought surely to
go charging off and inflict on the villainess some gorily appropriate revenge. We get to know her better instead, and she turns
out to be a wonderfully loony old girl, anxiously dithering in a
garret full of dusty notebooks—her incomplete and uncompletable
history of the world. And: this visit to the witch's garret, which
would have been satisfactory enough in itself, and certainly would
have contented a writer who only wanted to advance the plot, is
embellished by a couple of charming fables told by the witch, one
about the beginning of the world, one about its end—as if this were
a musical comedy, and one of the leading characters had stepped
forward to stage center and burst into song.

I'm trying to say that this is a work which shows evidence not
only of skill and intelligence, but of love. It's a rich, warm con-
fection of a book, full of unexpected good things. Don't miss.

3. CHUCKLEHEADS

MY PUBLISHERS have asked me to open this chapter by dealing with a hypothetical reader's hypothetical question: "If these books are so bad, why bother writing so much about them?"

I had to stop and think. I have been throwing bad tomatoes at worse performances for so long, and so entirely instinctively, that it had never occurred to me to think up a reason for it.

Why should anybody rip a bad work of art to shreds? Why, to find out how it is made.

The critical method is to take things apart. The critic uses the same sharp-edged tools on all stories, but good stories resist; bad ones come to pieces. One of these tools happens to be laughter; that's all. I should have thought it was obvious.

The Blind Spot, by Austin Hall and Homer Eon Flint, is an acknowledged classic of fantasy, first published in 1921; much praised since then, several times reprinted, venerated by connoisseurs—all despite the fact that the book has no recognizable vestige of merit.

Hall, who wrote 39 of the book's 48 chapters, had these faults: He was style-deaf. Sample, from the prologue:

> For years he had been battering down the skepticism that had bulwarked itself in the material.

Another, from page 273:

> . . . he had backtracked on his previous acts so as to side in with the facts . . .

He was totally innocent of grammar. This is not an exaggeration; Hall could not tell a noun from an adjective, or a verb from either. Two samples, both from page 20:

> She is fire and flesh and carnal— . . . at whose feet fools and wise men would slavishly frolic and folly.

He was so little at home in the English language that he could not lay hands on the commonest idiom without mangling it. Three samples, out of dozens:

> It was a stagger for both young men. (Page 264.)
> There was a resemblance to Rhamda Avec that ran almost to counterpart. (Page 172.)
> It was a long hark back to our childhood. (Page 30.)

He was credulous without limit. The myths solemnly subscribed to in this book—none of them having anything to do with the plot— include the intuition of women, the character-judgment of dogs, "animal magnetism," "psychic vibrations" and the influence of intelligence on the color of the eyes.

He had no power of observation.

> The men about him purchased cigars and cigarettes, and, as is the habit of all smokers, strolled off with delighted relish. (Page 1.)

He had no empathy, and, I might add, no sense of humor. This is his notion of writing like a woman:

> I am but a girl: . . . I should be jealous and I should hate her: It is the way of woman. . . . I am a girl and I like attention; all girls do. . . . I had all of a girl's wild fears and fancies. I am a girl, of course. . . (Pages 101-103.)

His knowledge of science, if he had any, is not discoverable in these pages. He used "ether," "force" and "vibration" synonymously. On page 85, a chemist refers to a stone's thermal properties as "magnetism." "Magnetic"—like "sequence," "almost," "intrinsic," "incandescense" (sic) and "iridescense" (sic)—is a word Hall kept tossing in at random, hoping to hit something with it eventually. For example:

> She [a dog named Queen] caught him by the trouser-leg and drew him back. She crowded us away from the curtains. It was almost magnetic. (Page 95.)

He was incapable of remembering what he had already written or looking forward to what he was about to write, except when it was inappropriate to do so. For example, the book opens with the introduction of a character known as Rhamda Avec. (Didn't I say Hall had no sense of humor?) "Rhamda" is a title, but the narrator does not know this, no one who uses the name in conversation knows it, and the reader is not supposed to find out about it until page 58. Nevertheless, Avec is consistently referred to as "the Rhamda." And then, on page 171, we get this:

> By this time Watson was convinced that the word indicated some sort of title.

This Rhamda is a mysterious personage who, it goes on to appear, has come through the Blind Spot—an intermittent passageway between the Earth and another world. Somehow connected with the Spot is a blue jewel of odd properties, which the Rhamda spends the first half of the book trying to recover from one of the four protagonists; but inasmuch as he refuses to tell anybody why he wants it, what it is, who *he* is, or what happened to kindly old Dr. Holcomb—who vanished through the Spot shortly after being seen with the Rhamda—it's not surprising that he never gets it.

Later on he gets lost somehow, an entirely new villain shows up —"the Bar Senestro," if you please—and it eventually turns out that the Rhamda had no ulterior motives at all, but simply wanted to do everybody a good turn by getting the jewel back where it belonged. This being so, it is hard to understand why he stalked around like a silent-movie villain for twenty-odd chapters, clam-silent and snake-sinister.

The behavior of the other characters is equally puzzling. Another tourist from the far side of the Spot is wandering around in the early chapters—"the Nervina." She also wants the jewel returned to the Rhamda but is angry at him—no reason given—and she won't tell anybody anything, either.

It becomes evident early in the story that the Rhamda can't or won't take the jewel by force, and yet two of the protagonists, in turn, wear it for months even though it is evidently killing them.

Still earlier, fourteen pages are devoted to the introduction of the jewel. On page 40, one of the protagonists shows it to two others; on page 54, he disappears into the Spot. In between, it occurs to nobody to ask, "Where did you get it?" and as a result nobody finds out until page 72.

"Hall," says Forrest J Ackerman's introduction, "contributed a great knowledge of history and anthropology, while Flint's *fortes* were physics and medicine." Flint's understanding of physics may be judged by this passage, from page 147. (The stone "inducts" sound. They seal it in an air-tight canister; the sound stops.)

"Ah!" cried Herold. "It's a question of radioactivity, then! . . ."

Flint's nine chapters, written in a gushing, mock-hearty style which is an immeasurable relief after Hall's illiteracy, do inject some bustle into the story and contribute a good deal of common sense:

"Work on that ring. I was a fool not to get busy sooner."

This is true, and applies with much greater force to protagonist number one, who, instead of following up the only lead he had, apparently spent twelve months mooning around the awful old house on Chatterton Place, reading the collected works of Madame Blavatsky.

But Flint's memory was as frail as Hall's. On page 149 an extraordinarily heavy lump of stone, which Herold can barely lift with a spade, is discovered for the first time in the pile of earth which Jerome had previously *dug up, sifted minutely, and tossed through a doorway* into the next room in the cellar.

Flint's numerous new characters do nothing, say nothing— although at great length—and now Hall takes over again, this time on the other side of the Spot, where we meet more new people, including a woman *with. . . a wonderful fold of rich brown hair, tastefully done . . .* Most of Hall's women have this oddity; in this case it sounds like something between an envelope and a crepe Suzette. We also rediscover Dr. Holcomb, comfortably established as the reincarnation of a local god, and the story winds up in a very conventional melange of pageantry, witchcraft and good clean sport, which Merritt might have written in an off week.

We learn from Dr. Holcomb the importance of the Blind Spot: "It will silence the skeptics, and form a bulwark for all religion"; working together, our friends succeed in restoring the missing jewels to their places, returning to Earth, and closing the Spot; the eligible members of the party are neatly married off, and all ends happily.

The Rhamda Avec, having been mislaid twenty-one chapters back, remains so. We are left to wonder where he is, who built the Spot, what in the world all the characters thought they were up to, what the story was about in the first place, and—most of all—why anybody, even Ackerman, even Moskowitz, ever took this schoolboy novel seriously.

Take equal parts of Austin Hall, Sax Rohmer and A. Merritt;

add a touch of H. P. Lovecraft; shake until addled. Yield: *Kinsmen of the Dragon,* by Stanley Mullen. Serves 1/2.

I think it was my friend Jim Blish who coined the term "idiot plot," defined as a plot which is kept in motion solely by virtue of the fact that everybody involved is an idiot. Here is a delightful specimen: Sir Rodney Dering, the Wise Old Man of the story, is an idiot; Franchard, its sinister villain, is a super-idiot; Eric Joyce, its handsome hero, is an idiot in spades.

Behold:

In the prologue, Joyce visits Dering in London (Joyce is a young American who, although the author does not say so, must have been in suspended animation since about 1920) and is conned into joining a crusade against Franchard, who—Dering tells him— is using a network of nut-cults for the purpose of "undermining what we have left of civilization."

Supposing Joyce to have any brain at all, he ought to ask, "Why?" He doesn't, and the question never comes up; apparently it hasn't occurred to Dering, either.

In Chapter 1, we find Joyce in London again after a quick trip to Paris made off-stage. A long black sedan (typus!) swoops down; in it are Franchard and his girl friend, Darla, who spray Joyce with bullets. This seems a little odd, since Joyce has done nothing to annoy them, but he takes it as a matter of course. Franchard's explanation is deferred until page 66, and it's a honey: "I don't know why I did it. Just a momentary impulse. . ."

The Paris trip turns out to have been equally odd. Joyce, acting on Dering's orders, has interviewed two or three people, read a couple of books in the Bibliotheque Nationale, learned nothing not already known, and accomplished nothing whatever; we are left to wonder what, if anything, the trip was *supposed* to accomplish. This is partially elucidated on page 27: the trip, Dering says, has "succeeded in its main object, that of drawing their fire."

This leads us to still another "Why?", but the only answer we are going to get appears farther down on the same page: "It's not like Franchard to be unworkmanlike. He had a sitting shot, too. . ."

This is not very satisfactory, but at least it's plain enough— Dering's object in sending Joyce to Paris was simply to get him shot dead.

Neglecting the perplexing question of Darla's motive in accosting Joyce in a Paris bar, getting offended two minutes later and walking out without having altered the plot in any way, let us pass on to Chapter 6. After some preliminaries designed to show that Franchard is an evil so-and-so, Dering has got the password to one of the nut-cults and sent Joyce to investigate it. Joyce witnesses a very dull ceremony, broken up in the middle by a husband with a grievance, whereupon the cult priests set fire to the place and Joyce is captured by Franchard, who remarks, "You puzzle and intrigue me, Joyce. What can you hope to gain by your childish attempts to thwart me?"

This is a good question; a better one is, *"What* attempts?"

Franchard, who is telepathic and clairvoyant, then has Joyce, who knows nothing about anything, tortured to extract unspecified information from him. He is about to use scopalamine for the same purpose, when Darla rescues Joyce and turns him loose. On the way, Joyce gets a small bottle handed to him in the dark, without a word spoken.

He promptly swallows its contents—which, surprisingly enough, turn out to be brandy. For all he knew, they might have been ink.

Following this, Joyce happens to bump into an old friend named Redwood—identified, two pages later, as a merchant seaman who has been missing and supposed dead for three years. You can tell he's an old salt: "'Funny things happen at sea. . . . On a ship, the captain is boss and nobody questions his orders.'"

They escape an ambush at Joyce's car and drive home, tailed by the usual black sedan—which, however, goes away without any further attempt on their lives. If the reader at this point has another "Why?" left in him, he can use it here.

Redwood, who is really Chick Watson of *The Blind Spot* in disguise, tells a tale apparently derived from an imperfect recollection of *The Blind Spot, A Descent Into the Maelstrom, Pellucidar,* "At the Mountains of Madness" and *The Moon Pool*; i.e., after boarding a derelict, Redwood and his companions pass through a dimensional doorway; are sucked down by a huge whirlpool; emerge in a subterranean world; wander in a city of Cyclopean horror; and wind up in the hands of a dismal gang of demonolaters headed by Franchard.

Redwood is puzzled by the efforts of Franchard's gang to drag information about nuclear physics out of their proletarian prisoners:

> But why, since *He* seemed to know everything else about our world, would *He* not know . . . about that?
> There was no answer.

. . . Then, or ever.

Franchard's men, it turns out, have infiltrated an atomic-weapons arsenal in Yorkshire; Joyce and two others go there to "investigate," get caught in the middle of a pointless raid by the cultists, and retire with the score tied at zero. This brings us to

Chapter 13, up to which point nobody, on either side, has advanced the plot an inch.

Now, however, another old friend of Joyce's turns up: this one just happens to have a well-staffed private submarine, with which he had been planning to explore the Arctic ice. Dering, persuasive as ever, enlists him and his crew to find the dimensional doorway described by Redwood, and attack Franchard on his home grounds.

The main curiosity here is that nobody has any notion of how the submarine crew is to get back to Earth—Redwood's return appears to have been an accident; he doesn't know how it happened —but this question never occurs to anybody. That isn't all. Watch these page numbers closely:

On page 261, after a battle with the cultists in the eldritch dead city, a trek up into the mountains to a city of lizard-people, and other irrelevant adventures, Joyce is interviewing a gentleman named Vor, the Red Archdruid. Franchard, it appears, is the Black Archdruid, and there may or may not be a third—the White —who holds the balance of power. Vor mentions casually that he has traveled between the worlds—ergo, by an easy deduction, he knows how it is done. Joyce pays no attention.

On page 263, it turns out Vor's method is "astral projection" —no good for Earthmen. Joyce still doesn't react.

On page 273, Vor volunteers the information that he *can* show Joyce how to return to Earth.

And on page 275, Joyce asks, "Is it within your knowledge to direct us to our own world again? . . ."

Yikh!

. . . At any rate, it is now about time for Joyce to be recaptured by Franchard; this accordingly happens, and we get the standard interview, during which Franchard remarks, "Your bungling efforts to thwart my plans have caused me no end of trouble." This, of course, is a barefaced lie.

There follows a touching scene between Darla and Joyce; Darla slips her bra down to show Joyce her tattoo, incidentally, and we learn that it's in a "hollow beneath her left breast." Carries kleenexes there, no doubt.

Some lizard-men rescue Joyce as he is about to be done in; the party climbs up a tunnel to reach Earth again (don't ask me how this works), and we find that Franchard, at any rate, has quit fooling away his time: he is setting fire to cities at a great rate and has entrenched himself with an army on (for reasons best known to God) a small island off the coast of Scotland.

Our heroes attack him here and are captured once more, just as Franchard is about to sacrifice Darla on a druidic altar; Darla, however, turns into the White Archdruid, kills Franchard, and saves the day.

In the process, it would seem, she has become dangerously radioactive, but this is a minor matter; all Joyce has to do is take her down the tunnel to the subterranean world and get her cured—which, as the story ends, he is preparing to do.

Try bicarbonate of soda.

"This eloquent novel," says the jacket of Taylor Caldwell's *The Devil's Advocate*, making two errors in three words, "is a dramatic presentation of life in America in the not-so-distant future. It is chiefly the story of Andrew Durant and how in the year 1970 he and the incredibly brave Minute Men worked secretly and ingeniously to overcome the awful tyranny of the dictatorship that ruled the country.

"The dictators were native Americans of the group that had been in power for over thirty years . . ."

To be precise, for 38 years: ever since the Presidential election of 1932. Other villains, besides Franklin D. Roosevelt and the Democratic Party:

farmers	psychiatrists	agnostics, atheists
workers	New Yorkers	scientists ("smirking")
executives	cattlemen	women in men's jobs
technicians	doctors	communists in the
teachers	liberals	cabinet
rich people	college students	journalists
	materialists	

Most of these groups are fingered one at a time by Miss Caldwell in a sentence which begins: "They had been among the very first to betray . . ." When the reader has encountered this formula for the eighth or ninth time, he begins to wonder whether anyone is going to be left out. But not *everybody* is guiltier than anybody else; Miss Caldwell likes:

the clergy, especially the Catholic clergy
the middle class
the Republican Party

The ingenuity exercised by the Minute Men in the 1970 revolution is of a class familiar to science fiction readers; they infiltrate the dictatorship until, in effect, they own it. Then, avoiding the prosaic coup d'etat, which would not make much of a novel, they slyly intensify the government's oppression until the public, which has stood with its finger in its mouth for going on forty years, Rises in its Wrath.

Miss Caldwell's style is of a piece with her plot. In narrative passages, among many other curiosities, she shows an ability to choose the word which does not merely understate a dramatic point, but mashes it completely flat: ". . . assassination of public officials *proceeding* by night and day" . . . "hordes . . . *applying* fire to public buildings" . . . "a blow in the mouth which had *removed* three of his teeth." [Italics mine.]

Totalitarianism is not intrinsically a funny subject, and I am not poking fun at this writer for dealing with it, nor for her opinions: Miss Caldwell to the contrary, it is not against the law in this country to be a Republican. Or a fathead, either. But it seems to me that anyone writing after Koestler on Koestler's subject must either parrot him, as Orwell did in *Nineteen Eighty - Four*, or attempt to refute him; Miss Caldwell writes as if he had never existed—as if, indeed, no fiction but her own had been written since 1910.

I don't say it is easy to interpret this century in prose, but Miss Caldwell has not made the first step essential to the interpretation of anything. She sees as in a Dewey button, darkly.

Miss Caldwell's second venture into the field covers a little more territory, and the catastrophe in *Your Sins and Mine* is more impressive: the Earth refuses to give forth its fruits; and this time, all of us are to blame.

The theme is terrifying enough, and in other hands might have made a notable book. But Miss Caldwell's ideas, like her characters, are as formless as dough: the tragedy of this story is three-quarters invisible behind a comedy of errors.

> And ye shall hear of wars and rumors of wars; see that ye be not troubled. For these things must needs come to pass; but the end is not yet. For nation shall rise against nation, and kingdom against kingdom; and there shall be famines and earthquakes in divers places. But all these things are the beginning of travail. . . . And because iniquity shall be multiplied, the love of the many shall wax cold. But he that endureth to the end, the same shall be saved.

This interpolated passage from Matthew (*xxiv.*, 6-8, 12-13) is the basis for Miss Caldwell's apocalyptic story. One dry spring, the fruit trees fail to blossom; the corn does not sprout, the wheat dies. Cattle grow lean; thistles invade the fields. In the farming community of Arbourville, the narrator's father (who "was what used to be called a 'fundamentalist' ") quotes Matthew to anybody who will hold still, but everybody else prefers a rosy Rotarian view. Newspapers, grange officials, heads of governments all keep up the fiction that the drought and famine are temporary and local. As the year wears on, Jehovah's patience with this obtuseness wears thin. New weeds of an almost Martian virulence appear. There is a plague, and a world-wide earthquake. The Almighty invents a brand-new insect, like a scorpion but nastier, to sting his children. "Local condition, ha-ha," says everybody but the narrator's pa. "Get better soon, yes sir. You bet. Got to keep smiling, boy. Keep that old chin up, shoulder to the wheel!"

As stockpiled food begins to give out, the local farmers band together to protect their seed corn and ration themselves. A native Communist agitator shows up, unaccountably talking like a Nazi out of a 1940 novel, but is quickly suppressed; and so forth, and so on. Miss Caldwell's explanation for all this is as follows:

> The land hated us, the violated land, the faithful land, the exploited and gentle land. The land had decided that we must die, and all innocent living things with us. The land had cursed us. Our wars and our hatred—these had finally sickened the wise earth.

Now, the curious thing about this is that it is not in the least biblical. Fundamentalist old farmer George appears to have forgotten that the events referred to in Matthew *xxiv.* are to be forerunners of the second coming of Christ (an event, and for that matter a name, not mentioned in this book). The author's alternative explanation—not Christian nor even patrist—invokes the ancient Goddess variously worshiped as Demeter, Ceres, &c.— the "Earth mother" aspect of the Triple Goddess. But on Christmas Eve, the Milky Way flows together into the shape of a cross, following the suggestion of Matthew *xxiv.,* 30: *"and then shall appear the sign of the Son of man in heaven."* (How mortifying for the author if it had been a crescent or a star of David instead!)

At any rate, on page 115 the narrator discovers (having done it once before, on page 37, and then sat on his hands for seven chapters) that all you have to do is kneel and pray, "Lord, be merciful to me, a sinner," and the weeds in your immediate vicinity will magically vanish, the earth be fertile again. This seems like a small price to pay, and accordingly everybody falls to. End of sermon.

The moral is not obvious, except that this country's unique theological contribution is still a wholly contemptible, watered down, dime-store religiosity. The tragedy, I suppose, is that Miss Caldwell is perfectly sincere: this saucer of weak tea really does plumb the depths of religious experience for her, and —evidently—for the "hundreds" of "priests, rabbis and ministers" who are said to have written her in praise of this work.

Starship Through Space, by Lee Correy, would appear to be Holt's answer to Robert A. Heinlein's Scribner juvenile series. Format and design are similar; so are the backgrounds; so is the plot—there are even recognizable chunks here from *Red Planet* (pages 15-18), *Farmer in the Sky* (page 48), "Gulf" (page 89), *Between Planets* (page 98), "Universe" (page 121), *Methuselah's Children* (page 164) and *Starman Jones* (page 166).

The book isn't entirely bad. For one thing, Correy, an engineer, makes his specialty vivid and interesting; for another, he has carried the saucer mystery into space, such an obviously good idea that I suppose at least twenty writers are now kicking themselves for not having thought of it first.

I want to say also that it's hard not to feel guilty for being as severe as this on a first novel. Heinlein's own first juvenile was nothing to be proud of; as for borrowing, although I think Correy has overdone it a mile, it's damnably difficult to avoid borrowing from Heinlein, who has so much to lend.

But this author has one overriding fault which makes me doubt that his second, or third, or tenth will be much better: Correy is half-literate.

Language and engineering are demanding and, perhaps, essentially contradictory disciplines; again and again in science fiction we meet the engineer who knows his subject, has story-telling gifts, is ambitious and productive; can build and service a hi-fi rig—and has a seventh-grader's understanding of that equally complex instrument, the English language.

Correy has made the incredible mistake here, among others, of exposing his idea of poetry: a character named Manning, who has been writing a symphonic suite for "a full *a capella* chorus, an electronic guitar section, and theremin" is persuaded to sing part of his score. There are three stanzas, of which the worst, by a hair, goes like this:

> We who have tasted alien stream
>   And done what others only dream;
> We who with earth-dirt on our shoes
>   Have walked the paths the sunbeams use;
> We will trod the Milky Way.

On the basis of this sample it can be definitely said that Manning is a worse poet than Lilith Lorraine; the only recent entry in science fiction that even comes near it is Milton Lesser's space-ranger song, in which "moons" is rhymed with "ruins." But it sends Correy:

"I like it very much," Marge said.

"So do I," Walt put in. "You can sell that, Marc."

"Perhaps, perhaps," Manning said modestly. "But my profession is astrogation. I have this sideline for relaxation. If other people enjoy it, too, I'm happy. . . . What's money? I have more personal satisfaction than any money could possibly buy me."

"I like your philosophy," Walt said sincerely.

The plot, which concerns the construction and maiden voyage of the first starship, with the two boy heroes accompanying their Big Cheese fathers, worsens steadily. In Chapter 7, Correy insanely introduces a cat into a control-room equipped with Heinlein's proximity switches. In Chapter 9, there is a foolish scene when the starship comes out of "high-drive" too close to Pluto: the pilot dangerously overloads the engines to decelerate, instead of steering out of collision course. (Reminds me of Moskowitz's ships that kept banging and clashing their way through the asteroid belt.*) And in Chapter 13, about the point where Heinlein usually injects a small and palatable dose of mysticism, Correy (if a little is good, the whole bottle is better) gives us this:

The starship has landed on a Centauri planet and found (surprise!) people. Descendants of a forgotten Earth expedition, naturally. Not from Atlantis—that would be bad enough, but it's out of style now, so this idiot has made the Tower of Babel into a spaceship.

The theme is developed with more piety than wit: the Centaurians' Bible is just like ours up to Genesis xi, but entirely different thereafter, meaning that the Babel story had to be set down as a running account ("the oldest history book terrestrial man had,") says Correy, apparently meaning the oldest newspaper) and that the writing of Exodus and Numbers, supposed by modern scholars to have been contemporary with that of Genesis, had to wait until the babbleship had taken off and the Israelites had gone back to their goats.

*My mind seems to have censored this, to make it sound more credible. Actually, it wasn't the asteroid belt; it was the rings of Saturn.

4. CAMPBELL AND HIS DECADE

Oh, the Dean Machine, the Dean Machine,
You put it right in a submarine,
And it flies so high that it can't be seen—
The wonderful, wonderful Dean Machine!

Oh, the therapy, the therapy
That Hubbard gave to JWC,
And it took him back to his infancy—
The wonderful, wonderful therapy!

The magnetic flow, the magnetic flow
That Ehrenhaft sold him so long ago,
And he swore up and down it was really so—
The wonderful, super magnetic flow!

Oh, the psi folderol, the psi folderol—
It never needs fixing, whatever befall,
For there's nothing inside it at all, at all—
The wonderful, wonderful psi folderol!

IN THE PANTHEON of magazine science fiction there is no more complex and puzzling figure than that of John Campbell, and certainly none odder. Under his own name, beginning as an MIT student in the thirties, he wrote gadgety, fast-moving, cosmic-scaled science fiction in the E. E. Smith tradition, and became, after Smith himself, its acknowledged master; as "Don A. Stuart," he began a one-man literary revival which eventually made that tradition obsolete. As editor of *Astounding*, he forced the magazine through a series of metamorphoses, not the least startling of which has been the evolution of its title—from *ASTOUNDING*

Stories to *ASTOUNDING Science Fiction* to *Astounding SCIENCE FICTION* to *ASTOUNDING SCIENCE FICTION*, and finally to *ANALOG Science Fiction — Science Fact*. More clearly than anyone, Campbell saw that the field was growing up and would only be handicapped by the symbols of its pulpwood infancy; he deliberately built up a readership among practicing scientists and technicians; he made himself the apostle of genuine science in science fiction . . . and ended as Dianetics' number one convert and fall guy.

As an editor, Campbell has never forgotten that, like a nation or an organism, the magazine which does not grow and change must wither. There have been periods, long enough to try the soul of the most faithful reader, when *Astounding* seemed to be dying on the vine; but always, up to now, it has turned out that Campbell was only incubating a new avatar.

In the hasty, ill-composed and ill-considered introduction to Shasta's *Who Goes There?*, Campbell says of the first Don A. Stuart story, "Twilight," that "it was entirely different from any science fiction that had appeared before." He ought to have added, "in Gernsback's *Amazing Stories* or any of its successors"; so qualified, the statement would have fallen at least somewhere near the truth.

"Twilight" is what Campbell says it is, a pure mood story— and as such is the lineal descendant of H. G. Wells' "The Time Machine," Rudyard Kipling's "A Matter of Fact" (both circa 1890), Stephen Vincent Benét's "By the Waters of Babylon" and many others. By the late thirties, when after a long decline the oldest magazine in the field had already died and been reincarnated as a dung-beetle, magazine science fiction was fast settling towards a dismal status as just another variety of pulp; Campbell's great achievement was to rescue it from its own overspecialized preoccupations and start it back toward the mainstream of literature. Although he later tried to nudge the pendulum the other way, the movement has continued; the revolution is a success.

The second Campbell - Stuart collection, *Cloak of Aesir*, contains seven stories that justify the author's cheerful boast: every one is a landmark in science fiction history. The germs of countless later stories are in them; indeed, it seems reasonable to doubt that the field ever could have developed as it has if they had not been written.

All these stories belong to what might be called the "Oh, yeah?" school of science fiction, though they are so cloaked in the Stuart mood-writing and in what still seems to me, in some of them, a real beauty, that probably few people realized it till Campbell himself pointed it out.

"Forgetfulness," for instance, is nothing at bottom but an irreverent iconoclast's-eye view of the proposition, "Machine civilization represents progress." So is "The Machine"; and "The Invaders" takes a similar look at "It would be awful if the Earth were conquered from outer space." "The Escape" is a "tragic" love story with a happy ending—and Campbell defies you to prove it isn't.

Campbell, a capable writer, never has been a stylist, and he didn't alter his natural prose style, with its short, blurted, agrammatical sentences, for the purpose of creating "Don A. Stuart." What makes the difference is partly the tone—a kind of high-pitched sing-song — and partly the point of view, a subtle thing that resists exact definition. The visual quality of every writer's work differs somewhat from every other's; probably it also differs, at least as widely, between one reader and the next, so that if I say that the Don A. Stuart quality, to me, is like a series of images shifting in and out of focus through a pearl-gray haze, nobody else is likely to sit up and say, "That's exactly it," least of all the author; readers who aren't visually oriented will not even know what I'm talking about. But the quality does exist and, I should think, is capable of being detected in some form by almost everybody; it's an important factor in making these stories what they are.

Clearly enough, the Don A. Stuart stories were only one experiment among many to Campbell; but modern readers may find in these two volumes his most important and lasting contribution to the literature.

People with a taste for the sharp-operator hero who flourished in American popular fiction during the thirties, and people with an insatiable appetite for bad science fiction will like Nat Schachner's old *Astounding* series, *Space Lawyer*. I confess to a sneaking fondness for it myself; the story moves fast and simply, as mechanically exciting as a pinball machine; it's wonderfully relaxing, because the author has done all of what little work there was, and nothing is required of the reader, not a moment's thought, not even an emotional response.

The formula is simply an amalgam of Mr. Tutt and Colin Glencannon, lifted bodily out of context and dumped into space. I wrote "into a spaceship" before I caught myself; actually it's clear from internal evidence that the vessels the author calls "spaceships" are oceangoing freighters—probably windjammers, at that.

No sooner had the ship blasted off than they set him to work. And what work! Scrubbing and scouring and restacking bales and cases every time the freighter took a steep curve. . . . (Page 24.)
  . . . The liner swerved toward her, and the buzzer sputtered, as the ship called for her to make radio contact. . . . The liner hesitated [with flapping sails?], then proceeded on its course. . . . (Page 137.)
  . . . She made some rapid calculations. If she kept her rockets on to hold to a steady three-hundred-mile-a-second gait [against a contrary wind, probably]. . . . (Page 139.)

And so forth. There's a dramatic moment in Chapter 10 when the hero, after accelerating steadily for thirty-five million miles out from Earth, turns on a dime and "retraces his steps" to rescue the heroine, becalmed in the Horse Latitudes and about to fall into the Sun; later on we encounter a description of radioactivity, all too obviously written when the works of A. Merritt had to serve in place of the unborn Smythe Report; but it doesn't matter —there's never a doubt that hero and heroine will steer safely at last through reef and shoal, in fair weather and foul, to the snuggest of all pasteboard harbors.

Science-fantasy addicts ordinarily shun other forms of pulp fiction as the plague; I still remember vividly the expression of horror on the face of one of them when—being then, through no fault of my own, the editor of a Western magazine—I tried to show him a copy of something with Stetsons and sixguns on the cover . . . So that until July, 1938, when *Astounding* published a short story called "The Dangerous Dimension," few of us had ever heard of L. Ron Hubbard.
Hubbard was the typus of a now-vanishing tribe of pulp-writers: like Tom Roan, who made occasional appearances in editorial offices wearing a ten-gallon hat and swearing like a muleskinner; like Norvell Page, who affected an opera cloak and a Mephistophelean goatee, Hubbard lived what he wrote. Big, swaggering and red-haired (like many of his heroes); sailor, explorer, adventurer; a man among men and a devil with the ladies, he cut a swath across the science-fantasy world the like of which has never been seen again.
In 1950, as the world knows, he catapulted to best-sellerdom and nationwide notoriety; a year later, trailing a cloud of lawsuits, he disappeared into the limbo of the Middle West, where at last report he remains.
He leaves behind an undiminished throng of admirers, a few friends and, I think, a rather larger number of enemies; a growing

body of legend; and upwards of ten short novels, most of them originally published in the early forties.

Here are two of them, both from the 1940 *Unknown*.

"Typewriter in the Sky" deals with the upsetting experiences of a dilettante pianist, Mike de Wolf, who is forced to live a role in a blood-and-guts pirate novel as it is written by his friend Horace Hackett—and not as the hero, either; as the villain.

The world around him is one completely subject to Hackett's whim: if Hackett says a man turns purple with rage, that's what happens. Hackett, moreover, is a very careless writer; de Wolf, moving willy-nilly through his paces as Miguel de Lobo, admiral of the fleets of His Most Catholic Majesty in the year 1640, finds himself playing Mozart on a piano plainly marked *Steinway, Chicago*.

The plot shuttles back and forth between Hackett, clad in a dirty bathrobe, grinding out chapters to meet his deadline, and Mike, fighting desperately to change the story and avert his own inevitable doom. The problem is a tough one, and Hubbard does not so much solve it as slide around it: the story-within-a-story winds up with a pointless final scene involving Mike and the heroine; the dream-world dissolves in earthquake and storm, and Mike is re-translated to the world of reality.

This weakness is more than compensated for by the ending of the story itself—three immortal lines:

> Up there—
> God?
> In a dirty bathrobe?

"Fear," as the author tells you plainly in a prefatory note, is not a fantasy at all—not, at any rate, in the addict's sense. It is written as if it were; the reader is led to believe that James Lowry's troubles stem from his having provoked the enmity of supernatural creatures, by writing an article denying their existence. And the story's plot, certainly, is fantastic enough: Lowry, having lost four hours and his hat, wanders in search of them into one hideous underworld after another. If he doesn't find them, he instinctively realizes, he will go mad; and if he does, he will die.

The second half of this credo is quite true; the first comes a little late: Lowry is already insane. At story's end, he regains his senses and remembers what happened during the missing four hours: finding his wife and his best friend together and misinterpreting the circumstances, he killed them both with an axe.

Haunted by his dead wife's scream ("Jim! Oh, my God! Jim!") Lowry spends the two days after the murder crossing and re-crossing the borderline of sanity. In his classes and at church, he is able to put up a fair appearance of normalcy. At home, refusing to let himself realize that his two victims are dead, he creates elaborate fantasies in which they speak to him, prepare dinner for him, and so on. (But he can't eat the imaginary food, because, when he tries to do so, the plate "moves" under his fork.) When he returns to the cellar in which the bodies lie, twice, to dispose of the evidence, his mind retreats altogether into hallucination.

The first of these episodes is the most effective passage in the story: the cellar stairs become an endless stairway incredibly opening from the sidewalk in front of Lowry's own house; he *has* to go down them, because each step vanishes behind as he descends; and, to help him forget where he really is, he creates a series of talkative phantoms:

> "If you please, mother, can't we come in off these stairs?"
> "You can't leave them. You walked up them, and now you'll walk down them all the way to the bottom. You must do it, that's all there is to it. You can sag and drag and gag and wag, but you've got to go to the bottom. All the way down. All the way, way, way, way, way, way, way, down! *Down! Down! Down!* Want some advice?"

After the second return, Lowry drifts still further into dementia, and here we get the most specifically clinical material in the story—a paranoid rejection of reality, and a recurring castration-anxiety fantasy in which the suppressed hatred for Lowry's ex-friend returns in a disguised form.

"Fear" is a good story that might easily have been a great one. Parts of it are magnificently written; a few passages, like the one quoted above, are pure dream-logic and dream-poetry, as good as anything in Carroll. Others are dull or irrelevant, and large sections are unforgivably bad.

The same is true of "Typewriter in the Sky"—and, indeed, of nearly all Hubbard's work.

Chapter 4 of "Typewriter" is a satirical and very funny dialogue between Horace Hackett and another writer. Toward the end of it, having bored each other with recitals of their current plots, and damned editors, the reading public and their profession indiscriminately, they drift into a reverent discussion of writing methods:

> "Sure. You lay out the beginning and know how it's going to end, and it wanders around as it pleases in the middle. ...
> "It's funny. ... I get spooky about it sometimes. It's—well, it's as if we were perfectly in tune with the story. We don't have to think about it, it just sort of comes bubbling out of us like music."

This is an accurate description of the commonest compromise
between plotting and inspiration (some writers plot everything,
in minutest detail; others simply reel the stuff out, without the
slightest notion of where they are heading) and of the ecstatic
feeling it sometimes produces. Nearly all writers rely to some
extent on subconscious processes to fill in the fabric of their
work; the ecstasy probably has something to do with the typical
writer's well-known reluctance to do any work himself.

The trouble with leaning too heavily on the subconscious is
simply that it has no critical faculty; it may lead you down temporarily attractive bypaths which end up miles from your story line;
it tends to be prolix; it often grasps eagerly at the approximate
word instead of the right one.

Hubbard must have worked submerged most of the time. He
wrote, we are told, on an electric typewriter, because no manually
powered one could keep up with him. In this volume and elsewhere, there is ample proof that Hubbard had an exquisite word
sense, when he wanted to use it; and equally ample proof that he
seldom bothered.

These two stories—particularly the second—are monuments to
a prodigal talent, prodigally wasted.

Conjure Wife, by Fritz Leiber, is easily the most frightening
and (necessarily) the most thoroughly convincing of all modern
horror stories. Its premise is that witchcraft still flourishes, or
at any rate survives, an open secret among women, a closed book
to men. Under the rational overlay of 20th-century civilization
this sickly growth, uncultivated, unsuspected, still manages to
propagate itself:

> "... I don't do much. Like when my boyfriend was in the army,
> I did things to keep him from getting shot or hurt, and I've spelled
> him so that he'll keep away from other women. And I kin annernt
> with erl for sickness. Honest, I don't do much, ma'am. And it
> don't always work. And lots of things I can't get that way.
> "... Some I learned from Ma when I was a kid. And some from
> Mrs. Neidel—she got spells against bullets from her grandmother
> who had a family in some European war way back. But most
> women won't tell you anything. And some spells I kind of figger
> out myself, and try different ways until they work. . ."

Tansy Saylor, the wife of a promising young sociology professor
at an ultra-conservative small American college, is, like most
women, a witch. She is also an intelligent, modern young woman,
and when her husband happens to discover the evidence of her

witchcraft (not his own easy advancement, which he ascribes to
luck, but certain small packets of dried leaves, earth, metal
filings, &c.) he's able to convince her that her faith in magic is
compounded of superstition and neurosis. She burns her charms;
Norman Saylor's "luck" immediately turns sour. But this is not
all—the Balance has been upset.

> This witches' warfare . . . was much like trench warfare or a
> battle between fortified lines—a state of siege. Just as reinforced
> concrete or armor plating nullified the shells, so countercharms
> and protective procedures rendered relatively futile the most
> violent onslaughts. But once the armor and concrete were gone,
> and the witch who had forsworn witchcraft was out in a kind of
> no man's land—
> For the realistic mind, there could be only one answer. Namely,
> that the enemy had discovered a weapon more potent than battle-
> ships or aircraft, and was planning to ask for a peace that would
> turn out to be a trap. The only thing would be to strike instantly
> and hard, before the secret weapon could be brought into play.

Leiber develops this theme with the utmost dexterity, piling up
alternate layers of the mundane and outré, until at the story's real
climax, the shocker at the end of Chapter 14, I am not ashamed to
say that I jumped an inch out of my seat. From that point onward
the story is anticlimax, but anticlimax so skilfully managed that
I am not really certain I touched the slip-cover again until after
the last page. Leiber has never written anything better . . . which,
perhaps, is all that needed to be said.

Lester del Rey's *Nerves*, revised and expanded from the 1942
Astounding novella, is still essentially the same great story of
suspense it was three years before the Smythe Report—and it's
still science fiction. Although actual atomic plants have already
surpassed del Rey's imaginary one in some respects—particularly
in the fields of automation, remote control and monitoring—this is
a story that might happen yet.

The 25-year-old National Atomics Plant in Kimberly, Missouri,
is under fire both from Congress and from the local citizenry,
stirred up almost to mob pitch by a vengeful newspaper owner.
In this tense atmosphere, a Congressional investigating committee
arrives. A minor accident occurs, increasing the tension: then
another, and so on down the inexorable chain to disaster.

Del Rey's wry point: there's an uncertainty principle in human
affairs as well as in subatomic ones. When you inspect a delicate
operation to see if it's safe—it isn't.

The story is told chiefly from the viewpoint of Doc Ferrel, head of the plant medical department. This device, which provides some high drama, is also one of the book's major faults: keeping the central action of the story invisible, behind the scenes, blurs and muffles a series of events which is none too easy to follow in the first place. Not until a third of the book is gone does del Rey let us see the trouble at first hand: a plant engineer named Jorgenson, buried by radioactive magma when an untried process goes wrong, fights his way to refuge in a lead sample box before he loses consciousness. In this one scene del Rey's muted story explodes with magnificent violence; its fury is enough to make up for all the slowness of the early chapters, and of others to come.

Now the main problem is fully developed: in the wrecked converter, what was supposed to be a harmless pest killer has turned into "Isotope R," a substance which in a few hours will break down into "Mahler's Isotope" — and Mahler's is an unimaginably violent explosive.

Jorgenson, the production man, is the only one who might be able to halt the reaction; and Jorgenson, though he has survived in his lead coffin, is in deep shock, his nerves jumping to the random signals of radioactive particles driven through his armor into the flesh. And, del Rey delicately suggests, Jorgenson's plight is a symbolic one: "Probably somewhere well within their grasp there was a solution that was being held back because the nerves of everyone in the plant were blocked by fear . . ."

Doc Ferrel is a rather gray figure, like other middle-aged del Rey heroes; the minor characters Jenkins, Nurse Brown, and Ferrel's wife Emma are more vividly sketched in; but Jorgenson, with his eternal caged anger at being the wrong size—"an angry, crippled god in chains"— is as vigorously and unforgettably real as the author himself.

Solomon's Stone, by L. Sprague de Camp, is a nostalgic reminder of the kind of smooth, expert tale de Camp used to spin in the early forties. Via a bungled experiment in black magic, it takes a near-sighted C.P.A. named Prosper Nash into a world of daydream figures. Each inhabitant is somebody's wish-I-were —cowboy, pirate, spaceman or what have you. De Camp is cheerfully irreverent and logical in everything from the tools of magic (he uses "virgin typewriter paper" instead of parchment) to the social ills of a community in which everybody is what he wants to be. As in Baum's *Tik-Tok of Oz*, there are more general officers than anybody, so a Private has the supreme command. There are Interplanetary Patrolmen, but no Interplanetary Patrol, because there's no interplanetary traffic. " '. . . So, as the first step, we formed a company to build a cosmobile. But there was the usual trouble . . . everybody wanted to be boss. They're splendid fellows, but they just couldn't realize that the management belonged to me, because of my natural gifts of leadership.' "

Nash, as "Jean-Prospère de Nêche," is an uneven mixture of the dashing chevalier and the methodical accountant. In a moment of emergency, he may find himself automatically skewering a footpad; but when he has leisure to think, his mind still runs cautiously to neat columns of profit and loss. In the best tradition of the farce-adventure, the story makes good use of each quality in turn—it's de Nêche who rescues the heroine from an Oriental fortress guarded by a saber-toothed tiger ("our little Smiley"); but it's Nash who worms his way into the fortress in the first place, by posing as a financial representative of the City.

There are battles and escapes, harem beauties (somewhat bowdlerized, as usual, by Avalon's unsubtle hand), monsters, comic Renaissance duellists (" 'Excuse me, Giacomo, I got business. I come back and kill you after, si?' "), a magic island, a demon, a talisman, all woven together into a deft, lively narrative. The ending is spoilt by *deus ex machina*, and by an anticlimax which ties up the loose ends in a perfunctory way, but the story is rewarding anyhow. They aren't writing them like this any more.

The Glory That Was is based on a pleasant conceit with which de Camp has amused himself before (in *The Carnelian Cube*): using historical reconstructions, hypnosis, and great gobs of money, an eccentric archaeologist recreates a city of the past— in this case, Periklean Athens—and in effect runs history over, either to see how it comes out, or to make it come out differently.

Into the pseudo-Athens come Wiyem Flin and Knut Bulnes, looking for Flin's kidnapped wife. The plot that now unreels is predictably and satisfyingly full of footpads, rascally innkeepers, intrigue, and the thorny parts of Greek grammar and folkways. The book is as easy and pleasant to read as de Camp's best work; his scholarly background is everywhere evident but nowhere intrusive. And yet something is missing; compared with *Divide and Rule*, *Lest Darkness Fall* and *The Incomplete Enchanter*, it seems somehow diffuse and incomplete. For what it's worth, I offer a possible explanation. The trouble is in the hero.

Knut Bulnes seems at first blush a typical de Camp protagonist, i.e., he is a young unmarried male, good at armed combat, girl-rescuing and other heroic business, but without that stupefying all-around virtue that makes you want to kick a classical hero. He is humanly imperfect, somewhat cynical and selfish, and may run like a rabbit if the situation seems to call for it. All this is refreshing to say the least, and Bulnes ought to be as attractive as Harold Shea or Howard Van Slyck. But he isn't, and I think I know why.

My notion is that sometime in the middle forties, without the author's awareness and surely without his intention, the de Camp hero became a victim of overspecialization. As the dinosaurs are said to have gone out of business when they got too big, and the saber-tooth when its fangs got too long, de Camp's hero grew too cynical, too selfish, too prosaically human to be admirable at all. In earlier stories, Shea's vanity, Van Slyck's selfishness and the like were little jabs at the reader to keep him awake, to make him sit up in surprise and say to himself, "Why, this guy's really human!". . . after which he could relax again and enjoy the sword-play. But Van Slyck, the spoiled young knight of *Divide and Rule*, was essentially an honest, idealistic and likeable man; the reader cared intensely what happened to him. Bulnes, although he goes through the motions, is simply—and sadly—not a man you can give a damn about.

It is no pleasure to me to make the admission, but Jack Williamson's *The Humanoids* is without doubt one of the most important science-fantasy books of its decade.

The story deals with a basic, immediate, and very probably in-soluble philosophical problem. A human scientist, embittered by mankind's ceaseless attempts to destroy itself, perfects and sets in operation the humanoids—a horde of efficient, respectful robot servants, all controlled by a single cybernetic brain, whose prime directive is "To serve and obey, and guard men from harm." But the first two clauses of this commandment are slighted by the humanoids' built-in interpretive mechanism; it is the third with which they are concerned, and they execute it to the last humor-less inch.

Wherever their expanding power touches, they guard men from any conceivable harm, even to the extent of depriving pathologi-cally unhappy people of their identities.

The rest of the story is occupied by the frantic attempts of the inventor and others to halt this monster, and change its interpre-tation of the prime directive so that the robots will actually serve and not rule . . . up until the final episode, wherein the book's un-happy protagonist learns that among the small group of renegades who are cooperating with the humanoids is the inventor himself, now a convert to the robots' present methods.

The story ends on a completely ambiguous note, the question unresolved—are the humanoids, in the last analysis, humanity's salvation or destruction?

The book is important, then, because its theme is important, and because Williamson's treatment is both honest and dramatically effective. It is also a most painstaking and conscientious job of writing, in everything from the plot structure to the pseudoscientific window dressing.

It pains me to admit all this, merely because the writing itself is so thoroughly, unremittingly and excruciatingly bad.

Williamson has the misfortune to be an exceptionally careful craftsman who grew up in one of the crudest eras of pulp fiction. The usual technique in those days was to grab the reader by his nose at the earliest possible moment in a story and never let go: thus, the hero invariably started out in a tough situation, which got progressively worse until the last scene, when, plausibly or not, the problem was solved.

Williamson, as a struggling young author, earned an impressive success by applying this system more thoroughly than any of his rivals. Williamson began each story by putting his hero in approximately the position of a seventy-year-old paralytic in a plaster cast who is required to do battle with a saber-tooth tiger —and, there being no place to go from there, kept him in the same predicament throughout the story, only adding an extra fang from time to time.

The years have polished this technique but have not altered it much; and the effect of it upon an even moderately sensitive ear is like that of an irritating sound repeated over and over and endlessly over.

Dr. Clay Forester, this novel's central character, is the victim of every torment Williamson could devise for him: he is fatigued to the limit of his endurance, sick with fear, frustrated by his work and his personal relationships, injured in his self-esteem by everyone around him, confronted by insoluble and vitally important problems—and his knee hurts—; and all this, very nearly without a letup, goes on throughout the story.

I read the book through for professional reasons, and came to the conclusion given above. But if I had been reading purely for pleasure, I would have breathed a prayer for Dr. Forester to break his neck somewhere during the second chapter, and turned to Dr. Dolittle.

5. COSMIC JERRYBUILDER: A. E. van Vogt

THIS CHAPTER CONSISTS mainly of a long essay, originally titled "The World of van Vogt," which I wrote in 1945 for *Destiny's Child*, an amateur magazine of Larry Shaw's. It predates my professional book reviewing by five years, and contains numerous crudities and at least one outright error; in spite of which it seems to belong here.

The inserted passages in brackets are from a second essay I wrote later, but never published: these compare the original magazine version of *The World of Ā* with the extensively revised and rewritten book version.

John W. Campbell has said editorially more than once that *The World of Ā* is "one of those once-in-a-decade classics of science fiction." I offer the alternate judgment that, far from being a "classic" by any reasonable standard, *The World of Ā* is one of the worst allegedly-adult science fiction stories ever published.

I'll try to prove that assertion by an analysis of the story on four levels: Plot, Characterization, Background and Style; to be followed by a brief comment on van Vogt's work as a whole.

Plot:
 The World of Ā, like all of van Vogt's longer work, is organized as a story-within-a-story-within-a-story—an extremely complex framework, vital parts of which are kept hidden until the end. It is, in fact, organized very much like a crime-detection novel—with two significant exceptions: that in a crime-detection novel, (a) all clues which are eventually used in solving the mystery must be given to the reader beforehand, and (b) all characters, no

matter how fantastic their actions may be caused to appear, must
be plausibly motivated.

The World of Ā abounds in contradictions, misleading clues and
irrelevant action. Shorn of most of these, and with the narration
sequence straightened out, this is what happens in the story:

The original Gosseyn discovers a process whereby he can reproduce his personality in a series of identical bodies. About five
hundred years before the beginning of the story proper, one of
this series of Gosseyns is mutated, developing an "extra-brain"*
which enables him to perform apparently miraculous feats—
teleportation and the like. This Gosseyn goes to Venus, where he
discovers that an extra-Solar race of humans has established a
secret base on that planet. This base is commercial, not military,
but is kept secret because its establishment is in violation of
agreements made by a Galactic League. The Gosseyn, realizing
that this base constitutes a threat to Sol, superintends the building
of the Games Machine in an attempt to remake the Solar population
into a completely sane and well-integrated race. Then he visits
other star-systems, presumably via the transportation system of
the aliens.

When he or his duplicate-successor returns, he finds that a
Terrestrial group, supported by Crang, Thorson and Prescott—
members of the alien staff on Venus—is plotting to destroy the
null-A system and the Games Machine. At the time the story begins, this group, by means of an alien invention called the Distorter, has forced the Machine to accept traitors for more than
half of all executive, judicial and police positions on both Earth
and Venus. The Machine knows what is happening, but is unable
to broadcast warnings because of the Distorter. Thus the revolutionaries' purpose is in fact accomplished; all that remains is to
destroy the Machine and formally take control.

The Gosseyn insinuates two spies into the traitorous group:
Patricia Hardie, daughter (?) of President Hardie (chosen for that
post by the Machine under the influence of the Distorter) and "X,"
a mutilated duplicate Gosseyn. Then he brings to life another
duplicate, Gosseyn I, who is the first protagonist of the story.
Gosseyn I's memory has been tampered with, as presumably the
others' have also, and he does not suspect his true identity.
Gosseyn I is now maneuvered by the dominant Gosseyn in such a
manner that he comes to the attention of the traitors, who believe
for some reason that he is tremendously dangerous to them. It is
never stated just who they think he is, but one clue (page 38, first

---

*By this puzzling word van Vogt, no grammarian, seems to mean simply "an
extra brain."

installment) suggests that they take him for the first mutated Gosseyn, the one who discovered the base on Venus and traveled among the aliens. At any rate, they torture him in an effort to find out what he knows; he escapes; they follow and kill him.

Gosseyn II comes to life on Venus, with all the memories of Gosseyn I except of what he had been told (false) about his identity. An agent of the Games Machine picks him up, tells him to allow himself to be recaptured by a certain member of the gang, which he does. The gang brings him back to Earth. He escapes, is recaptured, and the gang decides not to kill him again. He goes to the Machine, which tells him that he must kill himself, in order that Gosseyn III, whose extra-brain is fully developed, may come to life. He tries to do so, but meanwhile the Machine is attacked and destroyed, the body of Gosseyn III is accidentally killed, and his suicide attempt is frustrated by Patricia Hardie, acting for the dominant Gosseyn. Venus has been successfully invaded, he learns, and the traitors are openly in power.

Previously he has stolen the Distorter (which was in Patricia's bedroom all the time), and sent it to the Machine. He now retrieves the Distorter on Patricia's instructions, depresses one of its tubes—and finds himself again on Venus, with the Distorter. Here he is again captured by the gang, which now decides the thing to do is help him develop his extra-brain, keeping him under control by means of a "vibrator" which changes the atomic structure of everything around him so he cannot memorize it (sic) and effect an escape. Then they discover that the Machine had intended the Distorter to be sent to a certain place, and deduce that the "invisible chess-player"—the dominant Gosseyn—must be there. The leaders of the gang descend on the place with a horde of henchmen. The dominant Gosseyn, with Gosseyn II's help, destroys them—getting himself killed in the process. By this act, presumably, null-A is saved and the war is over except for mopping-up.

Therefore:

The dominant Gosseyn knows that by assassinating the leaders of the traitor group (whose identities and whereabouts are known to him) he can end or set in abeyance the threat to null-A.

He is able to do so.

Instead of doing so, he uses Gosseyn I and Gosseyn II to worry them and make them delay their coup. During the time thus gained, as far as the story tells us, he does not do anything whatever.

[Attempted justification: in the book version, Crang has been changed from a bona fide member of the enemy group to a null-A borer from within; on Thorson's death he will take charge of the invading army and so prevent enemy victory. This makes sense providing we can accept the entire plot as a necessary prelude to Thorson's death; otherwise not.]

The dominant Gosseyn knows all about the extra-Solar base and the civilization behind it.

He sends Gosseyn II to "investigate" it.

[Out, along with a mass of related nonsense.]

The dominant Gosseyn is able to produce as many duplicates of himself as he pleases, and is not obliged to wait until one dies to bring the next to life. (See page 178, last installment.)

He tells Gosseyn II, through the Machine, that he must kill himself in order to make way for Gosseyn III.

[Attempted justification: "But that's ridiculous," Gosseyn said jerkily . . . "Why can't this . . . third Gosseyn come to life without my dying?" "I don't know too much about the process," said the Machine. ". . . I have been told that the death of one body is recorded on an electronic receiver, which then triggers the new body into consciousness."

This is obviously untrue, since the dominant Gosseyn did not find it necessary to commit hara-kiri in order to give life to Gosseyn I. Elsewhere it is suggested that it wouldn't do to leave more than one Gosseyn roaming around at the same time, since the duplicates might become too powerful. This ignores all we have been told about the Gosseyns' null-A sanity and altruism.]

The dominant Gosseyn knows of the existence of the Distorter.

He makes no effort to find it and put it out of action.

[No change.]

After the Distorter comes into the possession of the Machine, which is then destroyed, the dominant Gosseyn realizes that the Machine's action in stamping his address on the crate constitutes a danger to him.

He sends Gosseyn II to retrieve the Distorter, but does not instruct him to destroy the crate.

[This has been justified by altering the plot, so that the dominant Gosseyn's basic purpose all the time is to lure Thorson to his lair where he can be killed. At the same time, complete, perfect idiocy is made of this proposition by having Thorson tell Gosseyn II that he has already visited said lair and destroyed the body of Gosseyn III.]

And therefore:

The acts of the dominant Gosseyn are the acts of a madman.

There is no valid reason for any act performed by either Gosseyn I or Gosseyn II, except one: Gosseyn II helps the dominant Gosseyn to destroy the gang leaders. This act would logically

have been performed at or before the time the story begins—
in which case there would have been no story.

These are by no means all of the major contradictions and
irrelevancies in the story. For example, the whole struggle between the dominant Gosseyn and the villains becomes meaningless
when we learn that null-A cannot be destroyed by armed attack:

> "Many will die. But I assure you, Gosseyn, we shall live
> through it. And now that the people of Earth know what is going
> on, the death-defying strength of the A system is going to start
> showing itself. . . The fools! . . . They have nothing that we can't
> take from them. And what we have—integration, superiority,
> consciousness of right—cannot be seized by force of arms."

[Justified by the above-mentioned change in Crang's role—
which, it seems to me, makes Crang the real hero of the story
and reduces the maneuvering with Gosseyns I and II to even pro-
founder meaninglessness.]

Again, there is a mass of material in the story concerning the
suspected existence of native intelligent life on Venus. There is a
long sequence where Gosseyn dreams he is seeing through alien
eyes — eyes which see things in a way no human eyes could possibly see. This has no conceivable reference to the extra-Solarians
later discovered on Venus, who are human beings.

[Out in toto.]

Some of the loose ends and inconsistencies, I think, are simply
examples of carelessness — as for instance the part Patricia
Hardie and her father (?) President Hardie play, which is either
self-contradictory or ambiguous from beginning to end. Others,
however, in particular the long passages which have no relevance
whatever to the rest of the story, are susceptible of a different
explanation:

Van Vogt is going to write, or has already written, a sequel.

I have not given this factor any weight in discussing the passages in question, because I believe that if it is so, it is no excuse.
I am writing under the assumption that a story, series or no, must
be able to stand by itself: that even if it is written as part of a
larger work, it must be at least coherent when read alone.

However, I think that a few predictions about the sequel might
be interesting when and if it appears. From what I know of the
way van Vogt's mind works, I suspect that some or all of the following will be brought out in the second story:

The original Gosseyn was born much earlier than the reader is
now supposed to believe. The Gosseyns may be identified with the
Wandering Jew, or even with Jesus Christ.

The battle for Sol is three-sided; there is a third force, more powerful than either of the others, which has not yet been revealed directly in the story. This force may be a race of beings who operate in the fourth dimension, or in "another aspect of reality."

The Gosseyns have been aware of this force, and their efforts have been directed principally against it, not against the small fry who appear in *The World of Ā.*

The Gosseyn who is dominant at any given time is in fact more powerful than the entire Galactic League put together. Gosseyn II has not yet learned who and what he really is.

Finally, I predict that when the entire Ā story has been told, it will be found to be very nearly as muddled and self-contradictory as is the first part by itself.*

Characterization:

Van Vogt tells us fairly clearly what all his major characters are like. Gosseyn I-II, besides being a superman, has a highly intelligent and well-trained mind. So do "X" and, in the final scenes, Patricia. Crang, Thorson and Prescott, although they lack the benefits of null-A, are intelligent and strong-minded representatives of a galactic culture. These things being established, the characters should act in accordance with their natures. They do not.

In Chapter IV, Thorson's agents have captured Gosseyn I and are taking him to the palace where he is to be examined and then killed. He is entirely in their power, and they are confident of their ability to dispose of him.

The agents have instructions to pretend, en route, that they are gangsters.

[Out.]

On page 15, second installment, Crang makes a long speech which is meaningful only under the assumption either that he is a Terrestrial, or that he wants Gosseyn II to think so. Since Gosseyn has no reason to suspect that the former is untrue, and no way of finding out, the false impression he receives is of no possible value except to mislead the reader — a motive which could hardly have influenced Crang.

[Out.]

On page 158, last installment, Thorson makes a long and completely irrelevant speech to the effect that human beings are the dominant race on tens of thousands of planets, and that phony evi-

---

*Van Vogt did write the sequel, *The Players of Ā*, which turned out to be so much more muddled and self-contradictory than the original story, as well as so much duller, that I couldn't make the effort to follow it.

dence of natural evolution has been planted on all these planets. I take this to be a hint toward what Campbell calls the "full implication" of the story which is supposed to strike the reader one or two days after he finishes it; but from Thorson's standpoint it has no purpose whatever.

[Out.]

On page 45, second installment, Gosseyn II is told by the Machine that it cannot broadcast warnings of the plot because the Distorter is focused on its public communications system. On page 65, last installment, Patricia says the same thing. Both times, Gosseyn II accepts the statement without question, in spite of the obvious fact:

The Machine is able to communicate with perfect freedom through at least some of its twenty-five thousand individual game rooms, as well as through "roboplanes" on both Earth and Venus —witness its conversation with Gosseyn II. Nothing would be simpler than for it to direct contestants or other persons to broadcast a warning.

[Several mutually exclusive justifications for this have been inserted throughout the story.]

Gosseyn II's prime motivation is a tremendously urgent desire to know the truth about himself. Yet:

On page 170, first installment, a "roboplane" sent by the Machine offers to answer any questions he wishes to ask. Gosseyn II spends more than three-quarters of a page in introspection, using up all the time available in so doing, although he has been told that the time is limited. He does not ask a single question.

[He's quicker on the trigger this time.]

On page 36, second installment, Gosseyn II has managed to frighten Prescott into talking, and Prescott is about to reveal where the gang got the Distorter. Dr. Kair returns, interrupting him, and Gosseyn allows himself to be sidetracked.

[See above.]

On page 64, Gosseyn II is closeted with Patricia, who has just revealed that she is an agent of the "invisible chess-player." Bursting with impatience, he demands that she tell him what she knows.

She evades his questions.

He does not press the point.

[New version substantially the same.]

Van Vogt's characters repeatedly commit the error known as the double-take. This phenomenon is funny because it represents a mental failure, just as a drunk's staggering represents a physical failure. Its cause is inability to absorb a new fact until a ridiculously long time has elapsed. In *The World of Ā* there are twelve examples in all, nine of which are Gosseyn's. Here are a few of them:

> "So this is the superman!"
> It seemed a futile insult. Gosseyn started to carry on with his examination of the man's physical characteristics; and then the import of the words penetrated.
> The man knew who he was!

[Altered out of recognition.]

> "Let's start at the beginning. Who do you think I am?"
> The moment he had spoken, he felt breathless. His muscles grew rigid; his eyes widened. He hadn't expected to utter the question just like that, without leading up to it by careful adherence to the laws of persuasive rhetoric.

[Out.]

> 'X' . . . laughed heartily.
> "You don't think we're going to tell you that. Dead men, of course, tell no tales but—"
> He stopped. He laughed again, but there was an edge of irritation in his amusement. He said:
> "I seem to have let something slip . . ."

[Out.]

> Gosseyn, intent on the possibility that he might be able to snatch one of his own guns, felt a vague puzzlement, a consciousness that there was something wrong with the words that he had heard. He gathered them together in his mind; and this time they penetrated.
> "You're going to WHAT?" he said.

[Minimized.]

> He was in the tunnel of the aliens.
> On Venus!
> (Half a page later:) He was about to climb to his feet when for the first time, the very first time, the transportation angle of what had happened, struck him. He who had been on Earth a minute before was now on Venus. !!!

(Exclamation points mine.)
["Transportation angle" changed to "magnitude," eliminating the double-take.]

Background:
"Null-A," generally speaking, is a rigor of logic; or else it is a system of mind training and/or mental-physical integration; or else it is a "semantic philosophy." Specifically, it includes the

"cortical-thalamic pause" plus a few rules of logic lifted from 20th-century texts, and it also includes fencing, breathing exercises and classical dancing. In short, it is anything having the remotest connection with pedagogy which happens to occur to the author.

And this gigantic and amorphous agglomeration is given a purely negative label: it is "not Aristotelian."

Aristotle was a philosopher who lived and died three centuries before Christ. His importance even today is purely historical; his influence has been filtered through twenty-three centuries of succeeding philosophers and logicians until it is no longer recognizable except to the student. Yet six centuries later, in van Vogt's world, it is sufficient to identify a supposedly radical new system of logic, to say that it is "non-Aristotelian."

(Here I revealed that, although I had been talking like a semanticist for years, I had never read Korzybski's [unreadable] pioneer work, *Science and Sanity,* and was not familiar with his coined term, "non-Aristotelian.")

The World of Ā takes place in 2560—fully 600 years after the invention of the atom bomb. In the 600 years preceding 1945, mankind progressed sociologically from feudalism to capitalism, economically from muscle-power to machine-power; technologically from wheelbarrows to jet planes. During this 600 year period, more than 30 times as many significant additions were made to man's scientific knowledge as were made in the 4,000 years preceding; and the progress to date shows a continual acceleration.

Yet in van Vogt's world the advancement over 1945, either stated or implied, amounts to no more than (a) a world government; (b) a handful of gadgets; (c) limited development of space travel; and (d) a scientific system of education—the latter developed by a superman.

This would be a plausible, if sketchy, background for a story laid from 50 to 100 years in the future. For a story which takes place 600 years from now, it is as bad as no background at all.

Furthermore, in van Vogt's world:

There are no more national barriers, and society is supposedly organized on a scientific rather than a political basis.

Yet there are still poor people ("They had been poor, working their small fruit farm in the daytime, studying at night") and people who live in palaces.

Space-flight has been technologically possible for more than 600 years; it has been an actuality for a large part of that time.

Yet no interstellar flight has been attempted, and only one

planet in the Solar system itself has been colonized.

Van Vogt's conception of his gadgets is worthy of note in itself. Study of the gadgets mentioned in *The World of Ā* reveals two things: first, van Vogt has not bothered to integrate the gadgets into the technological background of his story; and second, he has no clear idea of their nature.

Gadget 1: the electronic brain. This appears in two forms: the "roboplane" and the "lie detector." Even in the latter form, where its only function is one which a simple mechanical or even a chemical setup could perform as well, the brain is a highly complex one — it has both intelligence and volition, and speaks perfect idiomatic English. In the "roboplane" form, it has a sense of humor as well. No other part of the technology indicated in the story so much as approaches this achievement—mechanical duplication of the almost inconceivably complex human brain. It is as out of place in van Vogt's bumbling twenty-sixth century culture as a radio would be in pre-Roman England. It sells for thirty-six dollars, new.

Gadget 2: the "ingravity parachute." It's impossible to say whether or not this is out of place in the cultural level described, since the account of it adds up to precisely nothing. It is not a mechanism which counteracts gravity by applying force in the opposite direction, because this would be bulky, heavy, and dangerous. Neither is it a mechanism which counteracts gravity directly, because this is a fuzzy Aristotelian idea and manifestly impossible. What is it? It is "a metal harness with pads to protect the body."

Gadget 3: the Distorter. This, of course, has no relation to Solar culture, being an alien instrument, but its function appears reasonably plain at the beginning: it is a device which can be focused on and made to interfere with electrical currents at a distance. Having established this, van Vogt proceeds to ignore it: in the last installment the Distorter suddenly becomes a transport device and whisks Gosseyn II from Earth to Venus. It is as though a can-opener had abruptly turned into a conveyor belt; but the reader is apparently not expected to be surprised.

[No change.]

Style:

Examples of bad writing in *The World of Ā* could be multiplied endlessly. It is my personal opinion that the whole of it is written badly, with only minor exceptions; but this is a purely subjective judgment and is not susceptible of proof. Therefore, I quote below only a few of what I consider to be the worst examples:

He stood like that, eyes half closed, his mind in a state of slow concentration that made physical relaxation one of the important systems for the maintenance of sanity.

[Out.]

His mind held nothing that could be related to physical structure. He hadn't eaten, definitely and unequivocally.

[No change.]

Gosseyn compared his awareness of the night and the fog to the physical world as it appeared to man's senses.

[Out.]

Had she driven up in the car that afternoon KNOWING he would see her. If so, she knew that HE knew who she was . . . If THAT was true, then there was no doubt . . . (Et cetera, ad nauseam.)

[Out.]

He'd have to find that out for sure, of course, but the feeling that it was so lifted the sick pressure from his innards.

[Out.]

Gosseyn's intestinal fortitude strove to climb into his throat, and settled into position again only reluctantly as the acceleration ended.

[Out.]

Something closely akin to fire poured into his brain, and burned away there like a blazing beacon.

[Out.]

His brain was turning rapidly in an illusion of spinning.

[No change.]

There was a drabness about his surroundings that permitted thought.

[This one is lovely: "permitted" has been changed to "dulled."]

His leveling off on a basis of unqualified boldness permitted no prolonged time gap.

[Out.]

The final stairs led down *into* the dungeon; . . . After about ten minutes altogether, Gosseyn saw its source: Massive windows *in* a tree. . . . an immense garden *inside* the tree. . . . "I was so

unwilling to recognize that I was *in* this business that the first
thing I did was get myself killed." . . . He was in this affair, *in* it
as deep as he could go.

[No change.]

I have been progressively annoyed by van Vogt ever since *Slan*.
The first part of this article has vented much of that annoyance,
but there is a remainder: there are trends in van Vogt's work as
a whole which either do not appear strongly in *The World of Ā*, or
could not be treated in a discussion of that story without loss of
objectivity.

There is the regiphile trend, for example. It strikes me as
singular that in van Vogt's stories, nearly all of which deal with
the future, the form of government which occurs most often is
the absolute monarchy; and further, that the monarchs in these
stories are invariably depicted sympathetically. This is true of
the "Weapon Shop" series, the "Mixed Men" series and of single
stories such as "Heir Apparent"—the hero of the latter being a
"benevolent dictator," if you please.

I am attacking van Vogt on literary, not on political grounds,
so I shall not say what I think of a man who loves monarchies.
Neither do I think it relevant that these stories were written and
published during a time when both van Vogt's country (Canada) and
ours were at war with dictatorships, except insofar as it serves to
accentuate this point: Obviously van Vogt is no better acquainted
with current events than he is with ancient or modern history.

The absolute monarchy was a form of government which evolved
to meet feudal economic conditions everywhere, and which has
died everywhere with feudalism. Modern attempts to impose a
similar system on higher cultures have just been proven, very
decisively, to be failures. Monarchy is dead, and it can never
revive until the economic conditions which produced it recur.
It is no crime for van Vogt as a private citizen to wish that this
were not so; but ignorance, for an author, is a crime.

Another trend which appears in van Vogt's work is an apparently
purposeless refusal to call things by their right names. "Ā" and
"lie detector" are two examples; another is the term "robot"
which was employed throughout the "Mixed Men" series. Etymo-
logically the usage was correct; the word, as first used by Čapek,
meant an artificially created protoplasmic man; but it has since
been altered through wide use to mean a mechanical device which
performs some or all of a human being's functions. "Android"—
first used, as far as I know, by Jack Williamson—has assumed
the original meaning of "robot" in science fiction.

"Robot," in the aforementioned series, was a key word: to
garble its meaning was to render the entire story meaningless.
Van Vogt is certainly aware of the changed meaning of the word,
as shown by his use of the term "roboplane"; yet he did not hesi-
tate on that account to call his androids "robots." I do not pretend
to know why.

Still another trend is the plot wherein the leaders of two opposing parties turn out to be identical (*Slan*, "The Weapon Shop").
This trend, however, appears not only in van Vogt's work but in
that of several other *Astounding* writers; and I suspect that the
final responsibility for it rests with Campbell.

This plot device was used by G. K. Chesterton to beautiful effect
in *The Man Who Was Thursday*, and it was effective precisely
because the impression the author wanted to give was that of utter
and imbecilic pointlessness. In van Vogt's hands it gives the same
impression, but without Chesterton's charm.

In general, van Vogt seems to me to fail consistently as a
writer in these elementary ways:

1. His plots do not bear examination.

2. His choice of words and his sentence-structure are fumbling
and insensitive.

3. He is unable either to visualize a scene or to make a character seem real.

By a glib use of quotations, and, I think, still more by a canny
avoidance of detailed exposition, van Vogt has managed to convey
the impression that he has a solid scientific background. A moderately diligent search of his writings, however, will produce
such astonishing exhibitions of ignorance as the following:

> Journeys [to Venus] had been forbidden until some means was
> discovered to overcome the danger of ships falling into the Sun.
> That incandescent fate had befallen two ships. And it had been
> mathematically proven, not merely by cranks, that such a catas-
> trophe would happen to every spaceship until the planets Earth
> and Venus attained a certain general position with relation to
> each other and Jupiter. (From "A Can of Paint," *Astounding*,
> September, 1944.)

It seems to me, as a matter of fact, that van Vogt's reputation
rests largely on what he does not say rather than on what he says.
It is his habit to introduce a monster, or a gadget, or an extraterrestrial culture, simply by naming it, without any explanation
of its nature. It is easy to conclude from this that van Vogt is a
good and a profound writer, for two reasons: first, because van
Vogt's taking the thing for granted is likely to induce a casual

reader to do the same; and second, because this auctorial device is used by many good writers who later supply the omitted explanations obliquely, as integral parts of the action. The fact that van Vogt does nothing of the sort may easily escape notice.

By this means, and by means of his writing style, which is discursive and hard to follow, van Vogt also obscures his plot to such an extent that when it falls to pieces at the end, as it frequently does, the event passes without remark.

In the final scene of "The Rulers" (*Astounding*, March, 1944), for example, when van Vogt's hero is about to be done in by the villains, we learn for the first time that the hero just happens to have the power to make the villain's hypnotized henchmen obey his commands. This denouement is not based on anything which precedes it; it is simply patched on, in the same way that despairing hack writers used to bring in the U. S. Marines.

In "Enter the Professor,"* the hero is confronted by a dilemma —he's been injected with "seven-day poison" by the villains and must return for the antidote; but if he does, he can't squash them in time. Five pages before the end, the hero has a brainstorm and we are led to believe that the solution revolves around a character named Phillips, a double of the hero's who has been properly planted in the beginning of the story. The actual solution, however, turns out to be a bluff backed by an armed ship hovering over the villains' city, a thing which could have been done at any time—a solution of the dilemma by proving that there was no dilemma. The hero pulls some trickery involving Phillips, but this is completely extraneous; it has no bearing on the problem.

The hero's problem in "A Can of Paint"—how to get the perfect paint off his body before it kills him—is solved when he discovers that the "Liquid Light" in it is "absorbed" by a bank of "photo-converter cells" which he happens to have on hand; that is to say, that the doshes are distimmed by the Gostak, and how are you mr. jones?

Altogether, it is a strange world that van Vogt wanders in. In that dark and murky world, medieval rulers ride rocket-ships; supermen count on their fingers; the leader of the Left is also the leader of the Right; and every hero packs a .32 caliber improbability in his hip pocket.

In the absence of Heinlein, Hubbard, de Camp and the rest of *Astounding*'s vanished prewar writers, van Vogt stands like a giant. But he is no giant; he is a pygmy who has learned to operate an overgrown typewriter.

*By E. Mayne Hull, *Astounding*, January, 1945: but the voice is the voice of Jacob.

Empire of the Atom is a somewhat altered version of van Vogt's five "Clane" stories which ran in *Astounding* during 1946 and 1947. (The three-part serial, "The Wizard of Linn," which appeared in 1950, is not included.) An attempt has been made in Chapter 10, and in the genealogical charts used as endpapers, to justify the publishers' claim that the character of Clane is based on that of Lorenzo de' Medici. Actually, as James Blish pointed out at the time, the entire story is lifted almost bodily from the life of Claudius Caesar, and, more to the point, from Robert Graves' brilliant novel, *I, Claudius.* No serious effort has been made to efface the evidence — most of the names of principal characters are transparent disguises, Clane for Claudius, Tews for Tiberius, Lydia for Livia, &c. Van Vogt's Linn is Augustan Rome in almost every detail. (Even the coinage is in sesterces.)

The wonder is that, using such unlikely materials, and adapting them without a grain of common sense (nothing in the book suggests that van Vogt realizes there is anything more complicated about an expedition to Mars than about one to Gaul), the author should have produced a narrative on the whole so lively and readable. The references to atomics in the story are nonsense from beginning to end; so are those to strategy and tactics; even the multiplication is wrong; and yet van Vogt's single-minded power maniacs exert their usual fascination. You can at least be sure that a van Vogt character will never break down into sentimental altruism at a crucial moment; his villains are thoroughgoing bastards, and so are his heroes. In addition, the man does work on a grand scale: the magnitude of his backgrounds, and their massive movement, are engrossing in themselves. If you can only throw your reasoning powers out of gear—something many van Vogt fans find easy to do—you'll enjoy this one.

6. HALF-BAD WRITERS

THE HYPOTHETICAL READER who, looking up from one of the books dealt with in this chapter, should remark, "This isn't half bad," would be wrong. These books are half bad. They are the work of an infuriating small group of highly talented writers, who operate "by the seat of their pants," in the innocent conviction that their every word is golden.

A totally bad book is a kind of joy in itself, like a completely ugly dog; but these in-betweens, in which the author seems on alternate pages a genius and an idiot, are almost unbearable.

Take, for instance, a good, hard look at *I Am Legend*, by Richard Matheson. This story of the last live man, in a world where everyone else has become a vampire, has frequent moments of raw power: it's a theme perfectly adapted to Matheson's undisciplined, oh-my-God style, and he has developed it, in many places, with great ingenuity and skill. The book is full of good ideas, every other one of which is immediately dropped and kicked out of sight. The characters are child's drawings, as blank-eyed and expressionless as the author himself in his back-cover photograph. The plot limps. All the same, the story could have been an admirable minor work in the tradition of *Dracula*,* if only the author, or somebody, had not insisted on encumbering it with the year's most childish set of "scientific" rationalizations. For instance: vampirism is caused by a bacillus. Matheson's hero evolves this notion, apparently by opening a physiology text at random and stabbing with the thumb, and tests it by examining a specimen of vampire's blood under the microscope. He "proves" it by finding one—count it—one bacillus in the specimen. Previously, we are

*Of which Matheson writes, "The book was a hodgepodge of superstition and soap-opera cliches . . ."

told, the world's medical experts had failed to isolate the cause of the epidemic. Probably they were harder to satisfy.

On this slender foundation the hero erects a theory which has half the ten-dollar words of immunology in it, but does not make a nickel's worth of sense. Vampires can't be killed by bullets, for instance, because the bacillus causes the secretion of a—hold your hat—*powerful body glue* that seals up the bullet holes. (The bacillus also "provides energy," by the way, and makes the dog teeth grow.) Antibiotics won't work because—hold it again—the victims' bodies can't fight germs and make antibodies at the same time. It can't be done, believe him. It's a trap.

About a third of the book is taken up with this nonsense, which has been stuffed in with no gentle hand. The early part of it reads exactly as if Matheson had sat down with a first draft and an editor's letter beside him, copied off the questions (How does the hero, who knows no anatomy, always manage to hit the heart with his oaken stake? Why don't the vampires burn his house down if they want to get him out so badly?) and answered them with the first thing that came into his head.

This book has been well publicized as Gold Medal's first venture into science fiction. Those of us who write science fiction or read it for pleasure are now in the rather odd position of having no grounds for caring whether the book sells or not. If it doesn't, this important market will almost certainly be closed to us again. If it does, Gold Medal's editors will be confirmed in their present misconception that they know what science fiction is. The results will accordingly continue to be "horrid, all ass and no forehead..."

The novels of J. T. McIntosh (except for his first one, the inept *World Out of Mind*), have so many good things in them, and the things that are bad are so obvious and easily reparable, that it seems to me both the author and his publishers must be hagridden by halfwits.

In *Born Leader*, for example, the plot concerns two loads of interstellar colonists, fleeing from a doomed Earth, who have wound up independently on neighboring planets in the same system. The trip took them about 16 years at near light-speed; and a very minor segment of the plot turns on the exercise machines they used to keep their muscles firm during 14 years of free fall.

Didn't it occur to anybody that 14 years of zero gravity, for a colonists' vessel carrying livestock, is a practical impossibility —or that it could be avoided simply by spinning ship?

In the same book, the two planets are named Mundis and Secundis: good Latin, but the least unlikely translation is "to the worlds" and "to the seconds," which is pretty silly.

The contrast between the democratic, peace-loving Mundans and the tyrants of Secundis is a telling one—spoilt by giving the Mundans such a roster of "pure" Anglo-Saxon names as can't be found even in a random sampling of the British Isles.*

And so on. In Chapter 7 Phyllis Barton, a young Secundan and a very well-drawn character, hatches a scheme to cut the ground from under her superior, Commodore Corey. It works, even though Corey's cooperation, to a degree possible only to a suicide or an idiot, is a necessary part of it. The story progresses through a series of genuine and interesting problems—none of which, if you look closely, is solved. The author slides past every one and then tells you it's solved, when, with a slightly greater expenditure of thought, he could have shown you.

Like *Born Leader*, McIntosh's *One In Three Hundred* is a forthright, good-humored, dramatic tale that's remarkably easy and pleasant to read; it is also, like its predecessor, a painful collection of avoidable mistakes.

McIntosh is a gee-whiz writer.

Let me give you an example. A man sits down at his typewriter to outline a new plot. A solar flare (he writes) threatens all life on Earth. Gee whiz! There aren't enough existing spaceships to get everybody to Mars, so they build a lot of dinky little ships. Gee whiz! But even so, only one out of 300 can go, so they have to send these lieutenants (sic), the ones who are going to captain the ships (sic), around to all the towns to pick out the ones that are going to go. Well, we follow one of these dinky, rotten, little haywire ships that can only take 11 people. Well, as soon as they take off, the pilot notices that there isn't going to be enough fuel. Gee whiz! So he . . .

This is as good a place as any to stop and say let's-see-now. Build a lot of dinky little ships that can transport 11 people each? Great; this makes fully as much sense as building a lot of teaspoons to put out a fire with; or, let's say, building a lot of garbage scows to evacuate North America. (1) The "lifeships" are of a size and design for which there couldn't possibly have been any previous demand. Unlike larger passenger ships, they have to be designed and engineered from scratch. There will inevitably be bugs in them. (2) It is enormously wasteful of metal, of engines, of metering instruments, of crewmen, of everything necessary to

*This is probably carelessness rather than chauvinism. In the twenties no character in fiction had any but an aristocratic Anglo-Saxon name, unless he was either a comic butler or a ruffian; and a surprising number of writers haven't noticed that 30 years have elapsed since then.

a ship, to build 100 little ships rather than one big one. (3) The "lifeships," which McIntosh has taking off directly from Earth, have to be duck-designed—built for the wasteful short haul up from Earth as well as the long haul to Mars.

Take another look. Once our ship gets out into space, the passengers discover it is too well insulated; they are slowly being roasted to death by their own body heat, until they take a couple of insulating panels off. Gee whiz! . . . At the time of the story, the author would have us believe, we have been in the spaceship business for some years; we've got a colony on Mars and regular, if infrequent, passenger service thereto—and all this time, nobody has figured out a way to regulate the interior temperature of spaceships, until this very *moment? Really?*

Another crisis arises when somebody has to go outside in a spacesuit, and it's discovered that the helmet has "a jagged, irregular lump of metal" inside it which prevents it from being worn. Gee whiz again! But let's see now . . . could this happen to a machined helmet? Are you *sure?*

Faults like these are exasperating in a story otherwise so good. So—to name one more—is the effort involved in trying to forget that McIntosh's nice British characters are supposed to be natives of the midwestern U.S.A.

Most exasperating of all, not one of this story's flaws is essential to it. If they had all been corrected, the story would have been basically much the same; but it would have been a thousand times more plausible, a lot more fun to read—and beyond doubt it would have lived longer than it is now doomed to do.

McIntosh is a young and exceedingly promising writer: it would be remarkable if he had mastered all the demands of his craft in the few years he's been working at it. But when may we expect the editors of Doubleday to learn theirs?

Arthur Koestler's *Darkness at Noon,* probably the key novel of our century, defined the modern problem of conscience so sharply and explored it with such thoroughness that George Orwell, in his brilliant *Nineteen Eighty-Four,* had only to expand and project it. The conflict is the same, Ingsoc is only the Russian socialist state carried one step further; Winston Smith is the spiritual heir of the Old Bolshevik Rubashov, and even his occupation, in the Ministry of Truth, derives from one sentence in *Darkness at Noon:*

> . . . Rubashov remarked jokingly to Arlova that the only thing left to be done was to publish a new and revised edition of the back numbers of newspapers.

In the shadow of this double monument, David Karp, the Vanguard Press, the Book of the Month Club and Clifton Fadiman have combined their forces to lay a brick.

The plot of David Karp's *One* can be stated briefly: a man named Burden, professor of English at Templar College in an unspecified country, at some unspecified future date, is a part-time informer for the nameless authoritarian government of that country. Himself examined for heretical beliefs, he is found guilty; whereupon the Department of Internal Examination (Koestler's People's Commissariat of the Interior; Orwell's Ministry of Love) sets out to convert him. Partly because the D.I.E. inquisitor, Lark, is an amateur compared to Ivanov and O'Brien, and partly because Burden (in the author's opinion, though his own evidence does not support him) is made of tougher stuff than Rubashov or Smith, they succeed only by wiping out all their victim's memories and building up a totally new personality. Even then, the success is temporary; the new Burden, re-christened Hughes, sins again and has to be destroyed.

In this particular, *One* turns to an older model: Burden is redeemed, whereas the point made by *Darkness at Noon* and *Nineteen Eighty-Four* is precisely that for the 20th-century Faust there is no redemption, and no hope.

It would be pleasant to suppose that Karp is right, Koestler and Orwell wrong; even pleasanter to find the case argued plausibly.

But Lark's despair, when he discovers his failure with Burden, is unreal; the point is curiously pointless: the State does not stand or fall with Burden, as Lark unaccountably thinks. Like Rubashov, like Smith, Burden is a member of a vanishing class, a man old enough to remember another state of affairs and another set of values. The Rubashovs are replaced by Gletkins, the "Neanderthalers" with no memories and no traditions, "a generation born without umbilical cords"; the Smiths are replaced by Parsons; and the Burdens also have no heirs; they die and are replaced by the dehumanized young members of the Church of State, eager, conscientious, honest and unimaginative, who never say "I."

This latter invention, although it vitiates Karp's whole argument, is one of the chief virtues of his book; the description of the Church of State meeting is oppressively real. Similar flashes of imaginative insight occur here and there: Burden's childhood fear of being turned to stone if his father looked at him in anger, and his rage at the addition of fresh water to artificial flowers are true touches; they go deeper than logic, they're viscerally compelling. But this is a long book, and there aren't enough of them to go around.

One sentence of Clifton Fadiman's glib testimonial is worth quoting here: "Without any concession to sentimentality, Mr. Karp leaves us fascinated, exhausted, scared—but by no means despairing."

I'll buy that, all but one word. The book is fascinating; it has the one essential requirement of successful bad books: it makes you wonder what's going to happen next. It did leave me exhausted; I finished it in two sittings, and made two pages of irritated notes. It left me by no means despairing, even for the future of the American publishing industry; but it didn't, even for an instant, scare me.

It couldn't, because except for a rare page or paragraph at a time, no single character comes to life. Burden himself is a cardboard nincompoop; Lark shows signs of Machiavellian intelligence when interrogating Burden, and immediately spoils it all by talking like a schoolboy to his superior; the minor characters, nearly all of them, are names without faces. Worse still—and this is the central fault of the book—the real enemy, the State, cannot be judged, cannot be compared, and cannot frighten because it does not exist: it not only has no name, but no history, no philosophy, no doctrine of its own, no slogans, no catchphrases; it displaces no air and leaves no footprints.

A villain without a motive might as well wear handlebar mustaches and snarl, "Ah, me proud beauty"; the audience would at least know it was expected to hiss.

For Ivanov, the end justifies the means:

> "Have you ever read brochures of an anti-vivisectionist society? They are shattering and heartbreaking; when one reads how some poor cur which has had its liver cut out, whines and licks his tormentor's hands, one is just as nauseated as you were tonight. But if these people had their way, we would have no serums against cholera, typhoid, or diphtheria. . . ."

For O'Brien, the means justifies itself:

> "We know that no one ever seizes power with the intention of relinquishing it. . . The object of persecution is persecution. The object of torture is torture. The object of power is power. . ."

For Lark, who exists, himself, only in flickers, there is neither means nor end: he tortures Burden because he has been put there by the author to do so.

These comparisons are harsh, but the author has invited them and must take them along with his royalties. Perhaps the most curious thing about this book is that Karp has nowhere seized the opportunity, which placing his story in the future gives him, of implementing his tyranny with new technology; whenever it has been possible to advance a step beyond Koestler, Karp has resolutely taken one back from Orwell. The system of human informers in *Darkness at Noon*, for example, becomes a system of electronic informers in *Nineteen Eighty-Four*:

> For a moment he was tempted to take [the note] into one of the water closets and read it at once. But that would be shocking folly, as he well knew. There was no place where you could be more certain that the telescreen was watching continuously.

Carried one step further still, this becomes the system of narcotic informers, of self-betrayal; and indeed, Karp uses this method on Burden as a unique exception, without reflecting that it makes his human-informer system an anachronism twice over. Perhaps technology is not Karp's forte; there are several technical errors in the book, most of them common ones, so that it's hard to tell whether they're introduced deliberately, or whether it's the author himself who doesn't know that schizophrenia is not the same thing as multiple personality, that trained medical workers do not take pulses with their thumbs, that sexual congress is not the only way to contract syphilis.

Karp's style is precise and colorless, marred by a few self-conscious genteelisms—e.g., "place" for "put," usually at the expense of grammar and common sense.

Reprieve From Paradise, by H. Chandler Elliott, is an eloquent, muddy, perplexing first novel. The background, which involves a world-wide Polynesian culture dedicated to "breeding and feeding," is complex and intimately detailed; the satire, a funny-revolting extension of modern popular culture (love ballads and all) into a Way of Life, is wonderfully sharp. The style varies from a kind of heavy colloquialism (*"This* was *it!"*) through a kaleidoscope of elaborate awkwardness ("And his unfledged mind had found her a road to flaming revelation.". . . "The face of the woman, seated on a couch" . . .) to an occasional unexpectedly vivid image:

> The inhuman beauty of sky and hills was being swallowed in a living darkness, a cloak flung across the sky and swirled westwards as it lagged behind the wheel of the expanding latitudes that ringed the pole.

The plot takes Pahad tuan Konor, an instructor at the last of the great Universities, through a series of misadventures as predictable as they are unlikely—the standard beautiful spy, murder plot, stolen document, and so on—to a rebel utopia in the Antarctic, which turns out to be surprisingly convincing and desirable.

The hero, invincibly stupid like all his kind, fails to see what is under his nose and the reader's for ten long chapters; betrays the rebels to his own people; realizes his error at the last moment and has to turn traitor all over again, before the story can wind itself up in the usual rosy manner.

Two things, it seems to me, keep this story from coming to life for longer than a page or two, in spite of a carefully built framework, good character drawing, convincing scientific details and many other virtues: First, like nearly all the rest of the modern stories built on what Heinlein calls the "Man Who Learned Better" theme, this one fails on the question of guilt in apostasy. The hero switches sides—although so tardily that you want to kick him—as easily as a man crossing the street: and his realization, after the second betrayal, that he can never give himself wholly to any society, is admirable but comes much too late.

Second, I'm afraid, Elliott has simply bitten off more time than he could chew. The farther futureward a story goes, the more thoroughly divorced the imagined society gets from anything we now know, the harder it is for the author to bring his story to life. At any rate, the liveliest and most convincing episodes in this book are not those which belong to the far future of the story proper, but those which date much nearer the present, and are experienced by the hero as a kind of super-movie—a "neurreson" —merely to fill in the historical background.

The standard love story in this adventure novel is as flat and lifeless as usual; but it's only fair to add that Elliott's notion of love goes—a refreshing novelty—beyond clichés: the delicate, entirely innocent relationship between the hero and Elisis, an adolescent rebel girl, is a delightful thing.

Raymond Z. Gallun's science fiction stories first began appearing in 1929. He is a skilled and resourceful writer, who unfortunately has what is probably the clumsiest touch with the English language since Austin Hall's. Groping uncertainly, he pulls out a noun when he wants a verb; a verb when he wants a noun. His meaning shines blurrily, through a shimmer of approximate words. His narrative sentences tumble out jerky and double-jointed. His dialogue is exactly the same, so that his characters can never converse normally, but always seem to be making speeches to one another.

The far futures and alien intelligences of science fiction were Gallun's salvation in the thirties. If his characters spoke like nothing human, that only made them more plausible: and many of his stories of that period, such as "Old Faithful," "Davy Jones' Ambassador," and "Seeds of the Dusk," are among the most vivid and memorable stories about aliens ever written.

In the early forties, when science fiction was growing more realistic and somewhat less imaginative, Gallun dropped out of sight. He reappeared about 1950 and has kept turning up infrequently since, without attracting much notice. *People Minus X* is his first hardcover book, and his first novel-length science fiction work of any kind.

The story begins with a young man, Ed Dukas, staring at a letter he has been writing, on which an invisible pen is tracing the word "Nipper." Ed's astonishment is documented at some length, but unconvincingly (he not only doesn't try to touch the hand which is presumably writing, but doesn't even have to repress the impulse to do so).

Then we get a flashback which lasts for 64 pages.

Ed's Uncle Mitch, the only man who ever called him "Nipper," disappeared after being partly responsible for a catastrophe in which the Moon was destroyed, and 200,000,000 people killed. Among the dead: Ed's father, and a henpecked neighbor named Ronald Peyton. Neither had taken the then-common precaution of having his "body record" made. If they had, Humpty Dumpty could have been put together again: spanking new copies could have been manufactured, identical to the originals down to the last cell. As it was, copies were made anyhow, based on memories of the victims' wives, friends and acquaintances.

These revenants were the "people minus X" of the title: they were almost, not quite, acceptable copies. Something was missing: a decade or so ago, it would have been called the soul. Sometimes the changes were trivial, sometimes comic: Peyton's overbearing wife remembered him as a brute, so the copy she got *was* a brute.

Some of the copies were physiologically human; others, however, were put together out of a new substance called vitaplasm, and they were stronger, tougher and more adaptable than normal people. As the years passed, racial antagonism against "the Phonies" increased; rabble-rousers appeared, there were outbreaks of violence, and somebody began manufacturing vitaplasm monsters to stir up still more prejudice.

. . . Having remembered all this, Ed is arrested by police who have been spying on him with electronic eavesdropping devices, and who think he can lead them to Uncle Mitch. While Ed is in his cell, another message mysteriously appears on a scrap of paper he holds in his hand: "Nipper—argue police—you go Port Smitty—

at once." Ed accordingly goes, marrying his girl and taking her
along, and the police go too, keeping their distance like children
playing hare and hounds.

Now Uncle Mitch, as you might have guessed, has used micro-
miniaturization techniques (an idea that fascinated Gallun as long
ago as 1936) to create an invisibly small duplicate of himself.
It's this duplicate who wrote the messages, and who, riding along
with Ed, directs him to the concealed laboratory in the Martian
desert where his original body lies in suspended animation.

And here, 100 pages into the book, Gallun's story suddenly
comes to life.

Ed and his wife Barbara consent to use the apparatus Uncle
Mitch has left waiting, to make miniature duplicates of themselves. They lose consciousness in the tanks of the apparatus:
they awaken in a microscopic wonderland.

> Close by, everything was slightly blurred, as if [they] were far-
> sighted. Farther off, objects became hazed, as by countless
> drifting, speeding dots that weren't opaque but that seemed—each
> of them—to be surrounded by refractive rings that distorted the
> view of what lay beyond them.

Now by God, this is science fiction. It performs s.f.'s specific
function, to lift us out of the here-and-now and show us marvels.
No matter how badly it's written, if a story does that it is s.f.
A story that fails to do that, no matter how well written, isn't.

This story does it, eventually, with the vividness for whose
sake s.f. readers have always been willing to swallow a little ab-
surdity. [People in stories who blithely walk into matter trans-
mitters, to be "broken down into their constituent atoms, and
reassembled at the receiver," never seem to reflect that even
though, to the reassembled person, experience may seem to be
continuous, for the original person, experience stops—in effect,
it's death. In a similar way, Ed and Barbara seem blind to the
fact that in consenting to have tiny copies made of themselves,
they are dooming the copies to live out their lives in the world of
smallness. The only route of return is via another copying, which
is no return at all. As for vitaplasm, the stuff that enables the
micro-people to live and function even in vacuum (Gallun says it
is "capable of drawing its energy from sunlight or radioactivity"),
this is nonsense or magic, not science. But like Well's "Cavorite"
and a host of other improbable devices, it gets us to a place that
common sense can't reach.]

Dust motes, to Ed and his friends, are jagged crystalline stones,
or twisted masses like the roots of trees. When the police find the

hidden laboratory and force their way in, the event has a titanic grandeur: "It seemed then that the mountains opened, unfolded, grew taller, disgorged Atlases. . . ." And: "The face, briefly glimpsed, was a huge pitted mask, bearded with a forest of dark and tangled trunks."

Often enough, after this point, the story dips back into Gallun's muddled and pedestrian interpretation of the here-and-now. But in occasional passages, such as the heroes' epic, self-propelled journey from Mars to Earth, it touches the pure nerve of wonder. In places, even Gallun's leaden prose turns to poetry: "spoke without sound in the stinging silence" is exactly right.

The full meaning of the story appears only after the ostensible plot is all done with. The human-android conflict has been solved by leaving Earth to the humans: the androids can thrive anywhere. Spreading out, colonizing the planets of other stars, they are just beginning to realize the vastness of the experience ahead of them. Suns may turn cold and nebulas dim; the androids who are living now will still be there—changed, and yet the same—still on the move, still questing.

Gallun, who wrote this story once before, too ("Avalanche," by "Dow Elstar," in *Astounding*, December, 1935), sums up his vision in these words, near the close of the story:

> Inconceivably far off were other galaxies. Maybe Ed read her mind a little, as she thought of the vast, tilted swirl of the one in Andromeda. . . As a child she used to look at a picture of it and think that everything she could imagine, and much more, was there: books, musical instruments, summer nights, dark horror.

In *The Body Snatchers*, Jack Finney, author of several of the slicks' most beautifully made short fantasies (including the classic "I'm Scared") has put together a skilful Hollywood parody of science fiction.

In the little town of Santa Mira, California, a curious psychic epidemic occurs. Ordinary, sensible people will come to a doctor and doggedly confess they believe some member of their family to be an impostor. He looks like my Uncle Ira, they'll say, talks like him, knows everything he should—but it isn't Uncle Ira.

Young Dr. Miles Bennell turns his first case over to a psychiatrist friend and forgets it, until another friend calls him to witness an appalling sight: a human body, neither living nor dead, which isn't quite human—not fully formed, a blank waiting for individuality to be stamped on it. Slowly, they come to realize the truth—the people of Santa Mira are being systematically copied and replaced by strange vegetable pods from space, which have the power to reproduce any living thing to the last atom. To anticipate a little, this is how it works:

> "So it can happen, Doctor Bennell, and rather easily; the intricate patterns of electrical force-lines that knit together every atom of your body to form and constitute every cell of it—can be slowly transferred. And then, since every kind of atom in the universe is identical—you are precisely duplicated, atom for atom, molecule for molecule, cell for cell, down to the tiniest scar or hair on your wrist. And what happens to the original? The atoms that formerly composed you are—static now, nothing, a pile of gray fluff. . ."

The town of Santa Mira, where this horror happens, is so real that you can close your eyes and see it. The people, too, are solid, living and breathing: Finney writes so vividly that his story carries utter conviction—until you stop to think.

The quotation above is one very small example. In the second sentence, the key one, what Finney says about atoms is simply, flatly, not true.

If this seems trivial, take another example: the seed pods, says Finney, drifted across interstellar space to Earth, propelled by light pressure. This echoes a familiar notion, the spore theory of Arrhenius. But the spores referred to are among the smallest living things—small enough to be knocked around by hydrogen molecules in the upper atmosphere, and so escape into space; and small enough—with a surface-to-mass ratio so large—that light will propel them against the force of gravitation.

In confusing these minute particles with three-foot seed pods, Finney invalidates his whole argument—and makes ludicrous nonsense of the final scene in which the pods, defeated, float up into the sky to hunt another planet.

Worse, almost from the beginning the characters follow the author's logic rather than their own. Bennell and his friends the Belicecs, intelligent and capable people, exhibit an invincible stupidity whenever normal intelligence would allow them to get ahead with the mystery too fast.

When they have four undeveloped seed pods on their hands, for instance, they do none of the obvious things—make no tests, take no photographs, display the objects to no witnesses. Bennell, a practicing physician, never thinks of X-raying the pods.

And they destroy all four pods before these can come to maturity. This makes excellent sense from the author's point of view. *He* knows that allowing a pod to mature would mean the death of one of his chief characters: but *they* don't.

Bennell makes a phone call to a Pentagon officer he knows, and gets no satisfaction for obvious reasons; Belicec then tries to call the FBI, but discovers that the pod creatures are now in control of the local telephone exchange.

So they all pile into a car and run for it. The author's purpose in this is served once they get out of town—he wants to show you the deteriorating condition of the one feeder road that gives access to Santa Mira—so when they have got out, and slept overnight in a motel, they turn around and go back. Why don't they call the FBI from an out-of-town phone? No reason.

The big climactic scenes follow—all of them fine drama—as the pods' investiture of the town becomes complete. Bennell and his girl, the last two human beings left, are at least following their own logic in trying to escape—except when they visit a college professor because he can tell the reader something about the origin of the pods, and for no other evident reason. But the ending, also dramatic (and great for wide screen), leaves a sour taste.

> . . . the pods could tell with certainty that this planet, this little race, would never receive them, and would never yield. And Becky and I, in refusing to surrender, but instead fighting their invasion to the end, giving up any hope of escape in order to destroy even a few of them, had provided the final and conclusive demonstration of that fact. And so now, to survive—their one purpose and function—the great pods lifted and rose, climbing up through the faint mist, and out toward the space they had come from. . . .

Nuts. If Finney's nightmare had actually happened, and nobody concerned had had the God-given sense to holler cop, we would all be pods by now—and deserve it.

7. ONE SANE MAN: *Robert A. Heinlein*

ROBERT A. HEINLEIN has that attribute which the mathematician Hermann Weyl calls "the inexhaustibility of real things": whatever you say about him, I find, turns out to be only partly true. If you point to his innate conservatism, as evidenced in the old-time finance of "The Man Who Sold the Moon," you may feel smug for as much as a minute, until you remember the rampantly radical monetary system of *Beyond This Horizon*. One or two similar mistakes of mine are embedded in this chapter.

With due caution, then, let me say that in art, at least, Heinlein seems to be as conservative as they come. He believes in a plain tale well told. Although he fancies his own Yukon-style verses, or used to, he has no patience with poetry-in-a-garret. The people he writes about are healthy, uninhibited and positive, a totally different breed from the neurasthenic heroes of many of his colleagues. In a field whose most brilliant and well-established writers seem to flip sooner or later, Heinlein is preeminently sane.

Revolt in 2100 is the third volume in the Shasta Future History series: it includes a considerably rewritten "If This Goes On—," "Coventry" and "Misfit."

The original version of "If This Goes On—," published in *Astounding* in 1940, was Heinlein's first novel, and a massive addition to the structure he was beginning to build in science fiction.

Fifteen years ago, when this story was written, Heinlein must have been as happy as a pup in clover. He had discovered an interesting and lucrative occupation, most of whose practitioners were dunderheads. He had only to apply common sense, industry, intelligence—and an uncommon arsenal of knowledge—to turn science fiction upside down; and with something near the shortest apprenticeship on record, he set about doing just that.

Religious tyrannies in science fiction are a dime a dozen, each one less plausible than the last. It took Heinlein to show what might happen to Christianity in this country under given, perfectly possible, conditions—mass communications, a hysterical populace, and a backwoods gospel shouter for a catalyst; and if anyone here present is less frightened of that picture now than when the story was written, I wish he would try to convince me.

Revolution, as I've had occasion to mention elsewhere, has always been a favorite theme in science fiction. It's romantic, it's reliable, and—as a rule—it's as phony as a Martian princess.

Who but Heinlein ever pointed out, as he does here in detail, that a modern revolution is big business? And who but Heinlein would have seen that fraternal organizations, for thirty years the butt of highbrow American humor, would make the perfect nucleus for an American underground against tyranny?

The present revision is chiefly designed to make the hero and heroine more like people we know and less like the principals in a medieval romance. I'm afraid I regret the story-book romance between John Lyle and his Temple handmaiden, but I concede automatically that the new ending is more lifelike. Nearly all the new prose is a joy in itself: I'm especially appreciative of the added space given to Zebediah Jones, the wiseacre without whom no Heinlein story is complete.

One of the minor changes, though, makes me painfully conscious of my own drawbacks as a critic of Heinlein. In the original version, Lyle had to bail out of a stolen jet without shutting off the torch. Problem: how to keep from getting fried. Solution: He wraps himself in the seat cover, which "happens" to be made of asbestos. As you can see, this is from desperation, and Heinlein has now solved the problem more elaborately and much more plausibly.

The funny thing is that I miss the old version. I remember the flash of heat as Lyle went through that jet. I know it was hokum, but I don't care; I liked it. It *felt* right.

My trouble is simply that I was seventeen when this story was first published. My most impressionable age happened to coincide with a peak year in science fiction, and the effect seems to have been permanent. However, I've done my best to overcome this lack; I have collected every adverse criticism of Heinlein I could find. So far I have two: (1) His plots are weak. (2) He uses slang. Both of these statements are obviously true, and one seems to me about as unimportant as the other. So there you are. Either Heinlein is the nearest thing to a great writer the science fiction field has yet produced, or with all my pennyweighting I'm hopelessly biased on the subject; take your choice.

"Coventry"—if there's really anybody in the audience who hasn't read it—is a kind of footnote to the novel, and a bridge to the fas-

cinating world of *Methuselah's Children*. "Misfit" is, as even I
can see, an awkwardly written short story, chiefly notable because
it introduces the mathematical genius Libby, who later turns up
as one of the supporting players in *Methuselah*.

There is a note by Heinlein, "Concerning Stories Never Written,"
which partially satisfies my curiosity about (but whets my appetite
for) "The Sound of His Wings," "Eclipse" and "The Stone Pillow."
Still unexplained are "Word Edgewise," "Fire Down Below!" and
"Da Capo."

There is, finally, a remarkable introduction by Henry Kuttner.
That makes two out of three of these Shasta volumes whose intro-
ductions (by Henry Kuttner and Mark Reinsberg) have been of a
critical quality that we simply don't expect to find in this field.
Perhaps the subject has something to do with it.

Four of Heinlein's long novelettes appear in the Fantasy Press
volume, *Assignment in Eternity*. "Gulf" is Heinlein's superman
story from the November, 1949 "trick issue" *Astounding*: as ebul-
lient a mixture as he's ever written, hardboiled adventure, uninhibited satire, pathos, sober philosophy—and one of the most
thoroughly annihilating criticisms of another writer ever buried in
an innocent page of dialogue—all in one gorgeous bundle. "Jerry
Was A Man" is more vintage stuff: the emancipation of the apes,
written as no one else could have done it. "Lost Legacy" is the
parapsychology story—from which a cautious editor at Popular
Publications deleted all mention of Ambrose Bierce, fearing the
old gentleman would turn up and sue, I suppose—not quite incom-
prehensibly neglected till now; it's from the period when Heinlein's treads were still slipping occasionally. The story remains
the most logical and most breathtaking treatment of its theme, but
the plotline has a tendency to waver and collapse into triteness.
"Elsewhen" is a potboiler, the only really lifeless story of Heinlein's I can remember. It has some very pleasant porridge-
fantasy scenes; it's perhaps the kind of story Heinlein might have
written if he'd been born somebody else altogether, say a poetry-
loving drugstore clerk in Des Moines. Nearly every published
writer has some botches like this one clinging to his bootsoles
—some are completely covered with them—but I must say it's an
agreeable surprise to me to find that Heinlein has any.

The impersonation of a hero is, I suppose, one of the most overworked plot devices in fiction. There have been phony Tarzans
wandering around the prop jungle, phony Supermen strutting in
monogrammed tights; phony princes, presidents, &c., ad nauseam.
But in *Double Star* Robert Heinlein demonstrates again that the
boobs cannot put so many greasy fingerprints on an idea, that a

good writer cannot lift it out shining and new.

Problem: John J. Bonforte, leader of one of the two chief political coalitions in the Solar Empire, has been abducted just before a Martian ceremony at which he must appear. Solution: a double —an at-liberty actor styling himself Lorenzo the Great. The impersonation, at first planned to last only a short time, has to be extended again and again, and in the process Lorenzo—and the reader—learns what it is like to be the elected leader of eight billion people.

I confess to mixed feelings about this book. It's as hypnotically written as the best Heinlein; the characters are as strong, and in general the technical work is a joy to watch. Lorenzo, for instance, is not only an actor, which is refreshing—most doubles are merely long-lost twin brothers, or hoboes who when shaved bear a startling resemblance to Ronald Colman—but he talks like an actor and thinks like an actor, which is vanishingly rare. The politics, too, is real politics, and not the usual stale hash of ignorance.

But there's a point at which these virtues begin to give us an uneasy feeling that if they were only shaved and cleaned up a little, they would look like faults. Lorenzo's acting experience, for instance, seems to be less an extrapolation than a mishmash of modern-day stage, circus and TV. Bonforte might easily have been the premier of a somewhat smaller Empire, and even the Martian ceremony of adoption has a pretty obvious parallel in the recent political history of this country. What's left is science fiction—but there's very little left.

And yet, the Mars of *Double Star*, if it's less romantic than that of *Red Planet*, is absolutely convincing. The Martians themselves are, by far, Heinlein's most imaginatively alien non-terrestrials to date, and I regret their brief appearance in the story. The narrative is always exciting, sometimes deeply moving—and there are one or two surprises I haven't mentioned. Most of all, I think the book is rewarding for the cumulative sense of Heinlein's own philosophy which it gives you, particularly in the unforgettable last lines.

Heinlein's *The Door Into Summer* has a plot about as original as the Grimm fairy tale "The Golden Bird" (in which the good brother does all the work while the bad one gets all the credit), and about as convincing as Buck Rogers: Good Guy invents a flock of useful machines; Bad Guy and Bad Girl, his partner and fiancée, fleece him of same and plonk him into cold-sleep to get rid of him. Good Guy wakes up in the future, finds a professor who has in-

vented time travel (but is sitting on the discovery for reasons too
flimsy to mention), goes back to his own time, gets his revenge,
then cold-sleeps *again* in order to catch up.

I loved it.

Mind you, this is a shoddy novel. But look: when the story
opens, the hero is a morally defeated man with a galloping case of
self-pity and a cumulative hangover, looking in the bottoms of shot
glasses for the Door Into Summer. If anybody else had written it,
this guy's oozing sorrow for himself would have dripped until it
made you sick. (Turn the average writer onto the subject of self-
pity and you have an immediate autobiography.) But Heinlein's
hero, even in this sad state, has so much sheer gusto left over,
it's a pleasure to identify yourself with him.

Heinlein's greatest asset, I think, is this same perennial hero—
essentially he's Heinlein himself, and Heinlein likes himself. This
is a thing so rare in writers-by-necessity, who are insecure, self-
critical men, that every now and then a writer-by-accident who
has it, as Mark Twain did, cheerfully walks away with all the
prizes in sight.

As usual, this book shows the fruits of Heinlein's mature inquiring mind: he makes the spirit and practice of engineering
come so vividly alive that I almost wish I had been better at math.
Also as usual, the last third of the book is scamped. Heinlein is
like the young man from Japan,

> Whose limericks never would scan.
> When asked why this was,
> He answered, "Because
> I always try to cram as many words into the last line
> as I possibly can."

Fifteen years or so ago, the phrase "science fiction juvenile"
automatically meant two boys and their scientist-uncle roaring off
into some adventure in dimension more notable for its excitement
than for its scientific accuracy. This formula is probably nearly
as basic as boy-meets-girl; Heinlein used it unblushingly in the
first (and least) of his juveniles for Scribner's, *Rocket Ship Galileo*,
then abandoned it entirely, with magnificent results, in the next
four—*Space Cadet, Red Planet, Farmer in the Sky* and *Between
Planets*—then returned to it in his sixth, with embellishments, as
if to prove that it doesn't have to be bad. He makes his point;
The Rolling Stones, if it lacks some fraction of the adult appeal
its predecessors had, will probably be at least as satisfactory to
the teenagers for whom it was written.

The two boys are twins, Castor and Pollux Stone; the "uncle" of the formula is their father, Roger Stone; but the roll-call doesn't end there. Also present and very much accounted for are their mother, Edith Stone, M.D.; their grandmother, Hazel Meade Stone; their older sister Meade; and their small-fry brother Lowell. Counting the twins as a unit, and with the single exception of Meade, every one of the family is a distinct and by no means ordinary character.

This is a good place for me to eat a few words; I once wrote:

> . . . Most striking of all, these people are not preselected for their gigantic intelligence or their colorful personalities; they are simply a random sampling of genus homo. So far as I can recall, there is not a character in any one of Heinlein's stories who is not essentially ordinary. Some of them have eccentricities. . . but. . .

This "but" is the sound of a reviewer missing the point. It's true that Heinlein's characters tend to seem commonplace by contrast, simply because they're all healthy, physically and mentally, except for an occasional psychotic villain. Heinlein isn't interested in neurotic people, perhaps because he feels they are obsolescent, like the modern automobile (disposed of with great gusto in Chapter 4): but eccentricity is something else again:

> "Roger, have you ever met any normal people? I never have. The so-called normal man is a figment of the imagination; every member of the human race, from Jojo the cave man right down to that final culmination of civilization, namely me, has been as eccentric as a pet coon—once you caught him with his mask off."

The speaker is Hazel Stone, an engaging oldster who is among other things a top-flight engineer and a champion chess-player; who helped to pioneer the Moon and still packs a gun, although the charge chamber is now loaded with cough drops. Her son Roger, who admits to the lowest IQ in the family, is (a) also a first-rate engineer, and (b) a successful writer of space-opera for television; the twins are mechanical geniuses; and God knows what Lowell's going to grow up to be; at four, he licks Hazel consistently at chess, and nobody is quite sure whether it's because he reads her mind or not.

In outline, this is the story of the Stone family's pleasure junket from their home on the Moon to Mars, to a mining camp in the asteroids, and finally, as the book ends, to Titan. For excitement, there's a shipboard epidemic and an accident that leaves a space-scooter manned by Hazel and the baby drifting out of help's way. Older readers may be more interested in the twins' remarkably complicated attempt to sell Lunar bicycles on Mars, and in Heinlein's usual detailed, plausible picture of the future, convincing even when it is most startling—as in the case of the Lunar bicycles, and in that of the notion, obvious but unheard-of, that on a low-gravity satellite like Phobos you wouldn't have to climb or jump to reach the airlock of a grounded spaceship—you could simply walk up the side of it, like a fly on a wall.

In theme, perhaps more explicitly than in any of his previous books, this is the story that Heinlein, along with Homer, considers the greatest in the world:

> . . . the *Stone* trembled and threw herself outward bound, toward Saturn. In her train followed hundreds and thousands and hundreds of thousands of restless rolling Stones ... to Saturn . . . to Uranus, to Pluto . . . rolling on out to the stars . . . outward bound to the ends of the Universe.

Starman Jones, Heinlein's seventh juvenile, is, I think, one of his best—but except for the first, *Rocket Ship Galileo*, which was a sort of trial run, they've all been so good that it's difficult to choose among them—and impossible to find any precedent for them in this field. The Carl H. Claudy books, which I read in my teens, struck me as pretty hot stuff then, and I've often wondered why Grosset & Dunlap hasn't reissued them since the Boom; it seems to me they could still compete with great ease against Winston's nauseous line of trash.* But they were derivative— watered-down Wells, mostly—and I don't suppose adult science-fiction readers, then or now, would find much in them. Heinlein's are something else again. Is *Treasure Island* a juvenile, or *The Wind in the Willows*? All right, then so are these.

This is the first of the series in which Heinlein has ventured outside the solar system, and to do it, without the generations-long trip of "Universe" and without ignoring Einstein, he's assumed something called "anomalies" in space—sectors where multidimensional space is folded back on itself like a crumpled sheet of paper. *Not* "space warps," the hero indignantly explains to a groundling: "That's a silly term—space doesn't 'warp' except in places where *pi* isn't exactly three point one four one five nine two six five three five eight . . . like inside a nucleus." It comes to nearly the same thing, but not quite: and the difference makes for the tautest, most edge-of-your-seat control room scenes ever written.

Starman Jones is the story of a back-country youngster who

---

*This is funny: a couple of the Claudy stories did turn up in an anthology edited by Lester del Rey, and published by Winston.

dreams of going to space but hasn't a chance because of the rigid hereditary guild system of an overcrowded planet (about a century's worth more crowded than the Earth of *Farmer in the Sky*), and of how, incredibly and wonderfully, his dream comes true—and of much more besides. In these stories, I think, Heinlein is doing something more than just earning a living at the work he does supremely well: he's preparing a whole generation—the generation that will live to see the year 2000—for the Age of Space that's as real to him now as it will be, must be, to them.

Heinlein's eighth Scribner's novel, *The Star Beast*, is, like six of the others, only nominally a juvenile. Two of the central characters are minors, but neither of them is the hero of the book; nor, in spite of his-her vast appeal, is Lummox, the star beast. The hero, if there is one, is Mr. Kiku, Permanent Under Secretary for Spatial Affairs, surely the most likable and charming administrator in the entire universe. When Lummox (a six-ton pet) starts out innocently enough to eat a few rose bushes and a mastiff, and ends by involving the whole planet in the threat of annihilation, it's Kiku who has to pick up all the pieces. It's a pure delight to watch him at work. Heinlein's interest, as always, is in The Man Who Knows How, other types appearing only as caricatures, and if this makes for a distorted view of humanity, it also makes for close-textured, fascinating writing. Stories about know-nothings inevitably repeat the same stock motions; the repertory of competence is inexhaustible.

This is a novel that won't go bad on you. Many of science fiction's triumphs, even from as little as ten years ago, are unreadable today; they were shoddily put together, not meant for re-use. But Heinlein is durable. I've read this story twice, so far—once in the *Fantasy and Science Fiction* serialized version, once in hard covers—and expect to read it again, sooner or later, for pleasure. I don't know any higher praise.

As I have said before, I am not the man to write the definitive critical analysis of Heinlein, because I am a sucker for his work. However, I think I have finally hit upon something which has balled me up previously in reviewing Heinlein; I think it's the same thing that confused me about the Kuttners before I stopped trying to write about them as one person.

Heinlein's style, which I admire, is a flexible and efficient instrument, but so simple and conversational that it makes you think of Heinlein's work as a simple, standardized product, and of Heinlein himself as a simple, standardized man.

In reality, there are several Heinleins. One of them is a 19th century rationalist and skeptic, who believes in nothing he can't see, touch, and preferably measure with calipers. Another is a mystic, who strongly believes in the existence of something beyond the world of the senses, and keeps an open mind even toward the ragtag and bobtail of mystical ideas, flying saucers and Bridey Murphy.

All this is fairly obvious and has been said before. What struck me as a new notion, on reading *Tunnel in the Sky* and *Time for the Stars*, was that Heinlein's way of telling a story is a mixture, and not always the same mixture, of two things. One, which I have been taking for the only ingredient, is a perfectly open and natural narrative manner. Heinlein's first published story had it, and it has never changed much since. The other is the result of careful and labored craftsmanship.

A look at these two novels will show what I mean.

In each of them, the chief character is a junior edition of the standard Heinlein hero. In *Tunnel in the Sky*, he is Rod Walker, a high school senior who is sent, with others of his class, through a dimensional doorway to undergo a "final exam in Advanced Survival." In *Time for the Stars*, he is Thomas Paine Leonardo da Vinci Bartlett, who goes along on one of the first interstellar exploration ships as one half of a telepathic communications team. The other half, who stays behind on Earth, is his twin brother, Patrick Henry Michelangelo Bartlett.

In each case, the rationale of these unlikely events is elegantly and plausibly worked out. Heinlein's bourgeois matter-of-factness has a way of cutting a fantastic idea down to size, and suddenly making it more lifelike and interesting as a result. The subject of what real telepathy would be like, for instance, is one I had regarded as closed; George O. Smith's unnecessary typographical tricks, in *Highways in Hiding*, only pointed up how little Kuttner and Bester had left to be said. Heinlein, without detracting from their work, nevertheless shows that under the circumstances of his story, a telepathic communication would *necessarily* be perceived as speech.

In *Tunnel in the Sky*, the basic gadget, the transdimensional doorway, is a more unconventional speculation than Heinlein usually allows himself; but once having made the assumption, he treats it as soberly as if it were an everyday fact, including such usually ignored matters as allowing for the relative motions of the two planets connected by the doorway, and of getting them right side up with respect to each other.

At first glance, the associated idea of sending high school kids through these doorways, to live or die by their resources on savage planets, seems even more wildly improbable. But in the overcrowded world Heinlein postulates, when Earth's population increase is in full explosion, such callous practicality begins to seem not at all unlikely.

In both novels, as usual, the story line is long and meandering. In *Tunnel in the Sky*, Walker and his classmates are isolated by a failure of the doorway, and are left to lead a Tarzan-like existence in the jungles. *Time for the Stars* follows the travels of the starship *Lewis and Clark*. The shipboard romance in this story never comes to much of anything, like the contest for leadership between Walker and another boy in *Tunnel in the Sky*.

Heinlein stops both novels by running them into the same tree: in the next to last chapter, emissaries from Earth turn up to end the adventures and take the participants home. In each case there is an epilogue; Walker, having learned some not very apparent lesson from his sojourn in the wilderness, grows up and goes out again as a professional captain, leading a train of Conestoga wagons to another virgin planet.

Heinlein's star-travelers, in *Time for the Stars*, like van Vogt's in "Far Centaurus," find that progress at home has made them obsolete before they finish their journey. The captain winds up a victim of technological unemployment; Tom, who is younger and more adaptable, sells out his partnership with his now-aged brother, marries his great-grandniece, who was unborn at the time he left—another version of the curious paedophile plot Heinlein used in *The Door Into Summer*—and prepares to go out to the stars as a colonist.

Now, in their looseness of structure these are both fairly typical Heinlein novels; what gives them coherence is not so much any development of character or action, as the general scheme of the author's thought against which they are laid. In the classical sense, *Tunnel in the Sky* has no form at all—it starts off in an arbitrary direction, goes on cheerfully until the author has written enough words to fill a book, and then stops. The hero's family relations are quite perfunctorily sketched in; the sister, a member of the Amazons, is a delightful character, complete with plumed helmet and soldierly profanity, but she adds only local color, and the parents are cardboard figures.

Time for the Stars is a different case. From the very beginning, Heinlein has built up a carefully documented rivalry between the twins, first making it appear that Pat is somehow invariably the lucky one. For instance, it just happens to work out that Pat is tacitly accepted as the twin who is to go on the ship, leaving the unexciting part of the job, staying home on Earth, for Tom; and in fact, it is only when Pat has an accident while undergoing training for the job that Tom is chosen to go instead.

Then, slowly, Heinlein turns this picture around and shows you the other side. Tom, unaware of it himself, has been using his half-conscious antagonism toward his twin as a shield for timidity, almost cowardice.

This kind of slow unfolding of character and motive, plus the grotesque confrontation of the twins at the end of the book, gives the novel a structure which is firm and symmetrical enough to satisfy anybody. It is psychologically sound; dramatic; and complete: yet it rubs me the wrong way. Careful though it is, it seems an intrusive element; it does not belong in the story.

Heinlein's world is essentially one of naive vigor and optimism. His heroes are big and solid; his villains are unconvincing figures: his revolutionists in *Beyond This Horizon*, for example, were a totally unconvincing bunch of fatheads. In spite of profound democratic convictions, I think, Heinlein is a fastidious man who admires quality in a human being as much as in a piece of engineering. His patience with stupidity is vanishingly small; he has no sympathy with "the common man" or with "little people."

Although the division of Heinlein's novels into "adult" and "juvenile" is in many respects a joke, I think it is no accident that he has been so successful in the juvenile field. Almost invariably, his most convincing and attractive characters are adolescents in one sense or another. Lazarus Long, for instance, is several centuries old at the time of *Methuselah's Children*, but he has never quite grown up.

It seems to me that Heinlein's natural attitude toward the kind of Freudian probing he uses here ought to be the instinctive repugnance he shows toward modern art. I am guessing, and may be guessing wrong, but it seems to me that this is a thing Heinlein has begun mortaring into his stories, conscientiously but without conviction, because he thinks it will improve them.

At any rate, when it comes to Heinlein I am a conservative myself. Certainly we have enough writers already who will give you the textbook psychoanalytic interpretation of a character, from childhood up. I liked the old romantic Heinlein a whole hell of a lot better, and I have a hunch that in the end, he may even be nearer the truth.

Citizen of the Galaxy is longer and meatier than any of Heinlein's previous books in this series, and the way it is packaged suggests to me that Scribner's may be pushing it both as a juvenile and as an adult novel. If so, hurray; I don't see any reason why not.

The book is written in four almost equal sections. Part I takes place in a city called Jubbulpore, "capital of Jubbul and of the Nine Worlds, residence in chief of the Great Sargon." The story begins:

> "Lot ninety-seven," the auctioneer announced. "A boy."

The boy is a half starved, savage waif named Thorby, who bears on his back "white scar streaks, endorsements of former owners' opinions." He is no bargain at any price; through a combination of buyers' apathy and a blunder of the auctioneer, he is sold for two minims—less than the stamp tax on the transaction—to a one-eyed, one-legged beggar named Baslim.

Baslim cleans him up, feeds him, houses him in a well-equipped hideaway under the ruins of the old amphitheater, and slowly makes a human being out of him. The quasi-Oriental background of this section is pushed back almost out of sight: Heinlein's chief concern is with the developing father-son relationship, and he makes it fascinating. The early stages, when Baslim has to gain Thorby's confidence by the methods one would use on a wild animal, are touching and absolutely real.

Later, in spite of digressions into the art of beggary and the art of learning itself, it becomes clear that what Baslim has to teach is not technique but character. Baslim is an old-fashioned, stiff-necked moral individualist, who keeps undeviating standards for himself while insisting on absolute freedom for other people. He rules by love, teaches by example. Only by inference, almost casually, does it appear that he is something more than an incongruously educated beggar: he is a spy, smuggling out information about the space traffic of Jubbulpore.

When he dies, caught by the Sargon's police and "shortened" —beheaded—Thorby is adopted by one of Baslim's contacts, a Free Trader named Krausa. Part I ends. Part II takes place largely on the Free Trader ship *Sisu*.

The Traders are interstellar gypsies, speaking a "secret language"—in this case, Finnish—living only in their ships, and keeping their integrity by an elaborate formal culture. Heinlein's exposition of this is typically thorough and lucid; where almost anybody else would have gone into long, windy rhapsodies over the supposed wild freedom of the space gypsies, Heinlein tells you in detail about their phratry relationships and their fire-control systems.

Thorby's gradual evolution from a *fraki* (i.e., non-Trader scum) to an assimilated member of the crew is set forth plausibly; he nearly winds up in a political marriage contrived by the matriarch of *Sisu*; but Krausa, following Baslim's instructions to the letter even though it hurts, turns him over to the commander of the

Terran Hegemony Guard Cruiser *Hydra*.

Part II ends. Part III takes place largely on *Hydra*.

Once more Thorby has to begin from scratch in a strange environment; and along about here, you begin to realize that in spite of his apparently successful adjustments, Thorby is someone to feel sorry for: he has a real, tough "Who am I?" problem.

The Guard commander, trying to identify him through the resources of the Hegemony, fails just long enough to make the result seem in doubt. Then he succeeds: Thorby turns out to be a long-lost heir, and the Guard delivers him to his home on Earth.

Part III ends. Part IV takes place on Earth.

Thorby now finds himself a multimillionaire, "Rudbek of Rudbek," whose position has been usurped by a wicked uncle. This plot is so familiar (though unusual in science fiction) that its puzzle value is nil. The basic pattern is one of the strongest in fiction, but its use here has an inherent contradiction which Heinlein is too honest to duck. For real suspense, you need a tough problem, to be solved by the hero's own courage and resourcefulness. But in a problem of this kind, courage and resourcefulness are not much to the point: what the hero ought to do is hire a good lawyer; and that's what Thorby (a little belatedly) does.

The ensuing legal contest is treated in careful detail, but Thorby is hardly more than an interested spectator; and I think we have to call this section of the plot a failure in its own terms.

Technically speaking, *Citizen of the Galaxy* has two major flaws. The first and more serious is its division into four separate parts, each with its own distinct background and cast of characters. Only Thorby appears in all four sections; every other character stays strictly in his own compartment. This prevents the book from achieving any unity, or even continuity for more than half a dozen chapters at a time. Further, it disposes of the book's best character one-quarter of the way through. Baslim is by far the strongest, solidest, most plausible and interesting character; it seems to me a serious error to write him off so early. Still further, although the four-part division allows Heinlein to include more backgrounds, it does not give him space to develop any one of them fully. The *Kim*-like wicked Oriental splendor of Part I is shrugged aside; the backgrounds of Parts II and III are merely detailed vignettes—Thorby never becomes really a part of either the Traders' or the Guards' society, and his involvement in their doings is slight.

Second, nearly all the characters seem to be *in* but not *of* their environments. This is most strikingly evident in the case of Thorby himself. Twice in Part II, and again in Part IV, beautiful young ladies throw themselves at his head with about as much effect as if he were a mollusk. The plain inference is that Thorby has had so many cold showers and invigorating scrimmages, that he has got through puberty without so much as noticing the difference between the sexes. This is a pious convention in the upper-class literature of the early 20th century, which dealt with young men who actually got the scrimmages and cold showers: in a story about a slave boy, who has grown up in the gutters of an Oriental port, it is a stupefying incongruity.

I take this to be a restriction imposed on Heinlein by librarians' censorship, and for all I know he may have emphasized it deliberately to show how foolish it is. All the same, it is there, and other characters (particularly the young Traders) show a similar fault: forgetting who and where they are, they sometimes think, act and talk too much like mid-20th-century middle-class Americans.

But when you've totaled up everything that can be said against the novel, it remains an enormously entertaining, rich, satisfying story. Heinlein is a man who believes in good workmanship and honest measure: each of his plot-tight compartments is at least packed full.

The lucid discussion of the Traders' kinship system in Part II will undoubtedly lead some of Heinlein's readers for the first time into the fascinating field of cultural anthropology. The knowledgeable (and comic) descriptions of life aboard a military vessel may someday tip the scales for a Navy-minded man, one way or the other. Thorby's difficulties with the disappearing furniture in his "bunkie" aboard *Sisu* are funny and illuminating at the same time. The book is full of gentle ironies, from the name of the place in Jubbulpore where the slave auctions are held (the Plaza of Liberty), to the name of the woman anthropologist who is traveling with the Traders (Margaret Mader). Everywhere the story alights, however briefly, you have the feeling that Heinlein has done more work than was required.

Compartmented as it is, the plot does draw some continuity from the gradually emerging thread of Baslim's fight against the slave trade. Thorby's final choice among his four possible identities is adroitly and suspensefully handled.

The story ends inconclusively, with nothing actually solved or settled; the scale is too big for that—the whole galaxy, and centuries of time.

This may not be in any sense a great book, but it is a big one: it has the bigness that distinguishes science fiction at its best from any other form.

8. ASIMOV AND EMPIRE

FOURTEEN YEARS AGO, shortly after Isaac Asimov's first story appeared, he got a fan letter from a callow eighteen-year-old in Hood River, Oregon. Not to keep you in suspense, the fan was me.

Time passed; I grew older very slowly, grew an invisible mustache and shaved it off, learned to stay away from dry red wine and recovered somewhat from my enthusiasm for Ross Rocklynne and Edgar Rice Burroughs. But I still yield to nobody as an Asimov fan. Among writers of the purest and most difficult kind of science fiction, the serious "what if" story, I think he's approached by nobody but Heinlein. His robot stories put an end forever to the misbegotten series of clanking Adam Links that had infested science fiction for twenty years; his "Nightfall" is matchless of its kind, and I could name half a dozen others.

But as a writer of twice-told tales, I think Asimov is as dull as anybody. That's why I've been waiting, long and impatiently, for *The Caves of Steel*: because I wanted to praise Asimov, and because, if I reviewed *Pebble in the Sky*, *The Stars, Like Dust...*, *Foundation and Empire*, *The Currents of Space* or *Second Foundation*, I couldn't.

All five of these books are laid against much the same Galactic Empire background, a background which in Asimov's own words (slightly chopped to fit) is "simply the Roman . . . Empire written large." That phrase, to me, is an absolutely devastating criticism of any science fiction story, for two reasons. To take the least first: history does not repeat.

In his contribution to the symposium *Modern Science Fiction*, Asimov took up that statement from a fan-magazine article of mine and undertook to prove that for his purposes, I was wrong. He appended a table showing nineteen points of correspondence among the Civil War in England, the French Revolution and the Russian Revolution. The correspondences are indeed striking, and Asimov's presentation is ingenious, but the whole thing simply is not relevant: although there's a two-century spread between Charles I and Nicholas II, as Asimov knows perfectly well, they and Louis XVI lost their thrones and their lives in the identical historical process, working itself out a little later in France than in England, a little later in Russia than in France.

The ellipsis in the quotation above stands for "or British." The association was inevitable; the resemblance between the British and Roman Empires is probably the most frequently cited in support of that false platitude, "History repeats itself"—in the face of the plain fact that the correspondences between the two empires are insignificant compared to their differences.

The late-Empire Roman who attempted to use his own history to write a prophetic story about an empire of the British would have made an ingenious ass of himself. But Asimov's Galactic Empire is Roman.

The second and more serious objection to this kind of thing is simply this: It isn't science fiction—that is to say, speculative fiction—any more than the well-known Western with rayguns instead of sixshooters; any more than Frank Robinson's "The Santa Claus Planet," which transferred the Kwakiutl of Vancouver Island bodily to a fictional world; any more than Ken Crossen's endless transcriptions of *The Hucksters*. It's of the essence of speculative fiction that an original problem be set up which the author is obliged to work out for himself; if the problem is an old one, and he has only to look the answers up in a book, there's very little fun in it for anybody; moreover, the answers are certain to be wrong.

The Caves of Steel, then, besides being a delightful thing in itself, seems to me to vindicate Asimov as a writer and myself as a critic. Like his 1952 novella, "The Martian Way"—like very nearly all his work, in fact, except for that lamentable Empire kick—it is a brilliant, thorough, and above all an original exercise in speculation. The subject is one of the oldest stock properties of science fiction, the super-city of *Metropolis* and Wells' "Story of the Days to Come"; but just as—*pace* Moskowitz—Heinlein took the ancient and mishandled idea of the super-parasite and, in *The Puppet Masters*, buttressed it with such a mass of brilliantly imaginative detail that it came horrifyingly to life, Asimov has turned a clear, ironic and compassionate eye on every cranny of the City: the games children play on the moving streets; the legends that have grown up about deserted corridors; the customs and tabus in Section kitchens and men's rooms; the very feel, smell and texture of those steel caves in which men live and die.

The story, moreover, turns on murder and detection; it doesn't, like so many recent miscegenations, attempt to fuse science-fantasy and the murder mystery simply by jamming them together in one jacket: the larger story, the science fiction story, revolves upon the mystery. The movement is massive, swift and enormously exciting.

The book ends on a pious note which I found a little strained, and it solves the City's population problem in a way which—as, again, nobody knows better than Asimov—is no solution at all; but this is a matter of the last page only. If the book had five such faults, it would still be the impressive performance it is.

The title story of Asimov's collection, *The Martian Way*, is surely one of the best science fiction novellas ever published. The story's taking-off point is simple: If no miracle fuels or propulsion systems come along, but Mars is to be colonized anyway, then it will have to be done with step rockets. A-B-C. All right, then what happens to the discarded steps—hundreds of thousands of tons of salvageable steel? Asimov's answer: they drift on out across the Martian orbit, until Scavengers in tiny two-man ships come out to get them.

The drama of "The Martian Way" is in those ships. Asimov, writing compactly and with enviable control, makes every phase of them intensely believable—the irritation that grows in the cramped quarters, the squabbling "Scavenger widows" at home, the monotony of waiting, the excitement—like hooking God's biggest fish—of a fat strike.

A lesser writer, fumbling for something to say, would have made these men little tin heroes, tight-lipped and glint-eyed, with shoulders from here to there. Asimov's characters are good-natured, human, unextraordinary, wonderful joes.

And a lesser writer, dealing with the long voyage to Saturn which turns this story from a vignette into an epic, would have marked time with mutinies, sprung seams, mold in the hydroponics tanks and Lord knows what all else. Asimov, instead, has rediscovered the mystic euphoria and beauty of space travel. Of those who have written about this imaginary journey, how many others have even tried to make Saturn glow in the reader's eyes like the monstrous jewel it is ?

When you read this story, if you haven't already, you'll realize how much there is of heroics in run-of-the-mill science fiction, and how little true heroism. Asimov will make you feel the distances, the cold, the vastness, the courage of tiny human figures against that immense backdrop.

It's seldom that science fiction sticks as closely as this to its proper theme; if it happened more often, probably the respectable critics would have given in long ago.

Asimov's *The End of Eternity* is a curious patchwork, containing some monumentally good ideas and some startlingly uneven writing. In contrast to the intensely human pioneers of "The Martian Way," Asimov's characters in this one are gadgeted and double-talked almost out of existence: Twissell, the most readily visible character in the book, is little more than a collection of mannerisms; Harlan, the hero, is not even that.

The book has one more serious handicap, for which Asimov is to blame as much or as little as the rest of us.

The background is extremely complex, involving a race of Eternals with a self-appointed mission to doctor reality all up and down the time-line—with a technology, mores, anxieties, a world-view and a terminology to fit—none of which the reader has a fair chance to absorb before he is flung into the story proper.

This abrupt plunge into the action, though sanctioned by common practice, makes the first few chapters of the story perfectly unintelligible. What is all this blurred talk about Eternity and Time, Observers, Eternals, Reality Changes? Who is the girl with the funny name that the hero gets all tense about every now and then? The writer offers you no signposts; you have to pick your way as best you can, in the hope—justified, but after what effort!—that it will all become clear in time.

Once this barrier is passed, however, Asimov's story is a fascinating one. It has all the time-long sweep and mystery of Jack Williamson's creaky old "Legion of Time," plus an incisive logic that Williamson never had—and an occasional insight that's rare even in Asimov. Harlan's reaction when, by mistake, he all but meets himself, illuminates the doppelganger legend and the time-travel canon together, in one brilliant flash of subliminal understanding. Plot and counter-plot, in the best Williamson fashion, wind up spectacularly together, and there's a very acceptable happy ending.

This may be one of the last books of its kind. Science fiction is, pretty plainly, swinging away from its complex, cerebral, heavy-science-plus-action phase, toward a more balanced and easily digestible mixture of technology and human emotion. Only a writer trained in the days when s.f. was still a species of adventure pulp could write a novel like this one; and Asimov, whom I persist in thinking of as a rising young writer, is now one of the last of the Old Guard.

9. MORE CHUCKLEHEADS

TAKE THE FRESHEST, brightest book in the world, I don't care how good it is—take *Nineteen Eighty-Four* or *Gravy Planet*—an expert can turn it into a muddy cliche before you can say Western Printing and Lithographing Company. A real expert can take both of them, and Poul Anderson's "Sam Hall" to boot, and boil them down into one negligible novel; and that's what Ken Crossen has done in *Year of Consent*.

The result is one of the saddest things I know—honest conviction embodied in dishonest writing. There are a few isolated, quivering bits of this book that seem to me both original and good; I am bound to wonder if I have merely missed the models Crossen used. No single piece of the background he describes holds together with any other piece: we have relaxed sexual standards + plunging necklines + 1956-type divorce faking. We have a U. S. populace conditioned from cradle to grave, by transmogrified adman's techniques, + half a state full of Communists, deliberately maintained by the government for use as scapegoats. We have an "expediter" or government detective (the hero—who is also Paul Revere, the dauntless UN underground agent) who is always overworked because of a staff shortage, + assignments which give him nothing to do. We have a white-collared tyranny which ruthlessly persecutes the UN underground—and lets itself be conned into adopting Thoreau as required reading for campers—; this is about like Eisenhower passing out copies of Marx at a DAR meeting.

The writing itself incorporates every beginner's mistake known to man. The hero-narrator describes himself while looking in the equivalent of a mirror. He asks or answers impossibly stupid questions in order to communicate background material to the reader. His confederates act in a manner only possible to clairvoyants or maniacal hunch-players, and get away with it. And —please notice this battered, inside-out echo of *Nineteen Eighty-*

Four—the hero betrays himself in an apartment *which he knows to be wired.*

The dialogue between the hero and heroine has to be seen to be believed; I have watched a few TV soap-operas lately, and *they* haven't been this bad. After the usual chase, hero gets his choice of being shipped off to Australia with girl just as the revolution is about to start, or sticking around to do sixteen jobs nobody else can handle. He picks Australia, but has a change of heart at the last moment, and makes a speech *this* long about it . . . I can't go on.

Just one final note about this book as an example of sloppy writing jobs in general. In Chapter 2, a girl who is in bed with the hero gets out of it in the following manner:

> [She] came out of the bed with a single leap that carried her a
> good two feet into the middle of the room. She stood there on tip-
> toe, her eyes wide, her head thrown back, her body arched rigidly.

(And two pages later, well into Chapter 3, she hasn't moved a muscle.)

This is not merely picturesque, it is impossible.

Nobody wants a hard-working writer to spend years in research to produce one lousy little novel; but if the necessary research takes less than five minutes, I think the reader has a right to expect it. Take, for example, Jerry Sohl's *The Altered Ego*, in which a character sees his face clearly in a washbasin full of water. This happens to be impossible in a normally lighted room, and Sohl, supposing he knew where to look for a washbasin, could have found it out. Richard Matheson, having boned up enough for six jawbreaking sentences about antibodies, could have taken the trouble to learn how they are made. And Crossen could have gotten up off his rump, as I did, to see whether that position is as tough as it sounds. The exercise would have done him good.

Francis Rufus Bellamy's Crusoe-like *Atta* should delight the *Time* reviewer who announced, to no one's surprise, that Friday's footprint was preferable to my blob of green gelatin.* The burden of his criticism could have been expressed by "Why don't they write like that no more?" Obligingly, Bellamy has wrote like that, as nearly as a man can who is writing 200 years after Defoe's death; and the result is just as stale, windy and distempered as anyone but *Time*'s idiot might have expected.

*This reference is to *Time*'s review of the first *Galaxy Reader of Science Fiction*. The reviewer, to my annoyance, used most of his space talking about Robinson Crusoe.

The plot concerns a man who is hit by lightning and wakes up to find himself about half an inch tall. He strikes up an Androcles-like friendship with an itinerant warrior ant, name of Atta, goes to live with "him"—the word is Bellamy's, and sets the tone for the astonishing display of ignorance that follows—in a walnut shell, milks aphids, tames a beetle to ride on, uses a needle for a lance, visits Atta's home city and runs into trouble with the authorities, and so on and so on, until Atta, his only friend, expires, and apparently out of sheer grief the hero returns to normal size.

Aside from the author's archaic narrative style and his relentless disregard of natural history, the principal irritant in this story is the hero's absolutely impenetrable stupidity.

His situation is plain enough from the beginning, even without the tip-off thoughtfully provided by the blurb-writer; but the hero can't puzzle it out. He sees trees shaped like dandelions; he walks on soil of a texture never found on any continent or island of Earth; he meets a six-foot ant, in heaven's name, and this is not enough. Very well, says the reader, he is suffering from shock; it will take him a little time.

He takes shelter from pumpkin-sized raindrops in a discarded thimble: now, says the reader, it will dawn upon him. But no. He finds a giant needle and a piece of thread: *now?* No. So help me, it isn't until page 91, when the man stumbles across a tent-sized piece of metal foil marked "CHOCOLATE," that the great illumination comes.

This book could only have been written by a man who thought his idea was brand new. If he had read a little science fiction, he might have been disabused of this and several other misconceptions; but doubtless he took the word of some respected critic that no worthwhile fantasy has been published since 1719.

The only thing worse than a bad American novel is a bad British one. Something in the nation's towering literary tradition must give grubstreeters a reckless feeling; when a Briton lowers himself to write tripe, he does it with a will.

Timeliner, by Charles Eric Maine, is that sort of amateur flight of fancy that takes leave of its premises, and its senses, in the second chapter. Almost anything can then happen, except the unexpected. Here, the assumption is that a scientist working with "dimensional quadrature" is flung forward in time, to a period where his consciousness ousts that of another man; and when that man dies, the protagonist leaps forward again, and so on, always crowding out somebody close to a woman who resembles the protagonist's wife. Beyond this, the plot is not worth mentioning, but here are some random examples:

> Abruptly he saw the significance of that first incredible tran-
> sition: it meant he was dead! The real Hugh Macklin had perished
> in the capsule four hundred years ago. (Page 116.)

This has been obvious to the reader for exactly eighty-eight
pages.

> ". . . But we have no alternative. If you abolish compulsory
> euthanasia and the principle of social utility, then you must re-
> strict population by controlling birth. In twenty years, eighty per-
> cent of the people would be middle-aged and old, and there would
> be insufficient children to maintain the population level. Where
> does that get us ? (Page 154.)

Nowhere, inasmuch as the speaker (and the author) is using
"controlling birth" as if it meant "abolishing birth."

> "How did you come to travel through time ?"
> "By dimensional quadrature," Macklin replied. (Page 183.)

Beautiful: " By dimensional quadrature," i.e. by the fourth
dimension, i.e. time — or, " How did you travel through time ? "
"By time travel."

Since we seem to be well into the Age of Space, ready or not,
novels about the first steps up—satellites, and the Moon trip—
have a special interest and importance. Here is one, by a British
writer, designed to make any rocket engineer or space-flight en-
thusiast lie down and cry: *High Vacuum*, by Charles Eric Maine.
    The first manned Moon ship, *Alpha* (why is this the omega
of British writers' imaginations when they name spaceships ?)
unaccountably runs out of fuel just before landing in the Mare
Imbrium, and crashes, killing one of the four-man crew and
marooning the rest.
    The book is about vacuum, and the struggles of the *Alpha*'s crew
to survive in it. The first mention of it in the story itself comes
this way:

> He listened carefully as he tapped one boot against the floor
> —the clean sharp impact of the magnetic sole against the metal
> could be felt as a transient vibration in his leg, but there was no
> sound. (Page 2.)

No air, ergo no sound, because sound is transmitted only by air:
right ? My god, no.
    A little later, it develops that Kerry, the surgeon-navigator,

has had his radio "intercom" broken along with his leg, so they naturally can't communicate with him. Spacemen in s.f. stories have been talking to each other by touching helmets for thirty years, but it never occurs to these characters; Kerry goes speechless until he dies, c. page 109; and so help me, it isn't until page 114 that anybody discovers solids will conduct sound. Meanwhile, the stowaway who's been in the hold all this time has been hammering on the walls, "but there was no sound in the vacuum."

On page 14, a new peril crops up: the "Geiger equipment" is "giving a positive reaction." Patterson, the electronics officer, looks at the "spinning strobe" and announces, "Around two thousand gamma. . . It means . . . there's a lethal amount of radiation in this cabin." The whole crater, it appears, is one big uranium field: consequently the crew can't stay in *Alpha*'s cabin but must find a safe place, live there in spacesuits, and visit *Alpha* only once a day, for food and elimination.

Now this is just silly. The radioactivity of uranium ore is so slight that you couldn't get a lethal dose from it, without refining it first, if the whole Moon were made of pitchblende.

Swallow it for the sake of the story? Why? On page 15, Commander Caird asks Patterson, "Couldn't it be some kind of contamination from the atomic turbines?" Patterson says no, that "the turbines are intact." Tell me something: why couldn't he have said yes?

On page 33, the author refers to gamma "particles," thus revealing the full, gorgeous extent of his ignorance on this subject.

The next thing that happens is that the stowaway is discovered: she is Janet Vaughan, née Ross, the wife of the dead man. It was her added mass which caused *Alpha* to crash in the first place and kill her husband. This could have been a neat irony, if the author had paused to make elementary sense of it.

Item: Janet lived in a spacesuit, in *Alpha*'s hold, for six continuous days—a neat trick. She went without food or water for the same period, and ran out of oxygen just soon enough to be turning slightly blue when found and dragged out of her suit.

Item: her added mass could very well have made *Alpha* crash by using too much fuel; but the way Caird tells it (page 80), "What happened was that the fuel allocation in the main drive tanks ran out just a fraction too soon—a few seconds that's all." In other words, there was no safety factor; *Alpha* was supposed to run out of fuel at the exact instant she touched down. *Crikey!*

Maine's style is stiff and pompous, full of tautologies ("retrospectively into the past"; "On the surface he was laconic and

superficial"), but it moves the story along purposefully; his characters are oversimplified but vivid and forceful at times. The
story itself, as it narrows down to a contest for survival between
a paranoid woman and a radiation-poisoned man, takes on a classic
simplicity.

The book has passages of great strength and even of eloquence.
In between, it dips frequently into unintended farce, as when Patterson has to repair the ship's radar, two of whose *glass* tubes
have been broken.

The unpleasant details of the Moon-castaways' life are soberly
and realistically treated. There are bits of interpolated humor,
including a popular song bad enough to be genuine. There are
sudden poetic insights, as when the castaways grow so accustomed
to spacesuits that taking one off is like shedding a cocoon, to
emerge "soft and white and hairy." There are moments of real
horror—Vaughan's spacesuited corpse, pinned in the wreckage;
Patterson looking in the mirror, seeing the signs of advanced
radiation poisoning.

The only thing really wrong with the book, in fact, is the science
in it. Maine's physics is bad, his chemistry worse ("Incandescent
oxygen . . . a bubble of life-giving gas burning itself into inert
elements . . ."); his physiology is pathetic—he naively assumes
there is a calibrated, one-to-three relationship between monkeys'
reactions and men's.

For the record, again, I don't expect any science fiction writer
to do graduate work in physics before he writes a space opera.
If a writer makes a blunder in higher mathematics or theoretical
physics, he is safe from me—I am no expert, and will never notice it. The gross errors in this novel are in the area of common
knowledge (as if a Western hero should saddle up a pueblo and
ride off down the cojone): any one of them could have been corrected by ten minutes with a dictionary or an encyclopedia.

If Maine has no talent or taste for science, but is determined to
write s.f. anyhow, I admire his nerve, but for heaven's sake let
him get a collaborator—any fifth-form science teacher would do.

Even Jove nods, and even Ballantine can produce a genuinely
bad book. *Riders to the Stars*, by Curt Siodmak and Robert Smith,
is a stinker such as I have seldom had the privilege of seeing:
so thoroughly and concentratedly bad in every dimension, joint,
hinge, surface and detail that I cannot offhand think of a companion
piece for it.

The book was written, if that is the word I'm hunting for, by
someone named Robert Smith, or by someone retreating behind

that name, from the screenplay by Curt Siodmak. (You will be seeing this Ivan Tors production soon at your neighborhood theater,
unless you duck pretty damned fast.) I am reluctant to believe
that this can be the same Robert Smith who wrote *The Second
Woman* and other distinguished screenplays, but two possibilities
occur to me: either Mr. Siodmak and Mr. Tors farmed this job
out to the hungriest-looking local hack, for a cent a word and all
the peanuts he could eat, or to a small screenwriter with a large
cigar who undertook to prove he could dictate one of those piffling
little novels in an afternoon, and did it.

The plot goes like this: The government of the United States
has been sending up rockets with a view to establishing an orbital
satellite station, only to get a nasty shock: at an altitude of four
hundred and twenty-six miles, cosmic rays turn the rockets' steel
to crystallized chewing gum. BUT it is observed that meteorites,
composed mainly of nickel and iron, come through in great shape;
therefore there must be some mysterious surface coating on meteorites that protects them from cosmic rays but gets burnt off in
the atmosphere. How to find out what this precious stuff is?

The answer has the classic simplicity of all great thinking.
When the next meteor swarm comes by, three intrepid men will be
sent up in rockets equipped with jaws like a shark. Their heroic
job is to capture a virgin meteor—like this: fftGULP—and bring
it down for study.

The three men are those who survive a testing program that
uses up just under a third of the book; all the same, when the big
day comes, one of them flips his lid in space and another mis-
judges his meteor and gets blown up. The third, name of Richard
Stanton, keeps his equilibrium and comes down with the prize, because (this is explained in a tender epilogue) he had the love of a
Pure Woman to sustain him.

Early in the proceedings, someone remarks, "This is too much
like a movie."

That about sums it up.

From the jacket of *Mach 1, a Story of Planet Ionus*, by Allen A.
Adler: "This is Allen Adler's first novel, although it was he who
conceived the original story of *Forbidden Planet . . .* He produced
a revival of *Front Page*, has written both original stories and
screenplays for the motion pictures."

To get one misconception out of the way immediately, this is no
novel: it is a half-heartedly "novelized" screen story. The blank-
faced characters stand up and speak their lines woodenly, without
any perceptible motivation; of characterization, explanation, depth

of any kind there is none; the thing is a framework to be filled in by a producer, and a puzzle to be solved by a director.

As a screen story, it follows three tried and true principles, namely:

1. You can't beat the old malarkey.
2. Nobody but kids go to see these things.
3. Science is all double-talk anyway, so what the hell?

Operation Mach 1, at the San Diego Naval Base, consists chiefly of Admiral Buchanan, Commander Shawn, and Commander Jeb Curtis, all of whom spend their time shouting at each other nose to nose.

Also present are Lt. Janis Knight, meteorologist, and a civilian electronics expert, Martin Edmur. Martin likes Janis, but is too timid (after all, a *civilian*) to be much competition for rough, tough Commander Curtis, a John Wayne type.

The Mach 1 is a nuclear-powered torpedo boat, designed to exceed the speed of sound. It rides out of the water on a fin, and smooths a path for itself with a "tri-node" which emits "occulting current."

What is occulting current? " 'Well, it's much more powerful than either direct or alternating current. Its amperage can be made to build like an atomic chain. Its ray produces a peculiar molecular cohesion.' "

Blah. Well, Jeb takes the Mach 1 out on a super-secret test run, and disappears. So does Janis, who was on San Nicolas Island waiting for him. The Grid Space Mass got them.

I repeat, the Grid Space Mass. A space mass is a spaceship, only made of gas. It looks like "a monstrous clam composed of some form of tremulous gelatin."

The Grid are people whose names begin with K. They come from "planet Ionus," and look just like us, fortunately for Casting, except for their multi-colored hair and eyes. When we first see them, they're like photographic negatives, but that's because they're "accelerated."

Jeb and Janis are probed by a device which "records" their molecular structure, because only things that have been "recorded" can pass through "the barrier," and be prepared "to withstand the speed of light."

Gug. So the Grid take them to Ionus, which turns out to be a moon of Saturn; they learn that the Grid live in a big city thirty miles under the ice, because a monster named Karkong (out of Dr. Zarkov, by King Kong, I guess) has eaten up everything on the surface of the "planet." Karkong got to be the way he is by neglecting to discharge the "occulting current" which, by a funny coincidence, the Grid generate in their bodies.

Yikh. So Jeb and Janis look around and gather samples, and then the Grid take them back to Earth in the Space Mass, to "Demonstrate to your United Nations our need for atomic power." (To feed the monster.)

The monster, however, follows them back to Earth: there's a twist for you!

A point that seems to have eluded Adler is the energy required to propel a monster 700,000,000 miles at the speed of light. Since all the nuclear energy produced anywhere in the world would not do more than wet the bottom of that bucket, Karkong is like a fellow driving from Portland, Maine, to Portland, Oregon, to buy a half-gallon of gas.

Anyhow Karkong shows up, "an inverted bowl composed of turbulent air" a hundred yards wide. He sucks up electrical energy wherever he finds it, blacking out cities; and he emits lightning bolts and leaves a charred path behind him, which also seems wasteful for an energy-hungry monster.

In spite of efforts to dismantle all atomic plants in his path, he gets a taste of nuclear energy and likes it (the flavor?); he accordingly takes off for Russia to find more. The Grid in their Mass and Jeb, Martin and Shawn in the Mach 1 take out after him; meanwhile Admiral Buchanan dives out a window. Martin dies in firing the atomic torpedo which cripples the monster. (Karkong, now a thirty-foot tar baby, is felled by lightning bolts a little later, which does not make much sense but provides a sock finish.) Jeb gets the girl. The Grid go home. The End.

The Navy background, including the imaginary torpedo boat Mach 1, is competently handled and authentic-sounding. Two minor characters, Buchanan and a Mexican girl named Orquita, briefly show traces of life. The scenes of destruction (great for wide screen) are powerfully handled, although there's something a little obscene about real suffering used to provide a foreground for a cardboard monster.

The rest of the book, including all the "science fiction" part, is so bad that ordinary epithets will not do. It is incredibly, stupidly, loathsomely bad. The science double-talk is not only meaningless but incoherent. The action has the frantic and addled air (and the idiot prurience) of a comic-book story. The style is pretentious, ignorant and vulgar.

Some bad science fiction books get published through innocent enthusiasm or incompetence. The publication of this one is an act of contempt for science fiction readers—and a slap in the face for every honest craftsman in the field.

Judith Merril's novel, *The Tomorrow People*, deals with a sick spaceman, Johnny Wendt (who has come back demoralized by an experience on Mars), and his sweet, patient, self-sacrificing girlfriend, Lisa Trovi.

Doug Laughlin, Johnny's companion on the first Martian expedition, wandered off apparently to die in the desert, nobody knows why; four pages of the ship's log are missing, and Johnny can't even talk about what he is drinking to forget.

This puzzle-box remains in the background throughout most of Miss Merril's earnest, ungraceful book. When it is finally opened, it discloses a sticky marshmallow: Mars is the planet of Love. (If only a girl and a boy had been sent on the expedition, instead of two boys, everything would have been dandy.)

Lisa Trovi, the book's heroine, is a lovely, devoted, unselfish, talented girl who reads a lot about ESP; every man who sees her falls madly in love with her, but her heart belongs to Johnny, a boyishly attractive bottle-a-day man, who realizes all too well that he can never be worthy of her great love.

Johnny's interior monologues run mainly to virile profanity:

> *And what the Hell do you think you're proving?* he jeered at himself . . . What the Hell should *he* care? . . . The Hell with it. . . . What the Hell did he *want* her to say?

Other characters include Phil Kutler, a psychiatrist who is trying to cure Johnny (though hopelessly devoted to Lisa, of course); Dr. Peter Christensen, director of the All America laboratory on the Moon; Brigadier General Jethro Harbridge, and assorted other political types whose involved intrigues, occupying a substantial part of the book, remain totally incomprehensible to the last.

The science in this book can only be described as a shambles. Newcomers to the Moon find they can walk normally in magnetic-soled boots, and are troubled by no sensations of falling; when a lady scientist escapes from Red Dome on the Moon, she does so in a helicopter. (Think of that word, and the author who wrote it; the editor who read it, and copyread it, and proofread it.)

The author's use of scientific terminology is dependably cute and inaccurate, e.g., "Geiger-suits." (To insulate spacemen from dangerous high-velocity geigers?) Her syntax is no better:

> Every ship of all nations that lifts off of Earth . . . (Page 167.)
> . . . that no breath of suspicion sully his name or place in doubt (by a wary government) his suitability . . . (Page 12.)

At its worst, her style drops to the level of bureaucratese. Two ghastly examples:

The prevailing state of by-mutual-consent *laissez-faire* isolation was such an inherent fabric that. . . (Page 12.)
. . . an anachronistically solid-comfortable leather chair . . . (Page 60.)

Parts of this book are relatively painless to read; the only irritants in the dialogue are coyness, feminine overemphasis and an unaccountable sprinkling of 1960 jive talk. Phil Kutler, the psychiatrist, is well drawn and sympathetic for the most part; even Johnny Wendt becomes briefly poignant and believable.

What is objectionable in the book is its lack of any internal discipline, either in the writing or the thinking. Under the crisp surface it is soft and saccharine: wherever you bite it, custard dribbles out.

Is this the "woman's viewpoint"? I don't believe it; I think it is the woman's-magazine viewpoint, from which God preserve us.

Q.: What does the name of this book mean, Daddy?
A.: Hmm? *Point Ultimate*, by Jerry Sohl. Darned if *I* know. Let's see, a point is a dot, and ult—
Q.: Well, never mind. Gee whiz. So how does the book start?
A.: Once upon a time, along about 1995, there was a handsome youth named Emmett Keyes, and he lived on his Daddy's farm in Illinois. But Emmett was very unhappy, because everybody was so poor, and the Enemy and the Commies had taken over his country—
Q.: The Enemy *and* the Commies?
A.: That's what it says here. Well, anyway, the Reds had taken over back in 1969, and—
Q.: How they do that, Daddy?
A.: First they dropped big H-bombs on Washington, D.C., and Chicago. Then when the President went to drop H-bombs on *them*, he found out the Enemy had *an impregnable barrier against aircraft and missiles*. It says right here. Like a wall the planes and bombs couldn't go through. You see?
Q.: Sure. A force field. Over the whole goddam continent of Asia, Dad?
A.: I don't know. I guess so. Now it seems young Emmett was the only one that was immune to the awful plague the Reds had infected everybody with, so they'd have to have booster shots every month, or else get sick, or go crazy, or even die. Boy, this is exciting! They—
Q.: Hold on a minute. Emmett was the only one that was immune?
A.: That's what it says.

Q.: Okay, I just wanted to get that straight.

A.: Yes. Well, and besides that, the Commies made everybody wear identity strips under the skin of their forearm. See, these are not the same as the identity bracelets, later on—those are under the skin and all, but around the *wrist*.

Q.: Uncomfortable as the dickens, huh, Dad?

A.: You bet! Well, young Emmett wanted to fight the Enemy, anyway, so he left home and went looking for gypsies. Well, sir—

Q.: Whoa. Hold on. Just a minute. He went looking for gypsies?

A.: That's right. See right here? Gypsies.

Q.: Why?

A.: Well, because he had always heard that gypsies were immune to the plague, you see, and could travel around without—

Q.: Whup! Didn't you just get through saying—? Oh well, why bother? Clear ether, Dad—toe in and blast ahead.

A.: Okay. Well, he walked along the lovely fields in the sunshine, and by and by he came to a beautiful farm. Oh, it was pretty. New paint *all* over, and tended just *so*. Emmett never *saw* such a pretty farm! Well, he was thirsty, so he walked up and asked Farmer Tisdail for a drink of well water. And what do you think he found out?

Q.: What?

A.: Why, jolly Farmer Tisdail was a mean old collaborator who tried to kill Emmett with a wrench! Gosh! And so Emmett took his hunting knife and cut Farmer Tisdail's guts wide open, and serve him just right too! Then he and gloomy old Mrs. Tisdail had a nice chat over her husband's body while he washed the blood off his hands, and they made speeches to each other, and then she told him the sad story of her life, and then she gave him a brand new shiny sleep gun and a lot of money, and sent him happily on his way.

Q.: That was the farmer's wife, that did all that?

A.: No, his widow. So then Emmett met some jolly young people in the woods, but they wouldn't tell him anything, and he wouldn't tell them anything *either*. They just made speeches. So they let him go, and—

Q.: Just one question, Dad? If there don't nobody tell nobody nothing, what was the point of them meeting at all in them woods?

A.: Let me get on to where he gets captured by the Enemy, a horrible fat man named Gniessin who lives in a villa—

Q.: Gniessin?

A.: You heard me, Gniessin. —in a villa with a bunch of robots and a horrible cook and a nice, *nice* doctor who used to be an abortionist and takes dope, and they have wild parties every Saturday night—say, listen, I wonder if this is a book for you, after all.

Q.: Yeah, yeah, so?

A.: Hmm. Well, it does get pretty disappointing here, at that. So anyway, Gniessin just happens to die an entirely natural death in the steam bath, and Emmett cuts Gniessin's identity bracelet out of his wrist and sticks it into his own wrist, and—

Q.: He must be some surgeon, this Emmett boy, huh?

A.: No, no—he just hacks away with a piece of broken bottle, and then—

Q.: You mean he hacks through all those veins in the wrist, and doesn't bleed to death? Hoo boy!

A.: As a matter of fact, Mr. Smart Aleck, this is only the first time. Later he does it again, and—

Q.: Now I can believe anything. Okay, go on to where he flaps his arms and flies away, Dad.

A.: No, he steals a plane, see, and gets away, and *now* guess what? He finds the gypsies!

Q.: Go on.

A.: Yes, really, he does! So then he flashes this big roll of bills in the fortune teller's tent, and so the patriotic gypsies knock him on the head, but then he convinces them he's all right, and joins their carnival—

Q.: Their *carnival*? Dad, you mean carnies, not gypsies, right? Gypsies don't—

A.: Yes, they *do*, too. And it turns out these gypsies are the same ones he met in the woods that time, and they have an underground railroad where they sneak off pregnant young girls that the Commies won't let have babies, and—*Aha!*

Q.: Aha?

A.: They sneak them off to Point Ultimate. That's what it means. The last point on the underground railway, you see? It means the End of the Line.

Q.: So why don't they call it that, huh, Dad?

A.: Never mind. They all know a lot of Latin, those gypsies, is why. So then, the Enemy capture Emmett again and try to make him tell where this Point—

Q.: Listen, Dad?

A.: Umhmm?

Q.: You remember what I said about those kiddie comic books you bought me?

A.: Yeah. I ought to wash out your mouth—

Q.: Well, I take it back. Let's read about Cinderella and the mad scientist some more, shall we?

A.: Right.

10. WHEN I WAS IN KNEEPANTS: *Ray Bradbury*

RAY BRADBURY BEGAN writing professionally at the floodtide of the cerebral story in science fiction—in 1940, when John Campbell was revolutionizing the field with a new respect for facts, and a wholly justified contempt for the overblown emotional values of the thirties. Bradbury, who had nothing but emotion to offer, couldn't sell Campbell.

Bradbury didn't care. He adapted his work just enough to meet the standards of the lesser markets—he filled it with the second-hand furniture of contemporary science fiction and fantasy—and went on writing what he chose.

It's curious to look back now on those first Bradbury stories and reflect how far they have brought their author. Not many of them are stories at all; most are intensely realized fragments, padded out with any handy straw. The substance of "The Next in Line," for one especially vivid example, is in a two-page description of some Mexican mummies, as relentlessly and embarrassingly horrible as any tourist photograph. The remainder—the two American visitors, the car trouble, the hotel room, the magazines—is not relevant, it merely plumps out the skeleton enough to get it into a conventional suit of clothes.

On a story-a-week schedule, Bradbury sold prodigiously to *Weird Tales*, *Planet Stories*, *Thrilling Wonder*. One day we awoke to discover that he had leapfrogged over John Campbell's head, outside our microcosm altogether: his work was beginning to appear in *Harper's*; in *Mademoiselle*; in the *O. Henry Prize Stories*; on the radio; in *Esquire*, *Collier's*, *The Saturday Evening Post*.

Outside the huge, brightly-colored bubble he had blown around himself, "serious" critics reacted with rapture:

> . . . the sheer lift and power of a truly original imagination exhilarates . . . His is a very great and unusual talent.
>
> — Christopher Isherwood

Inside the bubble, we get at once a clearer and a more distorted view of Bradbury. Although he has a large following among science fiction readers, there is at least an equally large contingent of people who cannot stomach his work at all; they say he has no respect for the medium; that he does not even trouble to make his scientific double-talk convincing; that—worst crime of all—he fears and distrusts science.

. . . All of which is true, and—for our present purposes, anyhow —irrelevant. The purists are right in saying that he does not write science fiction, and never has.

To Bradbury, as to most people, radar and rocket ships and atomic power are big, frightening, meaningless names: a fact which, no doubt, has something to do with his popular success, but which does not touch the root of the matter. Bradbury's strength lies in the fact that he writes about the things that are really important to us—not the things we pretend we are interested in— science, marriage, sports, politics, crime—but the fundamental prerational fears and longings and desires: the rage at being born; the will to be loved; the longing to communicate; the hatred of parents and siblings, the fear of things that are not self. . . .

People who talk about Bradbury's imagination miss the point. His imagination is mediocre; he borrows nearly all his backgrounds and props, and distorts them badly; wherever he is required to invent anything—a planet, a Martian, a machine—the image is flat and unconvincing. Bradbury's Mars, where it is not as bare as a Chinese stage-setting, is a mass of inconsistency; his spaceships are a joke; his people have no faces. The vivid images in his work are not imagined; they are remembered.

Here is the shock of birth, in "No Particular Night or Morning":

> "Have you talked about this to the psychiatrist?"
> "So he could try to mortar up the gaps for me, fill in the gulfs with noise and warm water and words and hands touching me...?"

And the death-wish, Bradbury's most recurrent theme:

> . . . When I was living I was jealous of you, Lespere. . . Women frightened me and I went into space, always wanting them and jealous of you for having them, and money, and as much happiness as you could have in your own wild way. But now, falling here, with everything over, I'm not jealous of you any more, because it's over for you as it is for me, and right now it's like it never was. ("Kaleidoscope.")

> Forty-five thousand people killed every year on this continent
> ...made into jelly right in the can, as it were, in the automobiles.
> Red blood jelly, with white marrow bones like sudden thoughts . . .
> The cars roll up in tight sardine rolls — all sauce, all silence.
> . . . You look out your window and see two people lying atop
> each other in friendly fashion who, a moment ago, had never met
> before, dead . . . ("The Concrete Mixer.")

The gulf between Bradbury and the science fiction writers is
nowhere more clearly evident than in the lavish similes and metaphors that are his trademarks:

> The first concussion cut the rocket up the side with a giant can
> opener. The men were thrown into space like a dozen wriggling
> silverfish. ("Kaleidoscope.")

> . . . And here were the lions now... so feverishly and startlingly
> real that you could feel the prickling fur on your hand, and your
> mouth was stuffed with the dusty upholstery smell of their heated
> pelts . . . ("The Veldt.")

The aim of science-fantasy, more and more as it becomes what
it has always tried to be—adult fiction—is to expand the imagination, stretch it to include things never before seen or dreamed of.
Bradbury's subject is childhood and the buried child-in-man; his
aim is to narrow the focus, not to widen it; to shrink all the big
frightening things to the compass of the familiar: a spaceship to
a tin can; a Fourth of July rocket to a brass kettle; a lion to a
Teddy bear.

There is so much to say about Bradbury's meaning that perhaps
too little has been said about his technique. He is a superb craftsman, a man who has a great gift and has spent fifteen years labor-
iously and with love teaching himself to use it. "For here was a
kind of writing of which there is never much in any one time—
a style at once delicate, economical and unobtrusively firm, sharp
enough to cut but without rancor, and clear as water or air."
That's Stephen Vincent Benét, writing in 1938 about Robert Nathan;
the same words, all but the next to last phrase, might have been
written with equal justice of Bradbury. His imagery is luminous
and penetrating, continually lighting up familiar corners with unexpected words. He never lets an idea go until he has squeezed
it dry, and never wastes one. I well remember my own popeyed
admiration when I read his story about a woman who gave birth to
a small blue pyramid; this is exactly the sort of thing that might
occur to any imaginative writer in a manic or drunken moment;
but Bradbury wrote it and sold it.

Why Bradbury's world-line and that of the animated cartoon have never intersected, I do not know; perhaps because the result would necessarily scare the American theater-going public out of its underpants; but clearly, in such stories as "Jack-in-the-Box," Bradbury is writing for no other medium. The gaudy colors and plush textures, the dream-swift or dream-slow motion, the sudden dartings into unsuspected depths of perspective, or contrariwise, the ballooning of a face into the foreground—these are all distinctive techniques of the animated cartoon, and Bradbury uses them all.

As for the rancor, the underlying motif of much early Bradbury, the newer stories show little of it; this might be taken as a sign that Bradbury is mellowing in his thirties, and perhaps he is; I have the feeling that he is rather trying to mellow—deliberately searching for something equally strong, equally individual, less antagonistic toward the universe that buys his stories. I don't think he has yet found it. There's the wry, earthy humor of "En la Noche," the pure fancy of "The Golden Kite, The Silver Wind"; these are neutral stories, anyone might have written them. There are the moralistic tales; if you find the moral palatable, as I do in "The Big Black and White Game" and "Way in the Middle of the Air," these are sincere and moving; if you don't, as I don't in "Powerhouse" or "The Fire Balloons," there is a pious flatness about them. Then there is sentiment; and since Bradbury does nothing by halves, it is sentiment that threatens continually to slop over into sentimentality. At its precarious peak, it is a moving and vital thing: when it slops, it is—no other word will do—sickening.

It has been said of Bradbury that, like H. P. Lovecraft, he was born a century or so too late. I think he would have been a castaway in any age; if he would like to destroy airplanes, television sets, automatic washing machines, it's not because they make loud noises or because they have no faces or even because some of them kill people, but because they are grown-up things; because they symbolize the big, loud, faceless, violent, unromantic world of adults.

Childhood is after all Bradbury's one subject. When he writes of grown-up explorers visiting the sun or the Jurassic jungles, they are palpably children playing at spacemen or time-travelers. He writes feelingly and with sharp perception of young women and of old people—because, I think, he finds them childlike. But it's only when the theme becomes explicit that his song sings truest:

> The boys were playing on the green park diamond when he came
> by. He stood a little while among the oak-tree shadows, watching

them hurl the white, snowy baseball into the warm summer air,
saw the baseball shadow fly like a dark bird over the grass, saw
their hands open in mouths to catch this swift piece of summer
that now seemed most especially important to hold onto . . . .
How tall they stood to the sun. In the last few months it seemed
the sun had passed a hand above their heads, beckoned, and they
were warm metal drawn melting upwards; they were golden taffy
pulled by an immense gravity to the sky, thirteen, fourteen years
old, looking down upon Willie, smiling, but already beginning to
neglect him . . .

Learned opinion to the contrary, Bradbury is not the heir of
Poe, Irving or Hawthorne; his voice is the voice (a little shriller)
of Christopher Morley and Robert Nathan and J. D. Salinger.
As his talent expands, some of his stories become pointed social
commentary; some are surprisingly effective religious tracts,
disguised as science fiction; others still are nostalgic vignettes;
but under it all is still Bradbury the poet of 20th-century neurosis,
Bradbury the isolated spark of consciousness, awake and alone at
midnight; Bradbury the grown-up child who still remembers, still
believes.

The young Ray Bradbury wrote a story called "Skeleton," about
a man obsessed by the fact that he carries a horrid, white, grin-
ning skeleton inside him. The story was raw, exuberant, gauche,
pretentious, insulting to the intellect, and unforgettable. *Weird
Tales* published it, and later it appeared in Bradbury's first collection, *Dark Carnival*.

The story did not soothe its readers' anxieties nor pamper their
prejudices, nor provide vicarious adventure in a romantic setting.
Far from solving his problem by his own courage and resourcefulness, the hero let it be solved for him by a strange little man
named Munigant, who crawled down his throat, gnawed, crunched
and munched away the bones which had so annoyed him, and left
him lying on his carpet, a human jellyfish.

Time passed; Bradbury got a little older, stopped running quite
so hard. His stories acquired depth, smoothness, polish. Little
by little he stopped writing about corpses, vampires, cemeteries,
things in jars; instead, he wrote about civil rights, religion and
good home cooking. The slicks, which had begun buying him as a
curiosity when he was horrid, kept on buying him as a staple when
he turned syrupy.

Dandelion Wine consists of sixteen loosely connected tales without a ghost or a goblin in them; they are familiar in tone and
rhythm, but these stories are no longer what we mean by fantasy;
they are what Hollywood means by fantasy. The setting is an

imaginary Midwestern town, seen through the wrong end of a rose-colored glass. The period is as vague as the place; Bradbury calls it 1928, but it has no feeling of genuine recollection; most of the time it is like second-hand 1910.

Childhood is Bradbury's one subject, but you will not find real childhood here, Bradbury's least of all. What he has had to say about it has always been expressed obliquely, in symbol and allusion, and always with the tension of the outsider—the ex-child, the lonely one. In giving up this tension, in diving with arms spread into the glutinous pool of sentimentality that has always been waiting for him, Bradbury has renounced the one thing that made him worth reading.

All the rest is still here: the vivid images, the bombardment of tastes and sounds and smells; the clipped, faceless prose; the heavy nostalgia, the cuteness, the lurking impudence. The phrases, as before, are poignant ("with the little gray toad of a heart flopping weakly here or there in his chest") or silly to the point of self-parody ("lemon-smelling men's room"). The characters are as lifelike as Bradbury's characters ever were: bright, pert, peppermint-stick people, epicene, with cotton-candy hair and sugar smiles.

Maybe Bradbury, like his own protagonist in "Skeleton," grew uneasy about the macabre forces in himself: or maybe success, that nemesis of American writers, was Bradbury's M. Munigant. Whatever the reason, the skeleton has vanished; what's left is recognizable but limp.

11. THE VORPAL PEN: *Theodore Sturgeon*

THEODORE STURGEON is a phenomenon out of Philadelphia, a yellow-eyed thing with a goatee, a mortician's voice, and Pan's original smile. He clashed with high school. He ran away to sea, took up nudism, ran a bulldozer, got married and unmarried, wrote music, advertising copy and fantasy, smoked cigarettes in a long holder, got married again, tinkered with gadgets. His biographical note in *More Than Human*, as wild as anything he's written, ends with this sentence:

> He lives with his wife and son, twelve-string guitar, and hot-rod panel truck in Rockland County, where he is at present working on an opera.

Now there you are; that's Sturgeon. *Damn* the man!

> The idiot lived in a black and gray world, punctuated by the white lightning of hunger and the flickering of fear. His clothes were old and many-windowed. Here peeped a shinbone, sharp as a cold chisel, and there in the torn coat were ribs like the fingers of a fist.

That's from the first paragraph of *More Than Human*, and it will do for a sample of the best Sturgeon yet. Or this from page 43, when a little girl named Janie has just walked out on her mother.

> Wima knew before she started that there wasn't any use looking, but something made her run to the hall closet and look in the top shelf. There wasn't anything up there but Christmas tree ornaments and they hadn't been touched in three years.

. . . My God, it's *all* like that, violins and stained glass and velvet and little needles in your throat. Even after the first reading, you can dip into this book anywhere and have to haul yourself out by the scruff. The *Galaxy* novella "Baby Is Three" is the middle section of it, and that's all it is; if you thought it was complete in itself when you read it, you'll never think so again after you've finished *More Than Human*. It's a single story that goes from here to there like a catenary arc, and hits one chord like the Last Trump when it gets there, and stops. There's nothing more to be said about it, except that it's the best and only book of its kind.

Sturgeon hasn't always had his big voice under the control he showed in *More Than Human* and "Saucer of Loneliness." He's been practicing, trying this and that, and along with the pure tones a lot of sad squawks have come out. (When a really good voice goes just a little off key, it's a hard thing to take.)

But Sturgeon's failures, some of them, are as triumphant as his successes; they made the successes. Sturgeon is the most accomplished technician this field has produced, bar nobody, not even Bradbury; and part of the reason is that he never stops working at it. He tried writing about each character in a story in a different meter once—iambs for one, trochees for another—a trick, not viable, but it taught him something about rhythm in prose. He has cold-bloodedly studied the things that make people angry, afraid, pitying, embarrassed, worshipful, and mortared them into his stories.

And for the last few years he has been earnestly taking love apart to see what makes it tick. Not what the word means on the cover of a pulp magazine, but love, all the different kinds there are or could be, working from the outside in. "It is fashionable to overlook the fact that the old-shoe lover *loves* loving old shoes."* Some of the resulting stories have been as flat and unconvincing as others are triumphantly alive; but Sturgeon is learning, has learned more about the strongest theme in life or literature than anybody this side of Joyce Cary.

He writes about people first and other marvels second. More and more, the plots of his short stories are mere contrivances to let his characters expound themselves. "It Wasn't Syzygy," "The Sex Opposite" and "A Way of Thinking" are such stories: the people stand out from their background like Rubens figures that have strayed onto a Mondrian canvas: graphic evidence that Sturgeon, like Bradbury, long ago went as far as he could within the limitations of this field without breaking them.

For those who think they see an easy answer to the problem, here's a thought: Sturgeon *has* tried writing straight people-stories, without any fantasy in them at all. Two of them wound up

*Sturgeon's "Why So Much Syzygy?" in the Summer, 1953 issue of Redd Boggs' *Skyhook*.

in hard covers: but both were first published in science-fantasy
magazines. "Hurricane Trio" evidently failed to sell in its original, stronger form; Sturgeon had to dilute it with space-opera to
save it. "A Way Home" is not even remotely science fiction or
fantasy: it saw print, undiluted, in *Amazing Stories*, but only God
and Howard Browne know why.

   This is laughable on the face of it, but it happens to be true:
Cramped and constricted as it is, the science fiction field is one
of the best of the very few paying markets for a serious short-
story writer. The quality magazines publish a negligible quantity
of fiction; slick short stories are as polished and as interchange-
able as lukewarm-water faucets; the pulps are gone; the little
magazines pay only in prestige. There are no easy answers.

12. ANTHOLOGIES

OUT OF THE FOURTEEN STORIES in Robert A. Heinlein's *Tomorrow, The Stars*, by my reckoning, ten are A's, four B's; there are no stinkers at all. This is much too good to be true; it suggests that the collection may be dangerously unbalanced— if I like everything in it, there's sure to be somebody else who won't like anything—but considering that two of the stories were originally published in a magazine I edited, I don't see how I can legally complain.

Heinlein is one of those who draw a firm line between science fiction and fantasy; they are, he says in his introduction, "as different as Karl Marx and Groucho Marx." It's a pleasure to be able to disagree, for once, with a writer I admire so strenuously. Heinlein goes on:

> Fantasy is constructed either by denying the real world *in toto* or at least by making a prime basis of the story one or more admittedly false premises—fairies, talking mules, trips through a looking glass, vampires, seacoast Bohemia, Mickey Mouse. But science fiction, *no matter how fantastic its contents may seem*, always accepts all of the real world and the entire body of human knowledge concerning the real world as the framework for the fictional speculation.

Granting that the aims of "pure" fantasy and "pure" science fiction differ, are they two rigid compartments, or only the ends of a continuous spectrum? Heinlein concedes that much of what he calls science fiction (including nine out of the fourteen stories in this book) deals not with legitimate extensions of present-day scientific knowledge but with subjects about which we're allowed to speculate freely, because *nobody knows*—with time travel, for example, or intelligent, volitional robots—but not with an "admittedly false premise" like fairies or talking mules.

It seems to me that the distinction between a newly invented improbability and a traditional one is an essentially unreal and uninformative distinction; Heinlein in fact is claiming something for science which he has no right to claim.

We have no negative knowledge.

We don't know that time travel and humanoid robots are impossible; neither do we know that fairies, Carroll's looking-glass world, a literal fundamentalist heaven and hell, or Joseph Smith's golden tablets do not and cannot exist. To take examples from Heinlein's own work, we don't *know* that the universe is not a set of clever stage-illusions designed to mislead one man; we don't *know* that some whirlwinds may not have intelligence and volition; we don't *know* that witchcraft, properly applied, couldn't manufacture dresses and non-fattening desserts.

Who decides what is an admittedly false premise? Heinlein is in a peculiarly bad position to defend this point; if "Magic, Inc." is fantasy because, among other things, it deals with a genuine witch, then what is "Waldo," which deals, among other things, with a genuine Pennsylvania hex doctor? If "They" is fantasy because it takes solipsism seriously, what about *Beyond This Horizon*, which deals at least half seriously with the identical subject? And what about the reincarnation in the same novel?

Varied as they are, the stories in *Tomorrow, The Stars*—the ten A's among them, anyhow—have one thing in common with each other and with Heinlein's own work: each is a pretty good approximation of the last word on its subject. Nobody has ever improved on "Universe," although a good many reckless people have tried, because Heinlein said it all. For the same reason, these are stories that can be depended upon to last awhile; nothing written in the foreseeable future is likely to make this book a dead weight on your shelf.

Jack Finney's "I'm Scared" postulates a queer kind of involuntary time-travel, and builds it with infinite care into a genuinely frightening thing—a rarity in what Heinlein calls science fiction, or in what he calls fantasy, for that matter.

C. M. Kornbluth's "The Silly Season" is an outrageously logical formula for the invasion of Earth. This story has a history that goes back to the forties, when a group of threadbare young writers, including Kornbluth, Robert W. Lowndes and myself, were associated in a Manhattan kaffeeklatsch called the Futurian Society; it derives, if I am not mistaken, from an idea Kornbluth and I worked out together for a cops-and-robbers story Walter Kubilius

wanted to write.* Rather than try to get my one per cent out of
the author, I hereby relinquish all rights to my half of the notion,
which Kornbluth has improved out of all recognition anyhow. (The
original involved photoelectric beams, bats smuggled into a bank
in briefcases, and large quantities of pinochle-playing policemen.)

"The Report on the Barnhouse Effect," by Kurt Vonnegut, Jr.,
deals with a very old idea in science-fantasy, the notion that one
man of good will, armed with an irresistible weapon, could make
our society sane. C. S. Forester, R. De Witt Miller and others
have tried their hands at it, but I don't think it's ever been done
quite so compactly or with so much sparkle.

Bob Tucker, a fixture in science-fantasy fandom for twenty-odd
years, and more lately one of the most brilliant writers in the
business, immortalized my first contribution to any magazine in a
wonderful fanzine called *Le Zombie*. It would be nice to be able
to say that I bought his first professional story, but somebody, I
think Fred Pohl, beat me to it about ten years before "The Tourist
Trade" was written. Anyhow, this is a very funny story; it deals
with an irreverent aspect of time-travel which Tucker and John
Wyndham hit upon almost simultaneously; and without derogation
to Wyndham, a veteran science-fantasy writer and still one of the
best, Tucker's version is much the better of the two.

"Rainmaker," by John Reese, is what Heinlein calls it, "almost
a period piece"; it was first published in 1949, since when rain-
making has become as much a part of the mundane world as the
atom bomb; nevertheless, this is science fiction of the purest type
—and a thumping good story.

The spontaneous-human-mutation story, these days, is pretty
nearly dead, partly of a surfeit, but also partly because of some
spectacularly good writing. The major culprits are Henry and
Catherine Kuttner: like Heinlein, like any master craftsman, they
will not and cannot let a subject go until they have exhausted its
possibilities, leaving nothing for the next man to do but to go
and find a subject of his own. This one was a massive job, but
they killed it in sections, painstakingly exploring one aspect at
a time in such memorable stories as "Margin For Error" and
this volume's "Absalom."

"The Monster," by Lester del Rey, and "Jay Score," by Eric
Frank Russell, must have been selected and paired deliberately;
published ten years apart, both are based on the same trick-ending
gimmick—which has, besides, been used so often by lesser writers

---

*Lowndes reminds me that Kubilius *did* write the story, and sold it to *Science
Fiction Quarterly*; and as a matter of fact, I illustrated it. This shows you what
illustrators are like.

that experienced editors can spot it on the first page of a slush-pile submission—and yet each is so different from the other, and so very good in its own way, that they don't conflict even when placed side by side, as they are in this volume.

"Betelgeuse Bridge," by William Tenn, is typically wry, ingenious and witty, but it's a story which has always seemed to me in some obscure way disappointing. I think perhaps the trouble is that its development, wry, &c., as it is, is too conventional, too much What the Editor Thinks He Wants; and that the same author's more recent "Liberation of Earth" (*Future*, May 1953)—the funniest story he's ever written, and about as equivocal as a punch in the solar plexus—may have expressed what he really wanted to say all along. If I'm right, it merely proves what needs no proof, that Tenn is another artist who won't stop till he's had the last word.

Judith Merril's stories are of two types: the sweat-tears-and-baby-urine variety, which Judy apparently writes simply because some editors expect nothing else from a woman, and one paragraph of which is sufficient to make me feel unclean; and the cerebral, quietly competent game of wits with her readers, at which she works equally hard, often with brilliant results. "Survival Ship" belongs to the latter category; if you are one of the twenty million readers who did not see this story in its original publication, printed on second-hand pulp paper and distributed exclusively in Lower Slobbovia, you may try to guess what vital fact it is that Miss Merril is not telling you before she's ready to let you know; my money is on the author.

Murray Leinster, science-fantasy's Grand Old Man, evidently writes the stuff for love, since his alter ego Will Jenkins makes a great deal more money; however, he knows all the tricks in the game and uses them, too often, as a substitute for conscious attention. "Keyhole" is a conventional story written in Leinster's worst style, which is one precarious step above that of "Peter Rabbit"; it is by no means a bad story—if Leinster has ever written a stinker, it must have been long before my time—but it's neither the first nor the last word that will be written on its subject.

Isaac Asimov's contribution has an ugly but accurate title: "Misbegotten Missionary." It poses a difficult problem, develops it with skill, and solves it, regrettably, by accident; what disappoints me more in the story, which might have been a great one, is that it also suggests a very delicate problem of values, and not only does not solve it—I'll admit this would be too much to ask—but leaves it entirely out of account.

William Morrison, most of whose work has been cautiously conventional, has written in "The Sack" a very controlled and perceptive treatment of the "dangerous knowledge" theme—which is philosophical in nature, purists please note, whether it appears in a fairy tale or in *Tomorrow, The Stars*. My only major complaint here is that Morrison, who is a chemist and ought to know better, insists on inventing unlikely organisms and establishing them in even unlikelier places, without any attempt to justify either.

Finally there is "Poor Superman" by Fritz Leiber, who is at his brilliant best when sticking pins into some prominent member or other of the American Paranoids' Association—e.g., Mickey Spillane in "The Night He Cried," or, in the present case, our old friend Alfred van Vogt.

Star Short Novels, edited by Frederik Pohl, offers us a sobering spectacle; here are three novellas, by three distinguished writers —Jessamyn West, Lester del Rey, Theodore Sturgeon—only one of which turns out to be a finished piece of work.

That one, not surprisingly, is the third. "To Here and the Easel" was written at the very top of Sturgeon's range, on the same level as *More Than Human* and "Saucer of Loneliness" and a few others—a breathtaking display of sustained brilliance, all glitter and pop, never holding still an instant, with the velvet-covered fist hanging, hanging . . . here a pun with a bawdier one on top of it, here a sudden unexpected gallop of blank verse . . . until that damned fist comes down and squeezes the whole thing so tight that there's nothing more to say about it. I'm damned if I'll dissect it: *read* it.

Jessamyn West's "Little Men," which opens the book, is an exasperating fraud—no novella, but a rough sketch for a novel. The story begins when the adults of the world wake up to find themselves dwarfed, while their children have grown to man-size. The story also all but ends there, owing to the slowest narrative technique on record. Every now and then we get a tantalizing glimpse of the reversal-of-roles satire we had expected; but it's all two mirrors away, flickerings in the wrong end of a telescope. Miss West, for reasons best known to herself, has chosen to tell her story as the retrospective narrative, written sixty years after the event, of an intolerably windy old man. This hoary method has the sole advantage of making it unnecessary for the author to think up any explanations. In every other way it makes the worst of both worlds—we have neither the sense that the story is unfolding unpredictably as we read, nor the comfort of having been told all that we need to know.

West in the persona of the editor keeps complaining about the

windiness of West in the persona of narrator. This seems a futile
business; obviously she is not listening to herself, or else is determined to make a lively story into a ten-volume bore. Early in
the goings-on, for example, there is a big hassle when the gigan-
tified children fire off a sixteen-inch gun and sink a ship. You
would really think it impossible to make this event sound dull, but
West manages—with just two sentences of action, and two almighty
pages of remastication.

Lester del Rey's "For I Am A Jealous People" is even more
disappointing. Miss West's story, if it is badly and incompletely
developed, at least makes a snail's inch of progress before the
author poops out. Del Rey's is not developed at all.

The story begins with the assumption that Yahweh—the original
one-goat God of the Hebrews, spiteful, petulant and arbitrary—
really exists, and that He has found Himself a new chosen people
and turned against us. This is novel enough, and del Rey's solution
is neat, shocking and sensible. The two together occupy, legiti-
mately, about fifteen pages. The rest is vehicle, almost thirty
dismal pages of it, including a pointless escape-and-capture sequence that might have been lifted bodily from any two-bit action
novel. Del Rey, a high-production writer, can turn out this kind of
thing in any desired quantity. He can also write top-grade science
fiction, but he discovered a long time ago that few editors know
the difference, or care.

S-F, the Year's Greatest Science-Fiction and Fantasy, is the
first of an annual series of anthologies edited by Judith Merril.
Something of this kind was badly needed: an authoritative, perceptive, organized collection of the year's best, at a price everyone can afford.

Readers of Miss Merril's previous anthologies already know
that her taste is unfaltering. Five of the eighteen stories in
this one seem to me unimprovable—Avram Davidson's masterly
(and howlingly funny) "The Golem," Walter M. Miller, Jr.'s "The
Hoofer," Algis Budrys' "Nobody Bothers Gus," Shirley Jackson's
wonderful "One Ordinary Day, With Peanuts," and Isaac Asimov's
"Dreaming Is a Private Thing." Leaving my own entry out of
account (not for modesty's sake but the lack of it), there are seven
more stories—by Robert Abernathy, E. C. Tubb, Willard Marsh,
Mildred Clingerman, Kuttner-&-Moore, R. R. Merliss and Steve
Allen—eminently good enough to repay you if there were nothing
better in the book. There are five more which I mildly dislike, but
always for personal reasons of interest and taste. Mark Clifton's
psi story, "Sense From Thought Divide," although well written,

seems to me to demonstrate the hollowness of this much-touted subject; Sturgeon's "Bulkhead" has an over-emotional quality which somewhat repels me (but his very similar "Twink" made me want to bawl, so take your choice); Jack Finney's "Of Missing Persons" has a disappointingly trite ending; Zenna Henderson's "Pottage" and James Gunn's "The Cave of Night" seemed over-familiar to me: but I can't say that any of these is a bad story.

Taken all together, the eighteen stories (and the eighty honorable mentions in the back of the book) give an intriguing picture of science fiction, 1955. The spread of subjects is rather small; there are six space stories, three about robots or androids, two each about psi phenomena and supermen, and a scattering of others: but no cataclysm stories, no dangerous inventions, no time travel. The range of periods is correspondingly small: one story takes place in the past, the rest either in the present or the comparatively near future.

In spite of the light touch which may seem to dominate the book ("The Golem," "Junior," "The Ethicators" and a couple of others), the one thing that most of these stories have in common is their tragic mood. Miss Merril worked hard to keep this from overbalancing the collection, I know—one of the year's best but most dismal stories had to be jettisoned on that account—and yet all but seven of the stories which were finally chosen give a dominant impression of sadness; this is true even of stories with conventional happy endings, such as "The Stutterer."

I have the feeling that in spite of itself, science fiction is pulling in its horns. In these stories, we are visited three times by beings from elsewhere, but our own far traveling is limited to wistful glimpses of distant worlds (in "The Stutterer," the other planet is merely another battleground, and in "Of Missing Persons" it is a wonderful but unattainable colony). The flow of technological marvels has dried up. Of the eleven stories which make some use of the familiar "world of tomorrow" background, only one—Asimov's—explores the consequences of a new invention; the rest merely postulate the usual equipment, spaceships, robots or what have you, and go on from there.

In the space stories, the sense of destination is lacking. Sturgeon's "Bulkhead" takes place in a spaceship, but it might just as well have been a psychoanalyst's broom closet. Gone is the exuberance with which, in the thirties, writers peopled far planets with fascinatingly cockeyed life forms. Modern astronomy is no doubt partly responsible for this, but certainly there has been a change of mood among the writers, too. There was a certain light-heartedness in the way prewar writers used to destroy the

Earth by solar flares, invasions, earthquakes or inundation; but stories like "The Hoofer" and "The Cave of Night" seem to suggest a feeling that nothing so fortunate is likely to happen.

I am far from wishing to suggest that all this is evidence of the desperate plight of our times: to the contrary, science fiction was never more romantic and outward-looking than in the Depression years. What it does prove, if anything, is the desperate (and traditional) plight of writers. Another trend toward uniformity which Miss Merril had to combat was that in which the story's persecuted hero represents the writer himself, squeezed between a machine civilization and the demands of his art; and at least six such writers got themselves into the book in various disguises.

It's of more interest, perhaps, to note that in this year when the Boom collapsed, although many of the best old-guard writers were absent from the field, a lot of brilliant new talent was coming up. If I read the signs rightly, half a dozen of the bright young men represented here will be back next year—and that should be a collection to watch for.

As near as I can judge, the second *SF, the Year's Greatest Science-Fiction and Fantasy*, actually does contain all but about three of the first-rate science fiction stories published in 1956.

This is a compliment to Miss Merril's expert and painstaking winnowing job; but it also makes you stop and think about what she had to winnow from. To put it another way, she got two-thirds of all the first-rate stories: that is, six.

Six stories, plus three is nine—out of the total output of twenty magazines over a year's time. (The other three, incidentally, are not here because (a) two of them were snapped up by *F&SF* for its own annual collection, and (b) two—not the same two—are by authors already represented.

It may be that science fiction, which looks so flourishing, is coming to the end of its cycle. I crib this notion from Walter Kerr, who thinks our disillusionment with technological progress has already doomed our present theater, with its naturalistic conventions and its preoccupation with ideas drawn from science.

Maybe the same thing is happening to science fiction. Of the fifteen stories in this collection, three are upbeat in tone—"The Far Look," by Theodore L. Thomas, "Silent Brother" by Algis Budrys, and Zenna Henderson's wonderful "Anything Box." The rest range from the mild, almost cheerful pessimism of Mack Reynolds' "Compounded Interest," to the unrelieved gloom of my own "Stranger Station."

Our future, as depicted in these stories, is one in which a little old lady makes the world safe for silliness ("The Cosmic Expense Account," by C. M. Kornbluth); some aliens from the remote past cause a wholesale slaughter at a zoo, in the process getting themselves killed by lions and eagles ("The Man Who Liked Lions," by John Bernard Daley); an alien artifact terrifies a country doctor, who can't stand the idea that the universe is larger than our planet ("The Doorstop," by R. Bretnor); a man finds his rapport with a monstrous alien so painful that in struggling against it he kills them both ("Stranger Station"); and so on.

The point is not so much that the people in these stories come to sticky ends; I'm used to that. But never before have the futures imagined by s.f. writers seemed to me so thoroughly dismal.

A little of this goes perhaps a longer way than we have been realizing. All right, our confidence in the future has slipped a little, for good reasons, in the last decade; all right, science fiction is among other things a literature of escape and of protest: but surely we don't have to bang the same drum all the time.

(I have been writing gloomy stories for years, in a reaction against the silly convention that ruled in the magazines when I was a pup, that all stories must have happy endings. But I think a convention of gloom is just as silly as the other one, and you may expect me to turn optimist just as soon as I can retool for it.)

Last year, as Miss Merril notes in her summation, many of the stories had a common paranoid theme—the solitary hero in flight from a hostile world. This year, interestingly enough, there is a concentration of stories—four of them—built around the theme of multiple personalities. (Miss Merril insists on calling them "split-personalities," following a popular misconception. Multiple personality is not, not, not the same as schizophrenia, or "split personality"—the first is very rare, the second is the most common mental disorder.) In Thomas's "The Far Look," two men come back united in a mystic brotherhood from a tour of duty on the Moon; the same thing happens to a shipload of interstellar explorers in Budrys' "Silent Brother." In that story, the protagonist discovers that he has a "silent brother"—another intelligence inhabiting his body, who comes to conscious life when he sleeps. In Sturgeon's "The Other Man," exactly the same situation is dealt with in a fascinatingly different way; but in each, and in the Thomas story, and in my "Stranger Station"—where the mystic-brotherhood experience is supposed to happen, but doesn't —the message seems to be: *union is painful, oneness is bliss.*

What made four s.f. writers work so hard simultaneously at this theme, and exactly what it signifies, after all, are questions that have no place here, even if I thought I knew the answers: but it is a fact that, to my taste at least, the best and richest science fiction comes out of these curious group preoccupations. (Sturgeon had a pure multiple-personality story in last year's collection, by the way—"Bulkhead.")

My favorites this year are "Silent Brother," for its warm human portrait and its superlative techniques; Reynolds' "Compounded Interest," a wonderfully fresh and engaging new slant on time travel; "Prima Belladonna," by a new British writer named J. G. Ballard, who combines singing plants, psychogenesis, plant-human miscegenation and a lot of deadpan doubletalk into a misty, oddball story reminiscent of the vanished Venard McLaughlin; Sturgeon's "The Other Man" for his usual pyrotechnic style, and for a new system of psychotherapy that sounds both revolutionary and practical (but the people are not people, they are qualities—"good," "evil," "self-renunciation"—and that bothers me); and finally Zenna Henderson's warm little masterpiece, "Anything Box."

The other stories range from good to fair, beginning with C. M. Kornbluth's "The Cosmic Expense Account," which is wise, witty, funny, bitter and tragic, but ducks one of the hard basic questions of fantasy: "If this could happen once, why not twice?" Thomas's "The Far Look" suffers from a lack of characterization—the two principals have no faces and no individual differences, nor any personal reactions to each other—but is memorable for its careful, elaborate treatment of survival on the Moon.

John Bernard Daley's "The Man Who Liked Lions" has some effective passages of mood-writing, but uses stock s.f. gimmicks self-consciously and in places ludicrously: "It took time . . . to move along the pathways of time." Aiming at tragedy, it fails to establish sympathy for anyone concerned, and becomes pointlessly unpleasant. Bretnor's "The Doorstop" is a good minor idea, almost completely covered with chintz. "Each an Explorer" is very minor Asimov: a stock plot, treated perfunctorily. "Grandmother's Lie Soap," by Robert Abernathy, is whimsy muddled in with science fiction, a dreadful combination that affects me like a fingernail scraping a blackboard.

There is also a rather clumsy essay in future archaeology, "Digging the Weans," by Robert Nathan, which I could have done without, and a satire by Ray Russell, "Put Them All Together, They Spell Monster," which is funny, but no more belongs here than does Randy Garrett's verse parody, "All About 'The Thing.'"

Anthony Boucher once remarked that "the dividing line between 'mystery' and 'novel,' so clear for a couple of decades in the nineteen twenties and thirties, has become progressively vaguer.

(. . .) And the borderline is being crossed from two directions: mystery novelists have steadily improved until their best work has all the qualities demanded of any fiction, while some mainstream writers have found, in the structural techniques of the mystery, a valuably solid armature to shape their creations."

Something similar now seems to be going on in science fiction. More and more during the last ten years, the field has come to be dominated by writers who are interested in s.f. chiefly as a convenient vehicle.

Hardened old addicts have been watching this change a little dubiously. In style, depth of character, and other literary values, the new work is superior (that is to say, the top tenth of it — the remainder, according to Sturgeon's Rule, is, was and will be crud). But what we used to regard as the essential thing in s.f. —the technical idea, rigorously and imaginatively worked out— is almost as passé as the pure deductive element in the mystery novel.

This is dramatically shown by the contents of Judith Merril's fourth annual *SF, the Year's Greatest Science-Fiction and Fantasy*. The thirteen s.f. and fantasy stories are of high quality; but there is not one new s.f. idea in the book, unless you count Avram Davidson's madly ingenious notion about the life-cycle of the bisexual bicycle.

By my reckoning, there are two first-rate stories (McKenna's and Leiber's) in the book, and nine which in spite of some flaws carry a real emotional charge. (Short of top quality by a hair are Sheckley's "The Prize of Peril," which I find bitingly honest right up to the phony ending, and Sturgeon's "The Comedian's Children," which blunts its point with a clumsily unbelievable piece of misdirection.)

Unaccountably omitted: "Unwillingly to School," by Pauline Ashwell, surely the most brilliant and delightful first story by any newcomer of the last five years, and "Unhuman Sacrifice," an equally brilliant performance by old pro Katherine MacLean.

Of the fifteen stories, six are not classifiable as s.f. (including short satirical pieces by John Steinbeck and Richard Gehman which simply do not belong in the book at all). The other nine are distributed along a broad spectrum, from fantasy to mainstream: almost without exception, they are s.f. by courtesy. In "Pelt," by Carol Emshwiller, "The Prize of Peril," by Robert Sheckley, Thomas's "Satellite Passage," "Ten-Story Jigsaw," by Brian W. Aldiss, and "The Beautiful Things," by Arthur Zirul, it's clear the author's principal intent was to say something about people: the s.f. background, whether carefully handled or not, is only a convenience, or worse, a concession to the market.

As I noted earlier, "Casey Agonistes" by Richard M. McKenna, and "Space-Time For Springers," by Fritz Leiber, seem to me the strongest stories in the book. Both are pure fantasy. Almost invariably, where an s.f. gimmick appears in the other stories, it does so with an air of intrusion, and the story is weakened by it.

What we are still calling "s.f.," it seems to me, is at an awkward transitional stage. Either that, or (more hopefully), the field has drifted as far as it can go in the direction of indifference to science, and in the next few years we can expect a resurgence of space stories written by men who can tell the moons from the comets.

Bantam's reprint of Charles G. Finney's "The Circus of Dr. Lao" (in *The Circus of Dr. Lao and Other Improbable Stories*, edited by Ray Bradbury) is the first edition of this famous story which has reached more than a few thousand people, and it will be interesting to see how many find it worth the price. Shoals of critics, all the way from the erudite Mr. Boucher to the bumptious Mr. Moskowitz, have acclaimed "Dr. Lao" as a unique classic of fantasy. I may as well admit immediately that I have read it three times, each time with curiosity and disappointment.

I am willing to believe that I may be wrong, but I think this is a suit of the Emperor's new clothes. The story has intermittent merits; the vignettes about the mermaid, the hound of the hedges, the magician and the medusa are effective, funny in places, even occasionally moving. The style varies from good to atrocious; the construction is awful. One of the creatures in the circus appears to some people as a bear, to others as a Russian. Finney makes this primitive joke at length, eleven consecutive times.

The dialogue, where it seems meant to be funny, is as cute as Fitzgerald's worst. The characters pass unexpectedly from scholarly speech to slang—a sophomore trick, and Finney does it over and over. He smothers what story there is in repetitions and digressions, and finally shovels a pile of disjointed definitions over it. All this has its effect, certainly—a sort of cosmic pointlessness—but it's an effect bought by sleazy tricks that wouldn't work twice.

The other eleven stories in this collection are all classified by the editor as fantasies rather than science fiction. S.f., says Bradbury, is law-abiding; fantasy is criminal. S.f. balances you on the cliff; fantasy shoves you off. Being shoved off, he implies, is more fun. I don't think so, and not thinking so, I naturally don't care for this collection much.

There is one superb horror-adventure story in it, James H. Schmitz's "Greenface" (which however is science fiction by the rules I know), and two quietly effective chillers, "The Summer People" by Shirley Jackson, and "The Man Who Vanished," by Robert M. Coates. The first shoves you off, sure enough; the second pretends to, and then catches you: it has a happy ending and a rationale if you look for it, dangerous qualities in a lawbreaking fantasy. "The Pond" by Nigel Kneale is a silly weird tale of the kind that makes you snort with derision when you ought to be shuddering with horror; Roald Dahl's "The Wish" is another. "Earth's Holocaust," by Nathaniel Hawthorne, is a stodgy allegory, and what the *hell* is it doing here? "Buzby's Petrified Woman" by Loren Eiseley is one more of those damned is it/isn't it things that draw an equation between imagination and insanity; "The Limits of Walter Horton" by John Seymour Sharnik is about a fellow who turns into a piano virtuoso overnight.

"The Resting Place," a ghost story by Oliver LaFarge, is firstrate work, but has no plot—the ending simply falls over and dies. "The Hour of Letdown," by E. B. White, is funny, but the bar background is so ineptly done, you can't help thinking how much better Henry Kuttner would have written the same story—not the Kuttner of this volume's hackwork "Threshold," but the one who wrote "Don't Look Now."

I suppose nobody will believe me, because everybody knows that eminent writers are better than magazine hacks; all the same, Kuttner learned a few things about the short story, in a hard school, that nobody can learn from Henry James.

August Derleth's *Time to Come* offers a useful opportunity to moralize, not only about Derleth's shortcomings as an anthologist —about which I've written at some length elsewhere—but about the doldrums in which magazine science fiction presently finds itself.

Of the volume's twelve stories, here published for the first time, Robert Sheckley's "Paradise II" and Evelyn E. Smith's delightful "Baxbr Daxbr" are A's. Sheckley's, incidentally, brilliantly supplies the one major factor that's been lacking in his work: this, I think, is the first Sheckley story with people in it. Philip K. Dick's "Jon's World" and Clark Ashton Smith's "Phoenix," of which more in a moment, are B's in my reckoning. The rest— by Poul Anderson, Isaac Asimov, Charles Beaumont, Arthur C. Clarke, Arthur J. Cox, Irving E. Cox, Jr., Carl Jacobi and Ross Rocklynne—are trite, inconsequential, amateurish or all three together.

This book might have been designed as ammunition for those

critics who assert that all science fiction is ignorantly and badly written. In Irving E. Cox's "Hole in the Sky," for example, an amateur astronomer discovers a *black* object in the heavens near Jupiter. We'll pass that one, since the object turns out to be illusory: but when he reports the discovery, a professional astronomer's reactions are as follows: (1) Before looking: "It's probably a meteor." (2) After looking: "I'd guess it has a mass four or five times that of Jupiter itself . . ." A second professional astronomer, also after one look, comments that "It is a tremendous mass, and it is moving in an orbit that crosses Jupiter's." Gaw!

In "Keeper of the Dream" Charles Beaumont shows an entire ignorance of his subject, scientific inquiry, and ludicrously misinterprets his own fantastic data. Carl Jacobi's "The White Pinnacle" takes place on an asteroid with breathable atmosphere, Earth-normal gravity, vegetation, and native inhabitants (are you listening, Lord?). The major premise of Clark Ashton Smith's "Phoenix" is an impossible condition of the sun.

The last two stories are period pieces: they seem to belong on the gray paper of the thirties *Wonder Stories*, with blurred Paul illustrations. Jacobi's is a preposterous farrago of unexplained and unconnected creepy doings on a mysterious planetoid; but Smith's is something else again.

It takes place in that same never-never land, where the universe beyond Earth is whatever the author happens to feel like calling it. Viewed in terms of modern science fiction, it makes no more sense than the Jacobi: *but it means something*. It has something to say about love-and-death; it does something to the reader, doesn't simply pass through him like beets through a baby.

By "making sense," I mean telling a coherent story from one end to the other, without neurotic logic or kindergarten physics. Modern science fiction doesn't even do this often enough; it's unhappily true that most current science fiction stories neither make sense nor mean anything; but it occurs to me that as long as we're asking, we may as well ask for what we really want—the story, now nearly extinct, which does both.

Sam Moskowitz is a man I have disagreed with about as often as he has opened his hundred-decibel mouth. He has many admirable qualities; he's worked as hard for fandom as anyone living; he edited the foredoomed *Science-Fiction Plus*, according to report, with vigor and integrity beyond the call of duty. The only trouble with him, in fact, is his incredible talent for being wrong.

Editor's Choice in Science Fiction, edited by Moskowitz, sounds

like an obviously good, indeed, an almost foolproof idea; I picked
it up with the agreeable feeling that now, at last, I could say something nice about Sam.

No such luck. McBride, apparently engaged in a determined
effort to produce the most tastelessly selected, designed and
jacketed science fiction anthologies in the entire universe, has
done it again. To begin with, the innocent-looking title has two
fishhooks in it, namely: Which editor? And how much freedom
did he have to choose?

Let's see. Of the twelve stories in the book, one is from *Bluebook*; one from *Astounding*; one from *Amazing*; two from *Thrilling
Wonder Stories*; one from *Super Science*; one from *Unknown*;
one from *Astonishing*; one from the old *Wonder*; one from *Weird
Tales*; one from *Science-Fiction Plus*; one from *Famous Fantastic Mysteries*. Nine of these eleven magazines are defunct.
Galaxy is not represented.

Neither is *The Magazine of Fantasy and Science Fiction*.

Nor *Beyond*; nor *Fantastic*; nor *Space*; nor *If*; nor *Future*; nor
Planet.

If H. L. Gold, Anthony Boucher, J. Francis McComas, Lester
del Rey, Larry Shaw, Malcolm Reiss and Robert A. W. Lowndes
had to be left out, how did Donald Kennicott, Ejler Jakobsson,
Alden H. Norton, Dorothy McIlwraith and Oscar J. Friend get in?*

Of the stories themselves, by my reckoning, one is an A—Mona
Farnsworth's "All Roads," the *Unknown* fantasy of which Campbell
says truly that it should have been in hard covers long before now.
Seven are B's, and there are four stinkers: not an extraordinary
score, one way or the other. But there's still another word in that
title which doesn't mean exactly what it seems to. Of these twelve
stories two are technically science fiction—Clarke's "Wall of
Darkness," which however is straight fantasy in mood and treatment, and Kline's bit of hackwork, "Stolen Centuries." Every one
of the others qualifies as fantasy by the usual rule of thumb: each
excludes data admitted by science (in Kirkland's "The Wall of
Fire," the whole body of geophysics and stellar mechanics) or
admits data excluded by science (in Clifton's and Apostolides'
"What Thin Partitions," poltergeists; and in Johnson's "Far
Below," ghouls).

So who chose? As the introduction makes clear enough, these
are the selected editors' restricted choices, overruled by Moskowitz, overruled in turn by McBride's Otto v. St. Whitelock, and by
McBride himself. Again, this is not unusual procedure, although

*This still seems to me about the most spavined and knock-kneed list of
science fiction experts ever put together.

no publisher makes a point of it on his book jackets. The editor
who supervises an anthology project is responsible for it; it's his
job that will be in danger if, too often, the books don't sell.

The question is one of competence. Is Moskowitz competent
to overrule any science fiction editor? Is v. St. Whitelock competent to overrule even Moskowitz? The answer is no; and this
is the heart of the matter. For twenty-five years science fiction
has been plagued by men who neither liked nor understood the
stories they undertook to edit, and we are not done with them yet.
Mr. v. St. Whitelock's contempt for the field, in a reported statement, is explicit and quite typical: these gentlemen, almost without exception, blandly assume that since they feel superior to
science fiction, they're exceptionally equipped to deal with it.
Every one of them, I think, would indignantly reject the same
logic applied to sports fiction.

I mention sports fiction for a reason. I happen to dislike sports,
particularly team sports, with a virulence which is matched only
by Mr. v. St. Whitelock's dislike for speculative science. In 1950
I found myself editing a group of sports fiction magazines—
that is, copyreading, proofreading and all the other donkey-work;
the editorial decisions were made by the head of my department,
a man who is represented on the contents page of Moskowitz's
anthology. My former boss likes sports fiction, understands it,
and is a good sports fiction editor. With the best will in the world,
I was a bad one. Not, I am thankful to say, because I looked down
my patrician nose at sports fiction, those who write it or read it.
I found writers in this field whom I could admire as wholeheartedly
as I admire Heinlein and Bradbury—William Campbell Gault, for
one: a man who writes weak-tea science fiction, but is hell on
wheels on his own ground. I liked the characterization in those
stories; I liked the description; I liked the fist fights; I liked the
love interest. I liked everything about them, except what they
were all about.

In the same department, we produced a would-be science fiction
magazine. My boss also made the editorial decisions for that one;
and he liked everything about science fiction except the science.
I once asked him to have the art department delete the picture
of Saturn from the background of what was supposed to be an asteroid scene. I can still hear him saying, "But couldn't there be
some little thing shaped like that, floating around out there?"

He was and is a good guy and a good editor. But he killed that
magazine.

Men like him have been the death of other science fiction
magazines, some quickly, some by inches. In introducing Eando

Binder's 1939 clinker "I, Robot," the first of the godawful Adam (and Eve) Link stories, Howard Browne says this:

> Until 1939, such machines were invariably depicted as potential Frankenstein monsters, as trustworthy as a tiger and apt to turn upon their creators at any moment, with or without provocation. This approach became a tiresome pattern in science fiction until "I, Robot" was published in the January, 1939 issue of *Amazing Stories*.

Now, bad as "I, Robot" is, if Browne's statement were true, it would have some historical interest. But Lester del Rey's "Helen O'Loy" was published in 1938*; John W. Campbell, Jr.'s "Night" and Raymond Z. Gallun's "Derelict" in 1935. And Browne uses the phrase "Frankenstein monsters," apparently unconscious of the fact that "I, Robot" is nothing more or less than a clumsy pastiche of *Frankenstein.*

Aficionados like Moskowitz and August Derleth, who dislike modern science fiction but use its aegis to get themselves in print, can be borne; there is at least room for some honest disagreement about what science fiction should be, among people who have read enough to know what it is. But the burden of this other tribe of supercilious blockheads is too heavy. *How long, O Lord, how long?*

---

*Moskowitz pounced on me for this: he produced documents to prove that "I, Robot," in the January, 1939 *Amazing*, was on the stands two weeks earlier than "Helen O'Loy" in the December, 1938 *Astounding*. Touche! But I think my argument stands. Robert Moore Williams' gentle, wistful "Robots' Return" appeared in the September, 1938 *Astounding*, and there were others. My point was, and is, that Browne's statement showed his customary ignorance of any science fiction not published by Ziff-Davis.

13. HALF LOAVES

THIS CHAPTER CONSISTS of two essays, in each of which I paired off two s.f. books published at about the same time in order to contrast their faults and virtues. Writers hate this kind of treatment, and with reason, but critics love it and will do it every chance they get.

John Bowen's literate, profound and funny *After the Rain* begins with a refined crackpot named Uppingham, who proposes to make rain by a kind of reverse electrolysis—i.e., by sticking the hydrogen and oxygen molecules back together in the atmosphere. When he actually tries this, using a balloon inflated with hydrogen, he blows himself to flinders.
Whereupon it begins to rain, and doesn't stop.

> Now Noahs began to proliferate in Britain. There was a Plymouth Noah, a Bradford Noah, and a mad old man who lived just outside Luton. . . . The Luton Noah was prosecuted for stealing sheep; the Plymouth Noah put out to sea, and was lost without trace; the Bradford Noah worked to the dimensions and materials laid down in the Bible, and never finished his ark for want of cypress.

Meanwhile the narrator, John Clarke, an ex-reporter for a British imitation of *The New Yorker*, turns to writing flood-conscious ad copy. "One selling scheme of mine proposed that parasols turned upside down could be filled with food and towed behind boats in flooded areas, but it was rejected as far-fetched."
As the water keeps on rising, most of the arks founder, but Clarke and a girl named Sonya wind up on one that doesn't—a Kon-Tiki-style balsa raft, originally designed as a floating promotion stunt for Glub, the Ideal Breakfast Food: You Need No Other. The notion was for one Captain Hunter to drift around the Atlantic, subsisting on nothing but distilled sea water and "Glub Grits, Glub Cushions, Glub Toasties, Glub Flakes, Poppity Glub for the Little Ones, Glub Mash, and of course the new Glub

in a Matchbox—a Week's Nourishment in Your Pants' Pocket."

Clarke and Sonya find seven people already on the raft: Hunter, "a shirt-off kind of man," who took the Glub position after failing an exam for pub-keeper; Harold Banner, a clergyman without a vocation ("I was too young at that time, and lacked the proper academic background—I got a fourth, you know. It was not good enough to qualify me as a probation officer, but the Church of England was not so particular"); Gertrude Harrison, a gusher of helpfulness, who used to teach Voice and Dramatic Art in a back-street flat; Tony Ryle, the simple body-builder; Muriel Otterdale and her loony husband Wesley; and finally, Arthur Renshaw, the self-appointed leader.

Nearly all these people are marvelously real and undramatic. They are unsuccessful, resigned, faintly comic people. The near-est thing to a hero among them is Arthur: a gray stick of a man, thin-lipped, thin-haired, eyes agleam with intelligence behind his spectacles, who insists on cold-water shaving and keeps the men sleeping dormitory style in one room, the women in another. He is also, and at the same time, the nearest thing to a villain. The rest of the book is a slow, dismally fascinating demonstration of how the others go on giving in to this prim fanatic, purely through laziness and lack of will, until they are in so deep there is no way out except by bloodshed. The paradox of Arthur is what gives the book its curious power: he is thoroughly awful, with the sort of gray, colorless awfulness that only a Briton could invent; and yet he is in fact the savior of the rest. Bowen makes it perfectly clear that without him, the others would have starved to death.

The Enemy Stars, by Poul Anderson, follows a familiar pattern: spacemen go out, wreck their ship, undergo prodigious hardships to repair it and get back to Earth.

Anderson's version is chiefly notable for its painstaking scien-tific background. Almost alone among active s.f. writers today, Anderson is a man with graduate training in science, and this novel, like some of the stories of James Blish and Hal Clement, fairly bristles with accurate and abstruse technical reasoning. The propulsive system of his interstellar ship is explained in plausible detail, and so is the effect that causes it to fail in the vicinity of a dead star.

There are four in the *Southern Cross*'s crew. David Ryerson is a father-tyrannized young commoner from the Outer Hebrides. Terangi Maclaren is a dilettante astronomer, a member of Earth's hereditary "technic" class. Seiichi Nakamura, a space pilot, is from the human colony on Sarai, in the system of Capella. The fourth man, Chang Sverdlov, is a member of an underground movement plotting rebellion against Earth on another colonial planet, Krasna, in the system of Tau Ceti. All four begin as stereotypes—the stammering young idealist, the arrogant rich man's son, the over-polite Oriental with an inferiority complex, and the violent, bullet-headed Slavic revolutionary. But Anderson's compassion and understanding make them come alive as individuals. Watching each one painfully learn to live with the imminence of death is a moving experience.

The story does not always break free of its pulp origins; some scenes are melodramatic, and toward the end of the book all the surviving characters begin to mount soapboxes or pulpits. (In Chapter 12, Ryerson's young wife makes a speech to his father which could only have been memorized from a 1940 soap-opera script.) Anderson's prose is sometimes graceless, occasionally drops into pulp jargon. But at his best he is poetically penetrating: in one swift image he can show you the heart of a character, or spread a landscape before your eyes.

These two books are the products of utterly different traditions. Anderson's arises from *The Skylark of Space*, *Planet Stories*, and *The Moon Is Hell!* Bowen's descends through Dickens, Huxley, Orwell and Waugh. The American pulp tradition is a tradition of form: a Western novelette, in the pulps' heyday, was as rigidly structured as a fugue. A writer in the pulp tradition takes his form whole, and embellishes it as best he can. This is what Anderson has done, and done superlatively.

The British tradition, on the other hand, is a tradition of content. Where Anderson's wit and understanding are bent out of shape to fit the iron skeleton of his plot, Bowen's story is as limp as an old sack. One is "chop it till it fits"; the other, "pour it in till it bulges."

Where these traditions meet, something new ought to take shape. Anderson's novel is satisfyingly rigid in structure, but it is brittle and largely artificial. Bowen's is deeply genuine and unforced, but while the raft drifts aimlessly, the story does too: and like the raft, it never seems to arrive at any particular destination.

Does it have to be one or the other? Is it impossible to imagine form growing out of content, or at least content modifying form?

Tomorrow's Gift, by Edmund Cooper, is a collection of short stories by a young British writer. *The Monster From Earth's End*, by Murray Leinster, is a novel by the oldest pro in the business.

Either of these two books would do for a sample of what science fiction is like: yet put them side by side, and you wonder how one term can stretch to cover them both.

Leinster's story takes place on an island supply base a few hundred miles from the south polar continent, where a plane lands after some mysterious catastrophe on its way from an Antarctic scientific outpost. The plane's passengers and crew turn out to have vanished in mid-flight, all but the pilot, who promptly shoots himself.

When an invisible something then begins attacking dogs and people, the question becomes: What sort of monster did the plane bring in its cargo? And how can it be stopped, before it kills everybody on the island?

Leinster develops this situation methodically, in a workmanlike first-reader prose which has not changed much in the last thirty years. ("Splendid!" cries the American heroine.) The short, simple sentences carry the story forward in a sort of spiral fashion: one foot forward, two feet back to cover the old ground again, then another small advance.

The strength of the story is in its careful technical background and its clear-headed Apollonian good sense. Leinster's basic premise is clearly stated in this book. It applies equally to every-thing he has written:

> In a real world, everything follows natural laws. Impossible things do not happen. There is an explanation for everything that does happen. The explanation links it to other things. There are no isolated phenomena. There are only isolated observations, and sometimes false observations. But everything real is rational.

A less rationalistic writer might have accepted the invisibility of the monster and gone on entertainingly from there: Leinster effectively debunks it. His subsequent exposure and explanation of the real monster is a model of water-tight reasoning; it is also, except for a few effective moments, a little dull.

Leinster's carefully pedestrian narrative is overlong getting to its climax; the love story is unfortunately as clear-headed and reasonable as the rest; and above all, the reader can't help know-ing all along that everything will be explained calmly, rationally, and in a little too much detail.

(This does not include the original mystery of the empty plane and the pilot's suicide, which is unsatisfactorily dealt with in the last chapter.)

The story has the form of a horror tale, but the horror seems curiously thin and artificial. The story's strongest kick is the purely cerebral pleasure of watching Leinster work his puzzle out. And it *is* a pleasure: but it isn't (for my taste) enough.

Edmund Cooper's basic premise is also spelled out clearly. In "The Butterflies," one of the ten stories in his book, a character remarks:

> ". . . To us, as to the primeval savages, the unknown is always a little magical — in spite of science, in spite of reason and in spite of infallible robots."

These ten stories, widely varying in quality, have one persistent theme. They are about the irrational, the inexplicable, the wonderful and terrifying things that lie beneath the orderly surface of our universe. Cooper has the true mystic's vision, and can convey it with startling strength in a sentence or two. But the rational frameworks in which these glimpses occur are perfunctory, unconvincing, sometimes downright shoddy.

Cooper's heroes show themselves as incapable as Leinster's of feeling any depth of emotion, but with an effect altogether different. Watching their machines blow up, organizing murder, contemplating their own unpleasant deaths, they have the frozen calm of nightmare.

Some of them are not people but points of view; all of them are symbols. And the curious result is that Cooper can get more onto his canvas than a realist can. The murder of the heroine in "Tomorrow's Gift," an event that would have to take up the foreground in a realistic story, is casually strung onto one of Cooper's elegant Elizabethan dialogues: it occurs suitably, and adds to the pattern, and the story goes on.

Two of the ten stories seem to me really lifeless and not worth reading. One, the title story, about a rebel facing lobotomy in a tranquilized version of *1984*, is a minor masterpiece. One, a rather conventional super-child story, is unexpectedly funny; and one more, about the ironic meeting of a criminal lunatic and two childlike explorers from another world, compels respect by its very grotesqueness.

The rest are mostly space-opera, with many evidences of careless and indifferent writing: but even these are partly redeemed by their endings. After a frantic comic-book brouhaha, Cooper will abruptly turn to a paragraph of calm description, e.g. of a lunar landscape: and the hidden meaning of the story blooms.

All the same, this is to say that seven-eighths of a given story may be tripe; the proportion is too high.

We ought to be grateful for half loaves, and I think I am. But I thought it might be worth pointing out once more that sense and meaning are both important in science fiction; and that their presence in the same story is not an impossibility.

14. GENIUS TO ORDER: *Kuttner and Moore*

HENRY KUTTNER, who has written science fiction not quite as long as Murray Leinster and perhaps not quite as voluminously as Edmond Hamilton, takes second place to no one in the matter of versatility. In his time, Kuttner has done every kind of science fiction and fantasy that any editor has been willing to pay for, all the way from the involute, cerebral fiction of Campbell's decade down to a couple of bare-bosomed epics for the early *Marvel*.

The accumulating mass of his pseudonyms reached the critical point in fandom sometime in the middle forties, resulting in the so-called Kuttner Syndrome; a baseless report that Jack Vance was Kuttner, originated by Ted Dikty in 1950, is still being refuted at least once a month at this writing.

Robots Have No Tails, as everyone ought to know, is the saga of Galloway Gallegher, the mildly mad scientist whose inventive genius operates only when he is completely sozzled. This fact complicates Gallegher's existence almost unendurably, because he never remembers what he has been up to the morning after; and it's generally important to Gallegher's bankroll, not to mention his sanity, that he find out. In "The World Is Mine," for example, the problem includes a series of mutually exclusive corpses of Gallegher himself, all deceased at different ages, and three little rabbity creatures from Mars who insist on conquering the world. In "Ex Machina" there's a three-foot pyramid with blue eyes (Kuttner, whose eyes are brown, appears to find blue ones irresistibly amusing) and a small brown animal, moving too fast to be visible to anybody but Joe the robot, who follows Gallegher around and steals his liquor before he can drink it.

All these zany puzzles turn out to have perfectly logical, though not precisely humdrum, solutions. Every one of the five episodes in this book could have been written as a straight-faced science fiction problem story; it is our inestimable gain that Kuttner chose to use them instead as a mere framework for the uninhibited

doings of Gallegher, Grandpa and Joe. The style, which is frankly
borrowed, is one of the book's chief delights; if Thorne Smith had
not existed, it would have been necessary for Kuttner to invent him.
    Two samples:

> Just inside the door was a hideous iron dog, originally intended
> for Victorian lawns, or perhaps for Hell . . . ("Time Locker.")

> "How stupid you are. You're ugly, too. . . . And you're a col-
> lection of rattletrap gears, pistons, and cogs. You've got worms,"
> said Gallegher, referring, of course, to certain mechanisms in
> the robot's body. ("The Proud Robot.")

Gnome, which has an irritating habit of buying good material
from the magazines and then stirring it up with its own grubby
little fingers, has put the first story, "Time Locker," last. This
is evidently because the irrelevant and overcute title contains
the word "robots," and "Time Locker," belonging to the pre-Joe
period, doesn't. The excuse is inadequate.

    "Tomorrow and Tomorrow" and "The Fairy Chessmen," two
short novels from the late-forties Astounding, seem to have aged
poorly; they're full of the wrong guesses which were standard in
science fiction for a few years after Hiroshima—mutations, world
government, status quo, underground cities, robot warfare. Even
so, and in spite of strong aromas of van Vogt and Ray Cummings,
these two stories are a long way from dullness. Both, curiously
enough, open with the same situation: A man believes he may be
going insane, but is afraid to tell anybody.
    "Tomorrow and Tomorrow," the second and weaker of the two
concerns a post-World-War-II world in which an outgrowth of the
UN, the Global Peace Commission, maintains an artificial status
quo (a) by control of all atomic energy, and (b) by keeping a lid on
all new research which might upset the balance. Joseph Breden,
the protagonist, is the top nuclear physicist assigned to guard
Uranium Pile One; he has a recurrent dream in which he kills his
second in command and then detonates the Pile, whence his fear
that he's losing his sanity. He could go to the resident psychia-
trists in the Pile and be cured, but he'd also lose his job, which
is vital to him in his half-aware struggle for supremacy with his
mutant brother, Louis.
    The dream, it turns out, is the work of a revolutionary organ-
ization which wants Breden to explode the Pile and so overthrow
GPC, break the status quo. Through a mutant called The Freak,
they're in touch with an alternate-probability world in which GPC

failed to abort World War III, and in which as a consequence, after a good deal of necessary unpleasantness, man has reached a free and orderly existence, found a cure for cancer, and doubled his life-span.

The revolutionists eventually succeed in enlisting Breden, but too late—the psych board rules him unfit for duty and he's expelled from the Pile, which is finally destroyed by channeling "entropy potential" from one alternate world to another. As a final kicker, we learn that Breden's Earth isn't a future extension of ours— in his, Washington was destroyed during World War II by a "kamikaze fleet." Ours, it would seem, was one of the alternate Earths which blew themselves up with uncontrolled chain reactions.

> ". . . well, they arrived at their crossroads and were given a fair choice. And they committed suicide. So forget about them— they're not important now."
> Louis said, "Man got used to being given another chance. But there's no second chance with atomic power, is there? The failures—"
> "It's already too late," van Buren repeated. "They don't matter any more."

"The Fairy Chessmen" begins and ends with a line which is or should be as famous as "Yngvi is a louse!"

> The doorknob opened a blue eye and looked at him.

Robert Cameron, the victim in this one, is Civilian Director of Psychometrics in another post-World-War-II world: here, the third war has been started by a hastily invented and completely unconvincing imaginary nation, "the Falangists"; both sides have decentralized and sunk their vital equipment and personnel underground, and the war has resulted in a continuously expanding stalemate, with each side strenuously improving its technology in order to overthrow the other.

The Falangists now threaten to break the stalemate through the use of an equation donated by a troublemaker from the far future, one Ridgeley, who keeps popping up from time to time throughout the story. Our side has the equation, but since it uses variables that ought to be constants—e.g., the speed of light, the acceleration of gravity at the Earth's surface—it drives everybody insane who tries to solve it.

Cameron is the man who has to find the man who can successfully solve the equation; and therefore the Falangists, using the equation, are continually harassing him with oddities like the doorknob: a spoon kisses him with cold metallic lips; a cigarette

squirms out of his fingers and loops up his arm like an inchworm, burning his skin as it goes; invisible rain falls on him as he sits at his office desk; a clock, instead of chiming the hour, opens a sudden mouth and says, "Seven o'clock."

Partial success in solving the equation seems to be as devastating as failure; one man discovers the secret of antigravity (which involves the assumption that the Earth does not rotate); he thereupon becomes convinced that he's the corpse of Mohammed, suspended between heaven and earth—and imperturbably floats five feet above the surface of his sanatorium bed. Another giggles suddenly, shrinks to microscopic dimensions and disappears through the floor, presumably on his way to the center of the planet; a third, going farther, discovers the essential unreality of the entire physical world. Trying to explain this to Seth Pell, one of Cameron's assistants, he points a finger at him and says, "You don't exist!"—and Pell doesn't.

This third gentleman, having decided that he's God and become something of a menace, is tracked down and killed by Ridgeley; meanwhile the equation is solved by a mathematician whose hobby is fairy chess—chess with variable rules.

This solution has been widely criticized on the ground that all theoretical mathematics is flexible and independent of real constants; therefore on logical grounds it shouldn't have taken a man with this hobby to solve the equation, and previous contestants shouldn't have been driven insane.

The story winds up with a passage which, if it hasn't been much criticized, ought to be—Ridgeley is forced to give up the "counter-equation" by bombarding him with distortions of reality like those used to persecute Cameron, and finally by making use of a finagle factor introduced much earlier for just this purpose—a group of nonhuman entities appear to have journeyed backward through time to the era of the story, and, in dying, liberated energies which (pardon me, but this wasn't my idea) mutated a young man named Billy Van Ness in such a way that he can sense temporal extension—and is therefore hopelessly insane.

Projecting this special awareness into Ridgeley's mind first makes him use the counter-equation in self-defense and then drives him into catatonia. All this takes place while Ridgeley struggles to reach his copter and escape, and is perfectly inane: using the equation, our heroes could have destroyed the copter, immobilized Ridgeley, and dealt with him at their leisure—the villain, in short, never had a chance.

There's an ironic postscript: Cameron, having survived the crushing weight of his responsibility in the matter of finding the man to crack the equation, realizes that his next duties—civilian indoctrination—will lead inevitably to the total mobilized state which produced Ridgeley.

He's wrong — Ridgeley's interference has given the West a breathing space by defeating the Falangists; mankind can now turn from self-destruction to conquer the stars—but Cameron doesn't realize that. He's vulnerable now; the tension has relaxed too suddenly—and although the Falangists' persecution has been ended, Cameron turns to look at his office door, knowing what he will see:

> The doorknob opened a blue eye and looked at him.

This story, like its companion, is handicapped by the author's scrupulous attempts to keep a straight face; but in this one the attentive reader can at least detect the traces of Kuttner's boisterous (silent) laughter in the background.

When Kuttner married Catherine Moore in 1940, two seemingly discordant talents merged. Kuttner's previous stories had been superficial and clever, well constructed but without much content or conviction; Moore had written moody fantasies, meaningful but a little thin. In the forties, working together, they began to turn out stories in which the practical solidity of Kuttner's plots seemed to provide a vessel for Moore's poetic imagination. Probably the truth is a good deal more complex; the Kuttners themselves say they do not know any more which of them wrote what (and I've always been uncertain whether to review them as a single or double author); at any rate, the two elements still seem to be present, and separable, in their work.

The Ballantine collection, *No Boundaries*, gives only a taste of this blending: of the five stories, I take one, "Vintage Season," to be almost entirely C. L. Moore's, and two, "The Devil We Know" and "Exit the Professor," to be equally pure Kuttner.

To dispose of these first: "Vintage Season" is the hauntingly memorable story, from *Astounding*, about the brief visit of a group of cruel pleasure-seekers from the future, which fairly drips with a blend of love, luxury and fear—a specific emotional color, so intense that you can almost taste it. The story is a rounded whole, complete and perfect in itself, except for a rather awkwardly prolonged ending. In an unfolding puzzle story like this one, the argument and the physical action ought to come to a point at once, like the intersection of a fist and a chin.

"The Devil We Know" is a deplorable potboiler from *Unknown*, with one paragraph of good writing in it—the description of the demon on page 55—; the rest is bromides and desperation. "Exit the Professor" is one of the funniest of the unfailingly funny Hogben series; these, I have said before, belong in a book of their own.

The two remaining stories, "Home There's No Returning" and "Two-Handed Engine" are recent ones; the latter was published in *Fantasy and Science Fiction* for August, 1955; the former appears for the first time in this book. Both are about robots, a subject which has intrigued the Kuttners separately before.

Here it's no longer possible even to guess what part is Kuttner's and what Moore's: the hypnotically deft treatment of Deirdre's robot body in "No Woman Born" is clearly echoed in these stories, but so is the ingenious improvisation of ENIAC in "The Ego Machine." The result is a series of brilliant and penetrating images, in which the robot, that clanking servitor of hack writers, becomes a vehicle for allegory and symbol. The blunt weapon suddenly has a point so sharp and fine that it tickles you at the heart before you know you have been touched.

"Home There's No Returning" deals with the robot as savior, and has a stiff little moral at the end: "Two-Handed Engine" deals with the robot as destroyer—the Fury of Greek myth, who pursues a malefactor to his doom. Which of the two stories you like better probably depends partly on the meaning these symbols have for you, and partly on how far the emotional experience succeeds in distracting you from the details of the plotting. Stripped of their elaborations, both plots are banal; the sociological backgrounds are no better than they should be, and the other sciences are worse; in one, the physical action of the story is so arbitrarily arranged as to be flatly incredible. Yet these are stories you won't soon forget: probably because science fiction is so full of stories in which the technical data are correct and soundly handled, but the people are so many zero-eyed integers—as blank-faced, but not a hundredth part as meaningful, as the Kuttners' shining robots.

15. KORNBLUTH AND THE SILVER LEXICON

READERS WHO HAVE followed Cyril Kornbluth's work since the early forties, when (as Cecil Corwin, S. D. Gottesman, Kenneth Falconer, *et al.*) he was a heavy contributor to *Stirring Science* and *Cosmic*, do not have to be told that for more than a decade he has been one of the most promising young writers in this field.

Kornbluth must have been born with a lexicon in his mouth. Legend has it that once, when a motherly stranger bent over him in his perambulator and made the sounds that are usually made to babies, Kornbluth remarked, "Madam, I am not the child you think me." At any rate, he was about sixteen, and looked a prematurely aging twenty-six, when he wrote "The Words of Guru," a short fantasy which, for my money, deserves the place in the literature generally assigned to something by Dunsany.

Today, heavier than ever (and looking about as much like his jacket photo as an owl like an owlet), he is not only writing first-rate science fiction but getting paid accordingly—a factor which, like it or not, makes all the difference between promise and fulfillment. His first novel was *Mars Child*, written in collaboration with Judith Merril; his second, *Gunner Cade*, also with Miss Merril; his third, *The Space Merchants* ("Gravy Planet"), with Frederik Pohl. All three, judging by style and manner, were at least three-quarters Kornbluth*; each was better than the last; but none of them has one-half the stature of *Takeoff*.

Takeoff is a science fiction novel about the building of the first Moon ship. It is also a contemporary novel of science and bureaucracy, and a tough, realistic murder mystery. It functions brilliantly on all three levels; Kornbluth's Midas touch makes the en-

---

*This is probably unfair. A more recent novel on which Pohl and another writer collaborated seems to me full of the distinctive flavor of *The Space Merchants*.

gineering of the spaceship as fascinating as the mystery behind it, and the devious workings of governmental intrigue as engrossing as either. The incidental love story is less effective, but this is a hindsight criticism.

Other hindsights: I regret the plot necessity that killed off the book's most engaging and believable character less than halfway through, and altered another, barely believably, to a villainess. In the protagonist himself there are traces of pulp characterization not evident elsewhere.

These are all minor cavils. If there is any serious complaint to be made to Kornbluth at this point, it must be based, oddly enough, on the very prodigality of his talent. Kornbluth's career is like that of a very bright schoolboy in a dull class; he discovered early that he could do the things the others struggled to accomplish a great deal better and with much less effort; he has been doing them ever since, with his tongue in his cheek.

Brilliant as it is, there is not an idea or an attitude in *Takeoff* that is original with its author. It is simply the standard material of modern popular fiction, compounded with more skill than most of us can muster.

A still better book—Kornbluth's best novel, I think—is *The Syndic*. This is sociological science fiction, the exasperatingly difficult type of which more is talked and less written than any other. What passes for genuine sociological speculation is mostly counterfeit: crude analogy, gimmicked-up history, burlesque or parody. Kornbluth has written those, too, but this is the real thing —an imagined society that meets the test of a real one: that it's based on its own unique premises and has its own rationale; and this—wherein lies the trick—with such conviction that the reader can, indeed, must imagine himself living in it.

In *Not This August*, Kornbluth returns to the careful, workmanlike, and somehow disappointing style of *Takeoff*. If we make use of the word "unusual" for small prodigies—like unsuccessful Wyndham novels and poor Sturgeon collections—what can we say of a Kornbluth book which echoes, even by inadvertence, the plot of a Jerry Sohl epic?

The parallels are obvious, and we might as well admit them at once; in *Not This August*, (1) the United States has been conquered and occupied by Communist armies; (2) the people are starved and oppressed; (3) the active part of the plot concerns the hero's efforts to make contact with the underground opposition; and (4) the solution, in this book as in Mr. Sohl's *Point Ultimate*, involves a spaceship built in a secret cavern by the Good Guys.

Of these points, (1) is obvious fictional material and would have had to come from somewhere; remember the gleet of "Yellow Peril" stories—about an America conquered by Chinese or Japanese—that ended just before World War I? Item (2) is equally obvious; any other extrapolation would have been extremely odd as well as unsaleable; (3) is a stock novelistic device which I hope has not outlived its usefulness, and (4) is a Hollywood (or Madison Avenue) idiocy.

Kornbluth's treatment of all these things, even the ship-in-a-cavern, is roughly one thousand times more intelligent, factual, detailed and convincing than Sohl's. The author's remarkable talent for producing the inside dope or a reasonable facsimile on anything at all, from dairy farming to Red Army methods, is here evidenced on nearly every page. Heaven forbid this story should ever become actuality; but if it did, the chances are, no fictional forecast would be more accurate (up to Chapter 15) than this.

Further, the book is tightly constructed and continuously readable; it has several vivid characters, a lot of equally vivid dialogue and action, and the same taut, hard-boiled excitement that made *Takeoff* so successful.

But this novel is written almost entirely in Kornbluth's extensive Working Stiff and Slob vocabularies, acquired (evidently) in an effort to reduce the gap between that odd fish, the writer, and the rest of humanity. Like everything else Kornbluth does, the effort has been thorough: Kornbluth has the words; but he hasn't got the tune.

No working stiff, or slob either, he has had deliberately to suppress the sensitive, cynical, philosophical, irreverent top slice of his mind in order to counterfeit the tribal conventions of the boobs around him. The result is as craftsmanlike, well polished and hollow-sounding as a tin dollar. It satisfies, even in a limited way, only until you compare it with the same author's short stories.

"Gomez," which leads off Kornbluth's Ballantine collection, *The Explorers*, was written especially for it; "The Rocket of 1955" and "Thirteen O'Clock" first appeared as long ago as 1941. In between come "The Mindworm," "The Altar at Midnight," "The Goodly Creatures," "Friend to Man," "With These Hands" and "That Share of Glory." All of them are written with distinction, even the cut-and-dried potboiler, "Friend to Man."

The remarkable thing is not that these nine stories, written over a thirteen-year period, are uniform in quality—they aren't —but that the earliest and slightest of them will stand comparison today with the average product of our best magazines. Kornbluth starts there, and goes up.

Three of the best are the result of a serious attempt to graft the mainstream short story onto science fiction. I dislike these three on principle. The very best of the lot, "The Goodly Creatures," flunks the key clause of Sturgeon's definition of science fiction—"[a story] which would not have happened at all without its scientific content." The other two pass, barely, but are so close to mundane stories that they make me almost equally uncomfortable. "The Altar at Midnight" is about the gulf between generations, and the lure of destructive, well-paid occupations, and the guilt of scientists, and similar things, all of which strike familiar chords. The center of attention is a young spaceman, hideously deformed by his craft; I might have missed the mundane parallel, though I felt it, if Kornbluth himself hadn't spelled it out for me—the old used-up railroad men who congregate in a dismal bar in "Gandytown." "With These Hands" is merely the lament for hand-craftsmanship, already a cliché in the mainstream story, which Kornbluth has translated from book-binding to sculpture. But when I say "merely," I lie. Each of these stories represents the triumph of a master technician over an inappropriate form—as if, on a somewhat grander scale, Milton had written "Paradise Lost" in limericks, and made you like it.

I think these three stories explore a dangerous dead end in science fiction; but I'm unable to wish they had not been written.

16. THE JAGGED BLADE: *James Blish*

JAMES BLISH IS AN intense young man with a brilliant scholastic mind and an astonishing variety of enthusiasms—e.g., music, beer, astronomy, poetry, philosophy, cats. Until fairly recently he played two instruments and composed music; he still writes poetry and criticism for the little magazines, is a genuine authority on James Joyce and Ezra Pound, and an expert in half a dozen other fields. In college he was well on his way to becoming a limnobiologist when he discovered he was getting more A's in English literature—and selling the stories he submitted to such magazines as *Future*, *Cosmic* and *Super Science*.

One man is obviously not enough for all this, and there are really two Blishes: the alertly interested, warmly outgoing human being, and the cold, waspishly precise scholast. Up till now, in his prose work at least, I think the two have always got in each other's way; Blish's early stories are almost oppressively devoid of any human color or feeling; they might be stories written by an exceptionally able Martian anthropologist.

"Beanstalk," at least, is different. Sam, Sena, Dr. Fred—and in particular Maury St. George, the most fascinating science-fictional villain since Blacky DuQuesne—all the major characters are as big and as round as life; bigger, I suppose I should say, since all of them but Dr. Fred are polyploid giants. They are, if you like, supermen and women (and one dog, a bitch named Decibelle)—they're taller, stronger, longer-lived than their cousins with the normal human number of genes—but their story is a story of recognizable, believable people. There is a really fantastic body of technique in this short novel, but unless you are looking for it you will never notice it; it's submerged, where it belongs.

If a superman really is a superman, he ought to be able to neutralize the natural hostility of normal men enough to get along; this is the point made by Kuttner in the Baldy series and neglected by everyone else, from Stapledon to van Vogt, until now. Like Kuttner, Blish makes paranoia the Titans' greatest hazard. Take a world in which there has already been much anti-Titan legislation and one anti-Titan pogrom, add a paranoid Titan who equates "superman" with "master race"—the result is explosive, and this is only the beginning. I am not going to tell much more about the plot, or Blish will say "supererogation" to me again; but I am going to say a great deal about the structure that underlies it and is interwoven with it.

Not merely embedded in "Beanstalk," but inseparably united to make one coherent and symmetrical narrative, are whole exemplars or recognizable fragments of the following: a sports story; a love story; a Western story—plus, for good measure, a couple of panels from "Buck Rogers."

Since the last thing I want is to scare anyone away from this work, I'd better repeat that this difficult technical feat takes place entirely in the submerged levels of the story. Wildly incompatible as the above-listed elements are, not one has been dragged in by the hair; every one has been almost unrecognizably altered by the author's inventiveness; every one is essential. The sports fragment is a jet-powered, gimmicked-up Titan football game, necessary to pave the way for the Buck Rogers element, which is itself (a) indispensable and (b) brilliantly rationalized, down to the last silly flange on the flying-belt-borne superman's helmet.

One of Blish's most engaging traits is the habit he has of examining the most moth-eaten and idiotic kind of plot, with an interested expression, like an open-minded watchmaker inspecting a Rube Goldberg, and then carefully rearranging it so that, by hook or crook, it actually makes sense. For example, we have here Villain kidnaping Heroine, and Hero chasing off through black forest to the lonely mountain cabin where she is pent, guided by Faithful Dog.

This is pure nonsense from beginning to end, as nobody realizes better than Blish; so he has given the villain an odd but perfectly sensible reason (which, pardon me, I am not going to reveal) for snatching the girl, and he has made the dog a mutated specimen with more intelligence than a chimpanzee.

I haven't finished yet. I'll say once more, just to make it perfectly clear, that all these unlikely patchwork pieces have been totally absorbed; not a scrap is still Western, or murder, or love story; it's all science fiction.

As if this were not unlikely enough, Blish has proceeded to

make the science fiction itself a synthesis of nearly every major period in the history of the literature, from gadgeteering to sociological, and to match the masters of each on their own grounds; and again there are no seams; the whole is one.

There remains a word to be said about style. Blish's prose style has always been precise, flexible and eloquent, but in nearly all his earlier work I've found it somewhat harsh and edgy as well. In "Beanstalk," by contrast, the writing is enormously effective— rapier sharp in the dialogue, smooth as silk elsewhere, and with a poetic intensity which, oddly, I've seldom found in Blish's work before:

> For Sena, who was not yet forty, the whole small world was in the throes of an endless springtide; a youth that would last more than a century, with toy bridges and houses and roadplanes clustered at her feet, and more than time enough to learn everything one needed to know, and the high-browed, god-like figures of lovers striding through the narrow streets of diploid man . . .
>
> The world waited, flooded with delicate greenness that would never die.

His love of words for their own sake, and his prankish humor, still lead him to what I think are occasional excesses. At the end of "Beanstalk," when the villain's cabin collapses and slides down into the valley, Blish describes the event in a long Joycean catalogue, as inappropriate as it is unexpected. But if this is a fault it's a minor one, more than counterbalanced by a thousand felicities like this, from the same part of the story:

> Sam moved one hand. The hillside, the ledges of the valley, the hillocks, the grasses uttered giants; they stood everywhere, motionless, like the dragon's-teeth soldiers of Cadmus.

Plateaus of learning, commonly noticed in the early training of children, seem to occur in later ages and other fields as well; I was in one myself, as a writer, for ten years, and I like to suppose that I am in another now. If Jim Blish has just jumped to a new plateau, meaning that this story is not a brilliant exception but the starting-point for another slow, steady advance, I suggest that the incumbent Mr. Science Fiction get ready to move over.

Blish's *Earthman, Come Home* is a big, complex landmark of a book. It represents several years' work by one of the most painstaking and devious plotters in the business: full of second and third thoughts, it's as hard to take in at one look as an Edwardian-Georgian-Victorian mansion.

Most of it was originally published in the form of four novelettes, three in *Astounding*, one in *Two Complete Science Adventure Books*. But, piecemeal, it never had the impact it has here, as one bound-together entity; moreover, Blish's involute text is so dense, not to say opaque, that many readers may have failed, as I did, to make much sense of it the first time around.

"Once antigravity was an engineering reality," says the author's prologue, "it was no longer necessary to design ships especially for space travel, for neither mass nor aerodynamic lines meant anything any more. The most massive and awkward object could be lifted and hurled off the Earth, and carried almost any distance. Whole cities, if necessary, could be moved."

New York was one of those that were moved, and never came back. Set free by the antigravity "spindizzy," some hundreds of years after the fall of the West in 2105, it became a migrant worker city. This is its story, and by extension, the story of all the interstellar cities—the "Okies."

In form this is an epic, and the most revealing comparison in science fiction, I think—though it's not likely to please Blish [it didn't]—is the Zorome series by Neil R. Jones, which appeared almost endlessly in the old *Amazing* and later in *Super Science*.

Both groups of stories have the same cosmic scale, the same plot-limitation to a series of planetary stopovers—all of which exhibit certain similarities—; in both, the immortality of the voyagers contributes a curious dreamlike effect; and in both the dominant impression is that the chief characters are fine fellows off to have adventures, although Blish pretends that his space-going cities are hobos looking for work.

Add the recurrent conflict of Good-vs.-Evil, as in The Lone Ranger, *et al.*, and you have a formula that is probably as old as tale-telling, and I suppose as durable.

The difference, aside from Blish's considerably greater talent, lies in his insistence on imposing the Okie parallel—the idea referred to above, that light can be shed on the cities' career by comparing them with displaced migratory workers.

This is the deepest flaw in the book, and there's no way of justifying it within this framework—you simply have to accept it or forget it.

On the author's own showing, the space cities are virtually self-sufficient. They grow their own food, and manufacture it by cracking petroleum. They're equipped to mine and drill for any mineral they need. And what one Okie city can't handle, another can.

Blish has his Okies seeking out inhabited worlds: "Where there's people, there's work."

But the city doesn't need work: it needs petroleum, and it can get that—but perversely doesn't try—for the taking, on an un-inhabited planet. Blish's other answers to this question are not sufficient, either; the cities need repair and docking facilities? So they do, but they could and logically should run such facilities themselves, as the buccaneers did at Tortuga. They need anti-agathic drugs to prolong their lives? All right, but somebody has to grow the plants and extract the drugs—why not Okies?

Blish, in a talk* given at the Little Monsters of America con-vention in New York, July 1952, coined the terms "template series" and "evolutionary series" to distinguish those groups of stories which merely repeat themselves from those which develop and go somewhere. The Okie stories were his example of the latter type, and they do develop, do go somewhere—but there are template elements in them, all the same.

In each of the four long episodes which make up the book, the city is forced to land in an inhabited system of planets. In the first two, they land in the middle of a local war. In each of the others, not finding any, they stir one up. In all four cases, the Earth cops—inimical to Okies in order to fit into the parallel, and for no other evident reason—show up to complicate matters. In all four, Amalfi, the thousand-year-old mayor of New York (and by far the roundest and most likable character in the book), pulls a last-minute rabbit out of his hat and saves the city.

If this sounds to you uneasily reminiscent of van Vogt, you're right. In form the book is an epic; in method it's a van Vogt story. A born technician, Blish will pursue any technical device that in-terests him to its last gasp—in this case, what William Atheling, Jr., calls van Vogt's "intensively recomplicated" story. My own term is simpler; I call it the Kitchen Sink Technique.

Briefly, this consists of packing as much as possible of every-thing into a given space. I mean almost everything: plot, incident, background, allusion, confusion; character usually gets left out.

Some of it is wonderful. There's Blish's breathtaking descrip-tion of the Rift, for example—"a valley cut in the face of the galaxy"—so inconceivably vast that from its center the stars form a double curtain of haze: too far away even to be seen as individual points of light.

There's a poetry of courage in the city's venturing into that chasm, like the fantastic bravery of Kon-Tiki or Columbus' fleet ... but not for long. This is a Kitchen Sink story; the Rift, like the African jungle or the interior of the Earth in a Burroughs

---

*Reprinted as an article in Redd Boggs' *Skyhook*, Autumn, 1952.

epic, turns out to be as cozily populated with friends and enemies as a Broadway drugstore. And off we go.

I think this is a bad method: it makes spectacular trickery, but seldom a durable story. In Blish's hands, brilliantly effective as it often is, it results in an incessantly doubled-back plot that is often confusing and sometimes directly self-contradictory. Worse, as a subsidiary effect, the human changes are all sprung on you so suddenly that they're unbelievable. Blish's resolution of the Amalfi-Hazelton relationship, for example, is as unconvincing as it is unpleasant—and then, by heavens, he retrieves it with exactly the right symbol.

The whole book is like that. There's no time to puzzle over such questions as why Mayor Amalfi, with his "direct intuition of spatial distances and mass pressures"—and spindizzy fields, apparently—couldn't determine the location of the buried bindlestiff city on the planet He. Things are moving too fast; He is whirled off into intergalactic space, the bindlestiff destroyed, and before you know it, you're caught up again in the rapid, powerful movement that is the K-S story's one major virtue.

And gradually, in spite of all the repetition and confusion, the packrat crowding of irrelevant information, a symmetrical and moving story appears. Out of all the details in the book, some will be for you—not the same ones that hit me, very likely, but they will build up much the same impressive picture. Blish's scale is the whole galaxy, a view that has to be awe-inspiring if he can only make you see it: and he does, I think, more successfully than any previous writer.

VOR, by James Blish, is a novel which began its intermittent life some 17 years ago, as a short story of mine called "Mercy Death." I had what I thought was a hell of a problem, but I couldn't think of any way out of it, so the story remained about half written until c. 1948, when Jim completed it as a novelette. It was published in *Thrilling Wonder* as "The Weakness of RVOG." (All these initials refer to colors; the alien creature in the story has a color organ in place of a mouth, and his name was originally "Red-green-orange-violet," or "RGOV." Sam Merwin, then editor of *Thrilling Wonder*, switched the initials around for reasons best known to himself, and now Blish has simplified them to VOR.)

The essential part of the story, which is much the same in this new version as in the novelette, consists of my problem and Blish's solution—the problem being, "What do you do when an apparently indestructible being tells you to kill him, or he'll kill you?" For Blish's solution, see the book.

Whether there ever was enough meat in this story to be worth developing into a novel, I don't know; I'm inclined to doubt it. At any rate, what Blish has done is to keep the original story more or less intact, and pad it by introducing a new set of characters and a new story line. The original characters were VOR (to give him his latest name), two scientists and a couple of supernumeraries. The new ones are a gaggle of CAP pilots, notably one named Marty Petrucelli who has a war-caused phobia against flying, and is losing his wife to a brash pilot named Al Strickland on account of it.

The CAP background is authentic and impressively technical (Blish was for several years a member of a CAP squadron); so is Blish's marshalling of details about the AEC, radiation problems, atomic physics, and so on. Nevertheless, inevitably, this is a bad book.

The introduction of the CAP characters seems reasonable enough in the opening chapters: they're the nearest squadron to the site of the alien's landing. After that, in spite of heroic efforts on Blish's part to shoehorn them into the plot, they simply get in the way. As early as p. 50, for example, AEC Commissioner Holm confronts the alien, risking his life to try to open communication. If the story had been written from Holm's viewpoint, this could have been a scene of hair-raising suspense. As it is, it takes place almost invisibly offstage, while we get a worm's-eye view of Marty and his stone-cold love life.

In padding a novel, the problem is not to advance the story but to slow it down. This one is slowed to a crawl—one-sixth story, five-sixths the endless, repetitive emotional Laocoons that identify Blish's hack-work. The writing itself, except for one or two notably good passages (particularly Marty's flight with the scared Russian scientist in Chapter 9), is as tortuous and knob-jointed as Blish's worst. Nearly every sentence has too much information packed into it; and since most of it is unnecessary information, the result is the same as if it were noise.

Blish's first story collection, *Galactic Cluster*, contains eight stories, of which six are more or less frankly commercial pieces. Except for isolated scenes that show Blish's real talent (such as the madman's scene at the beginning of "King of the Hill"), these stories are not about people but about gadgets; they are full of ingenuity and technical language, but largely empty of everything else that makes a story worth writing. In contrast, "Common Time" and "A Work of Art" are as honest and artistically rewarding works as our field can boast. "Common Time," which I discuss at length in Chapter 26, is a story with an interstellar plot which turns into a free-associating fantasy, stunningly rich in unconscious symbols. "A Work of Art," nearly as subtle and powerful, deals with a 20th-century composer who is recreated in a new body two hundred years after his death; in Kornbluth's perceptive words, this is "the story of the man who was not Richard Strauss." Pure feeling is distilled by each of these works: in the first, aching and nameless regret; in the second, a triumph that rises out of resignation.

17. OVERALLS ON PARNASSUS: *Fletcher Pratt*

THE LATE FLETCHER PRATT was an odd fish about whom I wish I had written more—a tiny, goateed wisp of a man who used to be a professional boxer, and who wrote the notable Civil War history, *Ordeal by Fire*; his shirts were also noteworthy, and he kept marmosets—but except for the one dealt with here, the only books of his that came to me for review were potboilers.

"The Blue Star," which on several counts ought to have turned out to be the weakest story in Twayne's *Witches Three*, is nothing of the sort. Boucher and McComas brushed this novel aside with a reference to George U. Fletcher's *Well of the Unicorn*—which I haven't read, unfortunately, so I can't say; perhaps "The Blue Star" is derivative.* If so, I don't see that it matters; it's a magnificent job of writing, the last thing in the world I would have expected from the Fletcher Pratt of *Double Jeopardy*—a gem-perfect example of a branch of pure fantasy so rare nowadays that I was beginning to think it was extinct—the dream-world story. The distinction between this and all other types—utopias and anti-utopias, interplanetary stories, projections of the Earth into the distant past and future—is that the dream-world must be completely insular, self-contained, having no point of contact with the mundane universe either in space or in time; its appeal, seemingly, is dependent on the fact that it never was, never will be and never could have been on this Earth; one touch of reality withers it.

There has never been much of this—never, at any rate, enough to suit me. I have the impression that there used to be a fair amount in *Weird Tales* when that magazine was still being edited intelligently, fifteen or twenty years ago; more recently, the only magazine fantasy writer I can think of who has tried it is Jack Vance, in his brilliant *The Dying Earth*.

"The Blue Star" is presented frankly as a dream. In an urbane and witty prologue, three men begin by discussing the possibility

---

* "George U. Fletcher" is Pratt's pseudonym, as I might have guessed, but didn't.

of other inhabited worlds, and end by postulating a single one: a world in which "somebody might have found the key to something as basic in [the field of witchcraft] as gunpowder was to the physical sciences."

> Penfield got up and stepped to the window. . . . "I wonder if it really does exist," he said.
>
> Hodge laughed; but that night all three men dreamed; and it was as though a filament ran through the ancient rooms; for each knew that he dreamed, and dreamed the same dream as the others; and from time to time tried to cry out to them, but could only see and hear.

And from that sentence on, the reader too is caught up in the dream of a world strangely like ours, and strangely different— a world where witchcraft is real, but not, as he might expect, one where witchcraft rules. This is no fuzzy fairyland, but a clear and detailed projection of a society obeying its own laws, with its own manners, customs, religions, history. It's a quasi-medieval world in which magic, instead of being the Church Militant's fictive scapegoat, is a real force, suppressed, legislated against —and used.

The tale is that of two unwilling lovers: Lalette, the reluctant witch, and Rodvard the revolutionary, whose masters set him cold-bloodedly to seduce her and so obtain the Blue Star. This is one of the ironies of the true witchcraft, that its most potent weapon, the Blue Star, gives no power to the witch herself; but when she is united in the Great Marriage (i.e., first intercourse), it passes to her husband, who can use it to read the minds of others for as long as he is faithful to her.

Rodvard is in love with another woman, and Lalette, in the beginning, loves no one; but as the tides of fortune take them on separate, Candide-like journeys half across the world, the Great Marriage endures—and in the end proves stronger than what they take to be their own desires.

For the main section of the novel, not counting prologue and epilogue, Pratt has devised a special style and manner to embellish his subject. Although he uses several contrived stylistic devices—parenthetical asides, oddities of punctuation, and the like —the effect is not strained but astonishingly fluent and graceful. It seems a great pity that there's no magazine market for this kind of thing any more, and next to no demand for it in hard covers. I'm no great fantasy-lover; most of Merritt bores me to tears; so do Howard and Lovecraft; but if anybody would publish a magazine full of fantasy as good as this, I'd be a charter subscriber.

18. MICROCOSMIC MOSKOWITZ

IN 1930, THERE WERE three monthly science fiction magazines, and two fan clubs. One of the magazines was Hugo Gernsback's *Wonder Stories*; one of the fan clubs was called The Scienceers. When they met, the results were world-shaking. Sam Moskowitz tells the story in *The Immortal Storm*:

> . . . Gernsback ran a contest in *Wonder Stories*, offering prizes for the best reports on the question, "What am I doing to popularise science fiction?" A prize-winning entry by Allen Glasser mentioned his work in The Scienceers, and, impressed by the concept of fans forming clubs, Gernsback requested that the organization send a representative to visit him. . . . Glasser was chosen to act in this capacity, and he returned with the startling news that Gernsback had arranged for a group of authors to address the club at New York City's Museum of Natural History, all expenses paid.
>
> When the day arrived no less than thirty-five members had mustered out for the occasion. . . . Gernsback himself was unable to attend, but he had sent in his place David Lasser, then editor of *Wonder Stories*, [and] Gawain Edwards Pendray, author and rocketry expert, Dr. William Lemkin, also a well-known author, as well as lesser lights of the Gernsback staff. They lectured eruditely to the Scienceers on their individual specialties, and finally departed amid much pomp and ceremony. The day had been a heady one for most of the Neophyte fans, and they wandered to their homes in a happy daze.
>
> At the club's next meeting they were rudely awakened, however, for they were then presented with a bill for the use of the room at the museum. . . .

Trufandom was off, to an appropriately ambiguous start.

"Through some misunderstanding," Moskowitz goes on, "Gernsback had not paid the museum rental"; and, one gathers, he never did.

Debate over this and cognate questions grew so heated that the club had to be disbanded. However, the demoralized remnants of the Scienceers crept gradually out of hiding and drifted together by twos and threes. Along about 1932, Glasser, Julius Schwartz and Mort Weisinger discovered Conrad H. Ruppert and his wonderful printing press, and the first printed fanzine, *The Time Traveller*, was born. Early in 1934 the first fragment of the first issue of William L. Crawford's piecemealzine, *Unusual Stories* was mailed to helpless subscribers; and in April of the same year, Gernsback announced formation of the historic Science Fiction League. The dark ages followed, and the hektograph. Then came Michelism, the Fantasy Amateur Press Association, and at last, in 1938, the time was growing ripe for the crowning event, the first World Science Fiction Convention.

A photograph from this period, on page 61, shows a group of professionals—Campbell, de Camp, Binder, Long and others—lined up against a brick wall, looking for all the world like delegates to a Central European trades union congress. The resemblance is accidental, but suggests an interesting line of thought.

In his early chapters, Moskowitz gives a wealth of detail about the first fans and the wonderful mixed-up things they did — the grandiose projects, some of which actually materialized; the short-lived organizations with the long names, the pitiful one-issue magazines. But the largest part of this book is concerned with fan politics.

What kind of politics was it? Let's see.

There were the splinter groups. ("The membership never exceeded the original five, and since these five promptly split into two factions . . .")

There was the East New York SFL *putsch*, which Moskowitz describes in these terms:

> . . . The second meeting of the reorganized New York chapter was in progress, with Hornig presiding, in a New York school room. Suddenly the clumping of many shoes was heard, and in burst Sykora and Wollheim at the head of eight other youths (not all science fiction fans) recruited from the streets for rough action if necessary. Sykora . . . with the aid of his comrades . . . chased Hornig from the platform. Producing a gavel of his own . . . [he] proceeded to call the meeting to order in the name of the New York branch of the International Scientific Association.

That was in late 1935. A year later, Sykora and four other ISA members joined a rival group, the Independent League for Science Fiction, and proceeded to torpedo it by propaganda and group resignations.

So the comparison is not really as ludicrous as it sounds: This was European power politics in a hatbox—scaled down, but still a politics of force, deceit and treachery. The same types emerged: the Booster; the Organizer, who frequently became the Wrecker.

Moskowitz himself, who first enters the story in Chapter XX, is a Booster. Although he performed a minor miracle of organization in 1938, when almost single-handed he cobbled together a huge club called New Fandom, to win sponsorship of the Nycon from the Michelists, his central motive was not power, nor any fannish ideology, but simply the growth and greatness of science fiction fandom. Nobody who didn't take fandom with almost maniacal seriousness could ever have gone to the trouble to write this history: moreover, the test of the Organizer and Wrecker in fandom is that when power wanes and wrecking palls, he drops out. Moskowitz is still with us.

And yet, when Moskowitz found himself embroiled in a feud with Wollheim & Co., it was impossible to distinguish one side from the other by the tactics they used.

In 1938, the debate was being carried on in the pages of Olon F. Wiggins' mimeoed magazine.

> To both factions the problem was clearly one of discrediting or silencing the leading spokesman of the opposing group . . . In the next number of *The Science Fiction Fan*, editor Wiggins made a simple direct statement. . . : "Beginning with this issue there will be no more material by Sam Moskowitz in the pages of the *Fan*."

Moskowitz goes on to note that shortly thereafter, Wiggins, who coveted the presidency of FAPA, was elevated to that post by a series of sudden Futurian resignations; and he adds:

> Moskowitz himself was stunned by the ingratitude and callousness of Wiggins' decision.

But this is only half the story. It appears on page 190; for the other half, we must go back to page 128, where we find this:

> At this point Wiggins informed Moskowitz that both Wollheim and Lowndes had sent him long rebuttals of the "Reply to Wollheim." Moskowitz . . . realized that his opposition was rallying and that, given a little time, he might well be smothered by its very volume. So he induced Wiggins to drop the feud in the *Fan** (although it was tremendously interesting to readers), hoping that Wollheim would find difficulty carrying on outside its pages.

It's the September, 1938, issue of *The Science Fiction Fan* that

---

*He doesn't say how; we are left to infer that Wiggins' dependency on Moskowitz's Manuscript Bureau had something to do with it.

Moskowitz is talking about on page 190; it's the *March*, 1938, issue of the same magazine that he's talking about on the earlier page.

Moskowitz nowhere connects the two incidents nor acknowledges his own equal culpability. This is the moral failure of his book: in spite of an attempt, and I think an honest one, to write impartially, Moskowitz demonstrates that he's learned nothing from his own careful record-keeping.

The chapters on the Nycon and the celebrated Exclusion Act are the culmination of Moskowitz's story, and the most exciting, best written part of the book. But what emerges from this account, pretty clearly, is that the Futurians bluffed Moskowitz & Co. into excluding them from the Convention, with the object of making martyrs of themselves and so discrediting New Fandom.

If it happened that way, was this underhanded? Yes, indeed. Were Moskowitz and his associates more open in their dealings? The record does not show it.

All the same:

This is a monumental work, fit to put beside the *Checklist* and the *Index*. In spite of the author's comic pomposity ("There is little available information on Bloomer the man"), his innumerable misspellings and grammatical errors, his remarkable talent for the mixed metaphor ("an article no intelligent mind could stomach"; "to funnel new faces into fandom") and his healthy admiration for himself—or perhaps partly because of them—he tells an engrossing story, livelier than ninety-nine per cent of mundane history, and most novels.

Anyone who takes fandom seriously—even if not quite as seriously as the author does—will find *The Immortal Storm* an invaluable sourcebook; a mine of odd information (from the origin of *Thrilling Wonder Stories'* column title, "The Ether Vibrates," to the care and hand-feeding of professionals); and above all, fascinating fannish reading.

19. AMPHIBIANS

PROBABLY AN EXCELLENT case could be made for the proposition that even more bad science fiction has been written by dabblers in the field, proportionately, than by full-time specialists. All the same, as an honest man I am bound to admit that three of the decade's best science fiction novels have been written by men who took the time off from *Post* stories or best-selling biography —and then went back to their more lucrative trades.

Bernard Wolfe is the author of "Self Portrait," one of 1951's most brilliant short novelettes. Those who have the November, 1951 *Galaxy* on hand might reread this story, for reasons which will be clear in a moment, and for its own sake; it's a beautiful piece of writing.

After people, these are the subjects with which "Self Portrait" is concerned:

> cybernetics in general
> prosthetics and EMSIAC (Electronic Military Strategy Integrator and Computer) in particular
> war as a "steamroller"
> "moral substitutes" for war, including voluntary amputeeism.
> " 'Marx corrected by Freud . . . . to each according to his (masochistic) need.' "

These are also the subjects of *Limbo*. I don't know whether the novelette preceded the novel, or, as seems equally likely, was written while the larger work was under way; at any rate, although the times, places, people and incidents are all different, I think we may say that both are essentially the same story.

To begin with, *Limbo* is a big-scale, exuberant, pyrotechnic, tight-packed giant of a book; it is guaranteed to do something to you—excite, irritate, stimulate, anger or bore you, or all five in succession; it will not leave you indifferent. The one thing it is not is an artistic success, a rounded symmetrical thing-in-itself like "Self Portrait."

The reason is partly a question of focus. "Self Portrait" is told from the viewpoint of an utterly humorless, clever-stupid cybernetics engineer named Oliver Parks, a frighteningly comic figure, a buffoon with power. Nothing has to be stated, Wolfe's moral is clear; a man like Parks is capable of creating Frankenstein's monster because he *is* the monster; because he has no soul.

But in *Limbo* Wolfe wanted to explore all the possibilities hinted at in "Self Portrait," and to do it he needed a spokesman who could be on stage all the time; he chose Dr. Martine, a young brain surgeon who flees the EMSIAC war, leaving behind a notebook full of gallows humor; spends eighteen years among a tribe of primitive lobotomists, and returns to civilization to find that a Parks, reading the notebook, has managed to translate its jokes into reality: Immob ("No Demobilization Without Immobilization") and Vol-Amp ("Arms or the Man").

The trouble with Martine is just that he is a spokesman; although Wolfe works hard to give him human faults and failings, he is inevitably St. George vs. the dragon, Dr. Christian vs. the town gossips, Hopalong Cassidy vs. the rustlers; he is sometimes interesting, sometimes not, but he's never believable.

Again, the trouble lies partly in the scale of the book: it's a panoramic novel and a synthetic novel of ideas; it's over 400 closely printed pages long; half the length has before now been enough to make a polished short-story writer come a cropper. The novel is not an easy form, even if you play safe and tread carefully in your predecessors' footsteps, and Wolfe has done nothing of the sort.

EMSIAC, Immob and Vol-Amp are fascinating in themselves; Wolfe encysts them with lavish, intricate masses of philosophical apology and analysis, as luminous as anything in Koestler; the book is thoroughly peppered with puns, at least half of them good, and with sniper's shots at almost every target in our intellectual climate, poetic and penetrating.

This isn't a book for everybody, as you will have gathered if you've read many of the reviews. I think that, far as it falls short of perfection, it's a great achievement.

Norbert Wiener forecast the Second Industrial Revolution—the replacement of routine-skilled human labor by machines; James Burnham argued that just as the old land-owning aristocracy gave way to a mercantile elite, the merchants in turn must be

replaced by a new set of rulers—the managers and engineers.
In *Player Piano*, Kurt Vonnegut has combined the two to produce
an enormously plausible and enormously entertaining nightmare.

Vonnegut has carefully used no major devices that haven't
already been built or that couldn't be built today; the pivot of his
whole system is, as the title suggests, simply the player-piano
principle adapted to industrial production. (The whole fantastic
field of automation has bloomed into prominence since Vonnegut
wrote his book.)

Nobody planned it that way; it "just happened." During the
war—World War III, evidently—American know-how solved the
problem of production without manpower; and coincidentally, the
nation's resources were coordinated under Dr. George Proteus,
the first National Industrial, Commercial, Communications, Food-
stuffs and Resources Director. Quite naturally and obviously, the
holders of this title usurped supreme power, the Presidency (as in
Pohl's and Kornbluth's *The Space Merchants*) becoming vestigial,
an office commonly filled by a photogenic ignoramus.

Result, a slightly uneasy paradise. On the top, the "resolutely
monogamous and Eagle-Scout-like . . . engineers and managers";
under them, people who do the routine work which is still un-
economical for machines, and are repaid by the constantly expanding benefits of an expanding and mathematically efficient
economy; under them, a rather perplexing mass of people with
no indexed skills.

These latter fall, or are pushed, into two categories: the Army,
and the Reconstruction and Reclamation Corps—the "Reeks and
Wrecks." Nobody goes hungry, unclothed or homeless; the Army
seems to fare about as badly as ever, but even the Reeks and
Wrecks, judging by the example of Edgar R. B. Hagstrohm, Under-
coater First Class, are provided with more and better creature
comforts than the average factory worker today.

The only trouble is that the machines have left very little for
people to do with their time; filling in a two-foot chuckhole in a
roadway appears to require the services of a forty-man R&R
squad; elsewhere, other scores are continually occupied in flush-
ing out storm sewers . . . and from the managerial level down,
this problem is becoming progressively more acute. Dr. Bud
Calhoun, manager of the petroleum terminal in Ilium, New York,
puts himself (and seventy-one others) permanently out of a job in
Chapter 8, by inventing a gadget which does the work better, thus
eliminating his job classification.

This is the lemming-like compulsion of the American gadgeteer;
Calhoun's case is typical. There's also the barber who kept

worrying that someone would invent a haircutting machine and put him out of business; he had nightmares about it; it was on his mind so much that he worked the thing out himself, bit by bit, sold it for a hundred thousand dollars and royalties, and retired.

And in the Carlsbad Caverns, EPICAC, the electronic intelligence that regulates the whole shooting match, is getting bigger and bigger and bigger....

The main story line is that of Dr. Paul Proteus, son of the first National Industrial &c. Director, but we're also introduced to the aforesaid Edgar R. B. Hagstrohm, who likes *Tarzan* as much as his father did, and hates living in Chicago even more; to PFC Elmo C. Hacketts, Jr., who's looking forward to the end of his hitch, twenty-three years in the future, so that he can make an indelicate suggestion to the first officer who gives him an order; to the Shah of Bratpuhr and his sloe-eyed nephew and translator, Krashdrawr Miasma, who wander in and out of the story as unimpressed observers; and to a host of other characters, all big as life and twice as vocal.

Proteus, like many an anti-utopian hero before him, becomes progressively uneasy about the elite to which he belongs, and eventually winds up involved in an attempt to overthrow it. Revolution is a common theme, not to say a cliche, in stories of this type—so much so that I've often wondered when the FBI is going to get around to compiling an index of science fiction writers. It's very nearly unavoidable, simply because it's the most dramatic sociological process, and almost the only one that happens fast enough to be compressed within story limits; but until now it's always had one major drawback. The happy ending, a convention of magazine fiction, naturally demands that the revolution succeed and solve the problem, whereas in the real world an ideological revolution has yet to achieve its stated aims.

The revolution of *Player Piano*, well organized and planned, fails: the insurgents capture (and very nearly wreck) Ilium, Salt Lake City and Oakland; but not St. Louis or Chicago or Boston or New York.... Even if they had taken every major city in the country, it's clear that nothing would have been accomplished; in the interval between the battle and the surrender, the revolutionaries, fresh from a happy orgy of machine-smashing, find themselves tinkering with these same machines—with equal and opposite delight, making them work again.

Lord of the Flies, by William Golding, is not science fiction nor even fantasy as the terms are usually understood, but I would like to break a rule and review it here anyhow: it is so close to the field—and so remarkable a book—that I think fantasy readers will want to know more about it.

When the story begins, thirty or forty British schoolboys have somehow been unexpectedly set down on an uninhabited tropical island. Evidently a new war had started, and the boys were being flown out of danger: the plane was attacked, and the passengers dropped in a sort of detachable cabin. To this extent I suppose the book is science fiction, but that is as far as it goes; Golding's intention is to show you what happens to the boys after they get on the island, and it does not much matter how.

Particularly in the opening chapters, the book comes triumphantly alive. Golding's island has all the rock-solid vividness of Stevenson's or Defoe's: you can see the pure sunlight filtering through the leaves, hear the insects, feel the dry sand underfoot. Golding, an ex-Navy man turned schoolmaster, knows tropical islands, and boys as well. The half-dozen boys who occupy the foreground are absolutely believable—recognizable individuals, not stereotypes, genus *boy*—and the rest form a silent chorus in its own way equally convincing.

> Some were naked and carrying their clothes; others half-naked, or more or less dressed, in school uniforms, grey, blue, fawn, jacketed or jerseyed. There were badges, mottoes even, stripes of color in stockings and pullovers. Their heads clustered above the trunks in the green shade; heads brown, fair, black, chestnut, sandy, mouse-colored; heads muttering, whispering, heads full of eyes that watched . . . and speculated.

The opening chapters are like a boyish dream come true: a desert island, and no grownups. The most poignantly moving passages of the book occur in this time, when the boys are busy discovering their island and themselves: "that glamour, that strange invisible light of friendship, adventure and content."

But there is a Beast on the island. The littluns dream about it and wake up shrieking; the hunters sense it behind them in the forest. Never seen, it haunts them by its presence, and little by little, the dream turns into a nightmare.

Golding's point: Civilization is a hard-built thing that only grownups know; children are nearer to savagery, and the Beast.

Children need meat, and there are pigs on the island, but no butchers. Someone has to hunt, and kill. Someone has to be the first to stand over the prey, with his arms reeking red to the elbows.

Someone has to paint his face with clays, and learn to chant over the fallen enemy:

"Kill the pig. Cut her throat. Bash her in."

Like a chart slowly unrolling the wrong way, the boys' society moves back along a familiar path to the tribe, and the law of blood. Golding's grip seems to falter once or twice; there are spots here of confusion and even of falsity. The personification of the Beast in a dead airman who comes to rest at the top of the island, though it provides one moment of pure horror, is forced and becomes a nuisance to the plot; but the subsequent appearance of the Beast to the epileptic Simon, in the form of a dead pig's head, is viscerally right, hypnotically compelling.

And the retrograde movement of the story as a whole is so strong that everything seems inevitable, down to the moment when the hunters move across the island, painted and fierce in the pre-Columbian sunlight—stalking a two-legged prey.

Readers who remember John Wyndham's 1950 *Collier's* serial, *The Day of the Triffids*, and J. T. McIntosh's *The Fittest*, will have no trouble in recognizing the pattern of *No Blade of Grass*, by John Christopher. It's a peculiarly British export—a pattern so simple and elementary that American writers long ago discarded it as old hat. American editors, however, are suckers for it—it has twice put science fiction, or some reasonable facsimile thereof, into the major slicks.

But this is a riddle I leave to others to figure out. The immediate point is that Christopher has written the story better than anybody before him.

Wyndham and McIntosh showed civilization dissolving under the attack of intelligent beasts. Christopher quietly goes them one better. What would happen to our world, he asks, if a virus arose somewhere that would attack the family *Gramineae*—the grasses?

This hits so close to home that it hardly seems like science fiction at all: everybody has seen grass, and heard of viruses. In every possible way, Christopher makes his one small pill of speculation easy to swallow. The story, published in 1957, is laid in 1958, but Christopher never says so; he slides you into that year by an ingenious and almost unnoticeable trick. The story begins in 1933, when Hilda Custance returns to her father's Westmorland farm with her two sons, David and John. In this brief prefatory section, Christopher introduces the principal characters and the remote valley ("Blind Gill") which is to be the goal of the book later on. Then, Chapter One of the book proper begins with the words, "A quarter of a century later . . . ."

Thus, in one stroke, the reader has been shoehorned, as it were, a year into the future, and the groundwork for the whole human drama of the book has been laid. Moreover, where Wyndham and McIntosh had to hunt up refuges for their fleeing survivors at the last moment—refuges which inevitably seemed improvised—Christopher has planted his at the very beginning.

The book is full of unobtrusive touches like this, evidences of consummate craftsmanship. The material is sensational in places, enough so to make Ben Hibbs sit up straight in his chair, but the approach is consistently quiet and reasonable.

Christopher's people are undistinguished, ordinary Englishmen. With two exceptions, none of them stands out, none of them is what an American writer would call "well characterized"; and yet, with the same two exceptions—Pirrie and his adulterous wife—all of them are perfectly plausible. When they speak, they seem to be saying what they would naturally say, and not what the author has put into their mouths.

Their development as the book proceeds is a little less believable to me, particularly in the way John Custance and Roger Buckley seem to exchange characters, John acquiring Roger's cynical toughness while Roger falls back into John's rather passive idealism. Neither of these changes seems exactly impossible under the circumstances, but they don't seem necessary to the plot, either, and they bother me a little.

For most of its length, the book blithely ignores the American convention that a story must be told as much as possible from a single viewpoint. Since this is a story of a group of people, not of any one man, the result is a definite gain in clarity and simplicity. Toward the end, it's true, the story does focus on John Custance during his character change, from a civilized man to a ruthless autocrat, but this seems to me a lapse in taste. Very much as in John Masters' *Coromandel!*, this process tends to be unconvincing, because it's shown entirely from the viewpoint of the hero himself: and he can't see the changes, except as they're reflected in those around him; if he could, very likely, they wouldn't happen.

The texture of the narrative, the stream of small details which makes the difference between a fascinating story and an irritating or a dull one, is extremely good. The novel is continuously entertaining, and in some sense rewarding, although it never says anything particularly new or profound. It seems to have a beginning and a destination, and on reaching the destination you have a sense, not only of having been entertained along the way, but of having got somewhere.

Level 7, by Mordecai Roshwald, is a novel laid in the future, making use of many imaginary technological advances, and an imaginary society governed on unusual lines. Thus, according to our usual working definition, it's a science fiction novel.

This s.f. novel, then, was enthusiastically reviewed in the major newspaper book departments (and not in "Spaceman's Realm," either—up front). The reviewers were careful to say, at the very outset, "This is not really science fiction."

Is it?

Level 7 is written as the diary of a military officer who one day is summoned by the C.O. of his "Push-Button Training Camp," and told he is to go on leave after a brief indoctrination period underground. This turns out to be untrue. The narrator gets into a closed car, is driven to a tunnel guarded by "two huge natural boulders," and down the rabbit-hole he goes. The tunnel leads to a passage, the passage to an elevator, the elevator to another passage and a revolving door, the door to an escalator and the escalator to the first of a series of underground chambers.

Car, elevator, escalator and doors alike move only one way: down. In this curious series of reverse-order prenatal experiences, the narrator realizes, he and all his fellow inmates have been trapped. Like Alice (who never found a way back either—she woke up instead), they are down to stay. If war comes, they will survive the attack and press the buttons that launch retaliatory rockets. But even then, they can never come up; whatever happens, they will never see the sun again.

In the next few chapters, we gradually learn more about the underground world. Level 7 is completely self-sufficient, and has supplies to last 500 years. (Level 6 is that of the anti-missile push-button warriors; the five levels above are intended to house civilians of varying degrees of importance, up to Level 1, which is only 10 to 60 feet underground and will certainly be shattered in the first five seconds of attack.)

The inmates of Level 7 do not use names, only numbers: the narrator's is X-127. By the use of this and similar devices, Roshwald has managed to avoid giving any overt clue to the nationality of Level 7's builders. It is clear that his intention is allegorical; the book is dedicated "To Dwight and Nikita," and at one point the diarist muses that there is really very little inner difference between the opposing camps: "As for the other levels, there might be the difference that in one country the rich got the better shelter, and in another country the mighty. But was this really such a big difference? I wondered. The rich were mighty and the mighty were rich."

The point is trenchantly made, yet there is no possible doubt where this story takes place; it is as Slavic as blintzes. As in Zamiatin's *We*, the nightmare is the socialist nightmare of numbers; the suffocating sense that individual personality is being

crushed; that everybody above you is deceiving you, and himself
being deceived in turn.

In fact, although the author himself sees it as an anti-war tract
(and has turned the latter half of the book into a progressively
drearier sermon); and although the jacket of the British edition is
plastered with militant endorsements by Bertrand Russell, J. B.
Priestley and Linus Pauling, *Level 7*'s theme, and the atmosphere
in which it swims, is that of collectivist tyranny.

For those who have read Orwell but not Zamiatin, it should be
noted that the gloom of *1984* is British gloom. X-127 is a good-
natured and rather simple person, with that peculiar combination
of gaiety and innocent spirituality that we think of as Slavic; the
tone of his narrative is one of resignation and childish wonder

The first half of the book, at any rate, is not only absorbing for
its ingenious and complex background, but delightful in its unexpected humor. When, shortly after X-127's arrival, the ubiqui-
tous loudspeakers announce reassuringly, "You need not worry
about your friends and relatives outside. They will be notified that
you have been killed in a painless accident and that you left no
remains," you don't know whether to laugh or cry.

Or, for another example, when X-127 learns of the ingenious
arrangement whereby space left vacant by food consumed is filled
with dehydrated sewage, gradually shoving along a "sealed but
moving wall," he suddenly exclaims to himself, "What if the wall
leaks?"

If the earnestness of the apologists for Level 7 is sinister, it is
faintly comic too. The inverse logic that is purely horrifying in
Orwell becomes ironically delectable: "'Everybody can enjoy the
individuality which his personal number symbolizes.'"

Yet, after all is said, it is the symbol-haunted dream landscape
of *Level 7* that gives it its distinctive tone, in passages like this

> Sometimes when I try to relax, take a warm shower, unharness
> my thoughts from my daily duties and let them loose on the sunny
> meadows of my terrestrial past, I suddenly realize that my lips
> are silently forming words. I speak them out loud, and always
> they are the same words: "Attention, please, attention!"

Well, then, is this science fiction or not? I submit, regretfully
that it is not.

When the editors of Bantam Books tell us that a book is either
good or s.f., but cannot be both; when the reviewers of such novel
as *Level 7*, *A Canticle for Leibowitz* and *On the Beach* assure u
that in spite of superficial resemblances, these are not really s.f
they are perfectly sincere, and they are right.

Science fiction, as Kingsley Amis reminds us in *New Maps of Hell*, is a field distinguished and limited by a certain special interest. For us, *Level 7* is absorbing partly because of the highly ingenious methods Dr. Roshwald has contrived to keep his prisoners alive and moderately sane in their dungeons, partly because of the fascinating structures of logic and myth they erect to justify their imprisonment. For the general reader, these are incidental. Make a list of the "science fiction" books which have won wide acceptance in recent years, and you will find they have one thing in common: they are parables, warning of political or military disaster.

The remoteness of imagined worlds is what charms a science-fantasy reader: the immediacy of these books is what sells them to the public.

It is futile to be bitter when a reviewer says, "This is not science fiction—it's good!" From the general reader's stand-point, this is the simple truth. Therefore for God's sake let us either write parables of atomic doom, or else be content with our tiny (but growing) audience.

The Joy Wagon, by Arthur T. Hadley, is a farcical novel about a political campaign. It gets enormous mileage out of one simple but blood-chilling device: substituting for the human candidate a Machiavellian computer named Microvac—and as far as possible, letting the plot proceed exactly as if he were human.

The first twenty pages of the book, for some odd reason, are written in primer-sized sentences, and as awkwardly put together as possible—a line of wooden dialogue, then a paragraph of back-ground material, then another line of dialogue, like a man trying to start a balky Model T. On page 21, the engine catches when Hadley turns to the unorthodox love problems of a young uni-versity professor and a night telephone operator. ("The room could be locked from the inside, but there were only two small swivel chairs with upright backs. Interruptions from the board, though infrequent, were of a disturbingly random pattern. Kay, hinting at some past experience, was nervous about cleaning men with pass keys . . .") And away we go. Hadley went through the 1956 Presidential campaign as a member of Stevenson's staff, and met all the gorgeously varied fauna of a Presidential year—and here they are: Bryant W. Dangle, the egghead candidate, "who never split an infinitive or joined an issue"; Congressman Bates Newball, "the sheep's friend"; mad Nora Claggett ("In her hands she bore a nine-foot pole from whose top fluttered a gigantic green and blue pennant with a gold radio tube on it. Beneath the tube

were embroidered in scarlet the words, 'Prepare for Doom'");
TV camera crews everywhere ("Two heaving roustabouts were
snaking a heavy cable across the room. They flipped it over a
line of chairs, fetching the ladies in the next row an oily smack.
'Hands off dat cable!' they yelled crossly"); Indians ("'See,
Microvac got no head. All world know machine got no head. You
give bonnet to machine that got no head, you look silly to whole
world, Chief'"); hustlers, advance men, managers, and above all,
Mike itself.

Mike is a political manager's dream. It works tirelessly,
knows all the answers, has a dynamic handshake (engineered with
"delicate electronic pads" in its hands), never loses its temper,
never makes the same mistake twice. As thousands cheer, you
cheer, too: the best part of the joke is that you find yourself
wanting Microvac to win, because it's a more likable guy, a
greater American, a more forceful and intelligent leader than
either of the two regular candidates. It ought to win, too, if logic
means anything: instead the book ends with a last-minute disaster
which is clumsily contrived and abrupt; if, as I half suspect, this
"happy" ending was forced on Hadley by an editor, the editor ought
to be shot.

Walden Two, by B. F. Skinner, is an interesting and highly important novel which I missed when it first appeared in 1948.

A university professor named Burris has been feeling a vague
dissatisfaction since the war. "For several years the conviction
had been forcing itself upon me that I was unable to contemplate
my former students without emotion. (. . .) So far as I could see,
their pitiful display of erudition was all I had to show for my life
as a teacher, and I looked upon that handiwork not only without
satisfaction, but with actual dismay."

When two of these ex-students turn up, just out of the army, to
remind him of something he had said about Utopian societies, he
is first staggered ("And, good God, just what had I told them?")
then intrigued. Burris recalls with some effort the romantic ideas
of a colleague, T. E. Frazier, which he must have passed along
in an idle moment. Looking Frazier up, he discovers that in the
intervening years the man has apparently set himself up in the
sort of experimental society he advocated: his current address
is Walden Two, R.D. 1, Canton, in "a neighboring state." Burris
and the two students, Rogers and Jamnik, go to see what it's like

With them go Rogers' and Jamnik's girl-friends, and a philosophy professor named Castle. They find Walden Two a self-
sufficient farming community of about a thousand, living in

rammed-earth dwellings and organizing their activity by a system of "labor credits."

The little world Burris and his companions see during the next few days is charming and disturbing: with more time for leisure than work (they work an average four-hour day), the Waldenites are cheerful, relaxed, courteous. Even the very young children, brought up in crèches, are well-behaved. Fear and hunger as economic motives have been eliminated; there is no politics and no discord.

As Frazier points out, this differs from all other Utopias in being a feasible project, right here, right now, in the midst of "normal" society. Walden Two's women are set free by "industrializing housewifery"; its young men and women, not compelled to delay marriage for economic reasons, become parents at 17 or 18.

People who are repelled by the human waste and irrationality of present forms of society will find this an absorbing book, in spite of several flaws. As a novel, *Walden Two* makes its best showing in the first half: Burris and the other characters are warmly real, and Frazier in particular is such an exasperatingly ambiguous person that the reader never knows from one moment to the next whether to trust what he says or not. Near the middle of the book, however, all but the pretense of novelistic development is dropped, in favor of an outrageously extended Frazier monologue. This is unforgivable because it is dull, and because it turns the book into propaganda, the characters into straw figures.

As propaganda, *Walden Two* is disturbing in several senses. Discounting some features which are hard to get used to simply because of their novelty, and some others which are probably wrong guesses (the crèches, and the glass dinnerware), there's still one thing that bothers me very much: the communal *mystique* which grows toward the end of the book. It's one thing to organize an experimental society communally for reasons of economy, and another, it seems to me, to hymn the virtues of "Communal authorship, communal art, communal music."

All the same, this is (I repeat) a fascinating and important book. Some of Skinner's arguments may be open to question, but of one thing there does not seem to be any reasonable doubt: We *could* do this, here and now.

Gore Vidal's *Messiah* is a hard book to assess. To begin with, it has a quality so uniformly absent from science fiction novels that it comes here as a shock: conviction, the feeling that the story is in some deep sense true. This means that Vidal's plot is almost beyond criticism—the story does not impress you as plot, but as something that happened.

It follows that whatever means have been used to achieve so (for us) rare an effect must be accounted good means: yet in several ways this is an appallingly bad book.

It has the cardinal badness, it is dull. I don't mean the story, which is a perfect thing, but the story-as-told. Like Jessamyn West in "Little Men," Vidal has chosen for his narrator an old man, near death, recording the events of the story many years afterward. His recollections have the blurred light of decades on them; faces are in shadow; irrelevancies intrude; and around this mass of unsorted material the narrator, tireless and un-critical, winds the string of his endless Jamesian sentences. . . . Well, this is all very much like life, but it is hard not to wish it were a little more like art.

I mention these things because I think the reader ought to be warned that he has an eight-and-a-half-page introduction—full of teutonic philosophizing, and printed in italics—to get through before the story even begins; that he won't find out the narrator's name till page 30; and that it isn't until page 48—almost exactly one-quarter of the way into the book—that reader and narrator meet the central character, the Messiah, for the first time.

Against this, there's an occasional flash of wit; good potshots at Episcopalian bishops, Jungian analysts and other sitting ducks, an astonishing slow delineation of character that turns cardboard figures into creatures as obstinately themselves as anyone you know; and finally the story itself—simple, powerful, disturbing—and, I think, unforgettable.

20. NEW STARS

THIS IS A CATCH-ALL chapter. Actually, most of the authors represented here have been around for a long, loud while, but it's only recently, as old fans measure time, that they've blossomed out as novelists.

When he was working at it, some twenty years ago, nobody in this field was a match for Raymond Z. Gallun in the vivid and sympathetic portrayal of alien intelligences; "Old Faithful," "Son of Old Faithful" and "Derelict" are titles that still send remembered shivers up my spine. Since his return to the field a few years ago, Gallun has been working another patch altogether —one that abounds in clear-eyed, ham-handed, pinheaded young men with cowlicks and freckles. But for the last ten years or so a Cambridge science teacher who writes as "Hal Clement" has been quietly fortifying himself in and around the spot Gallun left vacant. His failings are a certain emotional blandness—no Clement character ever gets excited—and a low romantic quotient: where Gallun's monsters are alien and humanly sympathetic at the same time—a damnably difficult thing—Clement's often fail to convince simply because they're too human: more so, in fact, than some of the human characters.

His assets are a working knowledge of physics, chemistry, astronomy and mechanics—rare equipment for a science fiction writer—and an almost inhuman thoroughness. *Mission of Gravity* is the result of what must surely be the most back-breaking job of research ever undertaken to buttress a science fiction story. Moreover, the result is worth the trouble.

Nowhere before, bar such primitive examples as Dr. Miles J. Breuer's and Clare Winger Harris' "A Baby on Neptune," and the notably unsuccessful *Petrified Planet* volume, has anybody made a really serious effort to explore the problems of life on a planet much different from our own. Mesklin, where this story takes place, is wildly different—see the jacket illustration—and inexorably convincing: it's Clement's sober, careful projection of the superplanet of 61 Cygni, detected in 1943 by Dr. K. Aa. Strand. Clement's article, "Whirligig World" (*Astounding*, June, 1953), really ought to have been included in this book; if it weren't for the unreasonable prejudice against prefaces to novels, and the scarcity of books about whose writing problems there is anything to be said, it might have been. There should have been diagrams and maps, too; no amount of detail about this fascinating place could be too much.

The Mesklinites, to return to where we started, are a blend of Clement's virtues and failings: physically, they're as satisfyingly alien as anyone could want; mentally, there's less difference between them and Mr. Clement than between Mr. Clement and a modern Chinese. In spite of the continual annoyance of their familiar thought processes and their idiomatic English, however, the gartersnake-sized officers and crew of the *Bree* are interesting and likable; and by the end of the book, although there's not a sermonizing word in it, they've built up as strong a case for the Brotherhood of Creatures as we've ever seen.

John Wyndham—our old friend John Beynon Harris—has written in *Out of the Deeps* another exemplar of that careful blend of realism and fantasy which, if we are not careful, seems likely to become a Wyndham monopoly. Like his previous novel, *The Day of the Triffids*, this one goes all the way back for its inspiration to the masterworks of H. G. Wells.

The lesson is illuminating. Submerging his fantastic element even more than Wells did—almost as much as the tediously expert H. P. Lovecraft—and keeping his focus sharply on the human figures in the foreground, Wyndham works a curious household magic: You have to believe in the monstrous events of the story, because they're happening to people you know.

In this case, the events themselves derive from Wells, via Eric Frank Russell: interplanetary visitors from somewhere arrive on Earth, but don't exactly land—they dive into the ocean, and, securely hidden in the Deeps, begin a remorseless campaign against land-dwellers.

No one but the British can write novels like this, apparently, and they do it all too seldom. Like *The Day of the Triffids*, this story is told in the first person from the viewpoint of an interested observer; the narrator is invincibly cool and stiff-upper-lipped, he anticipates at the drop of a hat, neither his pace nor his tone varies once all the way through—and all this, which ought to be maddening, simply makes the book more convincing and more enjoyable.

It's a *very* British book. I can't forbear quoting two bits of it, one from page 17, when a rather pompous naval officer is giving a lecture on the equipment being used to investigate the sea bottom:

> "—here," he continued, "we have a new instrument with which we hope to be able to make observations at something like twice the depth attainable by the bathyscope, perhaps even more. It is entirely automatic. In addition to registering pressures, temperatures, currents, and so on, and transmitting the readings to the surface, it is equipped with five small television cameras, four of them giving all round horizontal coverage, and one transmitting the view vertically beneath the sphere."

—And one more, very Wellsian indeed, from page 115:

> Europe remained an interested spectator. In the opinion of its inhabitants, it is the customary seat of stability. Hurricanes, tidal waves, serious earthquakes, et cetera, are extravagances divinely directed to occur in the more exotic and less sensible parts of the earth, all important European damage being done traditionally by man himself in periodic frenzies. It was not, therefore, to be seriously expected that the danger would come any closer than Madeira—or, possibly, Rabat or Casablanca.

Wilson Tucker's *The City in the Sea*, as I said in a loud and irritated voice, was a bad book: his second science fiction novel, *The Long Loud Silence*, is not merely a better one, which after all wouldn't be so hard to achieve, but a phenomenally good book; in its own terms, it comes as near perfection as makes no difference. The plotting is close-knit without being contrived; the style is compact and eloquent; the characters, in Faulkner's words, "stand up on their hind legs and cast a shadow."

This is the story of what happens when the eastern third of the United States is quarantined, as the result of an atomic and bacteriological bombing that wipes out every major city east of the Mississippi and leaves its survivors permanently infected—plague carriers, each one a potential center of death and destruction. To prevent the plague from spreading to the rest of the nation, what's left of the government and the army sets up a *cordon sanitaire* along the Mississippi. From one point of view, those who are now dead are the lucky ones; the others have nothing to look forward to but a long slow fight for survival, whose end is foreknown.

The protagonist, ex-GI Russell Gary, is billed on the dust jacket as a "professional heel," which he isn't. Even disregarding the totally irrelevant and inaccurate adjective, Gary is no heel: he is simply a very ordinary American male, thirty years old, with a little more than average intelligence but no extraordinary aptitudes, interests or attainments, who wants to go on living even in the hell that virus and quarantine have made of the eastern United States.

> *A man would be either quick, or dead.*

That's the only choice Gary has; not a single thing he does is conditioned by anything else. This, in fact, is precisely the thing that makes the book as good as it is: Gary is no hero and no heel, neither superman nor subman; he is not a symbol of anything and he falls into no moralistic category—he's a human being, and he's completely believable.

He has a normal, human hunger for companionship, and a normal, human callousness toward the misery of others; the two are brilliantly combined in one of the most effective passages of the book.

Gary has settled himself for the winter in a farm household —tricking his hosts, in a sense, by carefully playing on their emotions, but making a fair deal: he guards them from marauders, they feed and shelter him. He sets up an alarm system of wires and bells, and prowls at night, sleeping in the day. After a week or so, he discovers the family has a radio that still works, run by a windmill-driven generator.

> ... He ran back to the radio, sank to his knees before it and excitedly twisted the knob... His burning eagerness to *hear* stopped his fingers, made him aware of the peculiar thrill the glow and sound had given him. A year, a year and a half ago, this was nothing, but now it was everything. . . . This was civilization, and sanity, and warmth, and food, this was one man on friendly terms with the next. This was what he had lost a long time ago and despaired of ever having again.
>
> . . . There was a strange tightness in his stomach as he touched a second control knob and moved it a fraction of an inch.
>
> A girl was singing.
>
> He found her in the middle of a word, on a syllable that at once brought the entire word into his mind as though he had heard it from the beginning, and that word and the next few cast the image of the entire sentence on his consciousness so that he could not remember where he had come in, could readily imagine that he had heard it all. She was singing a slow song, a sweet and sad

song about leaves of brown that tumbled down and somewhere behind her where it shouldn't have been interfering a bell tinkled faintly.

. . . A bell. He leaped to his feet and dashed for the door, snatching up the automatic shotgun as he sped through it.

. . . Gary flattened himself against the wall and inched his head past the corner. Down the slope a dark bundle of nothing lay on the ground. As he watched, a slow movement of an arm and hand seemed to detach itself from the mass, seemed to reach out probing fingers for the wires he had strung there. . . .

And behind him, although he could not hear it, he knew the radio was playing softly and a girl was singing to him. All for him. The sound of his shooting would stop her, would end the quiet contentment of the voice and the moment, as the family rushed from their beds and rushed into the room. . . .

. . . Feeling around on the floor, his fingers touched an iron rod and he picked it up, judging its weight and striking power. It would serve. . . Once more he took up his post at the corner of the barn, concealed in the shadows and impatient with the stranger for taking so much time to climb the slope.

Damn him, damn him, why didn't he hurry?

Gary wants to get back across the river, to the warm, familiar world that no longer exists on this side. Eventually, with resourcefulness, patience and single-minded determination, he does it—only to find, of course, that he spreads death wherever he goes. He leaves a widening track of corruption behind him; he can never stay anywhere longer than a day; he is as irrevocably cut off from humanity as before.

But the main thing is still to survive. He recrosses the river and, as food stocks dwindle and the hunter and the hunted inevitably become one, follows his narrowing path with an undiminished will to live. At the book's end, he again encounters the girl with whom he had a brief affair at the beginning—each of them stalking the other. From this point, there are only two likely conclusions, of which, possibly on the insistence of his publishers,* Tucker has chosen the less gruesome and perhaps slightly the less logical; but this minor weakness, if it is a weakness at all, is easily forgivable. The book is honest, courageous, deeply felt. From where I sit, it makes the future of science fiction as literature look measurably brighter.

The fiction writer who ventures outside the narrow circle of the times and places familiar to his readers has always had one knotty problem to resolve before he can put a word on paper.

*Earl Kemp tells me this guess is correct.

Reduced to extremes, it goes like this: He can address himself
openly to here-and-now readers, and explain everything unfamiliar
as he goes along—in which case he commits himself to a continual
breach of the reader's self-forgetful illusion; or he can write as
he imagines his protagonist would, for a contemporary audience,
and explain next to nothing—in which case, likelier than not, the
reader will trip over an unlighted piece of stage-furniture on
every second page until he gives up in disgust.

The first is the easiest and crudest method: all the early
utopian novels were written in the form of travelogues; historical
fiction used to be copiously peppered with footnotes and other
author-intrusions:

> The reader must remember, of course, that in the Nazareth of
> Jesus' time, there were no motor-cars at all. . . .

Between this and the second pole, luckily, there's a long series
of mixed solutions—all the way from stories in which the characters seize upon any pretext to explain the obvious to each other
(and the explainee usually says, "Oh, yeah, that's right; I forgot")
to such brilliant exercises in subtlety as Fritz Leiber's "Coming
Attraction."

The second basic alternative is just possible in historical
fiction: Robert Graves, with the aid of one simple device—writing
in the character, not of a contemporary story-teller, but of a
contemporary historian—uses it and frequently gets clean away.
(But in his one experiment with the future he prudently chose the
first method; so did Franz Werfel.) In science fiction—assuming
that the reader is expected to understand what's going on without
a guidebook and in one reading—it is flatly impossible.

Murder in Millennium VI, by Curme Gray, therefore, is a pro-
foundly perplexing book. Shasta's blurb-writer was clearly at a
loss:

> A first novel. A new name. Almost out of nowhere has come a
> PHENOMENAL performance. How will it be known? As the first
> of its kind . . . a new direction in imaginative work? As the most
> astonishing Future Mystery ever written?

And the author of the publicity sheet sent to reviewers was, I
would judge, typing with one hand and biting the fingernails of
the other:

> Unusual love interest. Economy of telling. Conception excludes
> any vestige of nature. Style has a remarkable "modal" flavor.
> Gave our book designer the feeling of ancient Egypt.

I venture to suggest that if "modal flavor" means anything, Shasta is as much in the dark about it as I am, and that the book designer's Egyptian feeling is attributable to something he ate; but I don't blame the publishers.

For sheer audacity and stubbornness, Curme Gray's performance is breathtaking. Although the story is set 6,000 years in the future—in a matriarchal society, whose customs and technology bear no resemblance to our own—there is not a word in the book that might not logically have been written by the narrator for the edification of his own posterity.

About three-quarters of the background can be puzzled out from the context: the matriarchy is based on physical superiority (females are flat-chested and bigger than males); it contains remnants of the Triple Goddess worship familiar to Graves readers; the world of Millennium VI lives on food pills and water, and has forgotten death.

The rest, including the most trivial details of stage-setting, is submerged. The book opens with a cipher moving in a vacuum:

> Her tall spare body wrapped in a robe, she came out of the bathroom.
> . . . Hilda smiled.
> Perfect and permanent, she was thinking, and created by woman. But now a male was butting in. And not just any male. That one. Stupid, too!
> She frowned.
> Damn it! Why?
> She strode toward the closed arch opposite her. The door slid aside into the wall. She heard a tapping in the hall, approaching on her left. Already dressed, Alec was delivering the next breakfast. Neither could see the other, and she ignored her ears. Her body hit his extended arms. Since he was a head shorter and only half as broad, he was spun about; the articles he carried went rolling along the hall. . . .

Persevering, the reader will eventually learn that the male referred to is Victor Mitchel, the story's narrator, who is about to be interviewed by the Matriarch for a secretarial position; that he is Hilda's brother, that Wilmot is their mother and Alec their father. But he never will find out why Alec and Hilda couldn't see each other in the hall.

Similarly, some of the means of communication used by the characters are made clear by context early in the story (telement, clairvoyance); others remain incomprehensible (communion, "neutral").

The effect of all this is a little like that of a shadow-play performed behind too many layers of gauze; or like a radio drama tuned in after the first commercial—nothing assumes any definite shape or color; cast and stage-settings alike have a dreamlike insubstantiality; the burden of visualization is almost entirely on the reader.

Victor Mitchel and Barbara Porter, two century-old youngsters, are both throwbacks—Barbara physically (she has breasts and a complexion), Victor mentally (in his instinctive distaste for the ordered, termite-like existence of Millennium VI). They want to marry, but can't till Barbara either is elected to an administrative post or finds a job in business; like the other young women of her generation, she's been hunting without success for thirteen years.

Wilmot, Victor's mother, Chairwoman of the Board of Business, is an ambitious woman who has been four times defeated in the contest for the Matriarchy.

Alec, his father, is a secret masculist whose hobby is ancient books; he owns the only three known to be in existence—*Palmer's Method*, *Hobbies* and a volume called *Crime, a History*, which Alec takes to be a history of the world.

Hilda, his non-identical twin, hates Victor because he was born first, and so ranks before her in one category of precedence.

Gertrude Franklin, Barbara's great-aunt, Deaconess of the Synod on Science, has a weak heart and a guilty secret: Barbara's mother mated outside the Stud, and outside her caste—an unheard-of double irregularity.

These are the suspects when, at what was to have been Victor's audience, the Matriarch is found dead. This is another irregularity; Alec, who's familiar with the subject from his reading and because his own entire pedigree died in a hushed-up accident two and a half centuries before, has to define and decline the word *death*; and even then it's a long while before the others can quite grasp the idea.

When it sinks in, everyone is in a tizzy for fear death will again become a custom—as it evidently was in the misty pre-Matriarchal days. Wilmot assumes the throne, being next in line according to law (although it's surely odd that there's a law of succession at all, since death is unheard-of?); and by manipulating the problem according to the strict formal logic of the times eventually turns up the possibility of murder.

Alec's *Crime, a History* includes an (incomplete) analysis of the sealed-room problem which first directs suspicion at him: he was the first to touch the body; the Matriarch might have been only stunned or sleeping, and Alec might have choked her while pretending to feel for the pulse in her throat. His motive, of course, would have been a desire to restore the patriarchy.

This bubble bursts when Alec, having barricaded himself and Victor in the living room of the Matriarch's suite, is found the next morning stabbed with a pair of scissors; suspicion next, naturally, falls on Victor—the theory being that he committed the first crime in collusion with Alec, and for the same reason; the second to keep Alec from informing.

Now, however, Wilmot announces that Alec has confessed the first murder to her, then presumably killed himself for fear of punishment. This seems to settle it. Concurrently, the secret of Barbara's pedigree having come out, Wilmot forbids her to meet or communicate with Victor.

Nothing is settled as far as Victor is concerned. He intends to marry Barbara in spite of his mother's edict and the putative bride-to-be's own recurrent attacks of coyness; as for the second murder, Victor is half convinced that he did it in his sleep. But Barbara first proves that he hasn't the necessary strength; and then, examining Alec's body, discovers a new clue (one wrist is slit, and there's a bloodstain under it—evidence that Alec was already dead when the scissors-blade was plunged into his chest).

After four chapters of doubtful relevance, Wilmot announces her intention of deleting Barbara's memory of Victor; Victor tells her that unless she reverses this decision he'll inform on Hilda, who appears to be the owner of the scissors. Wilmot's answer to this is to clout him on the jaw, knocking him out, and to remove his "remitter," the telepathic-clairvoyant-communion-neutral gadget with which everybody communicates.

When Victor comes to, he's under guard and the Mass at which Wilmot will first formally appear as Matriarch is about to begin. Victor has to appear, since failure to do so would be an irregularity; but without his remitter there's little he can do.

What he does, immediately after Wilmot takes the throne, is to call out, "Hilda, it doesn't matter whether or not you slit his wrist. He was already dead"; whereupon both Hilda and Wilmot incontinently drop dead.

Victor swipes Wilmot's remitter, overpowers Barbara, and drags her out. After a notably foggy chase through the building, he reaches The Switch and shuts down the power all over the planet, inaugurating Patriarchy Two; he then explains the whole puzzle to Barbara (I'll come to this in a moment); but their fadeout clinch is forestalled by Barbara's realization that the globe's heating system is also off.

Victor turns the switch on in time to keep the entire population from freezing to death, and in an epilogue we learn that there isn't going to be any patriarchy. History does not repeat; but evidently some sort of compromise is in the process of working itself out, and has been for two and a half centuries. As for Barbara, she'll enter the Matriarchal elections—and win, says Victor, or he'll pull the switch again.

Victor, in the interval between being slugged by Wilmot and appearing at the Mass, had tested a scissors-blade on his own wrist and discovered it was painful—therefore, he reasoned, it would have been impossible to kill Alec in this way without waking him up. He confirmed his suspicion by opening the couch-cover and finding that no blood had soaked through to the upholstery: ergo, neither the wrist-slitting nor the stabbing killed Alec.

The method used, by Wilmot, was "communion"; this is also the method by which she had planned to erase the lovers' recollections of each other. Wilmot slit the corpse's wrist to confuse the issue; afterward, Hilda—afraid that Alec would escape without punishment for the murder of the Matriarch (actually, of course, also Wilmot's doing and with the same weapon)—stabbed him with the scissors she found in his hand. Hilda knew all about "communion," except the fact that it could be used for murder; she guessed that when Victor called to her during the Mass; Wilmot guessed that she guessed, and each struck instantly—yes, via "communion"—to forestall the other.

Now this may or may not make sense, depending entirely on what "communion" is supposed to be; the process, frequently referred to, is never explained, any more than a mundane novelist would explain the telephone, or the Republican Party. The only clue offered, indirectly, is the statement that communion is commonly believed to be impossible between persons—which seems to put it in the same order of reality as van Vogt's ingravity parachute.

In short, as a formal novel of detection the story is a bust— as, by the rules, it ought to be. But as a Pole Two solution of the problem outlined at the beginning of this discussion—for my money a much more difficult *tour de force*—it's a prodigious three-quarter success. The reader's imagination (mine, at any rate) is seldom quite adequate for the strain Gray imposes on it, and at times it boggles completely; nevertheless, the very strictures that make the book hard to read also give it a curious authority. Gray's future world, where it's visible, is a masterly job—and the picture carries conviction even where (perhaps because) it's incomplete.

This is Curme Gray's first novel.

If, as I devoutly hope, he survives the traditional ordeal of writing a second, his third ought to be something to watch for.

In 1950 *Famous Fantastic Mysteries* published a novelette by Arthur C. Clarke, called "Guardian Angel," whose plot was simply this: Earth has been bloodlessly conquered and is being administered with benevolence and enormous intelligence by a race of Overlords who never come down out of their great ships and whom no man has ever seen—not even Stormgren, the Secretary-General of the United Nations, who governs the planet under the direction of an Overlord called Karellen. Although Stormgren's faith in the Overlords is unwavering, even he in the end succumbs to the puzzle of *why* the Overlords will not let themselves be seen. He has a few tantalizing hints—that the Overlords have been studying Earth for a long time, perhaps for thousands of years; that they may have shown themselves to man once before with disastrous results; that they themselves are not the ruling intelligence of the universe, but only Somebody Else's errand boys. Finally, at Stormgren's last meeting with Karellen before he leaves office, he uses a strong light to penetrate the one-way glass that separates them, and sees just enough before the door in the other room closes: a black, barbed, and very famous tail.

The point of outlining this story here is not to spoil Clarke's surprise—I don't think it can—but to point out an amazing achievement in reworking magazine material for hardcover publication: a business of which science-fiction readers have seen a great deal in the past few years. Clarke has taken this novelette, which seems to kill its own subject about as thoroughly as a story can, and without changing it at all except to lop off its tail, has used it as the first section of a genuinely distinguished novel—*Childhood's End*. Rejecting his original decision that the story ends with the solution of the puzzle, he has carried it forward to consider what happens after the bat-winged Overlords—having educated the human race out of its medieval superstitions—come down out of their ships: who they are: who and what their masters are: and the reason for their patient guardianship of Earth; and the story, beginning so leisurely and in so small a framework, gathers momentum until in one breathtaking sweep it encompasses not only the end of humanity's childhood, but the end, at once wonderful and terrible, of humanity itself.

It struck me as a curious thing, when I was making my notes for this review, that the elapsed time covered by a novel should be in itself any factor at all, let alone a major factor in judging the novel's worth—yet a major factor it certainly is; it's the thing that induces that pleasurably poleaxed expression on the reader's face as he closes a book; every critic takes it into account, usually signaling his reaction with the word "scope"; and although I've avoided the word, you can see above that I'm no more immune than the rest.

But it's clear enough when you stop to think of it that this reaction makes the best of sense: the novel, like the epic and the saga, exists precisely because this long elapsed-time treatment is possible in it; the novel is our paramount form of literary expression because it satisfies that time-binding instinct which makes our species unique; and finally, that here, not in any low-cut gowns or chrome-plated gadgetry, is the root urge that explains the popularity of the historical novel. . . and of science fiction.

Clarke has been a very good writer for a very long time now; "When I was around fifteen," he says in his autobiographical note, "I started writing short pieces for the school magazine. . . On turning up these articles recently, I was depressed to see how little improvement there had been in the interim." All the virtues of *Childhood's End* are discoverable in much of his earlier work, in a highly compressed state; here for the first time they are fully unfolded. The work has numerous flaws—e.g., the deliberate contrary-to-fact assumption, a little more irksome here than in the original novelette, that the traditional devil-figure, a medieval symbol constructed by adding bat's wings and a dragon's tail to the pagan-symbol of Pan, is "remembered" from a contact with the Overlords in prehistory. In spite of them, I think few who read the book will be able to resist the spell of what the Los Angeles *Times* reviewer aptly called its "mourning beauty."

In the monograph *Editors and Other Fungoids*, which I mean to write as soon as ever I can get around to it, one of my best exhibits will be the early work of Arthur C. Clarke. Like Ray Bradbury and a few other such grubby figures, Clarke toiled for years unsung; in fact, nobody ever noticed him at all until he was suddenly sprawling all over *Holiday* and the Book of the Month Club. The result is, first, that when Clarke's publishers start looking around for old material to plug up the gap, they find there is plenty of it under stones; and, second, that the previous-copyright notices in the resulting books read like a record of failures. . . . Ah, but whose?

Of the eleven stories in Ballantine's *Expedition to Earth*, three are from *Astounding* and one from *Amazing*—the new, regenerated *Amazing Stories*, not the old one.* The rest were first published,

---

*This was apt when written; now I would have to say the old *Amazing*, not the new degenerated one.

one apiece, in *Science Fiction Quarterly*, *Future combined with Science Fiction Stories*, *Thrilling Wonder*, *F&SF*, *Startling*, *Super Science* and *Ten Story Fantasy*.

In justice to the well-paid editors who presumably rejected more than half of these stories, not all of them are very good. "Second Dawn," for example, is a long and tedious account of some intelligent unicorn-type creatures, recited in a sort of nasal monotone like that of a Village poetess reading something about flahrs. "Loophole" is a trick-ending potboiler exactly like one thousand others that you wish you hadn't read. (This is one that a well-paid editor bought, by the way.) "History Lesson" is a very mild joke, the point of which was given away gratis by the unspeakable illustrator when it first appeared.

Others, though, are very good indeed: "Superiority"—recommended reading at MIT, and a good story all the same—; "If I Forget Thee, Oh Earth. . .", a slight but very effective mood piece; "Inheritance" and "The Sentinel," two perfect examples of that half-mystical yearning toward the stars for which Clarke is now noted; "Breaking Strain" and "Hide and Seek," from a period when Clarke apparently aspired, with some reason, to become the combined Kipling and Maugham of the spaceways. All the editors concerned may now whistle for more like these; Clarke is writing books.

Clarke's *Prelude to Space* is another revenant; it was first published by *Galaxy Novels* in 1951, at the height of the *Astounding-Galaxy* misunderstanding. If ever a novel was unfairly tucked away into a cranny, this one was; until an eyewitness account comes along, it's the definitive story of the first spaceship launching. Heinlein's "The Man Who Sold the Moon" is a romantic fantasy; this is how it might conceivably happen.

The book is a little pedestrian by the standards we're accustomed to; if you're looking for fist fights, crash landings, or torture chambers, you won't find them here. Its careful verisimilitude, however, is marred only by the inevitable pratfall Clarke takes when he tries to make his hero sound like an American. British writers will do this; I don't know why.

Those who read Clarke's short story, "The Deep Range," in *Star Science Fiction #3*, edited by Frederik Pohl, will remember it as a provocative glimpse into a future where whales are cattle, and the herdsmen ride in tiny one-man subs.

As he did with *Childhood's End*, Clarke has now built onto the end of this short story in order to make it into a novel. Don Burley, the hero of the original story and its only human character,

evidently turned out to be too ruggedly simple a type for the plot
Clarke had in mind; so, early in the book, a new character, Walter
Franklin, is introduced, and gradually nudges Burley into the
background.

This is not really the best way of organizing a novel, and for a
while the viewpoint bounces back and forth like a ping-pong ball.

In Chapter 18, somewhat to the reader's relief, Burley is buried
by an underwater avalanche, and thereafter Franklin has our full
attention.

The background, in this larger treatment, becomes much more
impressive and believable than it was in the original story.
Clarke has built up his Bureau of Whales, and its fascinating
undersea activities, with painstaking care, from the routine training of recruits, riding "torpedoes," like underwater surfboards,
to the production-line killing and slaughtering of the whales.

The novel, in fact, is nearly all background. Most of the time
the actors in the foreground are almost painfully inadequate, and
the motions Clarke puts them through are puppet-like. The whole
thing has the embarrassing solidity of a bad Hollywood adventure
film—until, toward the end, it suddenly turns into a good one.
The underwater rescue operation, when a submarine is trapped
on the ocean floor by a collapsed oil derrick, is superb drama;
and Franklin himself acquires stature in a most undramatic conflict between the Bureau and the Mahanayake Thero, a Ceylonese
Buddhist leader who is determined to end the Bureau's slaughter
of whales for food.

The moral problem thus posed comes as it were out of nowhere
to us beef-eating readers, who have learned to shut our eyes to
the same problem in our own time. Clarke makes a startlingly
effective argument for the Mahanayake's position. And, with
characteristic detachment, instead of narrowing the focus as the
story ends, Clarke widens it; and we see that his concern all
along has been, as it always is, with history rather than with the
transient concerns of individual men. Clarke's abiding sense of
the grandeur of creation may perhaps make him a poor recorder
of merely human character and emotion; but we need that wide
view—that breath from the macrocosm, cutting through the reeks
of our little sty.

The writer of these tall *Tales From the White Hart* appears in
his familiar book-jacket photo as a grim and terrifyingly intelligent gnome, all spectacles, complicated wristwatch and intent
eyes. In person, he is a large pink man, downy-thatched, with
the friendly and diffident air of a new chick. The real Clarke
is doubtless more complex than either, but there is more of

Mr. Peepers in him than of Odd John. These stories, ingenious and amiable, are the schoolmasterish jokes of a man whose first thought is to instruct; his second is to apologize for presuming to do so. The intelligence behind the glasses really is of frightening proportions, and is scientifically trained at that; but nobody could possibly dislike Clarke, even in this Age of the Twitch.

All fifteen of the stories are loosely framed as anecdotes told over tepid beer, usually by a British Münchhausen named Harry Purvis, in "the White Hart"—really the White Horse, the London pub where for a number of years British s.f. writers and their satellites gathered. Clarke's focus is almost always on the gadget rather than on the people: a process for extracting uranium from sea water, suitable for use on billionaires' pleasure craft; a phony iceberg off the coast of Florida; a Hollywood zap gun that really works. There's a touch of Wodehouse in some of the stories, others are reminiscent of Dunsany or of John Collier; but in spite of their wry endings (a physicist falls out of an interesting anti-gravity field and becomes a meteor; a wife who talks incessantly is defenestrated, i.e., pushed out of a window), the dominant effect is one of good-humored mildness. The stories are all minor by intention; some of them are entirely too flimsy, but most of them are good fun.

The City and the Stars is a curious two-period piece—Clarke's first novel, *Against the Fall of Night*, begun in 1937, and now re-written and expanded by a maturer Clarke. Some of the changes are certainly improvements—as for instance the interesting polyp-creature whom Clarke substitutes for the old man in the crater of Shalmirane. Others are at least doubtful, like the sweeping innovation by which, in effect, Clarke turns all the inhabitants of Diaspar into golems; others, like the introduction of Alvin's girl-friend Alystra, are pure padding; and still others, it seems to me, merely illuminate the original faults of the story in greater detail.

The virtues of this novel in its original, shorter version are considerable—the gentle, likable characters, the nostalgic flow of the narrative, and similar things, all of which might be summed up under the word "charm." Of plot the story—in both versions—has just enough to get along, of excitement almost none. An even more serious lack, perhaps, is the almost total absence of any specific sensory quality in the writing. Unlike real cities, Diaspar has no characteristic architecture, no dominant color or texture, no mood, no pervading sound . . . in short, it's exasperatingly thin; you can't touch, hear, see or smell it.

Much the same criticism could be made of the characters.

The differences between them seem to be mostly accidents of circumstance—one feels that they could all be put back into the Hall of Creation as raw material (the fate which Clarke has in mind for them, anyhow), and with a little suitable alteration in conditioning, re-emerge in other roles—Alvin as Jeserac, or Jeserac as Khedron, or anybody.

All the same, I find, the story has left vivid images in my mind— the golden grass of Lys, rolling in the wind; the jewel-brightness of the great insect Krif; the pulsing growth of the city of Diaspar, seen in speeded-up projection. However much the story invites you to cavil at it in detail—and there are a dozen places where I think Clarke is wrong—the whole is an evocative, oddly disturbing panorama. As in *Childhood's End*, I think, the smallness of the human characters is forgivable: the real protagonist is Time.

Chad Oliver is that rare bird, a trained scientist who writes readable fiction about his own specialty. "John Taine," a mathematician, wrote most often about biochemistry; Isaac Asimov, a biochemist, prefers psychology and sociology. But Oliver, a graduate anthropologist, is building up our field's most fascinating and comprehensive collection of anthropological science fiction. Six of his best stories (and one dud) appear in Ballantine's *Another Kind.*

"The Mother of Necessity" is a wry, witty, good-humored story about a social-engineering project that backfires: slight, but handled with surprising depth and maturity.

"Rite of Passage" is about the now-familiar "primitive" tribe that turns out to be a gang of supermen—unsurprising, since it's been done so often, but unusually well handled. This story, incidentally, contains the sentence which curdled William Atheling's milk, and which, I'm surprised and delighted to find, doesn't bother me at all. The sentence reads:

> Even here, Martin Ashley thought, so far from home, the night still came.

Nightfall is what Atheling calls it, a universal commonplace, but it's also a potent symbol of awe, exactly right in its context. Moreover, by heaven, this is exactly the kind of dazed, trying-to-grasp-it thing that *would* occur to a man landing on a strange planet. An over-refined writer would have rejected it as banal; it's to Oliver's special credit that he didn't.

"Scientific Method" is the dud. For my taste, at any rate, this variant of the "First Contact" theme is insensitive, over-derivative, and unconvincing.

"Night," although it is probably anthropological nonsense, is a deeply moving treatment of cultural impacts.

"Transformer" — the *F&SF* fantasy which deals grimly and wittily with the secret lives of model-train town "people"—is atypical Oliver, notably well written even in this collection, but minor in intent.

"Artifact," which begins casually enough, with a flint scraping tool found on the lifeless deserts of Mars, builds into the most massive, mind-widening shock ending in recent memory. This story contains the "sense of wonder," the feeling which science fiction exists to create, in such measure that it hits you with an almost physical jolt.

And "A Star Above It" is a painful collection of mistakes about time travel. The author, idiotically insistent on thinking of time as *both* fixed and plastic, trundles you over a whole series of jarring incongruities. What saves the story, barely, are the characters and the thoughtful, compassionate mood. The story does not make a nickel's worth of sense, but it means something.

In sum: Oliver's talent here shows itself as an even more impressive thing than it seemed in his first novel, *Shadows in the Sun*. At his best, as in six of these seven stories, Oliver has the kind of gift this field most sorely lacks—the ability to touch the heart of the human problem.

Frederik Pohl is a quiet, cadaverous man, amiable but withdrawn, whose restless ambition has traced out a curiously brilliant and erratic career. In 1940 he created *Super Science* and *Astonishing* for Popular Publications; as editor, during the next two years or so, he wrote prolifically for himself as "James MacCreigh" and as various percentages of "S. D. Gottesman," "Paul (for Pohl) Dennis (for Dockweiler) Lavond (for Lowndes)," Dirk Wylie and others. After the war (in which he served as an Army weatherman in Italy), he and the late Harry Dockweiler formed the Dirk Wylie Literary Agency, which had attracted most of the top-grade writers in the field at the time of its catastrophic demise; he then turned up as one-half of the strikingly successful novelistic team of Pohl and Kornbluth, and edited some notable anthologies for Ballantine and Doubleday.

Like one of John Campbell's psionics machines, the heads of Frederik Pohl's characters are empty except for little cards labeled "career soldier," or "con man," or whatever. In the stories collected as *Tomorrow Times Seven*, they gabble brightly at each other, pose and pirouette through the motions of frantic plots. Pohl's ideas are ingenious, his backgrounds carefully de-

tailed, his pace swift. Over and over again, his greedy people are
scheming, conniving, sweating to get their hands on something
of value—in "The Haunted Corpse," a mind-transferring gadget;
in "The Gentle Venusian," diamond-studded boomerangs; in "The
Day of the Boomer Dukes" and "Survival Kit," two bags of tricks
from the future; and in "The Knights of Arthur," a brain in a
prosthetic tank.   The eerie and disturbing thing about all these
stories (and about the dismally ill-formed "The Middle of Nowhere") is that in spite of all the emphasis on wealth and cupidity,
it quickly becomes plain that not one of these characters really
gives a damn.

Only in the impressive seventh story, "To See Another Mountain"—up until the last-minute gimmick that drains all the life
and warmth out of it—is there a character who seems really
human, who has any depth of feeling inside his skull: and I think
it's worth noting that only in this story is there anyone who loves
anybody else. The other stories have a host of minor virtues—
e.g., some have ingenious gostak-type opening lines, and one
("The Day of the Boomer Dukes") has a veritable rabbit punchline
of an ending—but even the best of them are as hollow as Christmas tree ornaments.

Six of the stories in this collection are a fair sample of what
Fred Pohl usually does; the seventh gives a glimpse of what he
can do.

Alternating Currents contains ten stories, of which the oldest
is "Let the Ants Try" (by "James MacCreigh," *Planet*, Winter,
1949); the others are mostly from the 1954-'55 *Galaxy*. The old
one is a fairly conventional time-travel story, not remarkable
for its ideas but for a certain unexpected wryness in the ending.
Among the newer stories, two trends seem to be at work. In about
half of these stories, Pohl has had a fresh idea and has developed
it, usually, with workmanlike but unenthusiastic competence. At its
best, as in "Happy Birthday, Dear Jesus," where it is combined
with the I-am-a-Philistine viewpoint of "Gravy Planet," this produces a memorable but faintly unconvincing story; at its worst,
as in the hideously insincere "The Mapmakers," the best thing to
do is forget it.

In the other half, the wryness is back; and these stories pack
a wallop. In "What to Do Till the Analyst Comes" with its deadly,
harmless little euphoric drug; or in "Pythias" with its bru-
tally concise disposal of the power theme; or most especially
in "Rafferty's Reasons," where a desperate little man tries to
assassinate a roomful of people with a cigar butt—although there
is not a startlingly new idea in the lot—there is a new Fred Pohl:

one who means what he says, and can say it with quiet, economical force.

Pohl's *The Case Against Tomorrow* is a mixed bag of six brilliant and incomplete stories, by one of science fiction's most scattered talents.

"The Census Takers" is a beautifully compact exercise in indirection. Entirely successful in its own terms, it plays one speculative idea (mass executions as a solution to overpopulation) against another (superior beings from the center of the earth) without wasting a word or a motion.

"The Candle Lighter" is negligible—a feeble paradox, with one of those impossibly stupid come-to-realize heroes. Also negligible is "The Celebrated No-Hit Inning"—a dismal attempt to combine science fiction with the slick funny baseball story, complete with dialogue by Ring Lardner.

"Wapshot's Demon" has a fascinatingly impudent idea in the "Semantic Polarizer." Pohl mixes it adroitly with murder; the story is compact and well visualized, and would rate at least a B in my book, if it weren't for the leaky logic of the ending.

"The Midas Plague" is a distressing example of the kind of story which became identified with *Galaxy* during the 50s; the inside-out future society, played poker-faced for snickers, in which the author, whenever he comes across an inconvenient fact or consequence, slaps a coat of paint over it and goes right ahead.

In this case, the thinking behind the story goes something like this: Expanding technology means overproduction. The solution to this is compulsory overconsumption, with ration points. Therefore the rich are poor, and the poor are rich.

This is good for one laugh, or possibly two, but there is something gaggingly irrational after a while in the spectacle of Pohl's hero choking down more food than he can eat. The question, "Why doesn't he flush the stuff down the drain?" comes up several times during the story, but Pohl never answers it, he only makes vaguely relevant-sounding noises and changes the subject. The alternate solution, that of putting robots to work using up all the stuff the hero is supposed to consume, comes thirty pages too late in the story, and is hailed by everybody as a revolutionary idea.

This is something new in idiot plots—it's second-order idiot plotting, in which not merely the principals, but everybody in the whole *society* has to be a grade-A idiot, or the story couldn't happen. Admittedly, this attitude toward amusing but intrinsically wobbly ideas gets a lot of stories written that otherwise would be discarded: but it also populates the future exclusively with lackwits.

The story proper is just as dull as it ought to be, but Pohl has embellished it with some additional scenes that are better than it deserves—fine, zany drunk episodes, involving a couple of very sharp minor characters and some highly agreeable mock poetry and politics.

The subject of "My Lady Green Sleeves" is race prejudice, and the story attacks it in a typical display of *Galaxy's* agonized irony, by substituting "wipes" (common laborers) for Jews, "figgers" (clerks) for Negroes, "greasers" (mechanics) for Mexicans, and, variously, "civil service people" and "G.I.'s" for white Anglo-Saxons. The point of all this, when we eventually get to it, seems to be that fostering class distinctions based on occupations has canceled out others based on race or religion—so that the heroine can ask, in honest ignorance, "What's a Jew?"

In its own corkscrew fashion, I suppose this is intended as a contribution toward racial egalitarianism. But it seems to me that rubbing the reader's nose repeatedly into racial hate-words in this way is the worst possible way to go about it. The story is such a mishmash of viewpoints that it's impossible to tell where (if anywhere) the author's sympathies lie; reading it as straight satire, it seems to me, you could easily construe it as an expression of bigotry. And on top of everything else, a pure racial stereotype turns up in the story itself, in the description of a man named Hiroko: "Beads of sweat were glistening on his furrowed yellow forehead." (For God's sake, Fred, "yellow man" is an epithet—Japanese have brown skins.)

When two writers collaborate, usually one writes a first draft, the other corrects and rewrites it. The Dickson-Anderson "Hoka" stories were written this way, and so were the joint efforts of L. Sprague de Camp and Fletcher Pratt.

Frederik Pohl and Cyril Kornbluth had a different method, one which involved a single draft and produced novels in jig time: the hot typewriter system. After plotting the story together, they would divide the outline into short sections. One collaborator would sit down at the typewriter and do section 1; when he was finished, he'd go downstairs, drink some coffee, read a newspaper, while the other man went up and wrote section 2.

This system has evident virtues, together with some defects. For instance, as in *Wolfbane*, by Pohl and Kornbluth, you may get a brilliant analysis of the Oriental life pattern, developed and projected onto a future civilization on this continent (1,500 calories a day: slouching gait, politeness, minuscule sub-arts—Water Watching, Clouds and Odors, Sky-Viewing . . . people named

Tropile and Boyne, in towns called Wheeling, Altoona and Gary, walking through an elaborate life-long ritual, purely and simply because their diet permits nothing better) and then when you are not looking the other man sits down at the typewriter, and you get an incredibly obtuse blurt like this: "as children account for gifts at Ecksmass with Kringle-San."

Nevertheless, *Wolfbane*, which appeared in a shorter form as a two-part serial in *Galaxy*, is one of the most entertaining jobs Pohl and Kornbluth did together. For breadth of conception, for the intellectual brilliance with which it ranges over Zen Buddhism, higher mathematics, machine shop practice, &c., &c.; for occasional fruitful ironies (e.g., the robots who wire people into the circuits of their computers); and above all for the unsentimental clarity with which it views mankind, the novel is a rewarding experience.

Jack Vance's *Big Planet*, which first appeared in *Startling* in 1952, shows this brilliant writer at the top of his form. Big Planet, where most of the action takes place, is as vividly compelling as the dream-world of Eddison's *The Worm Ouroboros*: and that's the highest praise I know.

Vance has imagined a world with Earthlike air and gravity, but 80,000 miles in circumference: a light planet, without surface metals, too big to be governed as a unit. In a period of Galactic expansion, colonies from Earth have settled here and there, each with its own crotchets and peculiarities. Except for a ban on modern weapons, Earth lets them alone.

The result is a gaudy patchwork world, as mixed-up and surprising as Burroughs' best. Set down by accident half a world away from their destination, nine Earthmen find themselves faced by an epic problem: a forty-thousand-mile march to the only safe spot on Big Planet.

After that, Big Planet itself dominates the book. Like Burroughs' Pellucidar, it colors every landscape with its own overhanging presence: "Looking to where Earth's horizon would lie, he could lift his eyes and see lands reaching far on out: pencil lines of various subtle colors, each line a plain or a forest, a sea, a desert, a mountain range. . ." Vance's descriptions, all as crisp and economical as this one, have a magical persuasiveness. Even his imaginary place-names, recited alone, have a compelling sound: Grosgarth, Montmarchy, Parambo; Lake Pellitante, the river Oust, the Blackstone Cordillera.

In Vance, as in Eddison, the background *is* the story. Even in scenes of danger and death, the heroes and their opponents alike

seem half bemused by the gigantic warm lap of a world in which
they lie: the journey on the monoline—trolleys suspended from
cables, swooping in long roller-coaster arcs from mountain to
mountain—is pure dream-world delight.

Vance's characters are defined by what they do. The narrative
is cool and detached; it's possible to believe in the heroic energy
and resourcefulness of Claude Glystra, and in his understated
romance with the Beaujolain girl, because everything is presented
as something that happens, take it or leave it: nothing is explained
or apologized for, at least until after the event.

The book is complicated, and in places I think spoilt, by an
overt rationale involving Glystra's search for an Earth-born
tyrant, Charley Lysidder, who is plotting to conquer Big Planet
with modern weapons. The last chapters turn into a gimmicky
ordeal story, also well done, but out of key with the epic form of
the story proper; here and elsewhere, when he descends to the
merely human level of tension, Vance weakens his story. Nevertheless, when the story is over, he leaves the reader souvenirs of
an unforgettable journey—twilight in Tsalombar Forest; the Tree-
men and the Beaujolains; the Cossacks and Atman the Scourge;
the fortress city of Edelweiss; the Magickers and the false gria-
mobot; the monoline; the Stanezi; the Rebbirs . . .

If you have a taste for pure, strong fantasy; if you loved the Oz
books, or *The Worm*, or Burroughs, or *Alice in Wonderland*, buy
this one.

Edgar Pangborn's first published science-fantasy story was
a novelette called "Angel's Egg" whose style and mood were
perfectly suited to the story and its narrator—a gently loving
old man who offers himself up, in a peculiarly moving kind of
self-immolation, to an "angel" from another star. The style is
leisurely and reflective; the mood is one of blended sorrow and
delight. The curious thing is that in Pangborn's two subsequent
novels, *West of the Sun* and *A Mirror for Observers*, style and
mood are precisely the same, although the first deals with the
adventures of colonists on a strange world, and the second with
the highly dramatic maneuverings of two sets of aliens, one Good,
one Evil, for the destiny of Earth.

To my mind the disparity between subject and treatment makes
West of the Sun a totally disorganized book: everything in it gives
an exasperating sense of obscured brightness; the author will not
get out of the way, but forces you to look through his own misty
substance at what he wants you to see. Even in *A Mirror for Observers*, whose Martian narrator is as elderly, as kindly and very

nearly as believable as Dr. Bannerman of "Angel's Egg," this
metaphysical cloud seems to me at times to dim the story. It is
as if the Martian eye—but this is equally true of all the stories—
sees only certain moral and emotional colors, and according as
they are present in greater or lesser degree in the landscape, its
vision passes through startling changes in depth and chiaroscuro:
rather like those pictures of What You Look Like to Your Dog.

Believing Pangborn to be human, we can only assume that he's
deliberately blinded himself in half the spectrum in order to see
more radiantly in the rest. Certainly nothing is lacking in these
stories for want of skill. It may well be that this is the only song
Pangborn was made to sing; and a mournfully beautiful song it is
—very like the thing that Stapledon was always talking about and
never quite managing to convey: the regretful, ironic, sorrowful,
deeply joyous—and purblind—love of the world and all in it.

Algis Budrys is the son of the consul general of the Lithuanian
Government in Exile; his last name, like "Stalin" or "Lenin," is
adopted: it means "sentinel." The first name is shortened, too;
its full version is Algirdas: Lithuanian is a thorny speech. Aside
from all this—and it is really irrelevant—Budrys is one of the
five or six self-directed s.f. talents to emerge since 1940. He is
like Sturgeon, not in being like Sturgeon, but in being uniquely
himself. Beyond doubt he is a leader of the new generation of s.f.
writers, and for better or worse he is going his own way.

In his first novel, *False Night,* he has taken the familiar
theme of America after a plague that destroys civilization, and
developed it neither as a Hollywood horror story nor as a Hollywood romance—but as history.

The narrative is kaleidoscopic: as the wheel turns, one character fades out to be replaced by another. The first of these is a
lone wolf named Matt Garvin; the last is his great-grandson, Jeff.
That thread—the Garvins—is one of the few that hold the book together, through about sixty years of elapsed time. But if there is
a nearly central character, it's the second-generation Caesar,
Ted Berendtsen. Here's the strength of the book: we see him as
a contemporary might—clear and sharp, up in the foreground,
at first, then more dimly as he rises in stature, hazier, as he
towers, and then only the mists that close around a legend.

Nobody but history is the hero. For those who like optimism
tempered with a little sanity, here it is—a broken world reeling,
through many violent changes, back slowly to "normality."

The writing is uneven, and so is the construction. Nevertheless,
and although Lion's hasty cutting job muddles the plot and leaves

loose ends dangling, the historic sweep of this novel is something
rare and memorable in science fiction. Any logorrheic amateur
can write a 60,000-word short story, and many do; but this, in
spite of its faults, is a novel.

Budrys' second novel, *Who?*, is ostensibly about an Allied
scientist named Martino who is captured by the Soviets after an
explosion which has severed one arm and nearly destroyed his
face. Four months later, the Soviets return a man with a metal
face and a metal arm. The question is, who is it—Martino, or
someone else?

To Budrys, this is a question transcending the individuals of
the story: "Martino," or call him "X," is an emblem of "face-
lessness." He is a dramatic metaphor, not a man; and Budrys
uses him to make a subtle and penetrating point about something
so basic in our thinking that it's ordinarily invisible to us: the
imperative need for identity, the inability of society to tolerate
a man who cannot be identified.

The human problem of X is one of enormous potentialities for
a writer of Budrys' gifts: here is a man locked inside a blank
mask of steel, unable to communicate his consciousness of his
own identity. He has just come from four months of prosthetic
surgery and Soviet interrogation. He has a thousand physical
adjustments to make to his new body. If he is Martino, his career
is in ruins; if he isn't, he is playing a tragic and dangerous game.
He is an object of horror, suspicion, repulsion.

But the symbol crowds all this out. Having decided in advance
that the question, "Who?" cannot be answered, Budrys is forced
to stay out of X's head. Even the normal human responses of
other people to the first experience of X are slurred over or
blanked out altogether. He appears on the scene, in what ought
to have been a majestic and terrible revelation, with an effect of
indifference.

The security problem represented by X is again one of potential
excitement. Martino was the key scientist in a project of great
importance to the Allies, a project which will have to be dropped
if his identity cannot be established. If X is Martino, he must be
returned to the project; if he isn't, he must be kept away from it.
Again, the symbol takes up too much room. Take the matter of
fingerprints, for instance. The prints of the fingers of X's remaining hand match those of Martino: but someone says, "His
right shoulder's a mass of scar tissue. If they can substitute
mechanical parts for eyes and ears and lungs—if they can motorize
an arm and graft it right onto him—where does that leave us?"

In other words, that X's right arm may have been removed and

Martino's substituted ... but an exploratory operation would determine whether such an operation had taken place; so nobody thinks of it. Nobody tries comparing the skin of that arm with the skin of his body. Nobody compares his fingerprints with his toeprints.

Not only that, but no one who ever knew Martino interviews X. Nobody even suggests it. The symbol demands that X be unidentifiable—so nobody tries very hard to identify him.

The scientific problems involved in giving a man servo-powered, nerve-controlled prosthetics are immense and could be made fascinating in their own right. Budrys skips over them, because, again, it is necessary to the symbol to imagine that you can't get X's skullpiece off. (Why not? Is it welded on? Riveted?) The design is arbitrary and fanciful, totally alien to the Soviet tradition of ugly functionalism. X has lips to form speech, *and* a gasket to hold a cigarette when he smokes, *and* a movable grille over that, *and* a rigid jaw over that, something like the front of a modern car. He has a power pile in his chest (for God's sake), and a blower instead of lungs. The insane resemblance to a modern automobile is carried farther: he's designed to make it impossible to repair him.

The symbol is too big. More than half of the implausibilities in this story are unnecessary to it. Any victim of a severe facial injury could be unidentifiable by his face. The metal arm contributes nothing to the puzzle, the power pile and the rest of the gadgets are superfluous. Identity can be hard enough to prove, even for whole men. The metal parts of X have just one function: they make it possible to call the novel science fiction, which essentially it is not.

The mid-part of the book demonstrates again the paralyzing effect of the symbol. Any plot development of the original situation would upset the balance; therefore Budrys is forced to alternate chapters of inept cops-and-robbers stuff, which do not advance the story, with chapters of narrative about Martino's early life, which do not advance it either, and do not even shed any light on X. They can't, the premise excludes it—X is a man who can't be identified. Young Martino is a singularly lifeless young physics student; his relatives are dull, his job is dull, and his girl friends are dull. When he meets one of them again, in the cops-and-robbers section, she makes speeches like a soap-opera heroine.

Only at the end of the novel does Budrys break his basic premise, and then only to say, in effect, that the question can be answered but the answer is meaningless. Here, finally, the symbol pays off, and the end of the story is moving and satisfying. Three characters, each briefly, come to life in the manner of

Budrys' best work: Rogers, the Allied security chief; Azarin, the Soviet security chief; and at the very end, X himself. Parts of the story are written in Budrys' usual workmanlike and lucid style; others are surprisingly gauche, full of mixed metaphors, tautologies and grammatical monstrosities.

This novel, I think, represents Budrys' first published attempt to get one foot out of science fiction. Bad novels often break the ground for good ones, and this may be Budrys' first step toward the critical and financial rewards he deserves. Meanwhile, I hope I may be allowed to say that diluting science fiction is not the way to improve it: that science fiction must be good in its own way, or it can never be good at all.

Who? was nine-tenths non-science-fiction. *The Falling Torch* is ten-tenths: it's the story of a Lithuanian boy, brought up in America, returning to his homeland to liberate it from the Soviets; and it would undoubtedly have been published in that form if the author could have found any publisher to buy it. Because he couldn't, the Lithuanians have been turned into "Earthmen," the Soviets into "Invaders," Lithuania into America, and America into the planet Cheiron, of "Alpha Centaurus" (*sic*). For the most part, only the nomenclature has been changed (with an occasional slip, as when a character refers to "international law" in speaking of the relations between planets).

Whether the "straight" version of the novel would have been successful in its own terms, it's impossible to guess. The novel as it stands is an uneven performance, from the brilliant opening and closing chapters, through the rather muddled thought and action of the main section, to some downright bad writing, hasty transitions, and inadequate motivations in the middle of the book.

In form this is a growing-up story, but it is never quite clear, at least to me, what turns the hero overnight from a callow youth into a magnetic leader of men. Muddy writing is partly to blame; I am inclined to suspect that muddy thinking underlies it. At his best, Budrys is brilliantly lucid and believable. The old man, the hero's father, who appears at the beginning and end of the book, is a moving, thoroughly convincing portrait.

The portrait is beautiful, because it is honest and deeply felt. At a guess, the main section of this novel is neither: Budrys does not really believe that Lithuania can be liberated by any remarkably gifted young man from America. Instead of writing what he thought would happen, he wrote what he thought the editor would like to read.

The impulse to inject a little hokum into a story like this is almost irresistible, as I can testify, when the author is so painfully aware that he is writing something that will be looked on with suspicion or incomprehension by most people. But what's the use of getting out (or partly out) of science fiction, if not to leave the hokum behind?

Flight Into Yesterday (reprinted as *The Paradox Men*) represents the brilliant peak of Charles L. Harness' published work; Harness told me in 1950 that he had spent two years writing the story, and had put into it every fictional idea that occurred to him during that time.

He must have studied his model with painstaking care. You'll find here the gaudy van Vogtian empire; the love story, crackling with the tension of love-plus-hatred; the brutal swiftness of the plotting; the mutant superman who's unaware of his own extraordinary powers, and who must contend not only with his enemies, but with his suspicious friends; the philosophical (or medical, or historical) system elevated into a Rule For Everything; yes, even the misplaced jocularity, the impossible but fascinating conversations, the double-takes, the stage asides and the exasperating nothing-statements that were typical of van Vogt at his height.

—And all this, packed even more tightly than the original, symmetrically arranged, the loose ends tucked in, and every last outrageous twist of the plot fully justified both in science and in logic.

For instance, the mingling of atomic power and swordplay in Harness' 22nd-century empire looks typically van Vogtian—until you notice that Harness has provided an elaborate and thoroughly convincing technological reason for the use of swords.

A basic premise of all pulp fiction, from which magazine science fiction is derived, is that only the fear of imminent, violent death can make the human psyche function at its full intensity. (And it might be argued that the wider incidence of just this fear since about 1945 has been a factor in the decline of the pulps.) Harness carries the consequences of this notion as far as they will go. Re-reading this book reminded me of Campbell's description of *The World of Ā*:

> . . . something like a 550 volt A.C. power line; it looks innocent, but once you get hold of it you can't let go till somebody shuts off the power.

The sheer quantity of violent events in the story is enough to hold you, even though they're so compressed as to be almost drained of emotional meaning. While falling apparently to his

death from a "mile-high" window, for instance, Harness' hero
Alar reflects:

> He would not live to tell his companion Thieves that his reaction
> to death was simply a highly intensified observation.

An atomic attack on America, destined to destroy the locale of
the story "to a depth of several miles" serves Harness for the
background to one brief climactic scene; the duel between Alar
and his most dangerous opponent takes place in a "solarion," a
sort of Solar raft, which is sliding to certain destruction in the
middle of a sunspot. Burned in an incinerator, tortured insensible,
stunned by explosions, run through in a duel, Alar merely bounds
on to more strenuous adventures, his pulse rate responding (in
advance!) to each mortal danger, but his brain ticking along like
a well-adjusted clock.

For every peril, the developing superman has a new and more
impudent answer. There's a limit beyond which this kind of thing
turns to farce, and Harness has passed it more than once. There's
the scene in which Alar is trying to escape from a guardsman by
emitting electromagnetic radiation from his eyes, and so trans-
mitting false orders to the guard's button radio.

> Alar's eyes were growing beady and feverish but nothing was
> happening.
> He knew he was capable of emitting photic beams in the infra-
> red with a wave length of at least half a millimeter. The U.H.F.
> intercom band certainly shouldn't exceed a meter. Yet his eyes
> were pouring out the electromagnetic spectrum from a few Ang-
> stroms to several meters, without raising a squeak in the receptor
> button.
> Something had gone wrong. He was aware of Keiris' body
> shivering near his side.
> Suddenly the button whistled. The officer stopped uncertainly.
> A bead of perspiration slid down Alar's cheek and dangled at
> his stubbled chin.
> "A.M.," said Keiris quietly.

Blackout! But even this is not enough to destroy the web of
compulsion Harness' story weaves. If you get a surfeit of the
sledgehammer plot, there's a highly technical scientific argument
to engage your attention; if that palls, there's the uncommonly
intense and evocative sub-plot concerning the heroine, Keiris
and if you should become bored with that, look out, George, here
comes the sledgehammer again!

. . . Plus the fact that, if you have read Harness before, you
know you can trust him to wind up this whole ultracomplicated

structure, somehow, symmetrically and without fakery.

Finally,.when it's all done, the story means something. Harness' theme is the triumph of spirit over flesh: again and again, his protagonists survive crippling mutilations — Follansbee in "Fruits of the Agathon" is blinded, Keiris in *Flight Into Yesterday* loses both arms — and press on, as cheerfully as if they had merely lost a slipper, to new peaks of experience—often as not, to death and transfiguration. This is the rock under all Harness' hypnotic cat's-cradles of invention—faith in the spirit, the denial of pain, the affirmation of eternal life.

21. CURIOSA

ROGER LEE VERNON'S collection, *The Space Frontiers*, is unique in several ways. First, it's an original paperback, published by a company we had learned to regard as a die-hard reprint house. Second, it is the work of a man who has never before published any science fiction anywhere; Signet identifies him as a high-school teacher who enjoys writing (fair warning!); nor is it a first novel, which would be common enough, but a first book of short stories. Third, it is the work of a man who, to all appearances, has not so much as *read* any science fiction for the last twenty years.

The first thing that strikes you about these stories is the astonishing archaism of their style; for ignorance, for awkwardness and for sophomoric enthusiasm, several of them are the very spit of a 1930 pulp epic.

"Battle," for instance, is a slam-bang chunk out of an altogether incredible future war—in which the airborne hero, cruising at 6,000 mph, slaughters the enemy by battalions in the air and on the ground (sighting on them by means of "a viso-screen with adjustable knobs"); escapes the frightful "Oscar beams" by "zig-zagging . . . contrary to their wavelength"; and finally gets shot down in one piece but completely covered with debris, reflecting philosophically that "There had always been battles and there would, perhaps, always be."

"Incident in Space" takes place in an area muzzily identified by the author as "the Outer Orbits," and is full of violently enthusiastic detail about spaceships. For instance:

> In the early days numerous ships had been torn into ribbons by meteorites. Ships would fly into a bed of the rapidly moving objects and be filled with holes. [Noble phrase!] Now the gravitation locator solved all such problems. . . This device spotted and accurately charted the course of every particle. . . when the object was still about three minutes away.

Farther on, we are told, "The fastest the earth ship could travel was L7, seven times the speed of light." And a little later, after an encounter with an alien ship, a character remarks, "No. They're gone. If they're over eight thousand miles out we couldn't see them with anything."

Gaw!

For the record, a ship moving at "L7, seven times the speed of light," would travel eight thousand miles, not in three minutes, but in about six thousandths of a second.

Whatever Vernon teaches, it can't be mathematics....

"Xenophobia" is a good deal better: it deals conventionally but competently with the problem of a future society which has split up into tiny, mutually antagonistic family groups. Overlong, and spotted with the bruises Vernon leaves on the English language (e.g., "a round circular-like thing"), the story nevertheless has something to say.

"The City and the Ship" is another muddled space-opera (containing a planet which on one page has an impossible atmosphere 6,000 miles deep, and eight pages later has another, equally impossible, "just inches from the surface"). In about twice the necessary length, it deals with the familiar theme of the robot civilization after its creators are dead.

"The Chess Civilization" is a sprightly satire, about a world whose dominant passion is chess. Except for the embarrassing 1930 pseudo-science Vernon has put into the mouth of his inventor, this story is readable and good fun.

"The Plant World," as full of Vernonisms as any of the rest ("So unafraid of the presence of danger as to be foolhardy"), is an intriguing van Vogtish treatment of the planetary intelligence theme. The story's logic is badly marred by the world-girdling plant's ambition to copy the Earth spaceship and so carry unbroken tendrils of itself to other planets: if Vernon's plant-thing doesn't know this is impossible, his spacemen ought to; but the denouement is satisfactorily ingenious and sensible.

In "The Stop Watch," Vernon takes H. G. Wells' classic "The New Accelerator" and waters it down into an adolescent fantasy. "Population Crisis: 2550" can only be discussed as a tract; as such, it's unnecessarily gloomy.

"The Death Seekers," the final story, though well scarred by Vernon's awkwardness, is not easy to dismiss. Vernon has here taken the problem of the benevolent tyranny of robots, only sketchily examined in Jack Williamson's *The Humanoids*, and developed it in fine, moody detail. Along with his 1930 faults, Vernon has this 1930 virtue: his stories are concerned with the great unsolved problems that perplex and delight us, rather than with extensions of the trivia that keep us earthbound.

What bothers me about this volume, in its occasional goodness as well as its overwhelming badness, is the feeling it gives me of having lost two decades somewhere. Granted, modern science fiction lacks some of the sincerity and inner meaning it once had; but to recapture that, is it really necessary to go back to kinder-garten?

Again, this book is not so bad if you only take the space-opera out of it: but Signet appears to think that the space-opera is what makes it worth having: title, cover design and blurbs all support this idea.

What I am afraid of is that Signet might be right. This kind of ignorant nonsense ought to be well adapted to the existing mental set of a reader to whom "space," "planets," "galaxies," are all words without any specific meaning, conveying nothing but a vague feeling of "out there." If so—if there is a vast untapped audience of unsophisticated (and uneducated) science fiction readers just waiting to be fed—then we may expect to see an immediate mushroom-growth of Vernons . . . out of whom, in another twenty years, a little coterie of polished science fiction writers will evolve, to sit and wonder why their stuff doesn't sell.

What a nightmare! Thank heaven I don't believe it for a moment!

Another most peculiar item is Jeffery Lloyd Castle's *Satellite E One*. This one was written by someone without the remotest idea of what a novel is: it's three-quarters treatise, all very correct and British, some of it remarkably astute, about the probable development of a space station project.

It is also, apparently, a book written by someone who has not read much of the previous literature on the subject; the publishers describe him laconically as "a scientist," which I suppose means he is an archaeologist or something equally irrelevant. Perhaps because of this, on the two occasions when the book suddenly (and briefly) becomes a dramatic story, although the situations are from stock—in one, the pilot of the first manned spaceship is trapped on it and has to be rescued; in the other, a man in a spacesuit drifts out of radio range—Castle has handled them with unusual freshness and vigor.

The only thing that unites the jumbled pieces of this book is the temporal progress of the space station project, and evidently Castle thought that was enough. It's written in fits and snatches, past tense changing to present, hero's viewpoint interrupted by narrator's, like an amateur film in which the action stops at interesting places to let the announcer harangue you.

This narrator, one of the three people who take turns telling the story, spends half his time explaining the ABC's of space-flight at great muddled length, and nearly the other half spinning out a fantastic series of bright ideas—e.g., two brand-new and wonderfully ingenious methods of simulating free-fall conditions on Earth; a logical but slightly breathtaking scheme for making use of waste products in the space station (they're delicious!); an absolutely convincing fugue undergone by the narrator when he first experiences free flight in a long closed tube—apparently he thinks he's a sperm again—and a lot more.

And yet, particularly in the early part of the book, this same writer delivers himself of one scientific and logical howler after another. Hero #1, for instance, wears an Egyptian-mummy kind of spacesuit not equipped with direct vision; instead, he has two little television screens, one for each eye, at a range of about one inch (!). Wearing this monstrosity, he is loaded into the rocket *face down* for the 8-g takeoff—meaning of course that he takes the weight on his well-padded facial bones, rib-cage, anterior pelvic bones, kneecaps and so on, while the delicate, fragile back and rump are tucked up out of harm's way.

It says a good deal for American publishing, I suppose, that so odd a book as this could find a patron. It would be nice if the same easy tolerance extended to the good ones as well.

If, like me, you have been bored or disgusted by previous saucer books, try *The Report on Unidentified Flying Objects*, by Edward J. Ruppelt.

Ruppelt is the former Air Force captain who, as head of Project Blue Book, was charged with investigating flying saucers from 1951 to 1953. In this big book, he tells the whole story of the UFO investigations, including the two eras that preceded his—Project Sign and Project Grudge.

The story of the investigation itself, never before told, is equally as fascinating as the UFO story imbedded in it.

Ruppelt gives the impression of a man with a strong sense of responsibility. One of the most attractive things about this book is the author's scrupulous avoidance of speculation about UFOs; he is trying to give you the facts, such as they are, and leave his opinions out of it. But behind the sober and responsible Ruppelt there is evidently a Ruppelt with a big grin—richly merited by the antics of the Air Force brass who (a) went overboard in 1947 for the view that UFOs are spaceships; (b) made a 180° turn in 1949 and declared that all UFO sightings were mass hallucinations; and (c) tried to end the problem by a publicity blackout, on the theory that if nobody mentioned them, the saucers would go away.

If this book adds up to any one conclusion, it is that the problem is not that simple. Project Blue Book and its predecessors have accumulated thousands of "good," i.e., credible and detailed, UFO reports—some 27 per cent of which, after the most rigid examination, cannot be checked off as sightings of known objects—planets, meteors, atmospheric illusions, balloons, &c. Included are radar sightings, and combined radar-visual sightings.

Not everybody who has studied UFOs thinks they are interplanetary. The report of the blue-ribbon scientific panel assembled in 1953 to evaluate UFO data said: "We as a group do not believe that it is impossible for some other celestial body to be inhabited by intelligent creatures. Nor is it impossible that these creatures could have reached such a state of development that they could visit the earth. However, there is nothing in all of the so-called 'flying saucer' reports that we have read that would indicate that this is taking place."

But people who have seen UFOs are nearly unanimous on one point: what they saw was something real.

Whatever they are, UFOs appear to have six things in common: brilliant appearance (white or metallic by day, bright lights by night); oval or spherical shape; completely silent operation; high speed; unapproachability; erratic motion (many reports mention the UFOs' "violent oscillation").

How much of this pattern is really useful in speculating about the nature of the UFOs, it's hard to say. The trouble is that there is still no hard evidence, nothing but the reports of observers and a few instrument recordings of doubtful interpretation. The incident of the Florida scoutmaster who claimed to have been knocked out by a ball of fire from a landed saucer has puzzling aspects, but probably most readers will agree with Ruppelt in classifying it reluctantly among the hoaxes: vivid as it is, the report simply does not have the feel of the bona fide UFO sightings.

Spaceships or not, why do the UFOs concentrate over "interesting" military and civil installations, rather than averaging out according to population density? Why is there an annual peak in UFO sightings in July, and another in December?

The investigation is still going on. We are not done with the saucers yet.

Here's a real curiosity—a primitive science fiction novel, whose plot in several ways strikingly resembles that of *The Sky-*

lark of Space: *My Journeys With Astargo,* by Perl T. Barnhouse. (Bell Publications, Denver, 1952; 212 pp., paperbound, no price listed anywhere.)

Unlike Dr. Smith's Richard Seaton, who found his motive power by accident, and financed the building of his spaceship simply by being pals with a multimillionaire, Jack McCune and his sidekick Clif Sumner earn what they get the hard way; the first 28 pages of the book are taken up with preliminaries.

McCune and Sumner—both cowboys and Army veterans—have, as the author puts it, both been bitten by the same bug—"cosmic energy." Meeting again after the war, they decide to team up in pursuit of this mathematical will-o'-the-wisp; later on they enlist a third partner, a Southern youth named Albert Stardorf, Star for short. Living on McCune's ranch at first, later working a mine acquired by McCune in an odd but perfectly plausible fashion, they acquire the knowledge and the capital they need; this takes them two years. Then there's the matter of certain minerals essential to the process; the world-wide hunt for these consumes seven years more—and finally, something like twelve years from the starting line, they're ready to begin building a spaceship.

The ship, like the *Skylark,* is spherical and is propelled by anti-gravity. Its construction is described with considerable precision, and includes solutions of several engineering problems which, to the best of my recollection, Dr. Smith overlooked. When it's built, the trio—with a carefully-winnowed crew—makes a trial flight to Mars via the Moon. (Mars, they find, has unpleasant weather but is well-populated; there are "rank tasting animals that must have degenerated from a cross of goat and camel, a kind of cony . . . a fleet but pugnacious swinelike beast . . . mice . . . jackals, bobtailed weasels . . . water insects, toads, and . . . wild ducks . . . .") They then decide to head for Sirius.

It takes them nine years to get there; when they do, they discover an Earthlike planet; land; and—again like Dr. Smith's voyagers—open communications with the inhabitants by means of a telepathic instrument, a "mentagraph." This was a local invention in *The Skylark of Space,* but the Astargonauts brought it with them; where they got it, I'm unable to discover. At any rate the planet—whose name is Garza—turns out to be unequally divided between two nations—the Ruzos and (surprise!) the outnumbered Amacans. The Ruzos, under a ruthless leader named (surprise!) Stalo, have a People's Republic, in which the proletariat has had its wits liquidated and its hide covered with fur in order to save expense and trouble; the Amacans are democratic and much nicer, but our friends don't discover this until they've spent some months in Ruzo. McCune, who must be nudging fifty by now, has undergone the Ruzonian rejuvenation and longevity treatment. Then, diplomatic relations becoming strained, they flee to Amaca and—again as in *The Skylark of Space*—aid in the overthrow of Ruzo and are repaid by the grateful Amacans with a bigger and better replica of their spaceship. This second ship is *Astargo*, the first having been christened *Pioneerer*; the genesis of the new name had better be explained in the author's words:

> ...we had named (the ship) by combining part of the word astral and argo, Jason's ship. Then too, the three syllables of the name, A-star-go, fitted the purpose of the ship pretty nicely.

...Anyhow, while *Astargo* is still abuilding, McCune becomes enamoured of the Emperor's daughter Maysel (Amaco, as I say, is a democracy; but the people have elected a temporary emperor, Roman-fashion, to deal with the threat of Ruzo) who, it turns out, has been promised in marriage to a stinker named Mertos. Mertos is blackmailing Maysel's old man by threatening to reveal some indiscretion committed in his gay-dog youth. While McCune is trying to persuade the Emperor to face the music, Mertos—still again as in *The Skylark of Space*, but about thirty chapters later—makes off with Maysel, and McCune is obliged to fly to the rescue.

Following this, the new ship is stocked and commissioned; McCune and Maysel are married (every other member of the ship's complement having already acquired a Garzan bride), rejuvenation treatments are handed out all around; and after another nine or ten-year journey, during which Maysel and most of the other brides become mothers, the augmented crew finds itself on another Earthlike planet, which they christen Earthonia.

Another six years, another star. On the way, McCune is tempted into dalliance with somebody else's wife, but his conscience asserts itself at the crucial instant; this is a disappointment in a way, but refreshing all the same—it's the sort of thing that never would have occurred to Seaton for three zillionths of a milli-microsecond.

The new planet, Perfecto, looks so good to the travelers that they elect to stay and build a permanent, self-sufficient settlement. With rare good sense, Barnhouse doesn't minimize the difficulties of this undertaking—four years go by before they're ready to build so much as a house, and six more before the colony can get along without supplies from the ship. Finally, twenty-seven years after the landing, the McCunes and seventeen other couples again take off in *Astargo*, this time heading homeward

Stopping off briefly at four solar systems on the way, they reach Earth approximately one hundred and fifty years after the maiden flight of the *Pioneerer*—only to discover that, like Garza, Earth has become a communist world-state. (They arrive in the year 2045, which, unless Mr. Barnhouse and I use different systems of subtraction, must mean they left circa 1895—in which case, among other difficulties, it's hard to say what American war McCune and Sumner could have been in.) This problem is short work for the Astargonauts, and would have been even shorter except for a curious lapse of judgment on McCune's part: repairing the ship on Mars after a disastrous and unnecessary shellacking, they return and bomb the living blazes out of Moscow, Prague, Budapest, Berlin, London, Ottawa, Washington, Honolulu, Tokyo and Peking. What's left of the world capitulates promptly and democracy is restored; but McCune & Co., finding that no trace remains of any of their families, decide to return to Perfecto, this time for good.

My Journeys With Astargo, as the reader may have inferred, has numerous faults; but it has a good many virtues too. McCune's story, told by himself—and unpolished by anyone with more knowledge of grammar—is good-humored and zestful. When he's writing about cattle-ranching, mining or structural engineering, he's clearly on familiar ground, and expresses himself well and concisely; and even when he touches on more abstruse subjects with which, equally clearly, he has no acquaintance, the gorgeous stews of five-dollar words he concocts are worth cherishing for their own sake.

Judging by the look of it, this volume was manufactured by a medium-sized job-printing concern, possibly at the author's expense; presumably the novel was previously submitted to trade publishers, and presumably it was rejected—but I must admit I can't see why. In style and plot it is no worse than, say, *When Worlds Collide*; and compared with *The Blind Spot*, it is as Shakespeare to Mickey Spillane.

Vaughan Wilkins' *Valley Beyond Time* is a peculiar product of eclecticism, put together from ill-matched pieces of this and that, some of them quite beautiful, some very odd. It has a long waggle-tailed plot with its back broken in several places, a cheerful gang of mutually incomprehensible characters (some of whom speak what Wilkins takes to be the American language), and many other bright-colored anomalies.

The first chunk is a perfectly ordinary puzzle story about a man who vanishes on the isle of Caldy and reappears seven years later, having been gone (as he thinks) only a night; this is com-

plicated by the fact that two of the characters—Senator Benaiah
Purvis and his secretary, Silver Honeyhill (*boy!*)—are supposed
to be Texans, while the rest are almost desperately British.

> "You know almost enough to send us to the lunatic asylum, Mr.
> Furrow," said Sir Henry, "so you may as well know that Miss
> Honeyhill's chauffeuse is in reality Lady Diana Belcombe, eldest
> daughter of the Duke of Cumber. She is the only child of his first
> marriage."
> "Good God!" exclaimed Mr. Furrow, obviously more shaken by
> this revelation than by any fourth-dimensional adventures.

It was at this point that I first noticed the book had turned
into a P. G. Wodehouse novel; but while I was still waiting for
the younger son to hide the diamonds in a flower pot, the scene
changed again, and the tone with it.

Now Purvis, "R. R.," the above-mentioned lady chauffeuse, and
a young viscount answering to the name of "Midge," have all
crossed the dimensional border into Elfhame, which turns out to
be a silly world tinted pastel like cakes of bathroom deodorant.
Honest Celtic legend turns up here intermingled with astonishing
bloopers, as when a local princess introduces Midge in turn to
her mother, whose name is Branwen, and her horse, whose name
is Arianrhod . . . both these names being those of Celtic love
goddesses, and one being about as appropriate for a horse as the
other.

Wilkins' style, incidentally, is fluent and colorful, with some
rewarding things in it—like the delightfully horrid description of
an American car on p. 75, or like this description of what it's like
to pass through the dimensional barrier: "There had been but the
sensation of a damp fluttering kiss, such as that of a bursting
bubble. That was all." . . . But for the most part Wilkins' writing
has the slippery, fluid feel of prose that has neither been forged
nor tempered, but has only slithered out half-aware. A lot of it is
nothing but elegant clichés, like this flatulent passage from p. 80:

> . . . So great seemed their isolation that it was as though they
> had reached the end of space and time and stood together—young
> woman and small boy — on the very verge of nothingness, or,
> perhaps, eternity.

There follows a long bit all about the other world, which is one
of those exasperating places where everybody talks like a cross
between Longfellow and a wooden Indian, and you *wish* to blazes
somebody, just once, would scratch his arse, or belch, or get a
charley horse.

Then it turns out that Midge and his princess friend are going to be separated, so they escape together back into normal space. And, with a wrench, the story changes still again, this time to a really dismal tragedy. Our friends seem to have gone into the other world for the sole purpose of returning with a jaundiced outlook on this one; and Wilkins bangs away at that one note, like the sound of a boot on a dented chamber pot, for what seems eternities. To his credit, he makes our civilization sound a thoroughly gloomy thing, full of the funereal ticking of clocks.

Then there's another mismated slice of fantasy, this one a rather glorious battle in the Senator's half of the other world; then another sliver of tragedy, followed by the butt-end of the other-world fantasy to cap the edifice. Senator Purvis and R. R., both transmogrified, have perished in the aforesaid battle, but Midge and his princess are reunited. Miss Honeyhill, who after marrying Midge's father, the Earl of Morfa, has turned into a wicked stepmother, is left behind, together with divers supporting characters, all wearing surprised wooden expressions, like puppets who had expected better of their creator.

I don't know what the bejesus the author thought he was up to: writing an American fairy tale, maybe.

Morey Bernstein is a young family-business executive of Pueblo, Colorado, whose hobby is therapeutic hypnosis. In 1952, he tried taking a subject in deep trance back beyond her own birth, into a previous life. The results made *The Search for Bridey Murphy*— that is, about half of it. Thirty pages are taken up by appendices —supplementary material about hypnosis—and the actual record of the experiment does not begin until page 106: until that point, the book is concerned with Bernstein himself and the steps by which he became interested in hypnosis, ESP and reincarnation.

During the original session, and on five subsequent occasions, the subject assumed the personality of one Bridey Murphy, born in Cork, Ireland, in 1798, deceased in Belfast in 1864.

The question is, was there a Bridey Murphy?

Due to the paucity of the records (and to Bernstein's inept questioning), this question can probably never be answered, and it will only irritate many people that it should have been asked at all. Since the subject also described her death and burial as Bridey Murphy, and her sojourn in an immaterial world before being reborn in her present body, the question is of some interest.

Between the discontinuance of the experiment and the hurried publication of this book, some superficial investigations were made by correspondence in Ireland. So far, one of the items which have been checked out in this way is astonishing, and several others are suggestive, but there is no solid evidence.

This leaves us the transcripts themselves, and they are just the same: suggestive in many places, astonishing once or twice, but never any proof. The author, who in places sounds like a prize jerk, has not done justice to this subject, nor have the publishers. The question remains open; all we can hope is that it may perhaps be a little more open than it was.

Like science fiction writers, medical hypnotists are a small, overlooked and misunderstood group of dedicated people, whose field, every so often, erupts around them into a popular sensation. It's hard to say which irritates them more, the ten years' neglect or the nine days' wonder. Qualified members of the Society for Clinical and Experimental Hypnosis labor for years, publish textbooks, journals and annual reviews. Nobody hears about it. A parlor hypnotist in Colorado blunders into an interesting trance phenomenon, endangers his victim's sanity, misstates, misquotes, misevaluates, misleads. He writes a best-seller.

A Scientific Report on "The Search for Bridey Murphy," a symposium written by Margaretta K. Bowers, M.D., Milton V. Kline, Ph.D., F. L. Marcuse, Ph.D., Bernard B. Raginsky, M.D., Harold Rosen, M.D., and Arthur Shapiro, M.D., turns Morey Bernstein's shabby conjuror's hat inside out, revealing ignorance,[1] recklessness,[2] egotism,[3] and thinly concealed aggression. Bernstein's own records, in particular the tapes of the Virginia Tighe sessions, demonstrate his ruthless obsession with what Bowers aptly calls "The Search For Morey Bernstein." Bowers, by the way, anticipates the discovery made by a Hearst reporter: "Is it impossible that Bridey is simply a very wonderful, meaningful memory of an old Irish neighbor who relived her youth in Cork or Belfast through the response of the child Ruth?"

Who was Bridey Murphy? (a) An Irish lady of that name who lived across the street from Virginia Tighe when she was a little girl. (b) A secondary personality, either dormant since childhood, or created by Virginia Tighe in response to Bernstein's urgent demand. Such acquiescence is typical of hypnotic subjects, who will obligingly produce "memories" of previous existences in Ireland, India, or even on other planets.[4] The un-

1. Bernstein confuses hypnotics with narcotics, narcoanalysis with narcosynthesis, hypnotherapy with hypnoanalysis.

2. He admits treating headaches by hypnotism with no knowledge of their causes.

3. There are 182 pages in Bernstein's book about Morey Bernstein; next to nothing about Virginia Tighe.

4. Cf. Flournoy's *From India to the Planet Mars.*

conscious mind appears never to forget anything, and can turn up useful fragments to fit any story. Hence the surface plausibility of "Bridey Murphy," and hence the flimsiness of the story under close examination. The medical hypnotists, working in their accustomed obscurity, are astonished that anyone should find this kind of material extraordinary, or should be deceived by it for a moment.

Now this argues a failure of communication at both ends of the scale. Bernstein is a stupid bright boy, what the Germans call *dummschlau*, and it is difficult to find any politer word for his publishers than "crooks"; but this is only half the trouble. Bernstein and Doubleday were able to impose their hoax on the public partly because the responsible hypnotists have been buried in their laboratories. The real story of medical hypnosis, as sketched in this book, is even more fascinating than the sideshow trumpery of "Bridey Murphy": is it too much to ask that somebody should have told it *before* Bernstein came along?

But the answer to that, I suppose, is partly in the gobbledegook of Raginsky's Chapter 1, and partly in a wry story told in Chapter 4 by Shapiro: A young Czech, apprenticed to a shoemaker, prescribed some simple remedies for his neighbors and soon got a wide reputation as a healer. Eventually the medical authorities challenged him to produce a license to practice medicine—and he did. He was a graduate of a Prague medical school, but the cost of setting up an office was beyond him, and so he had apprenticed himself to the shoemaker.

As soon as this became known, his popularity ended; he had been unmasked, you see, as a fake quack.

Überwindung von Raum und Zeit, herausgegeben von Gotthard Gunther. Karl Rauch Verlag, Dusseldorf und Bad Salzig, 1952; 237 pp., unschatzbar.

Dieses Buch—no, the hell with that—this book contains seven magazine science fiction stories by American writers. The list follows:

"Desertion," by Clifford D. Simak
"Nightfall," by Isaac Asimov
"Who Goes There?" by John W. Campbell, Jr.
"The Lotus Eaters," by Stanley G. Weinbaum
"Time and Time Again," by H. Beam Piper
"The Monster," by A. E. van Vogt
"Mimsy Were the Borogoves," by Lewis Padgett

The selections, as you can see, are excellent; even the van

Vogt is the product of one of those rare occasions when the old master managed to be entertaining *and* make sense.

Perhaps a more interesting consideration, for American readers, is the effect upon these stories of translation into the awful German language. I have spent some time on this question, and have looked into it thoroughly; and I believe no serious student will contradict me when I say that, on the whole, the German text represents an enormous improvement over the English.

Take, for example, the well-known first sentence of Campbell's "Wer Da?"

The place stank.

This is a short, skinny, pallid sentence; it understates; it is half ashamed of itself. But see what a robust, impressive, nose-filling thing it becomes in the German:

Der Raum war voller Gestank.

Even when our English-speaking writer is doing his best, as in Padgett's:

> "S-s-s-spit!" Emma shrieked, overcome by a sudden fit of badness. "*Spit.*"

—the Teuton can better him without even breathing hard:

> "Ssspucke!" schrie Emma in einem plötzlichen Anfall von Ungezogenheit. "*Spucke.*"

To be sure, there are inevitable difficulties, rifts between the English and the German Weltanschauungen; for example when a recently-revived corpse in "Wiedererweckung" mentions pink elephants, there is little to be done; the German, even with delirium tremens, never sees pink elephants; he sees white mice. And in "Die Lotusesser," although Oscar comes off fairly well with "To me I am a man to you," the whole thing breaks up in utter confusion when Ham is supposed to feed Oscar the word he needs by saying, "There's a chance that there is no word!" In German, "there's a chance" is *möglicherweise,* and "the law of chance" is *das Gesetz der Wahrscheinlichkeit,* and that is that.

The most serious deficiency in the German language is of course its entire lack of nonsense words; thus Padgett's glossatch is firmly pinned down as Schrank, which means cupboard; and whereas a French translation of "Jabberwocky" is enough to drive you out of your mind, the German is merely rather sad. The stanza which appears in the Padgett story, retranslated, goes roughly like this:

'Twas dampish, and the slippery stones
Slid tossing in the web;
Miserable were the burgherlegs
And whoever could not go must stay.

Gunther identifies the source of these lines, in his Kommentar at the end of the volume, as a Kinderbuch; quotes them in the English, and remarks:

Do you understand this? Naturally not; but rest assured, the Editor does not understand it, either.

This is a great pity in more ways than one—it means, for one thing, that Algis Budrys' delightful "The Weeblies" will never penetrate the language barrier; and, more generally, I assume it means that none of these stories, however capable the translations, will have quite the effect upon German audiences which the writer had in mind.

In his determinedly didactic commentary, Gunther explains "Mimsy Were the Borogoves" as a companion-piece to an anecdote about Shelley; I'm reasonably sure this will come as a surprise to Kuttner. The Kuttner Syndrome, incidentally, can now be considered an international phenomenon: under "Über die Autoren dieses Buches" appears a note beginning as follows:

Lewis Padget: Pseudonym für Henry Kuttner (anderes Pseudonym: Jack Vance) . . .

Gunther also takes the view that American science fiction is some sort of mystical forerunner of a new Metaphysik; this seems equally dubious to me, but now that the tales are being translated into German, I suppose, anything can happen.

22. B-R-R-R!

THE PLEASURE of being horrified, moderately and for a fee, is a rather peculiar one. There's an analogy with the thrill of a roller-coaster ride—it's fun to be scared, when you know you can get off at the end of the line.

But people ride roller-coasters every summer; the horror business is not so dependable. There was a flood of horror films and stories during the 30s and early 40s; then nothing—then, fifteen years later, along they came again.

All this raises a number of baffling questions. There's the riddle of horror's on-again off-again popularity, to which I'll come back later. There's the psychological puzzle of why it should be fun to be frightened at all; and there's the question, paramount from the writer's point of view:

How can you scare a reader with something that doesn't exist?

Put in this form, the question has a clear answer: You can't. If an imaginary monster doesn't correspond to something that already exists, if only in the reader's subconscious, obviously it isn't going to scare him.

For this reason, most of the stories in *The Macabre Reader*, edited by Donald A. Wollheim, strike me as tedious. They belong to the pseudo-Poe school with its rococo style ("The malignant influence seemed to have departed the vicinity") and its conviction that the horrible must never be described, only hinted at. The reader's own imagination is supposed to fill in the gaps: but mine doesn't.

Eight of the ten stories in *Br-r-r-!*, edited by Groff Conklin, don't scare me, either, although some of them are enjoyable in other ways.

But this hits me where I live:

It crawled out of the darkness and hot damp mold into the cool
of a morning. It was huge. It was lumped and crusted with its
own hateful substance, and pieces of it dropped off as it went its
way, dropped off and lay writhing, and stilled, and sank putrescent
into the forest loam. ("It," by Theodore Sturgeon.)

And so does this:

There was silence, or as much silence as the jungle ever holds.
My own throat went dry. And what I have said is insanity, but this
is much worse. I felt Something waiting to see what I would do.
It was, unquestionably, the most horrible sensation I had ever
felt. I do not know how to describe it. What I felt was—not a
personality, but a mind. I had a ghastly feeling that Something
was looking at me from thousands of pairs of eyes, that it was all
around me.

I shared, for an instant, what that Something saw and thought.
I was surrounded by a mind which waited to see what I would do.
But it was not a sophisticated mind. It was murderous, but inno-
cent. It was merciless, but naive. ("Doomsday Deferred," by
Murray Leinster.)

Sturgeon's powerful story, from *Unknown*, exploits the shuddery
old idea of growth in decay—worms in dead meat, flies in dung-
hills. "It walked unbreathing through the woods, and thought and
saw and was hideous and strong, and it was not born and it did
not live. It grew and moved about without living."

Here is the myth of anti-life that you see in the visionary
paintings of Hieronymus Bosch—the dread of darkness and death,
paradoxically animated by the squirming "aliveness" of carrion.

This irrationally compelling idea is built into our languages—
the sentence "He is dead" contains it—and it lies at the root of
nearly all our conceptions of the supernatural, from souls in
heaven to vampires, ghosts, zombies and so on.

Curiously enough, these conventional figures are almost entirely missing from both collections. "Legal Rites," by Asimov
and Pohl, in the Conklin book, is a ghost story, but is meant to be
funny. Out of sixteen stories intended to be frightening (excluding
three more of Conklin's choices, "Nursery Rhyme" by Charles
Beaumont and "An Egyptian Hornet" by Algernon Blackwood, which
are not even fantasy, and H. L. Gold's meant-to-be-funny "Warm,
Dark Places"), two deal with corpses, one with a dug-up Norse
god, and one, Roald Dahl's disturbing "The Sound Machine," with
the sufferings of plants. Four stories come under the heading of
magical transformations or possessions (e.g., Idris Seabright's
elegant "White Goddess"); and eight are stories about monsters.

Why monsters, especially? I think perhaps because the ghosts, zombies, vampires &c. of tradition are malevolent creatures: and for one reason or another we no longer take pure malevolence seriously.

A monster, in our tradition, is a creature at once horrible and pathetic. He's rounder and more believable than the magic-lantern figures of Victorian melodrama: we can shudder and sympathize at the same time.

"It was murderous, but innocent," says Leinster of his army-ant horror. And it's just this innocence of evil, I think, which makes both his story and Sturgeon's so compelling.

Like Karloff's monster in *Frankenstein*, drowning a little girl among the water lilies, Sturgeon's monster is not malevolent, only intent, curious, interested, as it tears a living dog apart.

The shuddering pleasure of identifying with a monster in story or film is precisely the realization that it's a creature out of nature, beyond good and evil: it can commit the most horrible acts and still be innocent.

But what need in us calls up these horrific images? And why should it lie apparently dormant for fifteen years?

Siegfried Kracauer's *From Caligari to Hitler*, a study of the German film between wars, offers a disturbingly plausible theory.

In essence, Kracauer's thesis is the Jungian one that popular art forms reflect changes in the mass psyche. Thus, the grotesque and horrible films the Germans were making in the late 20s and early 30s are held to be precursors of the grotesque and horrible events they helped manufacture in the early 40s.

This belief goes back to classical times and probably much further—the word "monster" itself is from the Latin *monstrum*, originally a divine omen of coming disaster. A monster in the classical sense is a creation out of the natural order—a grotesque combination, usually gigantic, of two or more different animals, e.g. the chimera, centaur, mermaid. And we still shudder, I think with a classical anxiety, when we see the snake man in the sideshow.

What Kracauer is saying, of course, is not that the same Germans who made the films were responsible for the horrors of Belsen and Lidice, but rather that the film-makers expressed a wordless, universal sense of horror at what they all felt was coming.

For what the coincidence may be worth, the previous horror-film-and-story cycle in America lasted from about 1930 to 1945. The present one has been under way since about 1955 . . .

All this is of course pretty far-fetched, and you had better not believe any more of it than you can help.

A disparaging remark I once made about H. P. Lovecraft brought several long letters of rebuttal from his partisans. Mrs. R. J. Snyder of Canoga Park, California, Allan Howard of Newark, New Jersey, and James Wade of Chicago all pointed out that I had erred in calling Lovecraft's monsters inexplicit. Fritz Leiber made the same comment, adding, "It seems to me that Arthur Machen made more use than Lovecraft of the idea of 'unspeakable' horrors—and with Machen one gets the idea that these horrors were unspeakable because they involved abnormal sex, being generally associated with some pagan or witch cult. (. . .) Of course Lovecraft did use the 'unnameable' device in a few stories like 'The Statement of Randolph Carter'—and 'The Unnameable'! —but I think the tediousness (for some readers) of his later stories comes from something else—chiefly his liking for writing stories as if they came from the pen of a rather fussy long-winded New England scholar . . . sort of Gibbonesque prose . . . something very apt to happen to the first-person narrative done by a thoughtful writer who has a hero rather like himself."

The Shuttered Room and Other Pieces, by H. P. Lovecraft & Divers Hands, gives me an opportunity to enlarge on this topic. Here are some phrases and sentences culled from "Dagon," a story which Lovecraft's followers consider one of his best:

"When you have read these hastily scrawled pages you may guess, though never fully realize, why it is that I must have forgetfulness or death" (p. 291); "the carcasses of decaying fish, and of other less describable things" (p. 292); "Urged on by an impulse which I cannot definitely define" (p. 294); "A closer scrutiny filled me with sensations I cannot express" (*ibid.*); "Of their faces and forms I dare not speak in detail; for the mere remembrance makes me grow faint" (p. 295).

In spite of these examples, which could be multiplied many times over from Lovecraft's other stories, it *is* true that as a rule, he did make a practice of bringing his monster or alien on stage once, near the end of each story, for one brief, static glimpse. In this respect, "The Shuttered Room," completed by Derleth from HPL's notes, is typical. The story broadly hints, over and over (until the protagonist's continued obtuseness drives the reader to chew paper), that a frog-like monster, capable of enormously increasing its size, is living in a boarded-up room in an old mill. At the end of the story, we meet this being:

> There, squatting in the midst of the tumbled bedding from that long-abandoned bed, sat a monstrous, leathery-skinned creature that was neither frog nor man, one gorged with food, with blood

still slavering from its batrachian jaws and upon its webbed fingers—a monstrous entity that had strong, powerfully long arms, grown from its bestial body like those of a frog, and tapering off into a man's hands, save for the webbing between the fingers . . .

At this point, the monster springs, and the protagonist pots it with a kerosene lamp. End of monster.

Now, this is my real objection to Lovecraft and his imitators (aside from their arthritic styles): the monster does appear, sometimes, but only as a sort of peepshow. It is never brought onstage, as Leiber's and Sturgeon's monsters are, to act and react against the other characters. Thus the story remains in embryo, is never developed; one of the primary requirements of fiction is not fulfilled. A story has a beginning, a middle and an end: Lovecraft's pieces are only endlessly retraced beginnings.

The Shuttered Room, nevertheless, will appeal to those who, like Anthony Boucher, find Lovecraft's life more interesting than his works. Besides the stories already mentioned, the volume contains two other well-known Lovecraft stories ("The Outsider" and "The Strange High House in the Mist"), one more posthumous collaboration with the busy Mr. Derleth ("The Fisherman of Falcon Point"), seven "Juvenilia and Early Tales," all pretty awful, and a miscellaneous collection of Lovecraftiana: essays, notes for stories, tabulations of his themes and the recurring figures of his invented mythos, and a series of personal recollections, from which a grotesque and curiously appealing picture emerges. Lovecraft was a neurasthenic recluse, scholarly, fastidious and prim; yet out of this grey figure, through his voluminous letters, flowed an astonishing warmth and generosity toward younger writers. That he was much loved is undoubted; that he was not exactly like anyone else is well shown by such episodes as that of the ice-cream-eating contest (in which Lovecraft and James F. Morton each consumed twenty-six pints at a sitting, while Donald Wandrei, who tells the story, pooped out after seven); or that of W. Paul Cook's cat. Cook, who was being visited by Lovecraft, wanted him to write an article for his amateur magazine. "Knowing his nocturnal habits, I settled him at my desk to make a start on it, when the lateness of the hour forced me off to bed to be ready to pull out and go to work next day. Just before I left him, I dropped a half-grown kitten into his lap. (. . .)

"Next morning I found Howard sitting exactly as I had left him —not one scratch on his paper, the kitten still asleep in his arms. And when I remonstrated because he hadn't got on with my article, he replied, 'But I didn't want to disturb kitty!'"

Night of the Big Heat, by John Lymington, is still another product of well-meant auctorial ignorance and inveterate publishing snobbery. Like David Duncan, Jack Finney and some other intruders, Lymington is a skilled and persuasive mundane writer; his principal characters, Richard Callum, his wife Frankie, the country people who hang out in their inn, the White Lion, and a sexpot-secretary, Patricia Wells, are agreeably if sketchily drawn, and if there were nothing more to the novel, their casual encounters, sexual and otherwise, would make passable hammock reading. The science-fiction element, such as it is—a heat-ray attack on the northern hemisphere, followed by a matter-transmitter invasion of monsters—is kept carefully and completely in the background from beginning to end. It begins as addle-pated speculation:

> "Evidence has been known over centuries of thought waves actually causing the materialization of persons at a point thousands of miles from where they are known to be. (. . . .) Telepathy is commonly accepted, yet radio is merely the mechanical-electrical form of it." (Page 87.)

Then we get a series of menacing shapes and sounds in the night:

> "It is somewhere in the darkness below me on the bank. If I could see I would know what form of creature it is, whether it had normal sight, hearing and responses. Whether it is savage or not . . . But I can see nothing at all . . ."

And finally the fields catch fire, the monsters are all burnt up, and so we never find out anything more about them. The End.

This is where both the snobbery and the ignorance come in.

The snobbery: That the quality of a science-fiction novel is inversely proportional to the amount of science fiction in it. (We have been surrounded at times by book editors who chose s.f. novels on just this basis, though they would rather have died than admit it.)

The ignorance: That science fiction is simply a gadgeted-up version of the classic story of supernatural mystery.

The late Fletcher Pratt, in his distinguished anthology, *World of Wonder*, spoke of a play of Dunsany's in which the awesome voices of gods are heard offstage—an impressive effect, until the gods come stumbling on and the audience sees they are only men.

This story illustrates a principle that guided all the classic weird-story writers: that "mystery" goes out when the lights go on. Masters of the macabre like H. P. Lovecraft tried so hard (and so successfully) to put off actually introducing any of their

eldritch horrors until the last moment, that the most dreadful
thing about these stories is their endless tedium.

This is my point: Dunsany would have done better to keep his
gods offstage, simply because he had none of the genuine article
to show. But in fiction, a really imaginative fantasy writer can
bring his monsters into full view, and make them terrifying: the
highly explicit horrors of such modern fantasies as *Conjure Wife*,
by Fritz Leiber, "It," by Theodore Sturgeon, and "Hell Hath Fury,"
by Cleve Cartmill (all from the lamented *Unknown*), are more
frightening than all the "unnameable," "indescribable," and "un-
thinkable" hobgoblins of the Lovecraft school.

"Mystery," I repeat, asks the questions; science fiction—and
modern fantasy too—gives the answers.

It's an exploded myth that dreadful and wonderful things cannot
be brought into the light without destroying their awe. The writer
who adopts this pose nowadays is making a confession of imaginative bankruptcy.

And the publisher who seizes upon this stuff, in the naive belief that he's doing the s.f. field a favor, is a museum piece like
Cthulhu and the shuggoth.

There is a convention in modern fiction that people and events
are comprehensible and can be reduced to diagrams. Thus, as a
rule, every major character in a 20th-century novel sooner or
later—usually sooner—gets off in a corner with some other character and starts pulling drawers out of himself like a bureau.
This goes on until the reader feels perfectly satisfied that the
character is fully exposed and predictable; then the story can
proceed in an orderly way—character A is a knight, and moves
two squares forward, one square to the side; character B is a
bishop, and moves any number of squares diagonally; and so on.

Looked at in this way, every story is basically a game, and can
be discussed in terms of strategy.

But to Shirley Jackson, people are enigmas, and the things that
happen to them are essentially inexplicable. So her stories don't
and can't follow the rules; and in fact it seems to me that even
using the term "novel" to describe *The Haunting of Hill House* is
stretching the word too far.

Although this is certainly a ghost story in one way or another,
it does not follow the ghost-story pattern, and its dominant note is
not terror, but a faintly disturbing sense of strangeness. Certain
rooms in Hill House are described as distressingly wrong in their
dimensions (like the room built by the N.I.C.E. for the corruption
of souls, in C. S. Lewis's *That Hideous Strength*); and yet this

is curiously unimpressive, whereas the kitchen, a large, bright room which merely happens to have three doors opening onto the veranda, has an inarguable sense of something wrong about it.

"No live organism," the book begins, "can continue for long to exist sanely under conditions of absolute reality; even larks and katydids are supposed, by some, to dream. Hill House, not sane, stood by itself against its hills, holding darkness within; it had stood so for eighty years and might stand for eighty more. Within, walls continued upright, bricks met neatly, floors were firm, and doors were sensibly shut; silence lay steadily against the wood and stone of Hill House, and whatever walked there, walked alone."

Whether or not the house is haunted (and if so, by whom) never seems to be the central issue. Dr. Montague, the investigator who brings the other three main characters to Hill House, does little except try to measure the curious "cold spot" outside the nursery door. His more energetic wife, who turns up later in the company of a bean-brained headmaster, is a comic character, full of esoteric misinformation ("You have no idea the messages I've gotten from nuns walled up alive.") The narrative drifts slowly and rather pleasantly, like a very long short story, toward its resolution as one of the characters sinks gently and rather pleasantly into madness.

Not one of the characters unbosoms himself, or ever becomes quite predictable; at the end of the book they are all, if anything, more remote and mysterious than ever. The question of Hill House is answered (if it is answered at all) only obliquely. What remains is Shirley Jackson's unique sense of the pervasiveness of evil: the intolerable reality that surrounds all our dream-worlds of lath and plaster.

23. DECADENTS

PHILIP K. DICK is that short story writer who for the past five years or so has kept popping up all over—in one year, 1953, he published twenty-seven stories—with a sort of unobtrusive and chameleonlike competence. To quote Anthony Boucher:

> By now he has appeared in almost every science fiction publication—and what's more surprising, in each case with stories exactly suited to the editorial tastes and needs of that particular publication: the editors of *Whizzing Star Patrol* and of the *Quaint Quality Quarterly* are in complete agreement upon Mr. Dick as a singularly satisfactory contributor.

Entering and leaving as he does by so many doors at once, Dick creates a blurred impression of pleasant, small literary gifts, coupled with a nearsighted canniness about the market—he writes the trivial, short, bland sort of story that amuses without exciting, is instantly saleable and instantly forgettable.

The surprise of a book like *Solar Lottery* from such an author is more than considerable.

This book is remarkable, to begin with, in the way its extrapolations have been handled. Dick writes of a future world in which the radio-and-television quiz has evolved into a system-wide game with all power as its stake: the tyrant, the Quizmaster, is chosen by a random twitch of the bottle that contains an equivalent of everybody's "power card."

In theory, therefore, anybody might rise to the top, at any time. In practice, most people are "unks"—unclassified—and have no p-cards; of those who have, most surrender them to the bosses of the Hills, the great industrial complexes, under medieval fealty arrangements. The masses of the people, without any cause-and-

effect principle to sustain them, have fallen back on "Minimax"—
the Theory of Games made into a nihilist philosophy.

> The M-Game player never really committed himself; he risked
> nothing, gained nothing . . . and wasn't overwhelmed. He sought
> to hoard his pot and strove to outlast the other players. The
> M-Game player sat waiting for the game to end; that was the best
> that could be hoped for.

In a science fiction magazine serial, this framework would be
crudely exposed and bunged into the reader's eye at every opportunity: the lead character would have long solemn thoughts about
"how wonderful the System is—or is it?"—and we would all grow
so tired of waiting for the boob to make up his mind that any distraction, even the average Ace novel, would be welcome.

Nothing of the sort happens here; Dick states his premises,
shows you enough of his crowded complex world to give you your
bearings—and then puts away his maps and charts for good. You
are in the world of the bottle and the Quizmaster, the Hills and
the legal assassins, and you see the living surface of it, not the
bones.

This is not the end of the wonder. There's the tension: Dick
has caught and intensified the bare-nerve tautness of our own
society at its worst, and put it on paper here so you can see,
hear, feel and smell it.

Then there's the plottiness—like van Vogt miraculously making
sense as he goes along: each new development not merely startling—anybody can startle—but startling *and logically necessary*.
This is architectural plotting, a rare and inhumanly difficult thing;
and who in blazes ever expected Dick to turn up as one of the few
masters of it?

And the characters: Verrick, the deposed Quizmaster, whose
singleminded aim to assassinate his successor gives this story
its tremendous drive; Eleanor Stevens, the telepathic secretary
who renounces her gift to stay with Verrick, Pellig the golem-
assassin, and more. These people are real; they carry conviction. Not the least of Dick's virtues is that he shows the shock
to the human nervous system of all these violent events; he fobs
you off with no icy supermen.

Verrick at his most impressive is still human—irritable,
clumsy, oafish. The agony of the ex-telepath girl is authentic.
Nothing—to labor the point a little more—nothing in Dick's magazine work prepares you for this; it's as if magazine taboos and
crotchets had trimmed him down from a powerful writer to a cute
one, a novelty vendor. Some of the small excesses and awkward-

nesses of this book are perhaps traceable to the same cause. The bare-breastedness of all the women in Dick's world is hard to account for on climatic, social, moral, esthetic or other grounds, except as a simple reaction against magazine prudery.

The book has other faults—the burning of the surplus goods and the use of medieval charms, for instance, seem to me errors in dialectics; the protagonist, Benteley, himself, almost inevitably, is not always as consistent and believable a character as the rest.

Yet even in the summing-up, that place where the author has got to try to say what his novel means and where he thinks it leads, never quite satisfactorily—because all novels with any life in them end too soon—Dick acquits himself wonderfully well.

Cartwright, the new Quizmaster, is explaining how he gimmicked the bottle—making the whole M-Game system meaningless—in order to get himself selected:

> "Was that ethical?" Benteley asked. "That kicks over the board, doesn't it?"
>
> "I played the game for years," Cartwright said. "Most people go on playing the game all their lives. Then I began to realize the rules were set up so I couldn't win. Who wants to play that kind of game? We're betting against the house, and the house always wins."

Unanswerable . . . And then you realize, while that speech resonates in your mind, that it isn't only the imaginary society of *Solar Lottery* that Cartwright is condemning: it's all society, including our own.

Like his first, Dick's second novel, *The World Jones Made*, is a spectacular, brim-full grab bag of ideas. The central story concerns a new and fascinating style of conquering villain, but Dick has skilfully woven in such diverse and unlikely elements as (1) a race of artificial mutants, pathetic little goblins brought up in ignorance of their own destiny; (2) the "Drifters"—mindless blobs of protoplasm that float in from space, to become the victims of Dick's savage parody of a pogrom; (3) world peace enforced by "Relativism": " '. . . we say simply: put up or shut up. Prove what you're saying. If you want to say the Jews are the root of all evil—prove it . . . Otherwise, into the work camp.' "

Uniting all this is the central idea, the tyrant who can see the future.

His name is Floyd J. Jones. When he first appears in the story, he's a sideshow performer, an ugly, sullen, disappointed young man with a talent nobody wants. No, not even a talent—a curse. To Jones, the future, one year ahead, is always more vivid than the present. The real horror of this peculiar kind of limited pre-cognition does not appear till the end of the book, and had better remain Dick's secret; but here's a sample:

> ". . . It's not so much like I can see the future; it's more that I've got one foot stuck in the past. I can't shake it loose. I'm re-tarded; I'm reliving one year of my life forever." He shuddered. "Over and over again. Everything I do, everything I say, hear, experience, I have to grind over twice." He raised his voice, sharp and anguished, without hope. "I'm living the same life two times!"
>
> "In other words," Cussick said slowly, "for you, the future is static. Knowing about it doesn't make it possible for you to change it."
>
> Jones laughed icily. "Change it? It's totally fixed. It's more fixed, more permanent, than this wall." Furiously, he slammed his open palm against the wall behind him. "You think I've some kind of emancipation. Don't kid yourself . . . the less you know about the future the better off you are. You've got a nice illusion; you think you have free will."

This is startling enough, but is only the beginning. One of the characteristic jolts you get from a Dick novel is the shock of falling through an apparently simple idea.

Another is the shock of recognition. In a field noted for card-board characters, Dick's people are bitterly, sharply, unforget-tably real. Jones himself is no stereotyped dictator; he's as intensely irritating as the boss' brother-in-law, or the slob who keeps bothering you in the elevator: you'll hate and pity him: he's real. So is Cussick, the Fedgov security agent, and so (incredibly) is his blonde young wife. When their marriage comes apart, it isn't just a mechanical turn of the plot; it's painful, it hurts you. As in *Solar Lottery*, Dick has made his future world a distorted mirror-image of our own. The distortion is what makes it science fiction: but the image is what strikes home.

Like a good juggler, Dick manages to keep dazzling numbers of objects all moving at the same time: story ideas that would serve another writer for a novel apiece, in Dick's hands become mere diversions. The product of this nimbleness almost never bogs down, as straight-line novels so frequently do; it's continually in movement, and as a rule, Dick's sure touch with character and dialogue makes the unlikeliest combinations come alive.

The Man Who Japed is unlikelier than most. Dick's post-Armageddon world of 2114 A.D. is ruled by Morec—"Moral Reclamation," a puritanical theocracy which enforces its blue laws by a world-wide system of mutual spying and accusation—

and by Telemedia, the government agency which controls all mass communications. From this double-barreled first assumption, the novel develops in two curiously discordant ways. One is heavy with *1984*'s brooding atmosphere of bureaucracy and despair; the other echoes *The Hucksters* and "Gravy Planet"—it's the drama of an ambitious agency man in flight from his own conscience. Dick produces some striking effects: for instance, the device of having all voices at the Morec kangaroo court sessions electronically disguised to resemble each other is startling and effective. Using scenes like this for contrast with the episode of the two hermits on Hokkaido—the nightmare of isolation vs. the nightmare of belonging—Dick builds the kind of neurotic, highly-charged tragic atmosphere which is his trademark. His minor characters, as usual, are little miracles of insight; the human relations are real, an extraordinary thing in science fiction.

The book has three serious flaws. First, the *Demolished Man*ish dual life of Allen Purcell—a convinced Morec agent by day, who "japes" (i.e., defaces) a patriotic statue by night—is itself imperfectly developed. The two personalities seem to be almost totally compartmented, so that when the rebelliousness seeps over into Purcell's daytime life, the effect is not one of conflict, but of error.

Second, Dick has piled onto his basic premises a handful of others, each more inconsistent than the last. The habitable parts of Earth in 2114 are one huge city, supported by food farms and manufacturing colonies on the planets of other suns. The technology implied here is utterly incompatible with the rest of Dick's world, and is internally improbable to boot. Dick's citizens fly in "slivers" and spaceships, but are unaccountably afraid to travel on the ground faster than 20 m.p.h.—in automobiles steered by tillers, for Pete's sake.

Third, the careful and reasonably honest conflict of personalities begins to break down into hack melodrama on p. 34, when an underground agent—a pretty girl, naturally—accosts the hero very oddly without arousing any surprise. The underground plot-thread is uninspired and unconvincing from one end to the other; the device of using Telemedia facilities to broadcast a fake Morec message (borrowed from Heinlein's "If This Goes On—") is contrived, not integral; and the hero's last-minute renunciation of escape from Earth is straight out of the ending of Ken Crossen's awful *Year of Consent*.

In spite of these faults and several others, the book is worth reading: at his intermittent best, Dick is still one of the most vital and honest working science fiction writers. I don't believe he has mastered his form as yet; but his journeyman work deserves our respectful attention.

Dick's fourth novel, *Eye in the Sky,* is an *Unknown*-style fantasy. What appears to be a science-fictional situation in the opening chapter—eight people fall from an observational platform when an atom-smashing Bevatron goes out of control—turns out to have nothing to do with the case. The eight wake up in a cockeyed world, but have not been translated to another plane of reality, as you might expect, by the Bevatron: they are images of themselves, wandering around in a dream-world belonging to one of their number, something like Alice in the Red King's dream. ("'If that there King was to wake,' added Tweedledum, 'you'd go out—bang!—just like a candle!'") Meanwhile, their bodies are still lying unconscious on the floor of the Bevatron chamber.

This section of the story takes the form of a satire on Jehovism, exemplified for safety's sake by a crackpot Islamic cult called Second Babiism. (The courageous editor can afford to thumb his nose at any Moslems who may chance to pick up the book.) For blaspheming, the hero gets stung by a bee; for lying, he is deluged by locusts. Applying for a job in a research electronics firm, he finds that "communications" now means a direct line to the deity; his qualifications are determined by reading a random passage from the holy book, *Bayan of the Second Bab*; and by turning the spiritual tables on a group of hostile young believers, the hero gets them damned on the spot—i.e., turned into apelike dwarves, while everything around them is withered and blackened.

This kind of thing is good fun for infidels, and Dick lays it on with a trowel (e.g., God Almighty delivers his own pulpit-thumping Sunday morning sermons on TV).

On p. 121, the proprietor of this fantasy-world, an old soldier named Silvester, gets cracked on the sconce by an imaginary bedpost, and the scene immediately changes—the rest of the characters don't go out like candles, but they do find themselves in a second and equally askew world of phantasm. This one turns out to be that of a feather-brained matron named Mrs. Pritchet, who keeps deleting from it anything she feels is not quite nice—beginning, of course, with sex; auto horns follow, modern composers, rude traffic cops, and so on down to clouds, water and air. Having abolished everything, Mrs. Pritchet winks out: fantasy-world #3 comes into being.

The book is divided in this way into four dream sections, with a prologue and an epilogue in the real world. At their best, the dream episodes almost achieve the chilling balance between reality and horror of Hubbard's "Fear"; but the pace is too rapid, the story thread too slight. Once the unreality of the action has been established, there is no real urgency in it: Dick has to keep on leaping agilely from one set of assumptions to the next, in order to sustain the reader's interest at all. The characters, who in any other Dick novel would have acquired substance from their background, are here like empty Jello moulds.

In the mundane sections, Dick has something to say, but all too little time to say it, about the Negro in America, about security systems, Communists and liberals. Perhaps the deepest fault of the book is that, in the dream sections, it dodges such living issues to tilt at straw men: back-street cults, 19th-century prudery, paranoid maiden ladies, 1930 parlor pinkery.

The formula for Alfred Bester's writing is given on page 71 of his collection, *Starburst*. It appears in "Oddy and Id": " 'We need a short-cut.' . . . 'What do you suggest?' 'Dazzlement,' Migg spat. 'Enchantment.' "

Dazzlement and enchantment are Bester's methods. His stories never stand still a moment; they're forever tilting into motion, veering, doubling back, firing off rockets to distract you. The repetition of the key phrase in "Fondly Fahrenheit," the endless reappearances of Mr. Aquila in "The Starcomber" are offered mockingly: try to grab at them for stability, and you find they mean something new each time. Bester's science is all wrong, his characters are not characters but funny hats; but you never notice: he fires off a smoke-bomb, climbs a ladder, leaps from a trapeze, plays three bars of "God Save the King," swallows a sword and dives into three inches of water. Good heavens, what more do you want?

These are all memorable stories, and a few of them are classics —"Adam and No Eve," for instance, "Of Time and Third Avenue," "Oddy and Id," "Fondly Fahrenheit." Pyrotechnic as his performance is, it nearly always seems to end up somewhere; only four of these eleven stories have crippled endings; and if you're a real Bester appreciator, you'll readily forgive him those.

The Stars My Destination, otherwise known as *Hell's My Destination, Tiger! Tiger!*, and/or *The Burning Spear*, is everything Bester's *The Demolished Man* was, only a little too much more so.

There is the extravagant future society (hedonist in *TDM*, Victorian in *TSMD*); the psi factor which alters the society (in *TDM*, telepathy; in *TSMD*, "jaunting"—i.e., teleportation); there is the ruthless and inhumanly strong-willed villain-hero (Ben Reich; Gully Foyle) with his secret need for punishment; there are the typographical tricks and the funny names, all cranked up to a more breakneck pace, a more hysterical pitch.

The villain-hero is now opposed by no image of good, but by a gang of ruffians more coldly venal and merciless than himself. The playful name-coining of *TDM* here becomes a kind of maniacal doodling (Jóseph, Moira, &c.). The controlled violence of *TDM* here runs unchecked: Bester, the caustic satirist of neurotic science fiction, has turned himself into a sort of literate maso-Spillane. Foyle is pulped, slashed, tattooed, burned, frozen, &c., &c., *ad naus*.

The novel piles idea on idea, some of them good as gold—the underworld jaunters who follow the darkness around the world; the Skoptsies, self-mortifying ascetics who have had their sensory nerves cut; Sigurd Magsman, the 70-year-old child telepath; and enough others to stock six ordinary novels. Not content with this, Bester has added enough bad taste, inconsistency, irrationality, and downright factual errors to fill six more.

Having described the book's heroine, Olivia Presteign, as a blind girl, Bester immediately reveals that she is not blind at all, but sighted in a peculiar way: she sees in infra-red wavelengths, "from 7,500 angstroms to one millimeter . . . heat waves, magnetic fields, radio waves, radar, sonar, and electromagnetic fields." (We will pass by the question of how she manages to focus all this assorted noise on her retinas; Bester says she does it.) . . . After which, he goes right on calling her blind, treats her as if she were blind, even to having her unable to jaunt, and finally reveals that she has turned corsair because of her bitterness at being blind.

In the opening section of the book, when Gully Foyle is adrift on an airless spaceship, Bester's assertion that "Much of the canned goods had lost their containers, for tin crumbles to dust in the absolute zero of space" would be idiotic, even if tin cans were made of tin. And the stream of debris that follows Gully as he moves, "like the tail of a festering comet," is picturesque but inexplicable, unless Bester thinks there are convection currents in a vacuum.

You tell me: is Bester kidding?

Then there's Presteign of Presteign, head of the clan, sept and family, who is so rich and proud that he will not jaunt like ordinary mortals, but uses old-fashioned means of transportation, and even has a private telephone system. (Bester's notion that jaunting would replace the telephone is peculiar enough, considering that nobody can jaunt to an unfamiliar destination; but taking that on faith, *whom* does Presteign call on his telephone?)

The horrifying thing about all this is that it does eventually get somewhere, and assume shape and meaning. Bester ties up the major loose ends, including some you would swear he had never noticed. His puppet characters take on a sort of theatrical brightness; and the ending of the book, in mystical penitence and transfiguration, is grotesquely moving. Like the California hobbyist who builds graceful towers out of old bottles and rusting iron, Bester has made a work of art out of junk.

Readers who remember Kurt Vonnegut's *Player Piano* with wistful pleasure are in for a surprise: Vonnegut's second s.f. novel, *The Sirens of Titan,* is nothing like that at all. *Player Piano* was subtle, ironic and cool, with a surface smooth as gelatin, and all the jags buried deep under. *The Sirens of Titan* is jazzy, impudent, sarcastic, and about as smooth as gravel pudding; in a style like Harvey Kurtzman trying to imitate Doc Savage and Alfred Bester simultaneously, it piles one deadpan extravagance on another: superlatives, shock-for-shock's-sake, epigrams, parodies, boyish vulgarity. The plot concerns a Groton type named Wilson Niles Rumfoord, who "had run his private space ship right into the heart of an uncharted chrono-synclastic infundibulum." This last sounds like a Sheckley bibble-bibble, but Vonnegut explains it:

"Chrono (kroh-no) means time. Synclastic (sin-class-tick) means curved toward the same side in all directions, like the skin of an orange. Infundibulum (in-fun-dib-u-lum) is what the ancient Romans like Julius Caesar and Nero called a funnel. If you don't know what a funnel is, get Mommy to show you one."

What this adds up to is that (a) Rumfoord (and his dog Kazak, who was also in the private space ship) is scattered in time and space along a helix with one end in the sun and the other in Betelgeuse; and (b) Rumfoord, who materializes on Earth and other solar bodies whenever they intercept his helix, can see all aspects of truth at once and has accordingly become a sort of highly refined (but nasty) demigod.

Some of this is funny as hell, some is grotesquely moving, some awful by any imaginable standards. ("But Fate spared him that awful knowledge for many years.")

Vonnegut shares one priceless quality with Bester (and van Vogt, and other innovators): whereas most writers use the same story pieces, and only try to put them together in mildly novel ways, Vonnegut's pieces are all different — e.g., (1) diamond-shaped, music-eating, paper-thin cave creatures on Mercury (they form harmonious patterns on the walls, and "reproduce by flaking. The young, when shed by a parent, are indistinguishable from dandruff"); (2) a financier who corners practically everything by interpreting the Book of Genesis as a coded series of buy & sell orders; (3) Schliemann Breathing (i.e., inhaling through the lower intestine when in airless places), and so on, and on.

You may not like all of it; you may not even be able to decide whether you like it or not; but read it.

Most of the stories in Robert Sheckley's *Citizen in Space*, like those in his earlier collection *Untouched by Human Hands*, are brief, brightly inventive and logically unstable. Sheckley's faceless characters chirp, twitter, whirl with captivating grace around an idea, but seldom settle down long enough to exercise ordinary intelligence upon it. At its worst, the stupidity of Sheckleymen is so astonishing, it completely overshadows the marvels the author is expecting you to gawp at. Thus, in "Hands Off," two interstellar burglars (did you trip? sorry!) take 17 gory pages to discover— what every reader knew on page 1—that a spaceship built for the comfort of aliens is not likely to work very well for people.

Bar this one failing, however, Sheckley's is one of the most promising new talents in many years. He has a unique touch with a wacky civilization, a clean, compact style, and a satirical wit that is dry without being bitter. Some of these stories, particularly the later ones, show traces of characterization as well. My favorites are "The Mountain Without a Name"—which, incidentally, neatly disposes of the theme of *Your Sins and Mine* in about one-eighth the space—; "The Accountant," a mad little story about a family of warlocks which has spawned an obstinately impractical son; "Hunting Problem" with its tentacled Boy Scouts; and the wry "The Luckiest Man in the World."

Sheckley is a solemn, plucked-looking young man with an undisciplined imagination and a penchant for boats. He came to science fiction in 1952; some two or three years later, somebody told him he was writing parables, and Sheckley believed it. The stripped quality of his subsequent work, and its utter divorcement from fact and logic, are traceable to this unfortunate influence.

If the fifteen stories in Sheckley's *Pilgrimage to Earth* have a common point, it is that man is less clever than he thinks himself. In "All the Things You Are," for instance, a well-meaning contact man on a primitive world (a) stuns the natives with his halitosis, (b) disintegrates a bridge with his loud voice, (c) accidentally hypnotizes the natives with his soothing gestures, (d) burns them with his sweaty handshake. In "Early Model," and again in "Earth, Air, Fire and Water," a man is nearly killed by an over-elaborate mechanism designed to protect him.

Man, Sheckley seems to be saying, could use a little less cleverness and a little more humility.

The moral would have more point, it seems to me, if Sheckley
gave cleverness a fair shake.

"It suddenly struck him that in all the time of mankind, nothing
had changed. Perhaps the cave was a little bigger, the flints a
little better, but man himself was no bigger, no tougher, no better
fit."

—And, unfortunately, in these stories, no brighter. Sheckley's
heroes weigh in at an I.Q. of about ninety, just sufficient to get
aboard their shiny machines, but not enough to push all the right
levers. In "Earth, Air, Fire and Water," from which the quotation
above is taken, a man is set down *alone* on *Venus* (my God!) to
field-test a *spacesuit* (Jehosaphat!). It is not cleverness which
promptly gets him into trouble, it is this initial idiocy.

In "Milk Run," AAA Ace's Arnold and Gregor ship a load of
extraterrestrial animals without bothering to find out anything
about them; in "The Lifeboat Mutiny," they trustingly buy an
alien-built lifeboat, again without asking questions, although this
same gaffe has got Sheckleymen into dire peril before. In "Bad
Medicine," a man buys a floor-model therapy machine which turns
out to be one designed for Martians. "I can explain that," says
Sheckley through a character named Follansbee; but he can't, and
doesn't.

These stories are deft and impudently funny, as when the man
with the Martian therapy machine winds up saying, "It's the
damnedest thing . . . but do you know, I think I *do* remember my
goricae!" Sheckley's trademark is his ability to spin this kind
of thing out of nothing. In "Protection," for instance, a man is
adopted by an invisible derg, who protects him against a gamper,
but then there are the grailers to worry about, and the leeps, the
feegs and the melgerizer.

Once in a great while, when Sheckley bothers to put something
under his slick surfaces, his work comes brilliantly and even
movingly to life. "Fear in the Night" is a beautifully expert and
chilling exercise in pure horror, with the real shock coming when
the fantasy element is dispelled. "The Body," in spite of its slip-
shod technical background, is a curiously pathetic story of a
scientist's mind (brain?) transplanted into a dog's body. "Pilgrimage to Earth" is a compelling romantic satire about a young
man who comes to Earth looking for love, an antique emotion
which Earth has turned into a paying proposition. The story is
grotesque and tender, poetic and ugly by turns. The only thing
that mars it for me is the bit about the shooting gallery with girls

for targets. Sheckley tells me he meant to imply that the girls
don't die when you shoot them, but he plainly says just the opposite, and it turns that part of the story into a joke. (Something
like: "Why do you let them kill you?" "Aah, it's a living.")

Sheckley, like Bradbury and Matheson, is a "science fiction"
writer who does not write about science. His engine rooms have
nothing in them but big rotating shafts; his "linguascene," which
magically translates unknown languages, is an empty box. He
identifies a planet as "near Arcturus," and even his references to
existing devices are childishly askew ("degermifier," "ossily-
scope"), as if to say, "See, I don't know anything about science, so
don't ask me."

I think this is essentially laziness. The writer of burlesque is
not immune from the demands of good workmanship. Guy Gilpatric took care to put a real merchant ship under his burlesque
hero, Colin Glencannon, and the stories are a hundred times
funnier than if he had botched the job.

Like it or not, what Sheckley does is art. But he could use a
little less art, and a little more craftsmanship.

Richard Matheson is a prim young man whose considerable
talent is usually submerged in an indiscriminate creative gush.
Like most of his literary generation, he has no sense of plot;
in each story he puts together a situation, carries it around in
circles until he gets tired, then introduces some small variation
and hopefully carries it around some more, like a man bemused
in a revolving door. His stories sometimes reach their goal by
this process, but only, as a rule, when there is no other possible
direction for the story to take; more often they wind up nowhere,
and Matheson has to patch on irrelevant endings to get rid of them.
Of the stories collected in *The Shores of Space*, "Blood Son,"
"Trespass" and "The Curious Child" are botches of this kind.
Other, slighter stories such as "The Funeral," "Clothes Make the
Man" and "The Doll That Does Everything" are almost as weak,
but are saved by Matheson's impudence.

Except for whimsy, Matheson's dramas are all domestic, not
to say banal, and their hero is almost always Matheson himself.
He has a profound interest in the trivia of his daily life and in his
own uninspired conversation, which he reproduces without irony.
(" 'Oh my *God*, it's hot.' . . . 'It's your imagination. . . It's not hot
. . . It's cool. As a cucumber.' 'Ha. . . What a month for driving
. . . I'm done on one side. Turn me,' " and so on, and so on.) At
its best, by sheer honesty and intensity of emotion, this kind of
thing turns into art, as in "The Test," Matheson's harrowing story

of an old man losing his grip on life. "Steel," although it is built on a creaking sports-pulp plot and an even creakier set of robots, achieves tragic stature.

At its worst, Matheson's bare natural style, with its corner-drugstore vocabulary and inflections, is thin and dull. Apparently realizing this, he makes frequent efforts to jazz it up; I would lay odds that he owns and uses a thesaurus. He cultivates George Meredith's "he said" avoidances: "the little man asided," "Marian sotto voiced," "he dulceted." He has a sure touch for the gaudy solecism ("Another right concaved his stomach"; "The Count bi-carbonated"), for the unnecessary word ("unwanted garbage"), and for unconscious anatomical humor:

> Across her face, the hot wind fanned bluntly, ruffling the short blond hair. (Page 1.)
> He blinked away the waves of blackness lapping at his ankles. (Page 3.)
> His coarse gutteral (sic) tongue sounded unnatural in his frail body. (Page 83.)

As for the science in his stories, the less said about it by Matheson the better. When he sticks to one implicit assumption (euthanasia in "The Test," or the one survivor of atomic war in "Pattern For Survival"), his work is often compact and witty. The Earth is apparently about to be destroyed by collision with a flaming comet in "The Last Day," but Matheson never says so, he merely shows you the red horror in the sky, and with hardly any effort you can forget the Victorian nonsense and concentrate on the astonishingly effective prig's-eye view of humanity under sentence of death.

When, on the other hand, he feels obliged to expound the science background of a story, the results are pitiful. (" 'That clinches it!' he said. 'Mars has two-fifths the gravity of Earth. They'd need a double heart to drive their blood or whatever it is they have in their veins.' ")

Like many another talented writer, Matheson got into this field more or less by accident, found that it paid, and never bothered to learn its basic techniques. It's hard to know whether to be more grateful to him for minor masterpieces like "The Test" and "The Last Day," or more annoyed by the piles of trash he has left for us to wade in.

24. BRITONS

ALTHOUGH SOME BRITISH writers are dealt with without any discrimination here and there throughout this book, I have lumped others together under this heading because it seems to me that the virtues and failings of their work have something peculiarly British about them. The bad ones and half-bad ones, in particular, are unlike any bad or half-bad American novel.

The Bright Phoenix, by Harold Mead, is not an ordinary failure, but a book so solidly built that it falls with a resounding thud. I think the book deserves our respectful interest, not only for its honesty and skill, but for its technical value as a limit. Bad American s.f. novels (and some good ones) tend to be too hasty, too full of action for action's sake. Here is the opposite thing, a novel that fails because it is too slow, too careful, too thorough.

The sense of a limit is a very valuable thing for writers, and a hard one to come by. People who, like me, have been bothered by problems of pace could do worse than to steer midway between The Bright Phoenix and, say, James Blish's Earthman, Come Home.

Mead's hero is a blunt, bearded, bad-tempered man named John Waterville, recently returned from a voyage of exploration to "the Island" (probably England, meaning that the mainland across the ocean would be North America). He is to go again with an advance guard of colonists, eugenically produced super-men and superwomen, to spread civilization in the name of the Human Spirit. The religion of this post-atom-war culture, like its politics, is sanitary, functional, non-violent and essentially nasty. Waterville's sense of this means that he has become mor-ally maladjusted, and ought to turn himself over to the Ministry of Health's thought police for a checkup; his failure to do so means that his maladjustment is serious. How serious, he realizes only when he meets a girl named Jenny, takes out an "A license" with her (permission to cohabit in a state-run house of assignation for two weeks, renewable for two more) and discovers he wants the impossible—an old-fashioned marriage for love, and for life.

To underline the hopelessness of this desire, Jenny is taken away from him and turned into "a reconditioned"—a brain-washed zombie, one of a class used for menial labor. Later, on the Island, she recovers her mind briefly (and implausibly), only to be killed as she and Waterville are about to escape: this seems excessive. The rest of the story, the gradual collapse and ruin of the colony, and Waterville's adoption by the friendly aborigines, is told at enormous slow length—deadly dull in spite of Mead's good writing and sharp insights.

Mead is an intensely visual writer, but the images in his work are all alike, all smothered in shadow: "Bobbing lanterns emerged from a lighted hut, the legs of those that carried them casting scissor-shadows on the ground. I heard the doors of the van clang open, and by the uncertain lights could tell that a small mass of humanity was emerging from the interior of the vehicle. Occasionally a face was vaguely illuminated, now a pair of bare legs, now an arm. I noticed, briefly outlined by a passing lantern, a squat figure standing with its legs apart, its back toward me. . ." These bright glimpses are dramatic, but in time grow irritating by their very incompleteness. Worse, in spite of the narrative's lagging pace, so much time is taken up by pure word-chewing that none of the characters really comes alive or reveals much of himself; like the faces in one of Mead's half-lit scenes, they are distinguishable but insubstantial.

Perhaps the central fault of the book, however, is its legacy from Orwell's *1984*: when a hero is too overwhelmed by society, too passive, there's no drama. As Walter Kerr says (in *How Not To Write a Play*), "Our instinct for story is aroused whenever we scent difficulty—the hard *choice*, the crippling *alternative*, the threat and the necessity for change." The italics are mine.

Hole in Heaven, by F. Dubrez Fawcett is the first in a series of British science fiction novels to be edited by Angus Wilson, who might have done better to label this one "superstition fiction." Its subject is nothing less than the possession, by a powerful bodiless spirit from Somewhere, of a dying man's body.

Fawcett's style is banal; his characters appear at first to be pure stereotypes—a stage Irish girl, a stage Jew, and a stage Scotsman, among others. His narrative is a patchwork quilt, with twenty different viewpoints to the yard, stitched together with summaries, anticipations, moralizing, anything handy.

And yet, as the author slowly builds up his gallery of grotesques

—Dr. Hyman, the dope-taking hospital head; publicity-mad Intern Leonidas Lipwade (who comes to a most horrible end), dog-faced Vicar Glassbrow, and the rest—the reader comes to the uncomfortable realization that they are really not grotesques at all, nor stereotypes either. The author has simply excluded the dedicated doctor, the selfless pastor, the crusading newspaper editor and other rarities about whom polite writers tell us so often, and has given us the remainder—the mediocre, the venal, the meanly ambitious with whom, as the editor rightly notes, we have to do in our daily lives.

The possessed man, Nemo, would do almost enough if he only stirred up this colorful ant's nest of little men; but Fawcett has developed him into a character of singular power in his own right. Nemo is that chilling and rare thing, a genuinely alien being. The conclusions he reaches in his study of our race are, as we would expect, cold-bloodedly accurate; and yet, alone among the supermenaces I can recall, he leaves the reader no sneaking wish at all for his victory over humanity.

The copious notes he leaves behind him are nearly all burned. I hate this device—it's so corny, and as a rule so unnecessary— but in this case, given the opportunity, I think I would have burned them myself.

If the weird movie cycle ever comes back into its own (leaving science fiction to say something, instead of scaring people), this story ought to make a gorgeous specimen.

The failure of most recent s.f. novels to say anything new and important, or even very interesting, makes a novel like Brian W. Aldiss's *Vanguard From Alpha*, flawed as it is, worthy of note.

Aldiss writes pointed, dry, highly stylized short stories that pack a great deal into a small space. His novels, those we have seen so far, are pot-boilers. This one opens with a dispirited comic-book sequence: three young spacemen, all with identical clean-cut faces and empty expressions, are sent up to the Moon to investigate something mysterious going on near the Rosk installation there. I'll explain the Rosks in a moment. In a scrimmage, Tyne Leslie is knocked out, and when he comes to, in the spaceship on the way home, Murray Mumford tells him that he, Murray, saved Tyne's life after the third man, Alan Cunliffe, panicked and threatened to shoot Murray if he didn't leave Tyne behind. Tyne refuses to believe this story, and makes up his mind to find out the truth.

Now. The Rosks are immigrants from another star, vaguely Malayan-looking humanoids, who by threats and diplomacy have managed to get themselves allotted a district in Sumatra, and another on the Moon, and to become a Rosk Problem. The exasperating complexity of this problem, compounded by stupidity, nationalist short-sightedness and other human traits, makes it all too believable: and the ambiguity of the Murray situation makes it equally interesting. If Murray is not telling the truth, what did happen on the Moon while Tyne was unconscious? And if Murray is lying, why such a clumsy lie?

Then we get another comic-book sequence, in which Tyne, after being delayed at the spaceport, charges off after Murray without stopping to tell anybody anything; *and* meets a mysterious undercover agent in a bar, *and* gets knocked over the head and abducted in a taxi . . . The rest of the chase, which takes Tyne to Padang, a Rosk hideout, a desert island, and to some hair-raising cliffhangers in a big automated plankton plant, alternates more or less regularly between thoughtful analysis and pointless action.

But even in his comic-book writing, Aldiss is more perceptive than most. The final solution of his puzzle is ingenious and reasonably satisfying; his future world has at least touches of reality, because it's as idiotically patched-together and complicated as our own. And at times Aldiss's gift for phrase-making triumphs over his plot. Two samples:

> The ocean (. . .) lay there flat as failure, stagnant and brassy.

> Absolute poverty, like absolute power, corrupts absolutely.

If this writer ever does a novel with his right hand, it will be something worth waiting for.

Edmund Cooper is another British writer whose short stories so far, have been more rewarding than his novels. *Seed of Light* has a fatuous plot in which all the British statesmen are heroic idealists and all the Americans clowns and demagogues. The writing is gassy, with an almost incredible concentration of cliché in some places. For contrast, Cooper has had the gall to interpolate this fuggheaded screed with passages from Ecclesiastes and Revelation.

Put in charge of the first manned satellite (for some impenetrably idealistic British reason), a mystic and a Communist argue over whether to bomb all satellite bases, or just all but the Soviet Union's. In the event, it doesn't matter, because they start World War III anyhow.

Dissolve to a generation or so later. All that's left of Earth's human population is in a few glass-roofed cities, all of which are now building spaceships in a frantic effort to escape the lingering death of the planet. (They build these spaceships inside the city domes, in such a way that the takeoff of each ship will probably mean the death of everybody left behind. This seems pretty asinine, but let us pass on.)

Well, these gigantic spaceships are to support generations of travelers, but the original complement of each is to be just ten— five men, five women. By "recycling their biological material" over and over, they can exist indefinitely without further supplies of food. We fade out on a scene from the Hollywood version of *When Worlds Collide*. Now we meet the crew of one starship, all of whom take silly-ass names on joining the crew (the men take the names of famous scientists, the women those of cities —presumably on the theory that if you ruled out courtesans and actresses, there wouldn't be enough famous women to go around), and we settle down to a dismally uninventive rewrite of "Universe."

All this changes radically c. page 130, when a third-generation mutant named Kepler tries to unite his own telepathic powers and those of his two wives, in an attempt to explore the precognitive memory of a newborn child—with the object of finding out before-hand whether Procyon will prove to have habitable planets, so that if not, the expedition can save years by turning aside earlier. This venture and its sequel have a Stapledonian sweep; the char-acters are as stiff and artificial as ever, but now they have found their milieu. Even Cooper's soggy prose seems to take on dignity. From here until the end, the book holds up beautifully; the epi-logue is a little sticky, but not enough to matter.

What alarms me is that this transformation takes place just about 13/15 of the way into the book. I know perfectly well that if I hadn't had a review column to do, I never would have got past page 5; and I seriously doubt that any adult reader, under normal circumstances, would have the patience to read as far as page 50.

Sometime, Never offers three oddly assorted entertainments by three highly accomplished British writers. "Envoy Extraordi-nary," by William Golding, is a satirical fantasy of what might have happened if an ingenious Greek had invented (a) the pressure cooker, (b) the steamship, (c) the mortar, and (d) the art of printing, in the time of the middle Roman Empire. Golding, whose forte is subtlety, has embedded his joke pretty deeply in a mass of eru-dition, irony, and well-bred understatement, but it is still very funny, and a shrewder blow at the romantic ideal of Progress than Ray Bradbury's "The Flying Machine."

"Consider Her Ways," by John Wyndham, deals with a future

world in which men have been wiped out by a mutated virus, leaving women to reproduce by parthenogenesis and build up a rigid ant-like society of Mothers, Servitors, Doctors and Workers, each class biologically tailored for its function. Wyndham drops a representative young 20th-century woman bang into the middle of all this by way of a soul-liberating drug called chuinjuatin, and pits her against a cultured lady of the time in an argument that may make you stop and think:

If the women of the future are happy and secure in their stable, peaceful world, what exactly have they lost, in losing romantic love? The story is beautifully written, fully realized in a way that few s.f. stories have been.

"Boy In Darkness," by Mervyn Peake, is a curious episode in the life of Titus Groan, the central character of two long Gothic-fantastic novels by Peake. Titus, here simply referred to as "the Boy," is the heir of a gigantic, nine-tenths deserted castle in a gloomy, decaying, tradition-ridden land. Very little happens to him, or to anybody in these stories, but Peake's lavish Victorian prose builds up memorable impressions of dusty gloom, of silence and decay. A painter and illustrator by profession, Peake uses words more for their colors than for their precise meanings. The results are sometimes awkward, always verbose, but ever and again, like a man sloshing paints together at random, Peake achieves striking and unheard-of combinations. This time, in his only outright fantasy to date—it is subtitled "The Dream" in this collection, and Peake seems to have meant it as that—he creates images that are perfect nonsense, and yet will chill your blood as you read.

Rex Gordon, author of *First on Mars*, has produced a companion volume of sorts, called *First to the Stars*. Like the earlier book, this is an impressively original work. More uneven than *First on Mars*, it's poor enough at its worst, but at its best it is very, very good.

Gordon has a knack, rare in these jaded times, for interplanetary adventure soberly and convincingly told. His thinking often seems to have as many holes in it as a Swiss cheese (e.g., after a remarkably convincing argument that the crew of the first spaceship would necessarily consist of one man and one woman, he spoils it all by having them paired at random, and so incompatible that they can barely take time off from quarreling to pilot the ship); but between the holes, his writing is full of mental nourishment.

The book is divided into four parts, of which the first is the poorest: taking off for Mars, the hero and heroine, with some perfunctory muttering about Einsteinian relativity, find themselves heading for the stars instead. (Does anybody remember Karl van Kampen's "The Irrelevant"?)

After this comic-strip beginning, sketchy in its characterizations as it is careless in its science (" 'By the general theory of relativity,' I said, 'a body traveling at the speed of light would acquire infinite size and mass' "), the ship crashes on an alien planet, and part two begins.

Part two, which deals with the man's and woman's grim struggle for race survival, is Gordon at his best. Slowly and soberly, unaided by dramatic tricks, he shows you what it would be like to begin at the bottom of the cultural ladder, without tools, without any hope except for your children. The ending of part two is so unexpectedly honest that it comes as a crushing surprise.

Part three takes the story to still another planet, inhabited by an alien culture, and here, though the novel loses much of its powerful simplicity, it gains in subtlety. The remainder of the story, including part four, which is a brilliant outgrowth of part three, is mature science fiction—conflict, danger, mystery, all against a sustained background of intellectual excitement. For adult consumption.

25. PITFALLS AND DEAD ENDS

THE PUBLISHERS DESCRIBE the Twayne Triplets, of which *The Petrified Planet* is the first, as "the first truly new idea in twenty years of science-fiction publication." The last time anybody made a noise like that, it was about a science fiction magazine with a comic book bound into it. I have a hunch that this one won't last long, either.*

The idea *looks* good. A hired scientist (in this case Dr. John D. Clark), mocks up the chemistry, climatology and biochemistry of an imagined planet; his description is handed over to three writers, who use it as background material in three independent novellas.

The trouble is that, no matter how interesting the background may be, there's probably at most only one dramatic way of using it in a story, and when you toss it up for grabs the best thing that can happen is that one out of three writers will use it effectively. The trouble is, further, that shoehorning the postulated background into three different stories does not unify them but makes them mutually contradictory. The result is interesting in a technical sense, like *Mr. Fothergill's Plot*, the outrageous volume to which about twenty writers—Chesterton was one—contributed independent versions of the same short trick-ending plot; but for people who do not care how the plumbing is put together, but only want to get a drink, it's a flat disappointment.

Fletcher Pratt's "The Long View" is a complicated story of petty politics in an absurd Scientocratic state, inhabited by long-winded puppets; it also contains one horrible blooper, which seems to be par for the author when he writes science fiction: "...Shigemitsu's voice came out, with that tiny suggestion of hissing accent that no one of Japanese ancestry ever quite lost..." I grew up among Nisei, and can testify, if any testimony other than common sense is needed, that this is chauvinistic nonsense.

H. Beam Piper's "Uller Uprising," hands-down the best of the

*It didn't.

three stories, is excellent writing largely wasted, for my taste, on a conventional native-uprising story—full of careful military-historical detail which I find no more bearable here than in a textbook.

Judith Merril's "Daughters of Earth" is a truly sick-making combination of soap opera and comic book, honest ignorance and deliberate hypocrisy. Merril has a respectable talent and is in private life nobody's fool, and certainly nobody's weepy housefrau; I *wish* she would stop pretending otherwise.

Of the three, Pratt's and Merril's have so flimsy a connection with Clark's background material that they could be chopped loose with a few strokes of a blue pencil. Piper uses it brilliantly, but even his story could be laid on an altogether different imaginary planet—or, for that matter, on Earth—without altering the plot a nickel's worth.

The single-background series in science-fantasy is a notable snare and delusion. The temptation to squeeze some more juice out of an already established background is all but irresistible, even to writers who know the folly of Plotto and the exasperating stubbornness of the Ouija board; I have fallen victim to it myself often enough, God knows, but editors or, more often, my own boredom have always slapped me down. Yet the suggestion that a group of writers should agree on one broad picture of the future, and adhere to it, crops up again and again.

Writers aren't wholly to blame; readers are in a continual ferment of encouragement for series stories—naturally enough; when you find something you like, you want more exactly the same —and editors want them because the readers do.

And yet it ought to be no surprise to anybody that each successive instalment of such a series is vaguely less satisfying than the last. The background—the set of assumptions that governs the story—*is* the story. It's the hardest work involved in writing speculative fiction, and the only thing that makes it worth doing at all. The more familiar the background, the less speculative: and then you wonder why the Lensman stories seem to be getting murkier and less interesting as they go along, why Asimov's Empire is getting so dusty, why even the Baldies seem to be marching around in a circle.

Mutant, by Lewis Padgett, is about as strong a case in point as could be asked for. The Kuttners habitually operate on a level of competence that most of us can only strain after; in "The Piper's Son" they reintroduced to science fiction the idea that a superman story need not be a paranoid's dream of Wagner, and in the three

stories that followed it in 1945—a vintage year—they developed
the theme honestly, vigorously and with enormous skill. In 1953
they produced a fifth story to finish the series off: and here they
all are, with an ingenious sandwich-filling between them to reduce
the reader's required thought processes to a minimum. The texture is even; you can open this book anywhere and find the same
whetted tension, the same economy, the same firm structure. And
yet only the first and last stories are memorable.

The last story, because it contains the solution; the first, because all the background is in it. Everything: the decentralization
after Blowup, the armed truce, the telepathic Baldies, the paranoids and their Green Man, the hostility of the normal population,
the duelling, Baldy occupations, Baldy home life. The first story
says it all. "Three Blind Mice," "The Lion and the Unicorn" and
"Beggars in Velvet" will not stick in your mind because they have
no substance. "Mice" captures your attention with a trick and a
gimmick: the typographical experiments with unspoken dialogue—
anticipating Alfred Bester's playfulness in *The Demolished Man*—
and the paranoids' secret wavelength. "Lion" and "Beggars" ring
skillful changes on the tragic love-lives of Baldies and non-
Baldies, paranoid and sane Baldies; they introduce one more
gimmick—the scrambler—and one plot device, the retreat underground. The three together advance the plot of "The Piper's Son"
by an amount the Kuttners would normally consider worth about
two thousand words.

But if the Baldy stories had been written as a novel to begin
with, wouldn't all the background have been in the first chapter
just the same? (a) Certainly not, and (b) despite Gnome's inspired
tinkering, this book isn't a novel; God Almighty couldn't make it
one without rewriting it from the beginning.

The difference is this: A novel is one structure, built toward a
known end. A series is an open-ended Tinkertoy chain; it can go
on as long as the editor's and the writer's patience holds out, and
you can chop it off anywhere, like liverwurst. Because the first
segment has to be complete in itself, it must either use up the
postulated background or be a poor story; and since the Kuttners
have not written a poor story within the memory of man, they had
no choice but to put the rest together out of scraps, pyrotechnics
and sleight of hand.

Not many could have done it as well; but nobody could have
wanted very badly to do it at all.

Grame, the hero of Margot Bennett's *The Long Way Back*, was
a young mechanical-repetitive worker who had taught himself

science; he longed to be a cosmic-ray investigator. But in the
static, bored civilization of Africa, centuries after the fabled
Big Bang, there was no room at the top; the machine refused to
regrade him. Three times in the last week Grame had hung the
Drunk and Angry sign on the door of his hut; he had sworn to become a physicist or die. But when he was thrown a scrap—a place
in the first post-Bang expedition to savage Britain—he took it.
Along with Valya the dedicated spinster, ugly Hep the zoologist,
and a faceless pack of others, he climbed into the Amphibian and
flew northward.

—And as they fly, this novel follows them out of the most fascinating imaginary civilization of recent memory, into a series
of jungle adventures which, in spite of all this charming writer
can do, are much like other jungle adventures.

The first three chapters are a continuous delight. In dagger-
sharp, feather-light touches, the author gives us the Africans'
social habits, religion (the Noble Abstraction), government—and
such casual glances at their history as this:

> "Have you heard the latest ghastly news ? A couple of domesti-
> cated lions have got loose in the nature reserve. If we don't watch
> out they'll breed. Can you imagine lions loose in the reserve!
> They might turn positively vicious. If something isn't done, they'll
> get through the fence and eat all our Boers, and then what will
> happen to anthropology ?"

Apparently feeling that to dwell too long with her Africans
would be to dispel their mystery, Miss Bennett has fallen into
the greater error of the Transition Ad Nauseam: instead of going
directly to her protagonists' destination, she takes them the long
back way around, through hardship, attack by animals, sickness and
then (for variety) hardship, attack by animals and sickness again.

This pit yawns for every writer who has misread Burroughs
or Haggard in his youth. In many a classic romance, adventures
in the wilderness were not padding; they were what the story
was about. In modern science-fantasy, when the subject is the
manners and morals of people in a future society, such arbitrary
plot-spinning is a method of wasting space.

Miss Bennett has wasted about nine chapters of it—more than
half the book. Midway, the story picks up again when the brown
explorers enter a melancholy village of cave-dwelling Britons,
with habits as peculiar in their own dismal way as the Africans'
own; but then off they go through that damned jungle, in which
every square inch is like every other.

Before this monotony, Miss Bennett's wit fades; the characters'

speech lapses—even at those times when none of them is dramatically delirious—into a kind of pidgin African:

> "Soon we'll be in Africa," he whispered. "Forever. Not for
> everyone's ever. Only for our ever. Other people's ever is very
> different, like their now . . ."

Having plucked the most interesting Briton out of his environment, so that (like all the others) he has nothing to do that any
other faceless character couldn't, the author is forced to fall back
on a tardy, hastily manufactured and embarrassingly phony love
affair between Valya and Grame.

—And all this just to discover in the end, what every reader
knew all along, that the Britons extinguished themselves with the
atomic weapons which the Africans are just developing.

At story's end, Grame, Valya and Hep are heading back to
Africa, where the reader, to his frustration, senses that they
will immediately become fascinating, believable people again.

If only we could follow them there—or if only they had never
left home!

John Wyndham's *Re-Birth* is his third novel, although in a
previous incarnation he wrote several more. The new Wyndham
—who, in 1949, "broke a bottle over his bows . . . and started in"
afresh—has turned out to be something remarkably like a new
H. G. Wells — not the wise-old-owl Wells, more interested in
sermon than story, but the young Wells, with that astonishing,
compelling gift of pure story-telling.

Written in the first person, like *The Day of the Triffids* and *Out
of the Deeps* (and like much early Wells), this book introduces us
to one of the most believable After-the-Atom societies on record.
It's a rural society, a world of almost-frontier farming—not very
exciting, except for occasional raids by the outcast Fringes people
—quite small and safe feeling, a world of earth and sunlight.
To young David Strorm, who has grown up in it, there's nothing
extraordinary in this world's ultra-Puritan religion or its preoccupation with mutations. Destroy people and animals who have
an extra toe, or the wrong color of hair or skin? Certainly!
Doesn't the Bible say, "And God made the beasts of the earth
after their kind, and the cattle after their kind, and everything
that creepeth upon the ground after its kind . . ." and, "God created
man in his own image . . ." ? And yet, equally naturally, farmers
are reluctant to destroy a valuable animal, or a field of grain,
that's only a *little* different . . . .

A heresy: *Is* the description of the Norm that's recited in church on Sundays, the description of man as he was before the Tribulation? How can anybody know?

It's a vital point to David, for the first time, because of an accidental discovery: his small girl friend, Sophie, has a sixth toe on each foot.

Here's all love and all morality compressed into one aching question. It's sharply real, because the people and their world are real. These first few chapters have the genuine autobiographical sense—that Wellsian retrospective clarity, the torment of writers who can't do it themselves.

More's the pity that Wyndham, for once, failed to realize how good a thing he had. The sixth toe was immensely believable, and sufficient: but Wyndham has dragged in a telepathic mutation on top of it; has made David himself one of the nine child telepaths, and hauled the whole plot away from his carefully built background, into just one more damned chase with a rousing cliché at the end of it.

Wyndham's unflaggingly expert writing, all the way through, only proves that there are no exceptions: this error is fatal.

It's the same trap into which Lester del Rey fell with "For I Am A Jealous People," and Margot Bennett with *The Long Way Back*. One forest is like another forest, one chase like another chase, one rescue like another rescue. Those who want to read stale derring-do don't have to come to science fiction: back issues of the pulps, at three for a quarter, are foundering full of it. Crooks chase man and girl who Know Too Much; lawman chases badman; over and over and over; why else do you suppose the pulps died?

Del Rey's story was in the church where the aliens installed their God; Miss Bennett's was in Africa; Wyndham's was on the farm at Waknuk. Each threw his story away (del Rey to pick it up again, but almost too late), to grasp at movement for the sake of movement.

A rolling story gathers no meaning. Most of the frantic physical action in science fiction, of which sophisticated critics rightly complain, is no more than a nervous twitch.

Let us sit still, and unroll our mats, and tell our tales.

Ballantine has been publicizing Wyndham's *The Midwich Cuckoos*, for reasons I cannot fathom, as a comic novel. Certainly the plot sounds comic enough: Something like a flying saucer descends on a sleepy English village; there is a 24-hour blackout during which nobody from outside can get in, and the inhabitants slumber; and a few months later it becomes evident that every fertile woman in the village is pregnant.

In the hands of a French writer, like the author of *The Scandals of Clochemerle*, I suppose this idea might actually have turned out to be funny; but Wyndham is nothing if not English, and his treatment is deadly serious, and I'm sorry to say, deadly dull.

The book opens promisingly, with a phlegmatic parade of Britons imperturbably vanishing into Midwich, and other Britons being sent to hunt for them. There are glimmers of humor later on, as when a character refers to "the Obstetrics Division of Military Intelligence." But about page 90 the story begins to bog down under layers of polite restraint, sentimentality, lethargy and women's-magazine masochism, and it never lifts its head long again.

To begin with, the narrator is purely an observer; he continually gets in the way of the story without contributing anything of his own. The central events of the story, partly for this reason, never come out. The golden-eyed, hypnotic superchildren grow up to a nasty teenhood and are then bombed to bits by a patriotic villager, which is just about what you would expect. (In 247 pages, the book reaches the point at which van Vogt's *Slan* begins.)

Who the "cuckoos" in the flying saucer were, and what the *hell* they thought they were up to, we never learn.

Wyndham's unbearably leisurely preparation consumes 145 pages before we get our first first-hand glimpse of a super-child; we do not hear one speak more than a couple of syllables until page 210, and the effect then is one of fraud—it's too late to convince us that they can talk like anyone else.

In Wyndham's *Out of the Deeps*, this same kind of arm's-length treatment was highly effective, because the invaders were down at the bottom of the ocean, and we could only speculate about them. But in *The Midwich Cuckoos*, the children are here; to keep them always half a mile in the background, as Wyndham does, is indefensible.

Good As Gold, by Alfred Toombs, has one of those ideas that start you laughing before you even begin the book: a backwoods scientist discovers a substance that will turn gold into dirt.

The "dirt," a by-product of atomic research, turns out to be a miracle soil conditioner, producing, as the story unfolds, monster grass blades, cacti &c. Its discoverer, John Henry Johnson, is a natural football for all the varied pressure groups of Washington, D.C.: so away we go, from one expertly contrived situation to another, swinging from wisecrack to wisecrack. And gradually you discover that it's becoming an effort to hold your face in that grin.

It's hard to say why. Toombs writes uncommonly well; he

knows his Washington; his characters are sharply drawn and fairly crackle with eccentricity; his situations are as novel as you could expect, and his gag-lines are funny. Except for the sex, in fact, this is almost like a good Thorne Smith novel . . . .

Just so. Except for the sex: which in Smith's work was not just a kind of bawdy icing on the cake, but the essential ingredient that gave it weight and solidity.

The word for a sexless farce like this one—which bored me to distraction, I couldn't finish the damned thing—is "sterile." Of course.

David Duncan, a talented mundane writer, has produced three would-be science fiction novels in which his talent and his confusion are equally evident.

Duncan's forte is people: he sees them with an inquiring, ironic, compassionate but unsentimental eye. At his best, the characters he draws are sharply individual, each one believable and distinct from every other. He fills up the scene with these moving portraits, and their intricate mutual relationships, effortlessly handled, make his book.

Coming late to science fiction, Duncan acquired one fundamental misconception which is still hampering his work: he took the basic substance of science fiction to be mystery.

This is one of those half truths that are sometimes more hurtful than falsehoods. "Mystery" as Duncan interprets it is a vast, cloudy unknown—a feeling of awe in darkness. That feeling is certainly at the back of every field of human knowledge, from physics to theology—an ecstasy of ignorance. But in front of it is the opposite, an ecstasy of understanding. In cosmology, for instance, we see "mystery" beyond the elegant and satisfying complexity of celestial mechanics.

In science fiction as in science, "mystery" alone is not the truth; moreover, it is not a thing that can be manipulated meaningfully in fiction. The unknown is the unknown; you can't elaborate it without explaining the mystery away; you can only state it, and in 70,000 words that gets damned dull.

Finally, as I'll show in a moment, this approach necessarily ends where science fiction has to begin.

The example before us is Duncan's third "science fiction" novel, *Occam's Razor*. At a naval base on Santa Felicia Island, Dr. Roger Staghorn keeps a complicated apparatus for the study of soap films. The base is the one where the first moon rocket, *Luna One*, is being prepared for launching. Staghorn is on the premises because his specialty, the theory of minimals, has a

bearing on the plotting of orbits. The excuse is pretty thin, but so
are Staghorn and his soap films; both are fascinating. I spent a
happy and incredulous half hour making wire frameworks according to the book's directions, and dipping them in soapy water.
(How many planes of soap film will there be on a cubical wire
frame? Six? Wrong—thirteen. Try it and see.)

Staghorn is a completely engaging character, a cadaverous
scarecrow of a man, with a compulsive rudeness toward authority.
During a demonstration, he so provokes a torpid young ensign that
when three films appear where only two are possible, the ensign
breaks the extra one; and the anomaly refuses to repeat itself.
Greatly upset, Staghorn goes back to his lab to tinker with the
big soap-film machine, and from there the base psychiatrist,
Cameron Hume, gets a phone call for help.

He finds the lab in darkness; two half-seen forms escape.
Staghorn is lying in the apparatus, knocked out. When he comes
to, it develops that he has amnesia and can't tell anybody what
happened.

Now we get a series of incidents in which other people see the
two who mysteriously appeared in the lab; through these repetitive glimpses we learn that the man looks like the Devil and the
woman like Eve. They are wandering around the base, obviously
bewildered; the man has great strength and kills several people
who try to stop him.

"The vital task," says the author on page 68, "was to learn the
secret of their arrival on the island, to learn how they had passed
through the radar and sonar screens and past a hundred electronic
eyes without being apprehended." Now, please note that Staghorn's
amnesia, that tired old trick, has been introduced here specifically to keep this question from being answered. The author's
purpose is to prolong the "mystery": but there is no real mystery
for the reader, except the one which can never be solved or even
discussed until the author stops pussyfooting around. The characters' endless wrong guesses about what the reader already
knows are boring,* and the only suspense takes the form "When
will Duncan get on with it?"

The horned man is trapped and leaps to his death; the woman
is captured. She is beautiful, and Hume falls in love with her.
This is routine, but Duncan's deft touch gives it some freshness.
Meanwhile, Staghorn comes out of his amnesia just in time to
prevent the novel from bogging down forever: he tells his story
on page 117—about sixty pages too late. The strangers came

*From page 90: "It was strange, under the circumstances, that so far no one had
suggested that the woman might have come from another planet." Yes, indeed!

through one of his soap films from another plane; time as we know it is a train of temporal quanta, and in the intervals between them there are other such trains—other universes existing side by side with ours. This is not an unfamiliar idea in science fiction; what is new is Duncan's gaseous and self-contradictory exposition of it. As in *Dark Dominion*, Duncan gives the uncomfortable impression that his science is too deep, not for the reader, but for the author.

The rocket-site background of the story, which has been supremely unimportant and neglected until this point, now gets some attention: when the dimensional crossing-over occurred there was a momentary suspension of time, which has bollixed up the *Luna One*'s "built-in timing calculators" (i.e., set its clock back half a second); this, Duncan tells us stoutly, will take "about a month's work" to fix.

It further appears that the same thing has happened to other rockets in preparation all over the world, and other nations are hopping mad about it: there is an ultimatum, an admiral's plane is shot down by a submarine, and war is about to break out any moment.

Against this unconvincing background, Staghorn repeats the experiment which brought the two strangers through; the C.O., who has just finished telling everybody that under no circumstances will he let the girl be sent back, lets her be sent back, and it turns out that the shock of the second crossing-over has knocked out rocket missiles all over the place, and nobody has any weapons to fight a war with. Hume, who might have been a little quicker on the draw, is thinking that he will go through the doorway next time, to "kneel at Lael's feet and ask for the right to remain in that land of freedom until he had won his horns and could clasp her to him forever."

End of book: beginning of story.

Under the aspect of "mystery," a plot has one basic assumption which is not revealed until the end: when the assumption is revealed, mystery vanishes, the book is over. Under the aspect of science fiction, a plot *begins* with its one basic assumption. "Mystery" is the question: science fiction always tries to give the answers.

"Mystery" can never really tell a story; it can only prolong a literary striptease as much as possible. A story is "what happens"—in the last analysis, we always see that in a "mystery" nothing has happened.

Duncan's assumption—the serial universe—is not new but is by no means worn out, either. The idealized pastoral world of which he gives us a glimpse or two looks moderately interesting; at least it would be fun to see if he could reconcile the wildly conflicting elements he has built into it. The question he poses could lead to any number of interesting answers: What happens after communication between worlds is established? What adventures would an Earthman have on Lael's planet? Or: what would be the effect on our society of another accessible, inhabited world? Or (this one is hinted at in one tantalizing chapter, and then dropped): what does our world look like, seen through Lael's eyes?

The direction a story takes is up to its author; the only unforgiveable thing is to go through all the motions without taking it anywhere.

This Fortress World, by James Gunn, is the author's second novel; like his first, *Star Bridge* (with Jack Williamson), it is full of good or at least acceptable fictional ideas, slowly and ineptly developed. Its basic framework is all too familiar: acolyte rebels against priestly tyranny founded on electrical "miracles"; helps overthrow same; meets girl; gets girl.

In this kind of thing, once you get your shmo-hero shaken out of his comfortable cell in the monastery, the plot cannot proceed until you have him meet somebody who can teach him the ropes, and, as a matter of course, enroll him as an underground member. In Leiber's *Gather, Darkness!* this person was Mother Jujy, a likable crone whose adoption of Brother Jarles was at least half-believable; in Heinlein's "If This Goes On—" it was Zebadiah, a fellow member of the Prophet's palace guard. This is the most plausible solution, and is at the opposite pole from two things that happen to Gunn's hero, William Dane: he is dragged in off the street by a professional killer, who educates him in the tricks of the trade (enabling Dane to kill him, one chapter later on), and subsequently, he Meets a Girl in a Bar.

Once off on this wrong foot, the story limps ever after: much of the action fails to advance the plot and nearly all of it is unconvincing. Two minor characters, the villains Sabatini and Siller, are briefly and unexpectedly vivid, and there are frequent touches elsewhere of the good writing we expect from the Gunn who wrote "The Misogynist" and "New Blood"; but not even the best of artistic second thoughts can save this commercially degraded story.

The book has one more thing seriously wrong with it, in common with other recent popular work: Spillanism—sadistic violence for its own sake. We have grown so used to this in our country that it comes as a shock when a European reader protests with honest revulsion. When that happened to me some time ago, I argued with my correspondent somewhat in this vein: "Violence exists, even sadistic violence, and is a factual part of the universe about which we write stories. Where do you draw the line between what is permissible to write about, and what isn't?" I couldn't think of any satisfactory answer then, but believe I know one now. The question is one of meaning.

The abortive first novel I started when I was nineteen was autobiographical; I wrote in the third person and changed all the names, but otherwise it might as well have been a diary. To my surprise and disappointment, this did not turn out to be a novel or to have any other virtues, and I dropped it after a few pages.

Probably most young writers have to go through this sobering experience; my point is that reality alone does not justify putting anything into a story: *fiction is reality plus meaning.* At nineteen, I had no understanding of my own life and had nothing to say about it; my "novel" was only a transcription. The author of *This Fortress World*, for whatever reason, has not said anything about evil; he has simply mortared in a chunk of the pure thing.

The reader will have to turn to an older work, C. S. Lewis' Perelandra trilogy, to find the moral: "evil" and "meaning" are opposite terms.

Horace Gold is an amiable, prowling kind of a man whose taste in shirts adumbrates a private hankering to be tall in the saddle. Interested, alert, alarmed, skeptical, ironic, anxious as a broody hen, he can no more keep from interfering with another man's story, once he owns it, than a saucer-eyed kid with a jam jar.

His gargantuan optimism, and the deeper pessimism that lies under it, have helped to make *Galaxy* the brilliant and sometimes bewildering magazine it is. His scorn for clichés has been a major influence in the modern growth of science fiction; his indifference to questions of content and conviction has done as much to vitiate the field. The same qualities have shaped his own work —5,000,000 words of it—confessions, fact detectives, radio scripts, comics, everything . . . including a little science-fantasy.

As " Clyde Crane Campbell," he was writing tersely titled stories for *Astounding* in 1934; under his own name, a few years later, he turned up as the author of the first *Astounding* "nova" story, "A Matter of Form," and as co-author of one of *Unknown*'s most convincingly frightening short novels, "None But Lucifer" (with L. Sprague de Camp).

In all, and excepting the stories mentioned above (plus a few more which I'll come to in a moment), he wrote surprisingly little and surprisingly bad science fiction. At least, it is surprising to me; but here, in Gold's own collection, *The Old Die Rich*, is a fair sampling.

One miraculous small masterpiece: "Trouble With Water." This warmly human tragicomedy about the Rockaway concessionaire and the water gnome is on many an all-time-best list, including mine.

Five good to passable short stories, containing chinks and flaws of various sizes. These range from almost-perfect light entertainment like "Man of Parts" and "The Man With English," through near-failures like "The Old Die Rich" (a fine idea marred by incredible characters, and the most bloated climax-and-solution in recent memory), to the distressingly inconsistent and unpleasant "No Charge For Alterations."

Six totally regrettable potboilers: "Love in the Dark," "The Biography Project," "At the Post," "Hero," "And Three to Get Ready" and "Problem in Murder." The one common denominator of these stories is artificiality: the plots are mechanical, the characters shambling dough-figures.

Gold's working notes, appended after each story, are about like any other writer's mumble-sheets, but they do throw some light on why and where Old Pro Gold went wrong. In at least one place, almost by accident, they evoke the very thing that's missing from the stories themselves.

> THEME: Walking in dismal rain toward editorial conference, me without an idea in my head . . . worried sub-vocalization sticks in groove of old song about walking between raindrops. Feeling of elation—how about a man whom water won't touch?

There it all is, in less than forty words, and without any technical tricks—sympathetic character, problem, mood, setting and a lot more.

And there's the answer, too, in capsule form: the essential ingredient of fiction doesn't come from technique, or earnestness, or a dozen rewrites: it comes in the simplest and most natural way imaginable, when a writer honestly tries to tell what he knows and believes.

Preferred Risk, by Edson McCann, is the vastly disappointing winner of the *Galaxy*-Simon and Schuster contest. Apparently it's tougher than anybody realized to find an unpublished novel which (a) is not committed to another book publisher, and (b) satisfies the requirements of a *Galaxy* serial. The mountain has been laboring since February, 1953, and here is your mouse.

To begin with, the story slavishly copies *Galaxy*'s "Gravy

Planet" (*The Space Merchants*), which has already been copied
once by the original proprietors, as *Galaxy*'s and Ballantine's
Gladiator-at-Law. The third, and I trust the last in this cooky-
cutter series, it substitutes medical-insurance companies for the
advertising industry of #1 and the housing industry of #2; otherwise the tune is much the same, but the performance is very flat.

There is a tendency for the heroes of long *Galaxy* stories to
be shmoes; I do not know why, although I have contributed to the
trend myself; I suspect the editor likes them and sends out ema-
nations to that effect. At any rate, the hero of "Gravy Planet" was
a sharp apple, perfectly unscrupulous and entirely believable in
his environment. It was later complained that this made his climactic conversion to the forces of light rather hard to swallow.
Perhaps for this reason, the hero of *Gladiator-at-Law* is a social
zero, neither bright nor dull, honest nor crooked, tall nor short:
Mr. Who? This apparently worked well, as a character like that
can be converted to anything, twice a chapter if necessary, without
arousing any incredulity.

And for whatever reason, the hero of *Preferred Risk*, a claims
adjuster named Tom Wills, is a shmo to end all shmoes.

> "I know for a fact," Gogarty said bitterly, "that Zorchi knew we
> found out he was going to dive in front of the express tonight. . ."
> "Mr. Gogarty," I interrupted, "are you trying to tell me this
> man *deliberately* maims himself for the accident insurance?"
> Gogarty nodded sourly. "Good heavens!" I cried, "that's disloyal!"

This will give you some idea. The whole front half of the book
is like that: evidence parades across the middle ground in a
steady stream that the Company is run by a bunch of corrupt
no-goods and tyrants, &c., &c., and Wills stomps around through
it all, with a regulation smile on his face, uttering platitudes.
His only function in the novel, in fact, seems to be to demonstrate
this essence of shmoeness; he is totally unimportant to the plot.

Curiously, all three books hinge on the idea of inheritance of
power. In "Gravy Planet," the protagonist, unknown to himself,
turned out to be the heir apparent; this was a surprise. In *Preferred Risk*, exactly the same thing happens:

> He sighed. "I seem to have been wrong about you, Thomas.
> Perhaps because I need someone to help, I overestimated you.
> I thought long ago that under your conditioning you had brains."

This is incredible.

Only one character in the book has any vividness, and he briefly:
Zorchi, the "human jellyfish" whose ability to grow new limbs

enables him to defraud the Company over and over. This throws an ingenious monkey wrench into the orderly actuarial world, and for the first couple of chapters the man is enormously believable and entertaining. Later he blurs into the general grayness, as if another hand had taken him over.

The extrapolation holds up brilliantly in some places, as in the anti-war and disease policies, with their unexpected concomitant, the suspended-animation chambers; in others, it's nonsense, as in the "transportation policies" ("as the cab driver clipped my coupons . . ."). The plot development is logical and ingenious, but uninspired.

Leigh Brackett's *The Long Tomorrow* is a startling performance from the gifted author of so much, but so entirely different, science-fantasy. Miss Brackett is celebrated among fans for her intense, moody, super-masculine epics of doomed heroes on far planets, all extremely poetic and fantastical, and all very much alike.

The present novel takes place on Earth, about eighty-five years from now—two and a half generations after the atom war that destroyed the cities. The world, in almost a century, has healed over but never grown back. No longer half godless, America is chockablock with sects like the New Mennonites:

> . . . Back in the Twentieth Century, only two generations before, there had been just the Old Mennonites and the Amish, and only a few tens of thousands of them, and they had been regarded as quaint and queer because they held to the old simple handcraft ways and would have no part of cities or machines. But when the cities ended, and men found that in the changed world these of all folk were best fitted to survive, the Mennonites had swiftly multiplied into the millions they now counted.

Speculation as brilliantly sound as this no longer seems like speculation at all, but simple truth; and all this is as real, as intimately detailed and as warmly sympathetic as if the author herself had lived it. Here's young, flat-hatted Len Colter, for instance, just after he and his cousin Esau have seen a man named Soames stoned to death by religious fanatics.

> Len turned his head and looked at Esau. He was crying, and his face was white. Esau had his arms folded tightly across his middle, and his body was bent over them. His eyes were huge and staring. Suddenly he turned and rushed away on all fours under

the cart. Len bolted after him, scrambling, crabwise, with the
air dark and whirling around him. All he could think about was
the pecans Soames had given him. . . .

Just so, my God!
And here's Gran, who was a little girl when the cities were
still there:

"Seems like this is the only time you see real colors any more,
when the trees turn in the fall. The world used to be full of
colors. You wouldn't believe it, Lennie, but I had a dress once,
as red as that tree."

The book is full of similar poignant touches, each unexpectedly
penetrating and absolutely right. The author follows Len and Esau
from boyhood through young manhood with such warm wisdom that
you find yourself continually saying, " Yes, that's so . . . Yes,
that's so! . . ."
Unhappily, as the story progresses, it seems more and more
to support Koestler's assertion that literature and science fiction
cancel each other out. Most of the book, particularly the early
part, is compellingly written, but not speculative—communities
just like this one were common not so long ago, and some, as Miss
Brackett reminds us, still exist. Where the smallest flavoring
of speculation is mixed in, as in the passage quoted above, it
heightens the effect; but increasingly, as the invented elements
of the story grow more important, the vision dims.
Perhaps Koestler is right after all, and there's no help for it.
At any rate, Miss Brackett has dealt conscientiously with the
speculative element—a hidden town, now half-legendary, where
the descendants of government scientists are trying to find a way
to bring atomic civilization safely back. Two thirds of the novel
are occupied with Len's and Esau's search for " Bartorstown,"
and with the ordinary, miraculous, tragic things that happen to
them along the way. And when they finally reach their goal, they
find no Hollywood supermen dressed in chrome and black leather,
but ordinary people, in a dismal shanty town, laboring desperately
at a problem too big for them.
All the same, in spite of good craftsmanship and good intentions,
somewhere along the line, all the reality has leaked out of the
story. Miss Brackett's occasional sharp character sketches are
now all in the background; the foreground figures we now meet
are totally unconvincing, and so, I regret to say, is Len himself.
The story line, which had seemed to flow as naturally and inevitably as real life, gradually begins to waver into the same old

comedy of divided loyalties we have been through so often: having lost the drama, the author has fallen back on dramatics.

Like Wyndham's *Re-Birth*, this novel illustrates a problem which science fiction writers are going to have to solve before long: how to write honestly about a mildly speculative future without dragging in pseudoscientific props by the carload.

The mildly speculative future is a legitimate area of interest for literature, and one that's so far been notably neglected. The future-tense novel, for want of a better term, may in time become as common as the contemporary and past-tense novels; but it will have to give up hiding behind the clichés of science fiction first.

26. SYMBOLISM

HERE IS WHAT IS LEFT of a curious venture into symbolic analysis of s.f. stories. I wrote this essay for *Science Fiction Forum*, a short-lived amateur magazine edited by Lester del Rey and myself in 1957. The essay was to have been the first of two, but the second part never got written; I was so taken aback by reader reaction to the first part that I wrote a defense of it instead; then the *Forum* expired, and my notes for the second part—dozens of little slips of paper in a cardboard carton—were lost in moving.

I don't know quite what to make of all this now. Through the *Forum* experience, and at a session of the first Milford Conference, I found out that many writers have a strong resistance to the idea that there is or could be any unconscious symbolism in their work. I think it is there, nevertheless. The *Forum* debate on this topic was inconclusive, but I will say that I challenged Lester del Rey (one of the doubters) to produce an analysis of Jim Blish's "Common Time" showing that it is really about a man eating a ham sandwich on rye—and he did it.

People who write on this subject generally seem to begin with what amounts to an apology for bringing the matter up at all. Freud, in *Leonardo da Vinci: A Study in Psychosexuality*, goes out of his way to disclaim any intention "to blacken the radiant, and to drag the sublime into the mire." Ernest Jones's *Hamlet and Oedipus* opens by speaking of "the fear that beauty may vanish under too scrutinizing a gaze, and with it our pleasure."

Writing for a specialized audience, and about twenty years later, I think I can afford to ignore this kind of oversensitivity. There's another kind, though, that turned up to my great surprise at the first Milford S. F. Writers' Conference. A couple of people vigorously opposed any discussion of unconscious symbolism; not because they thought there were any bogies in their own minds, but because they were afraid of insights which would "cure" them and leave them happy and healthy, but no longer able to write.

I very much doubt my ability to write anything which would suddenly transform a neurotic, successful author into a normal nobody. There seems to be some ground for believing that I'm not likely to hit upon anybody's personal, private symbols, even by accident. Common symbols communicate; private ones don't.

I get embarrassed when I find myself talking about a high-order abstraction as if I had been there in person, and counted the knobs on it, and chipped off a piece to take home. I do not think I know much about the unconscious. But I am certain I have one, because I use it (or it uses me) every day; it does about ninety per cent of the creative work I put out. My unconscious gets ideas (as opposed to gimmicks); "I" never do. My unconscious dictates the form and mood of stories, and often supplies whole scenes and characters. I am just the scribe; I tinker with the work as it goes along in order to give it surface coherence and logic, but I have to keep in touch at intervals with the unconscious as I do so; if I don't, the product gets very flat indeed.

It's a commonplace of criticism that great writing has a richer texture of meaning than could ever have been deliberately woven into it; the unconscious of the writer has not only determined the form of the work, but has fleshed it out too. I hope to show that this is also true of tolerably good writing, and of some tolerably bad writing as well.

There are some axiomatic assumptions embedded in this work, and I may as well state them here for the benefit of those who will disagree with them. I believe that "the unconscious" is in a sense a misnomer; that the submerged portions of our minds are aware and govern our thinking to a larger degree than we usually realize. I believe the activity of the unconscious is structured, not random. I believe that in translating unconscious expressions we can demand a high order of coherence, and get it. To sum up, I think the images that recur in our creative work are not the products of a child or a moron; neither are they illegible riddles—they are exasperatingly hard to decipher, but that seems to be because of a conscious habit of looking the other way. I believe that the symbols which animate our best work are healthful, and that finding out more about them can only make us better artists.

I owe very grateful thanks to Jim Blish, whose insights in this field surround mine on every side; to his ex-wife, Virginia; to my ex-wife, Helen; to Algis Budrys, Phil Klass, Cyril Kornbluth,

Lester and Evelyn del Rey for invaluable suggestions, reproofs, and shoves in the right direction.

Mysteries of Birth

To find an unconscious symbol in art, look for something that affects you powerfully without your knowing why. Not every symbol will do this to everybody every time. Here's one that sometimes does it to me:

> A sense of elation swept through him. He felt as he had once felt standing alone at dusk in a wind-tossed forest. He could not speak. His breath stopped...
> ("The Far Look," by Theodore L. Thomas.)

What I feel when I imagine this scene is the shadow of something I've experienced directly in similar times and places—a particular kind of emotional tension; "anticipation" is the nearest word I can find for it, but anticipation at a very high pitch. It is not what I would call pleasure; it seems to belong at the moment just before pleasure. It has suggestions of joy and anguish in it. Apparently it's a very common human experience. It seems to be one form of what C. S. Lewis is talking about as "joy" in his autobiographical *Surprised by Joy*.

Here it is again, this time in an eyewitness account of a hurricane:

> Two minutes had scarcely elapsed, when the whole forest before me was in fearful motion... Turning instinctively toward the direction from which the wind blew, I saw, to my great astonishment, that the noblest trees of the forest bent their lofty heads for a while, and unable to stand against the blast, were falling to pieces... Some of the largest trees were seen bending and writhing under the gale; others suddenly snapped across, and many, after a momentary resistance, fell uprooted to the earth.
> ("The Hurricane," by John James Audubon.)

Now, what is it about the idea of a wind in a forest that calls up such a response? One explanation might be that when you are in imminent danger of your life, during such a natural catastrophe as a hurricane, you may feel a kind of exhilaration, which is fear turned inside out.

> I drove on. The wheat would have been as tall as your waist. It went undulating up and down the hills like a great green carpet, with the wind rippling it a little, kind of thick and silky-looking. It's like a woman, I thought. It makes you want to lie on it.
> (*Coming Up For Air*, by George Orwell.)

I am suggesting, with due caution and qualification, that this is a procreation symbol. Intuitively, the resemblance of the two experiences seems to me very striking. Traditionally, the earth and its foliage have feminine associations that go back as far as we can trace human thought. The wind's symbolism is equally ancient: it is the male life-giving principle, the "pneuma." The Greeks believed the wind could impregnate mares; the Egyptians had a similar belief about vultures.

These scholarly comparisons may seem remote, but they aren't: we are all pagans, in spite of two thousand years of Christianity, tight collars and cold baths. Nobody teaches us the religious beliefs of the ancient world, except as a series of quaint myths— but the forest is a chapel to us, all the same.

The story which originally aroused my interest in the symbology of science fiction was Jim Blish's "Common Time." Summarized as briefly as possible, the plot went like this:

A man named Garrard is the pilot and sole passenger of an experimental interstellar ship, the "DFC-3,"* bound for Alpha Centauri. Two previous ships of the same class have failed to return from the same journey. Garrard is put into the ship anesthetized (n.b.); he wakes up after the ship has gone into "overdrive," to the mental reminder, *Don't move.* (The story begins and ends with these two words.) The reminder saves his life. Garrard finds that ship time seems to be almost stopped relative to his consciousness; he can move, but with long delays between impulse and muscular response; he is not breathing. Imprisoned in his own body, he estimates the relationship between ship time and subjective time (by counting seconds between successive jumps of the clock's second hand) and calculates that the ten-month trip will take him 6,000 years, subjective time. When he has almost resigned himself to this horror, he finds that ship time is speeding up until it equals and then surpasses subjective time. He again loses control of his own body, and as the differential increases, he goes into "the pseudo-death."

He awakes when the ship nears its destination and comes out of overdrive. Hovering around his hammock is a dreamlike being or group of beings calling itself "the clinesterton beademung" it speaks to him in dream-language, which he understands perfectly: viz., "Let me-mine pitch you-yours so to have mind of the rodalent beademung and other brothers and lovers, along the channel which is fragrant to the being-Garrard." From this point the narrative becomes equally dreamlike and is written in the

*Kornbluth points out that this stands for "Distinguished Flying Cross." Probably it's a wry Freudian pun, combining intercourse with the agony on the cross.

same terms, giving the impression that Garrard's experiences with the beademung are wonderful but indescribable. This ends when the ship's automatic controlling mechanism is about to take it back to Earth; Garrard once more goes into the pseudo-death, and does not come out of it this time until the ship nears Earth. He lands safely, but learns that he can never go back: no other interstellar ship will go out in his lifetime. He cannot even remember any more what the beademung was like, or even if it was real; he has only a haunting sense of loss: "He had returned to humanity's common time, and would never leave it again."

Now, on the face of it, except for some ingenious manipulation of the differential time problem in the first half of the story, this is not a science fiction story at all; the plot is extremely simple, not to say half-formed, and I could not see why the story hit me as hard as it did. Blish and I had been discussing the supposed womb symbolism in his stories; I took a second look from that standpoint, and was astonished to discover a whole series of puns, running all through the story, which could be tabulated under two headings, like this:

INTERCOURSE   DEATH

Page*

306   "Common time,"
i.e. common rhythm, or: . . . . . length of life; common
term in that sense, or:
as the genital contact; common divisor in both senses; common measure (six inches, or . . . . six feet).

306   "Don't move,"
i.e., at the moment of orgasm, or: after the moment of death.

307   "Calendar: stopped,"
(in both senses)

308   "Not breathing,"
(in both senses)

309   "plunged into Hell":
followed by a description that would serve equally well for orgasm, or: . . . . death.

310   "vessel of horror,"
i.e., the womb, or: . . . . . . the uterine abyss of death.

310   "trickles of reason,"
i.e., during orgasm, or: after physical death of the brain.

*Page numbers from *Shadow of Tomorrow*, Frederik Pohl, ed. (Permabooks, 1953).

310   "eternity in hell had taken three seconds,"
i.e., the suspension of time in love, or in death: cf. "his
                              whole life passed before his eyes."

311   "transports of love,"
           paired in a sentence with "agonies of empires."

314   "The normal human hand movement, in such a task as lifting
a pencil, took the pencil from a state of rest to another
                   state of rest . . ."

316   "come up with the solution to the Problem of Evil"

317   "put his finger on the First Cause!"

317 "the situation demanded someone trained in the highest rigors

319   "the pseudo-death"

321   "clinesterton" from Greek *klino* + *sterto*, to snore in bed? *

321   "the All-Devouring"

322   " 'on Earth as it is in Heaven' "

326   "old and compressed, constricted"

327   "found myself in [a] box"

327 "The whole situation was now utterly rigid—and, in effect,
                   I died."

As the Blishes point out in a letter, "to die" is a wide-spread
popular usage for orgasm; it is still current in French, and turns
up in English poetry as late as Shelley's "Indian Serenade":

                   O lift me from the grass!
                   I die, I faint, I fail!
                   O let thy kisses rain
                   On my cheeks and eyelids pale!

So what we have here is apparently only a highly expanded
metaphor: "death" as orgasm, which is what the story seems

*Most of this dream-talk is fairly easy: for instance, *rodalent* is evidently a
combination of radiant and redolent. *Beademungen* stopped me, though, and I
appealed to Blish for more light. Between them, he and Virginia came up with
this: " 'Beademungen,' as it turns out, is not essentially German; the weak
German ending is a piece of dream-work designed to turn the Latin verb 'to bless'
into a noun, 'the Blessed.' Thus, 'the clinesterton beademung' turned into a
proposition reads: 'Blessed are they who snore in bed,' and the text goes on to
say in English, 'on Earth as it is in Heaven.' "

to be about. But look at it more closely again, and it again becomes puzzling. If intercourse is taking place in the story, who are the partners? Garrard seems to be a part of the male act, but is completely passive; the female appears nowhere unless as the ship: and this relationship, we see at once, is the wrong one. Clearly Garrard is *inside* one of the organs engaged in copulation; sometimes he seems to visualize himself as an unborn child, sometimes as a kind of analogue of the penis.

I think there is one clear answer to this, one which also satisfactorily explains the metaphor itself. "To die" is understandable as hyperbole: but the adult male partner in intercourse doesn't really die, as a rule. There is just one male human creature for whom orgasm is literally death; that's the sperm.

I'll come back to this, and answer some possible objections, in a moment. First, let me read one other Blish story into the record.

Intrigued by the string of puns I had pulled out of his "Common Time," Blish began browsing through the rest of his stories. He found that in most of them—particularly in his best-liked and most-reprinted stories—for the last fifteen years he had been writing what seemed to be the same covert plot, over and over. Blish's name for this theme was "Being Born," and he anatomized it for me in a story called "Solar Plexus." It was his ninth published story, and technically was pretty crude.

Ostensibly the story is about a man in a floating space observatory out near Pluto, who is approached by a pirate ship and lured aboard it. Following light signals* down empty corridors, he reaches the control room but finds it also empty: the ship's pilot is a renegade scientist who has had his brain surgically removed and its nerve-endings connected to the electronic "nerve system" of the ship. ("Where am I? I'm all around you. . . I'm the ship.") This villain proposes to use the hero's brain to manufacture another such robot, and incarcerates him with a second captive. Here the hero learns, by kicking the wall, that the brain can "feel" shocks of this kind. The two join forces and succeed in reaching the control room again, where the hero smashes the ship's autopilot. The autopilot turns out to be analogous to the villain's solar plexus; the blow hurts, the brain "faints," and the hero seizes control of the ship.

As Blish points out, this story is made up of passages through tunnels from one chamber to another; each of these repeated episodes could be regarded as a birth symbol. But look again: the hero (1) is expelled from a hollow sphere down a long tube, at

*Blish suggests these symbolize pain or muscular contractions.

the end of which he sees light; (2) is drawn by successive waves of light down a second long corridor, at the end of which (3) he finds himself in another empty chamber, which he learns is part of the body of a being who means to take him apart, and from which he is expelled to (4) still another, where he finds an organism like himself, with whom he combines forces, and (5) returns to the second chamber, where he causes the imprisoning being pain by kicking it in the abdomen.

It seems to me that birth is the only step in this sequence which does *not* happen symbolically in the story: The hero, a sperm, is expelled from his hollow sphere (the testis), down a long tube (the epididymis), down another long tube (the inguinal canal) into an empty chamber (the uterus), from there to another cavity (the space between the ovary and the oviduct) where he joins forces with a second captive (the ovum); and together they return to the uterus, where they grow more powerful and kick mama.

I had better say here, for the benefit of nervous people, that I don't think all this is any sort of evidence for Hubbard's engrams, or Jung's archetypes, or prenatal memory in any form.   Blish is a highly sophisticated reader and critic who has some reputation as an expert on James Joyce's multi-punned *Finnegans Wake*; he is also a scientifically oriented man who studied to be a limno-biologist in college; he could probably draw the complicated internal plumbing of the male genital organs from memory. (I had to look it up.) But I must insist that these chains of symbols were not deliberately written in as a prank or a Joycean exercise. Blish did not even suspect they were there until I pointed them out. Since then, I may add, I've been on the receiving end of this same experience, and it is startling.

I don't think Blish can remember his own experiences as a sperm, but I don't actually care whether he can or not; it isn't necessary to the hypothesis. In fact, if this notion should get logically into the argument, I would do my best to clear it out again: the idea of blind and compulsive recapitulation would make the whole process revoltingly meaningless. If there is any one dominant impression which every analyzed symbolic story gives, it is one of immense meaning.

A more serious objection, it seems to me, is this one: If Garrard, the hero of " Common Time," is a sperm, and the story chronicles his journey from testis (the Earth) to uterus, where he meets an ovum (the beademung), what about the return journey?

Watch out; here comes another hard, fast one. I think the first part of the story, containing all the intercourse symbolism, is told backward.

Look again at the list of puns on pp. 269-270, and this time read it from bottom to top. Omitting the bottom three items (which are taken from Garrard's recounting of the outward trip), first you find a cloud of passive images; next a clear series of erection puns ("the highest rigors," &c.); then the intercourse and vagina symbols themselves begin; and finally, at the top of the list, you reach the orgasm and the terminal pun, "Come on time."

For confirmation, here's another note from Blish:

"About the Greek: very evidently it had more to do with the intercourse theme you spotted than I had any idea it had up to now. The reference to the Alpha Centauri stars as 'the twin radioceles' obviously comes from *varicocele*, a common form of hernia involving the testicles, and I think now that the whole thing was suggested by the Earth-Moon balls on the cover around which I wrote the story. The main Alpha Centauri star and Proxima Centauri stand in about the same relationship as the Earth and the Moon, and both pairs might be described as one-hung-low. Also, the story *is* about love-and-death; it says it is. But I'm just now beginning to believe it. Writing frightens me. I don't know why I do it."

This one story shows every sign of being inexhaustible, but let's pursue it a little farther. The inverted time scheme I propose here is not really as unlikely as it seems; it turns out to be common in science fiction, as I'll show in a moment: but even granting that, why should one part of the narrative run backward and the other part forward?

The time inversion, and the whole sperm fantasy, express a longing to return to the beginning. But this is an impossibility; it can only seem to happen by the trick of telling the story backward. Once that has been done, then the story must unreel the other way, as if to emphasize that the reversal was an illusion. This is what the story is really saying: *You can't go back.*

In the synopsis of "Common Time," I asked you to notice that the hero was anesthetized before being put into the spaceship, so that in effect he woke up without any knowledge of how he got there. This curious little trick turns up repeatedly in science fiction. My guess is that it's a death-or-birth symbol* and accordingly a signal, when it happens to an adult hero, that the story is being told backward. I have used the device myself without knowing why in "Stranger Station" and elsewhere. Something very similar

---

*Cf. Auden's *Age of Anxiety*: ". . . there's a white silence
Of antiseptics and instruments
At both ends. . ."

occurs in Christopher Morley's *Where the Blue Begins*: At the beginning of the story, the protagonist, a dog named Gissing (all the characters are Disney dogs), is leading the life of an elderly well-to-do bachelor, although, we are told, he is only a few months old. The rest of the plot lends some support to the notion that the story runs backward—Gissing becomes in turn a business magnate, a lay preacher, an escaped criminal, and winds up a stowaway on a ship, which he appropriates by a trick and sails off by himself; the ship turns into a toy boat on a pond, and Gissing briefly becomes a real dog, worshiping at the feet of a tramp.

Morley was a writer you might expect to do a thing of this kind intentionally; he was a sophisticated and excessively whimsical artist with a nostalgic preoccupation. But Blish thought he was writing space opera. So did I. Entirely without conscious intention, I wrote in "Four in One" the story of a cell-division in reverse; four people enter a single living cell, are stripped down to their essential components, merge, and only two of them get out alive.

The hero of my "Cabin Boy" is an active gelatinous ovoid, who propels himself by an ion stream, and who lives with others of his kind inside another living organism who is his father. Again, I thought I was writing space opera, this time with a dirty joke for the punchline. But I don't know how you could ask for a clearer description of a sperm in the testis.

One of the puzzling repeated motifs that I noticed while accumulating material for this article was the *longing for union or communion with an alien being*. It turns up all the time in my own work, but a better example is Raymond Z. Gallun's classic "Old Faithful." As you may remember, this story describes the efforts of some Terrestrials and a Martian astronomer to get into communication with each other. Forbidden to waste any more energy in so useless a pursuit, the Martian finally builds a spaceship and by "hitching a ride" on a comet succeeds in reaching Earth. However, he's injured in the landing and dies shortly after; his friends preserve him in alcohol.

The Martian is one of Gallun's most elaborate and convincing aliens: Gallun describes him chiefly by indirection, but here is the scene in which the Martian, Number 774, visits his son in the communal nursery:

> The floor was covered with thousands of boxes of clear crystal; and in each box was a purple gob of something feeble and jellylike and alive.
>
> . . . He had dismounted from his automaton, and now, creeping forward, he thrust a slender appendage into the crystal case.

> A score of nerve-filaments, fine, almost, as human hair, darted
> out from the chitinous shell that protected them and roved caress-
> ingly over the lump of protoplasm. Immediately . . . its delicate
> integument quivered, and a thin pseudopod oozed up from its jelly-
> like form and enveloped the nerve filaments of Number 774. For
> minutes the two remained thus, perfectly motionless.

This is not a description that seems calculated to inspire
affection; yet it does. The whole impact of Gallun's story is in
the affection it creates for an apparently unlovable object.

Notice in the quotation above the repeated suggestions of soft-
ness, strengthlessness, and so on. These are typical, not only
of the young Martian, but of Number 774 himself. The effect, it
seems to me, is foetal, and I think that is the explanation of its
ambiguous appeal.

Beginning with Wells' *War of the Worlds*, the monsters who
have landed on Earth in science fiction stories have frequently
had this boneless, pickled-specimen character. I think it is safe
to postulate that "an alien lands in a spaceship" is dream-talk for
"a baby is born," and that the passengers of such ships are bound
to be foetal.

It goes almost without saying that stories of this character are
not confined to science fiction. They are, however, so frequent
in fantasy and allied fields that it would be next to impossible to
catalog them all. Here's one example which some of you may
remember from "Miss Mulock's" *Little Lame Prince*:

> When I was a child, I used often to think how nice it would be
> to live in a little house all by my own self—a house built high up
> in a tree, or far away in a forest, or halfway up a hillside—so de-
> liciously alone and independent. Not a lesson to learn—but no!
> I always liked learning my lessons. Anyhow, to choose the lessons
> I liked best, to have as many books to read and dolls to play with
> as ever I wanted; above all, to be free and at rest, with nobody to
> tease or trouble or scold me, would be charming.

This passage provides the clue, if any were needed, to the symbolic sense of the lame prince's long confinement in a lonely
tower in which,

> Within twenty feet of the top some ingenious architect had
> planned a perfect little house, divided into four rooms—as by
> drawing a cross within a circle* you will see might easily be done
> . . . here was a dwelling complete, eighty feet from the ground,
> and as inaccessible as a rook's nest in the top of a tree.

*This odd floor plan, I believe, is a primordial womb symbol. Something very
like it obtruded itself obsessively into my story, "Stranger Station," in which the

Regression in size, as in the English Tom Thumb legend, is another common type. Tom, "as big as his father's thumb," goes through a series of repetitious womblike situations: he falls into a bag filled with cherry stones, a hot pudding, a cow's mouth, a salmon's stomach. His sojourn with the queen of the fairies, who sends him back into the world dressed in green, suggests that he was originally a Dionysus, dying and being reborn each spring.

The numerous man-among-the-ants stories in science fiction belong to this type; also the man-in-the-atom stories, and the dwarfed men of "Little Hercules" and others of Neil R. Jones' remarkable "Durna Rangue" series.

Some stories, like H. G. Wells' "In the Abyss," make the regression to the womb into a chilling horror. (A unique example, so far as I know, is Victor Endersby's "Dispossessed," in which an inversion of gravity occurs—the protagonist falls *up*, into the uterine abyss of the sky.) Not exactly horrible, but queerly disturbing, is Edison Marshall's "The Star That Fell." Marshall builds up casually and deftly the story of a feature writer's acquaintance with an old man who has only one dull story in him: how when he was a little boy, on a sea voyage home with his father, the ship put in at an island and he met a man who must have been somebody important. At the end of the story, when you realize that the island was Elba and the man Napoleon, you get a sudden sharp shock—like touching a live wire into the past.

Time travel, either into the future ("the womb of time") or the past, is of course the classic expression of the theme. Historical novels—regressions to the past cultural stages—fall into this category; this probably explains the curious persistence of medievalisms in science fiction. Nostalgic stories and articles, even autobiographical works, I believe, make the same basic appeal. Author and reader alike are seeking one thing: the everlasting summer of childhood.

---

womb symbolism was important and deliberate. The diagram ⊕ itself is one of the oldest written symbols; it's one form of the astrological symbol for Earth, another form of which is ♁; the first is said to represent the four quarters of Earth, and the second, the cross and globe as symbols of authority. Both of these, like the crux ansata ♀ as the sign of immortality, seem to me to be late interpretations, although not far from the original meaning, which I take to be a simple schematic rendering of foetus and womb.

27. WHAT NEXT?

LIKE ALL MINORITIES, I think, science fiction addicts spend a lot of their time wistfully thinking how nice it would be if they were a majority. At various times evangelical movements have been hopefully launched ("If each of you will introduce one more reader to *ASTOUNDING* . . ."), and I think we have all felt an occasional foolish joy when someone Outside took notice of our microcosm—when Winchell mentioned it, or George Pal made a movie, or a serious *Saturday Review* critic solemnly got it all wrong. Even as late as 1956, writing in *Science Fiction Stories*, Robert A. W. Lowndes took the line that it doesn't matter much what outsiders say about us, so long as they notice.

Probably all of us, consciously or not, have been thinking that science fiction is a good thing which only needs to be sold to the public to become a big thing: hence our delight when the slicks began publishing (bad) science fiction stories, the hardcover houses (worse) science fiction books, and Hollywood began to produce (incredibly awful) science fiction movies. Never mind about the quality: at least They were noticing Us, and the rest would soon follow.

We had forgotten that a previous boom in magazine science fiction was accompanied in Hollywood, not by movies about adventurers in spaceships, but by something quite different: movies about the drafty old castle, the eerie flasks and retorts, the crashing sparks, the deformed servant, and above all, the shifty-eyed scientist. ("Isn't it true, *Dr.* Foulfingers, that you were hounded out of Peoria in 1929 for practicing vivisection?").

The humbling truth is that science fiction is only for the small number of people who like to think and who regard the universe with awe, which is a blend of love and fear. "The public" does neither; it wants to be spoon-fed by its magazines and movies, and it regards the universe with horror, which is a blend of fear and hate.

The moment we get any part of science fiction across this gulf, it turns into something else. It seems altogether likely, as I write, that the two most successful "science fiction" books of 1956 will turn out to be *The Power*, by Frank M. Robinson, and *The Shrinking Man*, by Richard Matheson. *The Power* has already gone into a third printing; it was published in a shorter version in *Bluebook* and was telecast by *Studio One*. *The Shrinking Man* was bought by Universal-International before publication, and Matheson himself wrote the screen-play. These are matters to make the average science fiction writer's tongue hang out; so it seems important to ask, "How did they do it?"

For one thing, by avoiding the "science fiction" label. The Matheson book is introduced simply as a "tale of horror"; the Robinson as "a novel of menace." So much for the science fiction boom.

The Power is about a mystery man named Adam Hart, who appears to have assorted malignant powers. He can read minds, transfer thoughts, erase memories. He can control another person's muscles, causing spastic convulsions, or heart failure, or what have you, up to and including championship basketball. He also has a useful defensive trait: everyone who looks at him sees a different Adam Hart, but always an object of love or admiration—for instance, a teen-aged girl sees a bobby-soxer's dream; a college professor sees an intense and brilliant student; to a coach he's the perfect athlete, and so on.

William Tanner, chairman of the Navy Committee for Human Research at a Midwestern university, discovers that Hart exists and is a member of the nine-man committee. Hart accordingly marks him down for death, and the rest of the book is concerned with Tanner's struggle to survive long enough to find out which of the eight suspects is Hart.

This question is the teaser on which the formal structure of the novel is built, and it takes delicate handling: if it were resolved too soon, there wouldn't be enough novel. So Tanner avoids the obvious sensible things to do (for instance, he never gets each committee member to describe each of the others, or looks up their dossiers in the university files). The matter is eventually settled by a process of elimination: at book's end, most of the prime suspects have been killed by Hart.

Robinson is a gifted and sensitive writer: his evocations of Chicago at night, early in the story when Tanner and his invisible pursuer are roaming the lonely streets, are persuasively scary.

But *The Power* has one other built-in flaw: as in Norvell W. Page's similar "But Without Horns" (*Unknown*, June, 1940), it's necessary at the same time to build up the superman as an overwhelming terror, and to keep the hero alive to the end of the book.

Since one serious effort on the part of the superman would do Tanner in, Hart has to throttle himself down to a campaign of petty persecutions. In spite of all Robinson's care, this is not in the least credible, and the story becomes less frightening the longer it goes on.

The manipulation of the suspects is competent but predictable, and the question from page 33 on is not so much "Who?" as "How?"

This straitjacket of plot gradually squeezes out everything good in the book: the characterizations, for instance, which are sharp and memorable at the beginning, are cheapened one by one. As a formal novel of detection and suspense, *The Power* is neither better nor worse than the average lending-library product; its appeal as science fiction is minuscule. The explanation of the book's peculiar strength lies elsewhere.

The Shrinking Man, written with much less care and integrity, is the story of one Scott Carey, a young man who suddenly begins shrinking exactly one-seventh of an inch every day. The story proper begins when he is five-sevenths of an inch tall and has been marooned in his own cellar forty-four days, with five more to go before he becomes zero inches tall and whiffs out like a candle flame.

Previous stages in his descent are told as interruptions: the focus is on Carey's last five days, his loneliness and hardships, his struggles to get food, and his occasional encounters with a grudge-bearing black widow spider. The spider has only seven legs; Carey has previously knocked off the other one with a stone, like an Ahab in reverse.

At five-sevenths of an inch, Carey is just about one one-hundredth of his former six feet; everything around him, therefore, ought to appear one hundred times its former size. This seems like a simple enough relation to bear in mind— 1 ft = 100 ft —but Matheson writes, on page 24: "Twelve inches, and yet to him it was the equivalent of 150 feet to a normal sized man."

On the next page, we find Carey staring up awe-struck at the towering height of a refrigerator, "as high as a ten-story building" —i.e., 100 feet, or exactly twelve inches on Carey's scale. The wicker table beside it is "half as high," or six inches; a little later it turns out to be 150 feet tall on Carey's scale, meaning a

foot and a half. Even so, this is not much of a wicker table. But
from this foot-and-a-half height Carey has to climb a further
seventy-five feet to the top of the refrigerator—that is, nine
inches, making the refrigerator two and a quarter feet tall—still
not much, but an improvement.

The cellar episodes vary from unintentional comedy like this
("'Son of a bitch!' he yelled, and he kicked the cracker to bits...")
through long stretches of boredom, to occasional incongruous bits
of truth, as when Carey is shocked and stunned by the impacts
of gigantic water drops. The most striking lapse in logic, for
readers who have seen this subject handled before in science
fiction, is Matheson's neglect of the square-cube law.

Other things being equal, a small object has proportionately
less volume (and therefore less mass) than a large one. If our
measuring sticks were to shrink at the same time, there would
be no difference, but they don't: atoms and molecules provide
an absolute standard of size, and in practice, so do the minimal
sizes of living cells, and the fineness of muscle fiber. So a flea
can perform gymnastic feats on spindling legs, while an elephant
lumbers clumsily on massive ones. It follows that a man Carey's
size could jump like a grasshopper, and could lift objects many
times his own weight. But Carey pants and struggles to carry a
pin, and toils up a wicker chair as if it were Everest. When, near
the end of the book, he finally realizes he can fall long distances
without being hurt, and does so, the event is totally incredible
because nothing else in the book prepares you for it: earlier,
when Carey tries a much shorter fall, Matheson would have you
believe the shock is agonizing.

A few drops of genuine feeling are distilled from this brew, as
when, on his last night, Carey faces extinction without hope or
fear: but the following scene, when he wakes up still alive and
still shrinking, is perfectly ludicrous—evidently the author has
some vague idea that minus numbers and microscopic sizes are
the same thing.

Like Matheson's first Gold Medal novel, *I Am Legend*, this one
is a drama of alienation. In the former book, everybody but the
hero was a vampire; in this one, everybody else is a giant. *The
Shrinking Man* is at one point strikingly reminiscent of *Alice in
Wonderland*: when Carey is the wrong size to climb the cellar
steps, the door is open; when he's the right size, the door is shut.

In the before-cellar episodes, Matheson, using quantity of emotion as a substitute for quality, runs through a kind of bathroom-
sink collection of vulgarities which, if written and published about
a real person, would be called yellow journalism. The story line

is purposeless and repetitive; about seven tenths of it is padding, but every now and then Matheson succeeds in registering the eerie scenic effects for which he is noted. In one short passage, when the forty-two-inch hero hitches a ride from an aging, drunken homosexual, Matheson's prose and his characters come brilliantly to life, as if the author wanted to prove that he really *can* write, when not churning out this sludge.

The rest of the book, like much of Matheson's work, is a dismal interior monologue, endlessly reflecting the author's own stream of consciousness at its most petty and banal.

Why did the movies buy this bad book? Because it has a Creature in it—the aforesaid black widow spider. But this only leads up to another question: How did it happen that the big science fiction movie boom turned itself into a Creature cycle?

To answer by indirection, let's look again at *The Power*. The revelation that Adam Hart is a member of the committee comes about in the following way: All the members have filled out experimental questionnaires but have not signed them. One of these questionnaires shows that the subject "has never been sick, never had any serious personal problems, never worried, and has an IQ close to the limits of measurability." One of the committee members, the neurotic John Olsen, insists the questionnaire be taken seriously: to humor him, Tanner proposes a test. He balances a tiny umbrella-shaped bit of paper on the point of a pin. "I'm assuming that our . . . superman . . . has mental powers such that he could make this paper revolve on the pin merely by concentrating on it . . ." All the members try simultaneously to make it move, and it does: ergo, the superman exists among them.

Please notice, first of all, that Tanner's peculiar assumption is not even remotely suggested by the questionnaire. Second, note that if anybody really cared to identify the subject of the questionnaire, it could have been done by elimination in five minutes. Third, note that this power—telekinesis—is irrelevant to the powers actually used by Hart and is never used again in the book until a similarly irrelevant test at the end. I think the effect is deliberate: Hart is not *a* superman, he is the idea, Superman. Superman can do anything; therefore Hart can do anything. Ordinary human beings must be helpless before Superman; therefore, whatever logic may suggest, they *are* helpless.

Hart is not a man but a symbol: he's danger walking faceless down a dark street; danger, lurking invisible somewhere in the mechanical hum of the city. Hart is the wise guy that wants to kill you.

He's the man with the keen eyes who uses the big words you

can't understand, who juggles with dangerous things that you can't even see. He's the man who invented the V-2 and the Bomb. The Scientist, Professor, Egghead.

Matheson's ignorance and distrust of science are as profound as Bradbury's, but Robinson is almost the type of the pure science fiction writer; he majored in physics at Beloit, spent his Navy hitch as an electronics technician. It is not accidental that two such different writers should produce books so essentially similar. This is *not* just bad science fiction; it's something else altogether.

It's anti-science fiction: a turning away, not merely from the standard props of science fiction (which are retained as vestiges) but from the habits of thought and belief which underlie science itself—the assumption that things can be put into categories (note how Hart's "Power" resists classification); that things can be measured (cf. Matheson's indifference to common arithmetic); the assumption of cause and effect (Matheson's almost contemptuously perfunctory "explanation" of the shrinking man: "radioactive spray" plus insect spray, uniting by a kind of magical miscegenation into a toxin). Logic goes, too: Adam Hart's actions are not logical if you assume he is a man, even a superman; but their very irrationality makes him more horrible if you see him as a formless menace.

It's hardly necessary to point out that the black widow in *The Shrinking Man* is not a real spider. Matheson has evidently read the *Britannica* article on black widows, and tells you toward the end of the book that, "naturally reticent and secretive, they build their webs in the most dark, secluded corners"—this after having the same spider chase Carey all over the cellar like a dog after a chicken. There's no rational motive involved when Carey reverses roles to go hunting the spider, on his last day, and Matheson's attempts to make sense of the event in these terms are palpably false. But:

> . . . That spider was immortal. It was more than a spider. It was every unknown terror in the world fused into wriggling, poison-jawed horror. It was every anxiety, insecurity, and fear in his life given a hideous, night-black form.

And here's William Tanner, in *The Power*:

> He shivered. It would be so damned easy to get the shakes and end up in a blue funk, just knowing what was after him. Not *who*. Not a person, not somebody he could fight, not somebody he could flush out into the open.
> Not *who*, but *what*.

In a grisly scene, Matheson's hero destroys the spider by impalement. ("The ghastly, piercing screech . . . was like the distant scream of a gutted horse.")

Spiders don't scream, as even Matheson might know; but gutted scientists do.

Throughout *The Power*, Tanner takes elaborate precautions at night—changing his lodgings, and so on—but seems to feel he's perfectly safe during the day. The symbolic nature of this feeling is evident, but Robinson attempts to justify it logically on page 169: "He had never thought that Hart would attempt [psychic violence] in public, that he would run the risk of giving himself away." This is obvious nonsense, since Hart's weapon is invisible and intangible, leaves no traces, and can be used from a distance. What Robinson seems to be saying is: *Safety in numbers*. To be precise, safety in a mob.

—This is more than disturbing, and so is the "logic" of Tanner's method of testing suspects: if you try to kill a man, and succeed, then it wasn't Adam Hart. (If you duck an old woman, and she drowns, then she wasn't a witch.)

This way to the bandwagon—which way to the pogrom?

The foregoing lines, written ten years ago, constitute an effort at prophecy which I am glad to admit was a failure.

At this writing (March, 1966), the boom of the 60s shows every sign of accelerating. The sickness of overspecialization in the magazines of the 50s has largely healed itself. The book editors who oppressed us have gone to their just rewards, or to other jobs, and their places have been filled by people who actually like science fiction and know something about it. Science fiction is accepted, not only by librarians, but by an increasing number of critics and by the public at large.

H. Bruce Franklin, in *Future Perfect* (Oxford, 1966), points out the curious fact that before 1900 science fiction appeared in all the leading literary magazines, and every major 19th century American author wrote it. (Nine tenths of it, of course, was crud.) Some other scholar will have to try to establish just what happened then—whether s.f. ceased to be respectable because it was taken up by the dime novels and pulp magazines, or the other way around.

Either way, it is clear that science fiction has gone through more than half a century of concentrated development under-ground, in the ghetto world created by publishers like Hugo Gernsback. There are some indications that it is now emerging from this microcosm into the mainstream. If so, a decade from now the survivors of our little group may be rich and famous, but they will probably be scattered. Cult science fiction will have become collectible in the same sense that Chippendale is, and future literary historians may look back on us as a remarkable flowering of American eccentricity.

A TESTAMENT

Now, therefore, believing as I do in human mortality, I hereby give and bequeath:

To Ray Palmer and John W. Campbell, radar beanies.

To Hugo Gernsback, incense in a golden bowl for fathering our microcosm, and a flourish of kazoos for his notion that s.f. authors should be able to patent their fictional ideas.

To Leo Morey, a lead medal for fifteen years of consistently dismal s.f. art, and to T. O'Conor Sloane, a glass eye for preferring him above all others.

To Earle Bergey, a monument in the form of a chromium brassiere.

To George O. Smith, Sam Moskowitz, Mack Reynolds, and Lee Correy, an English grammar; and to Avram Davidson, a spellynge boke.

To Hans Wessolowski the one-eyed and Lawrence Stevens the color-blind, my admiration.

To young writers, three admonitions: love your work; read your contracts; make friends when you can.

DAMON KNIGHT

ACKNOWLEDGMENTS

TO THE FOLLOWING PEOPLE, the publishers wish to express their thanks and most sincere appreciation for aid and encouragement in the preparation of this volume: Harry Altshuler, Redd Boggs of *Skyhook*, Lester del Rey, Ted and Judy Dikty, Harlan Ellison, Lloyd Eshbach of Fantasy Press, Don Fabun of *Rhodomagnetic Digest*, Nicholas Falasca, Lewis J. Grant, Jr., Nancy Kemp, Morris B. Levine of Hillman Periodicals, Robert A. W. Lowndes of Columbia Publications, Howard and Patricia Lyons, Edna Robbins of Edwards Brothers, Larry Shaw of Royal Publications, Noreen Shaw, William Thorsen of *The American Book Collector*, Walter Willis of *Hyphen*, Willis Kingsley Wing, and John Stopa, from whose collection a substantial portion of these critiques was selected.

In addition, we would like to express our thanks to the editors, the publishers and the respective staffs of the following magazines, within whose pages the bulk of this volume originally appeared: *Destiny's Child, Dimensions, Dynamic Science Fiction, Future Science Fiction, Hyphen, If: Worlds of Science Fiction, Infinity, The Magazine of Fantasy and Science Fiction, Rhodomagnetic Digest, Science Fiction Adventures, Science Fiction Forum, Science Fiction Quarterly, Science Fiction Stories, Skyhook* and *Worlds Beyond*.

Portions of chapter 5 originally appeared in *Destiny's Child*, 1945, reprinted through the permission of Mr. Larry Shaw.

Portions of chapters 3 and 12 originally appeared in *Dimensions*, August-October, 1954, copyright 1955 by and reprinted through the permission of Mr. Harlan Ellison.

Portions of chapter 20 originally appeared in *Dynamic Science Fiction*, copyright 1953 by Columbia Publications, Inc.

Portions of chapters 4, 16 and 21 originally appeared in *Future Science Fiction*, copyright 1953 by Columbia Publications, Inc. Portions of chapters 2, 4, 6, 9, 11, 12, 20 and 25, copyright 1954 by Columbia Publications, Inc. Portions of chapter 20, copyright 1955 by Columbia Publications, Inc. Portions of chapters 2, 6, 21, 25 and 27, copyright 1956 by Columbia Publications, Inc.

Portions of chapters 6, 9, 12 and 18 originally appeared in *Hyphen*, Numbers 11, 12 and 13. Reprinted through the permission of Mr. Walter Willis.

Portions of chapters 19 and 25 originally appeared in *If: Worlds of Science Fiction*, copyright 1958 by Quinn Publishing Co., Inc. Portions of chapter 16, copyright 1959 by Quinn Publishing Co., Inc.

Portions of chapter 23 originally appeared in *Infinity*, copyright 1955 by Royal Publications, Inc. Portions of chapters 4, 7, 12, 14, 20, 23 and 24, copyright 1956

BIBLIOGRAPHY

The following bibliography is limited in most cases to first serial publication, first U.S., British, and Canadian clothbound editions, and first U.S. paperbound edition. Book titles are in capitals, story titles are in quotations, and magazine titles are in italics. The abbreviation [ed] indicates Editor, and pb indicates paperbound.

Adler, Allen A. MACH 1. New York: Farrar, Straus & Young, 1957. Toronto: Ambassador, 1957. New York: Paperback Library, 1966 pb [as TERROR ON PLANET IONUS].

Aldiss, Brian. VANGUARD FROM ALPHA. New York: Ace Books, 1959 pb.

Amis, Kingsley. NEW MAPS OF HELL. New York: Harcourt, Brace, 1960. London: Gollancz, 1961. Toronto: Doubleday, 1961. New York: Ballantine, 1961 pb.

Anderson, Poul. THE ENEMY STARS. *Astounding*, Aug., Sept., 1958 [as "We Have Fed Our Sea"]. Philadelphia: Lippincott, 1959. Toronto: Longmans, Green, 1959. New York: Berkley, 1959.

Asimov, Isaac. THE CAVES OF STEEL. *Galaxy*, Oct., Nov., Dec., 1953. New York: Doubleday, 1954. Toronto: Doubleday, 1954. London: Boardman, 1954. New York: New American Library (Signet), 1955 pb.

———. THE END OF ETERNITY. New York: Doubleday, 1955. New York: New American Library (Signet), 1958, pb.

———. THE MARTIAN WAY AND OTHER STORIES. New York: Doubleday, 1955. Toronto: Doubleday, 1955. New York: New American Library (Signet), 1957 pb. London: Dennis Dobson, 1964.

Barnhouse, Perl T. MY JOURNEYS WITH ASTARGO. Denver: Bell Publications, 1952 pb.

Bellamy, Francis Rufus. ATTA. New York: Wyn, 1953. Toronto: Copp Clark, 1953. New York: Ace Books, 1954 pb.

Bennett, Margot. THE LONG WAY BACK. London: John Lane, 1954. New York: Coward-McCann, 1955.

Bernstein, Morey. THE SEARCH FOR BRIDEY MURPHY. New York: Doubleday, 1956. London: Hutchinson, 1956. Toronto: Doubleday, 1956.

Bester, Alfred. STARBURST. New York: New American Library (Signet), 1958 pb.

———. THE STARS MY DESTINATION. London: Sidgwick & Jackson, 1956 [as TIGER! TIGER!]. *Galaxy*, Oct., Nov., Dec., 1956, Jan., 1957. New York: New American Library (Signet), 1957 pb.

Blish, James. "Beanstalk." [in FUTURE TENSE, edited by Kendell Foster Crossen] New York: Greenberg, 1952. [Same] Toronto: Ambassador, 1952. [Same] London: Lane, 1954. *Science Fiction Stories*, January, 1956. Revised and expanded, as TITAN'S DAUGHTER. New York: Berkley, 1961 pb.

——. EARTHMAN, COME HOME. New York: Putnam, 1955. Toronto: Allen, 1955. London: Faber & Faber, 1956. New York: Avon, 1958 pb.

——. GALACTIC CLUSTER. New York: New American Library (Signet), 1959 pb. London: Faber & Faber, 1960.

——. VOR. New York: Avon, 1958 pb.

Bowen, John. AFTER THE RAIN. London: Faber & Faber, 1958. Toronto: British Book Service, 1958. New York: Ballantine, 1959 pb.

Brackett, Leigh. THE LONG TOMORROW. New York: Doubleday, 1955. Toronto: Doubleday, 1955. New York: Ace Books, 1962 pb.

Bradbury, Ray. DANDELION WINE. New York: Doubleday, 1957. London: Hart-Davis, 1957. Toronto: Doubleday, 1957. New York: Bantam, 1959 pb.

——. THE GOLDEN APPLES OF THE SUN. New York: Doubleday, 1953. London: Hart-Davis, 1953. Toronto: Doubleday, 1953. New York: Bantam, 1954 pb.

——. THE ILLUSTRATED MAN. New York: Doubleday, 1951. London: Hart-Davis, 1952. New York: Bantam, 1952 pb. Toronto: Doubleday, 1958.

——. THE OCTOBER COUNTRY. New York: Ballantine, 1955. London: Hart-Davis, 1956. New York: Ballantine, 1956 pb.

—— [ed]. THE CIRCUS OF DR. LAO AND OTHER IMPROBABLE STORIES. New York: Bantam, 1956 pb.

Budrys, Algis THE FALLING TORCH. New York: Pyramid, 1959 pb.

——. FALSE NIGHT. New York: Lion, 1954 pb. Revised and expanded as SOME WILL NOT DIE. Evanston, Illinois: Regency, 1961 pb.

——. WHO? New York: Pyramid, 1958 pb. London: Gollancz, 1962.

Caldwell, Taylor. THE DEVIL'S ADVOCATE. New York: Crown, 1952. Toronto: Ambassador, 1952. New York: Macfadden-Bartell, 1964 pb.

——. YOUR SINS AND MINE. *McCall's*, May, 1954. New York: Fawcett (Gold Medal), 1956 pb. Caldwell. Idaho: Caxton, 1959. Toronto: Copp Clark, 1959.

Campbell, John W., Jr. CLOAK OF AESIR. Chicago: Shasta, 1952.

——. WHO GOES THERE? Chicago: Shasta, 1952.

——. WHO GOES THERE? New York: Dell, 1955 pb [also contains stories from CLOAK OF AESIR].

Čapek Karel. WAR WITH THE NEWTS. New York: Putnam, 1937. London: Allen & Unwin, 1937. Toronto: Nelson, 1937. New York: Bantam, 1955 pb.

Castle, Jeffery Lloyd. SATELLITE E ONE. New York: Dodd, Mead, 1954. London: Eyre & Spottiswoode, 1954. Toronto: McClelland, 1954. New York: Bantam, 1958 pb.

Christopher, John. NO BLADE OF GRASS. London: Michael Joseph, 1956 [as DEATH OF GRASS]. Toronto: Collins, 1956 [as DEATH OF GRASS]. *Saturday Evening Post*, April 27 - June 8, 1957. New York: Simon & Schuster, 1957. New York: Pocket Books, 1957 pb.

Clarke, Arthur C. CHILDHOOD'S END. New York: Ballantine, 1953. New York: Ballantine, 1953 pb. Don Mills, Ontario: Longmans, Green, 1963.

——. THE CITY AND THE STARS. New York: Harcourt, Brace, 1956. London: Muller, 1956. New York: New American Library (Signet), 1958 pb.

——. THE DEEP RANGE. New York: Harcourt, Brace, 1957. London: Muller, 1957. Toronto: Longmans, Green, 1957. New York: New American Library (Signet), 1958 pb.

——. EXPEDITION TO EARTH. New York: Ballantine, 1953. New York: Ballantine, 1953 pb. London: Sidgwick & Jackson, 1954.

——. PRELUDE TO SPACE. New York: Galaxy Novels, 1951 pb. London: Sidgwick & Jackson, 1953. New York: Gnome, 1954. New York: Ballantine, 1954 pb.

——. TALES FROM THE WHITE HART. New York: Ballantine, 1957 pb.

Clement, Hal. MISSION OF GRAVITY. *Astounding*, April, May, June, July, 1953. New York: Doubleday, 1954. Toronto: Doubleday, 1954. London: Robert Hale, 1955. New York: Galaxy Novels, 1958 pb. New York: Pyramid, 1962 pb.

Coblentz, Stanton A. UNDER THE TRIPLE SUNS. Reading, Pennsylvania: Fantasy Press, 1955.

Collier, John. FANCIES AND GOODNIGHTS. New York: Doubleday, 1951. New York: Bantam, 1953 pb.

Conklin, Groff [ed]. BR-R-R-! New York: Avon, 1958 pb.

Cooper, Edmund. SEED OF LIGHT. London: Hutchinson, 1959. New York: Ballantine, 1959 pb.

——. TOMORROW'S GIFT. New York: Ballantine, 1958 pb.

Correy, Lee. STARSHIP THROUGH SPACE. New York: Holt, 1954.

Crossen, Kendell Foster. YEAR OF CONSENT. New York: Dell, 1955 pb.

Davenport, Basil, et al. THE SCIENCE FICTION NOVEL: IMAGINATION AND SOCIAL CRITICISM. Chicago: Advent, 1959. Chicago: Advent, 1964 pb.

De Camp, L. Sprague. THE GLORY THAT WAS. *Startling*, April, 1952. New York: Bouregy (Avalon), 1960. Toronto: Ryerson Press, 1960.

——. SOLOMON'S STONE. *Unknown*, June, 1942. New York: Bouregy (Avalon), 1957. Toronto: Ryerson Press, 1957.

Del Rey, Lester. NERVES. *Astounding*, Sept., 1942. New York: Ballantine, 1956. New York: Ballantine, 1956 pb.

Derleth, August [ed]. TIME TO COME. New York: Farrar, Straus & Young, 1954. New York: Berkley, 1958 pb.

Dick, Philip K. EYE IN THE SKY. New York: Wyn (Ace), 1957 pb.

——. THE MAN WHO JAPED. New York: Wyn (Ace), 1956 pb.

——. SOLAR LOTTERY. New York: Ace Books, 1955 pb. London: Rich & Cowan, 1956 [as THE WORLD OF CHANCE].

——. THE WORLD JONES MADE. New York: Wyn (Ace), 1956 pb.

Duncan, David. OCCAM'S RAZOR. New York: Ballantine, 1957 pb. London: Gollancz, 1958.

Elliott, H. Chandler. REPRIEVE FROM PARADISE. New York: Gnome, 1955.

Fawcett, F. Dubrez. HOLE IN HEAVEN. London: Sidgwick & Jackson, 1954.

Finney, Jack. THE BODY SNATCHERS. *Collier's*, Nov. 26, Dec. 10, Dec. 24, 1954. New York: Dell, 1955 pb. London: Eyre & Spottiswoode, 1955.

Flint, Homer Eon, and Hall, Austin. THE BLIND SPOT. *Argosy*, serial, May 14, 1921. Philadelphia: Prime Press, 1951. London: Sidgwick & Jackson, 1953. New York: Ace Books, 1964 pb.

Gallun, Raymond Z. PEOPLE MINUS X. New York: Simon & Schuster, 1957. New York: Ace Books, 1958 pb.

Gold, Horace L. THE OLD DIE RICH AND OTHER SCIENCE FICTION STORIES. New York: Crown, 1955. Toronto: Ambassador, 1955. London: Dennis Dobson, 1965.

Golding, William G. LORD OF THE FLIES. London: Faber & Faber, 1954. Toronto: British Book Service, 1954. New York: Coward-McCann, 1955. New York: Putnam (Capricorn), 1959 pb.

Golding, William, *et al.* SOMETIME, NEVER. [Contains "Envoy Extraordinary," by William Golding, "Consider Her Ways," by John Wyndham, and "Boy in Darkness," by Mervyn Peake.] London: Eyre & Spottiswoode, 1956. Toronto: McClelland, 1956. New York: Ballantine, 1957 pb.

Gordon, Rex. FIRST TO THE STARS. New York: Ace Books, 1959 pb.

Gray, Curme. MURDER IN MILLENNIUM VI. Chicago: Shasta, 1951.
Gunn, James E. THIS FORTRESS WORLD. New York: Gnome, 1955. New York: Wyn (Ace), 1957 pb.
Gunther, Gotthard [ed]. ÜBERWINDUNG VON RAUM UND ZEIT. Dusseldorf und Bad Salzig: Karl Rauch Verlag, 1952.
Hadley, Arthur T. THE JOY WAGON. New York: Viking, 1958. New York: Berkley, 1960 pb.
Hall, Austin. See Flint, Homer Eon.
Harness, Charles L. FLIGHT INTO YESTERDAY. *Startling Stories*, May, 1949. New York: Bouregy & Curl, 1953. New York: Ace Books, 1955 pb [as THE PARADOX MEN].
Heinlein, Robert A. ASSIGNMENT IN ETERNITY. Reading, Pennsylvania: Fantasy Press, 1953. New York: New American Library (Signet), 1954 pb. London: Sidgwick & Jackson, 1955.
———. CITIZEN OF THE GALAXY. *Astounding*, Sep., Oct., Nov., Dec., 1957. New York: Scribner's, 1957. Toronto: S. J. R. Saunders, 1957.
———. THE DOOR INTO SUMMER. *The Magazine of Fantasy and Science Fiction*, Oct., Nov., Dec., 1956. New York: Doubleday, 1957. Toronto: Doubleday, 1957. New York: New American Library (Signet), 1959 pb.
———. DOUBLE STAR. *Astounding*, Feb., Mar., Apr., 1956. New York: Doubleday, 1956. Toronto: Doubleday, 1956. New York: New American Library (Signet), 1957 pb. London: Michael Joseph, 1958.
———. REVOLT IN 2100. Chicago: Shasta, 1953. New York: New American Library (Signet), 1954 pb. London: Gollancz, 1964.
———. THE ROLLING STONES. *Boy's Life*, Sep., Oct., Nov., Dec., 1952 [as "Tramp Space Ship"]. New York: Scribner's, 1952.
———. THE STAR BEAST. *The Magazine of Fantasy and Science Fiction*, May, June, July, 1954 [as "Star Lummox"]. New York: Scribner's, 1954. Toronto: S. J. R. Saunders, 1954.
———. STARMAN JONES. New York: Scribner's, 1953. London: Sidgwick & Jackson, 1954. Toronto: S. J. R. Saunders, 1954.
———. TIME FOR THE STARS. New York: Scribner's, 1956. London: Gollancz, 1963. Toronto: S. J. R. Saunders, 1963.
———. TUNNEL IN THE SKY. New York: Scribner's, 1955. London: Gollancz, 1965.
——— [ed]. TOMORROW, THE STARS. New York: Doubleday, 1952. New York: New American Library (Signet), 1953 pb.
Howard, Robert E. THE COMING OF CONAN. New York: Gnome, 1953.
Hubbard, L. Ron. "Fear," *Unknown*, July, 1940. "Typewriter in the Sky," *Unknown*, Nov., Dec., 1940. TYPEWRITER IN THE SKY AND FEAR. New York: Gnome, 1951. FEAR. New York: Galaxy Novels, 1957 pb.
Jackson, Shirley. THE HAUNTING OF HILL HOUSE. New York: Viking, 1959. London: Michael Joseph, 1960. New York: Popular Library, 1961 (?) pb.
Karp, David. ONE. New York: Vanguard, 1953. Toronto: Copp Clark, 1953. London: Gollancz, 1954. New York: Lion, 1955 pb [as ESCAPE TO NOWHERE].
Kline, M. V. [ed]. A SCIENTIFIC REPORT ON "THE SEARCH FOR BRIDEY MURPHY." New York: Julian Press, 1956.
Koestler, Arthur. DARKNESS AT NOON. London: Jonathan Cape, 1940. Toronto: Nelson, 1940. New York: Macmillan, 1941. New York: New American Library (Signet), 1948 pb.
Kornbluth, C. M. THE EXPLORERS. New York: Ballantine, 1954 pb. London: Michael Joseph, 1955 [as THE MINDWORM].
———. NOT THIS AUGUST. *MacLean's* (Canadian) serial, 1955. New York: Doubleday, 1955. Toronto: Doubleday, 1955. New York: Bantam, 1956 pb.

———. THE SYNDIC. New York: Doubleday, 1953. Toronto: Doubleday, 1953. *Science Fiction Adventures*, Dec., 1953, Mar., 1954. New York: Bantam, 1955 pb. London: Faber & Faber, 1964.

———. TAKEOFF. New York: Doubleday, 1952. Toronto: Doubleday, 1952. New York: Bantam, 1953 pb. *New Worlds* (British), April, May, June, 1954.

Kornbluth, C. M., and Pohl, Frederik. WOLFBANE. New York: Ballantine, 1959 pb. London: Gollancz, 1961.

Kracauer, Siegfried. FROM CALIGARI TO HITLER. New York: Noonday, 1959.

Kuttner, Henry, and Moore, C(atherine) L. NO BOUNDARIES. New York: Ballantine, 1956. New York: Ballantine, 1956 pb.

———. MUTANT [by Lewis Padgett]. New York: Gnome, 1953. London: Weidenfeld & Nicholson, 1954.

———. ROBOTS HAVE NO TAILS [by Lewis Padgett]. New York: Gnome, 1952.

———. "Tomorrow and Tomorrow," *Astounding*, Jan., Feb., 1947. "The Fairy Chessmen," *Astounding*, Jan., Feb., 1946. TOMORROW AND TOMORROW AND THE FAIRY CHESSMEN [by Lewis Padgett]. New York: Gnome, 1951. THE FAIRY CHESSMEN [as CHESSBOARD PLANET]. New York: Galaxy Novels, 1956 pb.

Leiber, Fritz. CONJURE WIFE. *Unknown*, April, 1943. New York: Twayne [in WITCHES THREE], 1952. New York: Twayne, 1953. New York: Lion, 1953 pb.

Leinster, Murray. THE MONSTER FROM EARTH'S END. Greenwich, Connecticut: Fawcett (Gold Medal), 1959 pb.

Lovecraft, H. P. THE SHUTTERED ROOM AND OTHERS. Sauk City, Wisconsin: Arkham House, 1959.

Lymington, John. NIGHT OF THE BIG HEAT. London: Hodder & Stoughton, 1959. New York: Dutton, 1960.

McCann, Edson. PREFERRED RISK. *Galaxy*, June, July, Aug., 1955. New York: Simon & Schuster, 1955. New York: Dell, 1962 pb.

McIntosh, J. T. BORN LEADER. New York: Doubleday, 1954. Toronto: Doubleday, 1954. London: Museum Press, 1955. New York: Pocket Books, 1956 pb.

———. ONE IN THREE HUNDRED. [Composed of "One in Three Hundred," *The Magazine of Fantasy and Science Fiction*, Feb., 1953; "One in a Thousand," *ibid.*, Jan., 1954; and "One Too Many," *ibid.*, Sept., 1954.] New York: Doubleday, 1954. London: Museum Press, 1956. New York: Ace Books, 1955 pb.

Maine, Charles Eric. HIGH VACUUM. London: Hodder & Stoughton, 1957. New York: Ballantine, 1957 pb.

———. TIMELINER. [Based on "Highway i," *Authentic* (British), Nov., 1953. Same story as "Highway J," *Planet*, Nov., 1953.] New York: Rinehart, 1955. London: Hodder & Stoughton, 1955. New York: Bantam, 1956 pb.

Matheson, Richard. I AM LEGEND. New York: Fawcett (Gold Medal), 1954 pb.

———. THE SHORES OF SPACE. New York: Bantam, 1957 pb.

———. THE SHRINKING MAN. New York: Fawcett (Gold Medal), 1956 pb.

Matson, Norman. FLECKER'S MAGIC. New York: Boni & Liveright, 1926. London: Benn, 1926. Philadelphia: Lippincott, 1959 [as ENCHANTED BEGGAR]. Toronto: Longmans, Green, 1959 [as ENCHANTED BEGGAR].

Mead, Harold. THE BRIGHT PHOENIX. London: Michael Joseph, 1955. New York: Ballantine, 1956. New York: Ballantine, 1956 pb.

Merril, Judith. "Daughters of Earth." See Pratt, Fletcher, *et al.*

———. THE TOMORROW PEOPLE. New York: Pyramid, 1960 pb.

——— [ed]. S-F: THE YEAR'S GREATEST SCIENCE-FICTION AND FANTASY. Hicksville, New York: Gnome, 1956. New York: Dell, 1956 pb.

——— [ed]. SF: THE YEAR'S GREATEST SCIENCE-FICTION AND FANTASY. Hicksville, New York: Gnome, 1957. New York: Dell, 1957 pb.

—— [ed]. SF: THE YEAR'S GREATEST SCIENCE-FICTION AND FANTASY. Hicksville, New York: Gnome, 1959. Toronto: Burns & MacEachern, 1959. New York: Dell, 1959 pb.

Moore, C(atherine) L. [Mrs. Henry Kuttner]. See Kuttner, Henry.

Moskowitz, Sam. THE IMMORTAL STORM. *Fantasy Commentator*, Fall, 1945-Spring-Summer, 1952. Atlanta: Burwell, 1952. Atlanta: ASFO, 1954.

—— [ed]. EDITOR'S CHOICE IN SCIENCE FICTION. New York: McBride, 1954. Toronto: McClelland, 1954.

Mullen, Stanley. KINSMEN OF THE DRAGON. Chicago: Shasta, 1951.

Oliver, Chad. ANOTHER KIND. New York: Ballantine, 1955. New York: Ballantine, 1955 pb.

Padgett, Lewis. Pseudonym of Henry Kuttner and C. L. Moore. See Kuttner, Henry.

Pangborn, Edgar. A MIRROR FOR OBSERVERS. New York: Doubleday, 1954. Toronto: Doubleday, 1954. London: Frederick Muller, 1955. New York: Dell, 1958 pb.

——. WEST OF THE SUN. New York: Doubleday, 1953. London: Robert Hale, 1954. New York: Dell, 1966 pb.

Peake, Mervyn. "Boy in Darkness." See Golding, William, *et al.*

Piper, H. Beam. "Uller Uprising." See Pratt, Fletcher, *et al.*

Pohl, Frederik. ALTERNATING CURRENTS. New York: Ballantine, 1956. New York: Ballantine, 1956 pb.

——. THE CASE AGAINST TOMORROW. New York: Ballantine, 1957 pb.

——. TOMORROW TIMES SEVEN. New York: Ballantine, 1959 pb.

—— [ed]. STAR SHORT NOVELS. New York: Ballantine, 1954. New York: Ballantine, 1954 pb.

Pohl, Frederick, and Kornbluth, C. M. See Kornbluth, C. M.

Pratt, Fletcher. "The Blue Star." In WITCHES THREE. New York: Twayne, 1952.

Pratt, Fletcher, *et al.* THE PETRIFIED PLANET. [Contains "The Long View," by Fletcher Pratt (*Startling*, Dec., 1952); "Uller Uprising," by H. Beam Piper (*Space Science Fiction*, Feb., Mar., 1953); and "Daughters of Earth," by Judith Merril.] New York: Twayne, 1952.

Robinson, Frank M. THE POWER. *Bluebook*, March, 1956. Philadelphia: Lippincott, 1956. Toronto: Longmans, Green, 1956. London: Eyre & Spottiswoode, 1957. New York: Bantam, 1957 pb.

Roshwald, Mordecai. LEVEL 7. London: Heinemann, 1959. Toronto: British Book Service, 1959. New York: McGraw-Hill, 1960. New American Library (Signet), 1961 pb.

Ruppelt, Edward J. THE REPORT ON UNIDENTIFIED FLYING OBJECTS. New York: Doubleday, 1956. Toronto: Doubleday, 1956. London: Gollancz, 1956. New York: Ace Books, 1964 pb.

Schachner, Nat. SPACE LAWYER. New York: Gnome, 1953.

Sheckley, Robert. CITIZEN IN SPACE. New York: Ballantine, 1956. New York: Ballantine, 1956 pb.

——. PILGRIMAGE TO EARTH. New York: Bantam, 1957 pb.

Siodmak, Curt, and Smith, Robert. RIDERS TO THE STARS. New York: Ballantine, 1953 pb.

Skinner, B. F. WALDEN TWO. New York: Macmillan, 1948. New York: Macmillan, 1960 pb.

Smith, Robert. See Siodmak, Curt.

Sohl, Jerry. POINT ULTIMATE. New York: Rinehart, 1955. Toronto: Clarke, Irwin, 1955. New York: Bantam, 1959 pb.

Stevens, Francis. THE HEADS OF CERBERUS. *Thrill Book*, serial, August 15,

1919. Reading, Pennsylvania: Polaris Press, 1952.

Sturgeon, Theodore. E PLURIBUS UNICORN. New York: Abelard Press, 1953. Toronto: Nelson, Foster & Scott, 1953. New York: Ballantine, 1956 pb. London: Abelard-Schuman, 1960.

——. MORE THAN HUMAN. New York: Farrar, Straus & Young, 1953. New York: Ballantine, 1953 pb. London: Gollancz, 1954.

——. A WAY HOME (edited and introduced by Groff Conklin). New York: Funk & Wagnalls, 1955. London: Mayflower, 1955. New York: Pyramid, 1956 pb.

Toombs, Alfred. GOOD AS GOLD. New York: Crowell, 1955. Toronto: Ambassador, 1955.

Tucker, Wilson. THE LONG LOUD SILENCE. New York: Rinehart, 1952. London: John Lane, 1953. Toronto: Clarke, Irwin, 1953. New York: Dell, 1954 pb.

Vance, Jack. BIG PLANET. *Startling*, Sept., 1952. New York: Bouregy (Avalon), 1957. Toronto: Ryerson Press, 1957. New York: Ace Books, 1958 pb.

Van Vogt, A. E. EMPIRE OF THE ATOM. Chicago: Shasta, 1957. New York: Wyn (Ace), 1957 pb.

——. "The Players of $\overline{A}$." *Astounding*, Oct., Nov., Dec., 1948, Jan., 1949. New York: Wyn (Ace), 1956 pb [as THE PAWNS OF NULL-A].

——. THE WORLD OF $\overline{A}$. *Astounding*, Aug., Sept., Oct., 1945. New York: Simon & Schuster, 1948. Toronto: Musson, 1948. New York: Ace Books, 1953 pb.

Vernon, Roger Lee. THE SPACE FRONTIERS. New York: New American Library (Signet), 1955 pb.

Vidal, Gore. MESSIAH. New York: Dutton, 1954. Toronto: Smithers & Bonellie, 1954. New York: Ballantine, 1954 pb. London: Heinemann, 1955.

Vonnegut, Kurt, Jr. PLAYER PIANO. New York: Scribner's, 1952. Toronto: S. J. R. Saunders, 1952. London: Macmillan, 1953. New York: Bantam, 1954 pb [as UTOPIA 14].

——. THE SIRENS OF TITAN. New York: Dell, 1959 pb. Toronto: Houghton Mifflin, 1961. London: Gollancz, 1962.

Wilkins, Vaughan. VALLEY BEYOND TIME. New York: St. Martin's, 1955. London: Jonathan Cape, 1955. Toronto: Clarke, Irwin, 1955.

Williamson, Jack. THE HUMANOIDS. ["With Folded Hands . . .," *Astounding*, July, 1947; and ". . . And Searching Mind," *Astounding*, March, April, May, 1948.] New York: Simon & Schuster, 1949. Toronto: Musson, 1949. London: Museum Press, 1953. New York: Galaxy Novels, 1954 pb. New York: Lancer, 1963 pb.

Wolfe, Bernard. LIMBO. New York: Random House, 1952. London: Secker & Warburg, 1953 [as LIMBO '90]. New York: Ace Books, 1963 pb.

Wollheim, Donald A. THE MACABRE READER. New York: Wyn (Ace), 1959 pb.

Wyndham, John. "Consider Her Ways." See Golding, William, *et al.*

——. THE MIDWICH CUCKOOS. New York: Ballantine, 1957. London: Michael Joseph, 1957. Toronto: Thomas Allen, 1957. New York: Ballantine, 1959 pb.

——. OUT OF THE DEEPS. New York: Ballantine, 1953. New York: Ballantine, 1953 pb. London: Michael Joseph, 1953 [as THE KRAKEN WAKES]. Toronto: Collins, 1953 [as THE KRAKEN WAKES].

——. RE-BIRTH. *Argosy* (British), serial, 1955 [as "The Chrysalids"]. New York: Ballantine, 1955. New York: Ballantine, 1955 pb. London: Michael Joseph, 1955 [as THE CHRYSALIDS].

Zamiatin, Eugene. WE. New York: Dutton, 1924. New York: Dutton, 1959 pb.

INDEX

Abernathy, Robert, 122, 126.
"Absalom," 119.
"The Accountant," 237.
Ace Books, 229.
Ackerman, Forrest J, 24, 25.
"Adam and No Eve," 234.
Adler, Allen A., 101-103.
AFTER THE RAIN, 134-136.
AGAINST THE FALL OF NIGHT, 191
"Age of Anxiety," 273.
Aldiss, Brian W., 127, 243-244.
ALICE IN WONDERLAND, 198, 280.
"All About 'The Thing,'" 126.
"All Roads," 131.
"All the Things You Are," 237.
Allen, Steve, 122.
"Altar at Midnight, The," 148, 149.
ALTERED EGO, THE, 96.
ALTERNATING CURRENTS, 194-195.
Amazing Stories, 35, 116, 131, 133f,
    153, 188, 188f.
Amis, Kingsley, 7-8, 173.
Analog Science Fiction—Science Fact,
    35.
"And Three to Get Ready," 260.
Anderson, Poul, 95, 129, 135-136, 196.
"Angel's Egg," 198, 199.
ANOTHER KIND, 192-193.
"Anything Box," 124, 126.
Apostolides, Alex, 131.
Aristotle, 55.
Arrhenius, Svante, 74.
ARROWSMITH, 5.
"Artifact," 193.
Ashwell, Pauline, 127.

Asimov, Isaac, vi(f), 90-94, 120, 122,
    123, 126, 129, 192, 221, 249.
ASSIGNMENT IN ETERNITY, 78.
Astonishing Stories, 6f, 131, 193.
Astounding Stories, 34-35.
Astounding Science Fiction, 4, 34-35,
    36, 37, 42, 60, 61, 62, 73, 76, 78,
    131, 133f, 144, 153, 178, 188, 189,
    259,
"At the Mountains of Madness," 27.
"At the Post," 260.
Atheling, William, Jr., 154, 192.
ATTA, 96-97.
Auden, W. H., 273f.
Audubon, John James, 267.
"Avalanche," 73.
Avalon Books, 44.

"Baby Is Three," 115.
"Baby on Neptune, A," 177.
"Back for Christmas," 15.
"Bad Medicine," 238.
Ballantine Books, 100, 144, 148, 188,
    192, 193, 253, 261.
Ballard, J. G., 126.
Bantam Books, 11, 128, 172.
Barnhouse, Perl T., 210-213.
"Battle," 206.
Baum, L. Frank, 43.
"Baxbr Daxbr," 129.
BAYAN OF THE SECOND BAB, 233.
"Beanstalk," 150-152.
Beaumont, Charles, 129, 130, 221.
"Beautiful Things, The," 127.
"Beggars in Velvet," 250.

Bell Publications, 211.
Bellamy, Francis Rufus, 96-97.
Beloit College, 282.
Benét, Stephen Vincent, 35, 110.
Bennett, Margot, 250-252, 253.
Bergey, Earle, 284.
Bernstein, Morey, 215-216, 216f.
Bester, Alfred, 4-6, 84, 234-236, 250.
"Betelgeuse Bridge," 120.
BETWEEN PLANETS, 32, 80.
Beyond Fantasy Fiction 131.
BEYOND THIS HORIZON, 76, 86, 118.
BIBLE, THE, 252.
Bierce, Ambrose, 78.
"Big Black and White Game, The," 111.
BIG PLANET, 197-198.
Binder, Eando, 132-133.
Binder, Otto, 161.
"Biography Project, The," 260.
Blackwood, Algernon, 221.
Blavatsky, Madame, 25.
THE BLIND SPOT, 22-25, 27, 213.
Blish, James, xii, 4, 26, 135, 150-157,
    241, 265, 266, 268-274, 270f, 271f.
Blish, Virginia, 266, 270f.
Bloch, Robert, 4-7.
"Blood Son," 239.
"Blowups Happen," 5.
"Blue Star, The," 158-159.
Bluebook 131. 277.
"The Body," 238.
THE BODY SNATCHERS, 73-75.
Boggs, Redd, 115f, 154f.
Book of the Month Club, The, 67, 188.
"Boredom of Fantasy, The," 2.
BORN LEADER, 64-65.
Bosch, Hieronymus, 221.
Bott, Henry, vi.
Boucher, Anthony, 126, 128, 131, 158,
    224, 228.
Bowen, John, 134-136.
Bowers, Margaretta K., 216-217.
"Boy In Darkness," 246.
Brackett, Leigh, 262-264.
Bradbury, Ray, 108-113, 115, 128-129,
    132, 188, 239, 245, 282.
BRAVE NEW WORLD, 2.
"Breaking Strain," 189.
Bretnor, Reginald, x, 5, 125, 126.
Breuer, Miles J., 177.
BRIGHT PHOENIX, THE, 241-242.
BRITANNICA, THE, 282.
Browne, Howard, 116, 133, 133f.
BR-R-R-!, 220-222.

"Buck Rogers," 151.
Budrys, Algis J., 122, 124, 125, 199-203,
    219, 266.
"Bulkhead," 123, 126.
Burnham, James, 165.
BURNING SPEAR, THE, 234-236.
Burroughs, Edgar Rice, 90, 154, 197,
    198, 251.
"But Without Horns," 279.
"Butterflies, The," 138.
"Buzby's Petrified Woman," 129.
"By the Waters of Babylon," 35.

"Cabin Boy," 274.
Caesar, Julius, 236.
Caldwell, Taylor, 29-31.
Campbell, Clyde Crane, 259.
Campbell, John W., Jr., xi, 34-36, 47,
    60, 108, 131, 133-139, 161, 193,
    203, 217, 218, 284.
"Can of Paint, A," 60, 61.
"Candle Lighter, The," 195.
CANTICLE FOR LEIBOWITZ, A, 172.
Čapek, Karel, 11-12, 58.
CARNELIAN CUBE, THE, 44.
Carroll, Lewis, 39, 118.
Cartmill, Cleve, 226.
Cary, Joyce, 115.
CASE AGAINST TOMORROW, THE,
    195-196.
"Casey Agonistes," 128.
Castle, Jeffery Lloyd, 208-209.
"Cave of Night, The," 123, 124.
CAVES OF STEEL, THE, 90-93.
"Celebrated No-Hit Inning, The," 195.
"Census Takers, The," 195.
Cerf, Bennett, 15.
Charles I, 91.
"Chaser, The," 15.
CHECKLIST OF FANTASTIC LITERA-
    TURE, THE, 163.
"Chess Civilization, The," 207.
Chesterton, G. K., 60, 248.
CHILDHOOD'S END, 187-188, 189, 192.
Christopher, John, 169-170.
"Circus of Dr. Lao, The," 128.
CIRCUS OF DR. LAO AND OTHER
    IMPROBABLE STORIES, 128-129.
CITIZEN IN SPACE, 237.
CITIZEN OF THE GALAXY, 86-89.
"City and the Ship, The," 207.
CITY AND THE STARS, THE, 191-192.
CITY IN THE SEA, THE, 179.
"Clane" series, 62.

Clark, John D., 19, 248, 249.
Clarke, Arthur C., 129, 131, 187-192.
Claudius I, 62.
Claudy, Carl H., 82, 82f.
Clement, Hal, 135, 177-178.
Clifton, Mark, 122-123, 131.
Clingerman, Mildred, ix, 122.
CLOAK OF AESIR, 35-36.
"Clothes Make the Man," 175.
Coates, Robert M., 129.
Coblentz, Stanton A, 9, 12-13.
Coleman, Sidney, xii.
Collier, John, 13-17, 191.
Collier's 108, 169.
Columbus, Christopher, 154.
"Comedian's Children, The," 127.
"Coming Attraction," 182.
COMING OF CONAN, THE, 19-20.
COMING UP FOR AIR, 267.
"Common Time," 156, 265, 268-273.
"Compounded Interest," 124, 126.
"Concerning Stories Never Written,"
    78.
"Concrete Mixer, The," 110.
CONJURE WIFE, 40-42, 226.
Conklin, Groff, vi, 220-222.
CONNECTICUT YANKEE IN KING
    ARTHUR'S COURT, A, 12.
"Consider Her Ways," 245-246.
Cook, W. Paul, 224.
Cooper, Edmund, 136-138, 244-245.
COROMANDEL!, 170.
Correy, Lee, 32-33, 284.
Corwin, Cecil, 146.
Cosmic Stories, 146, 150.
"Cosmic Expense Account, The," 125,
    126.
"Coventry," 76, 77.
Coward-McCann, x.
Cox, Arthur J., 129.
Cox, Irving E., Jr., 129, 130.
Crawford, William L., 161.
Cromwell, Oliver, 2.
Crossen, Kendell Foster, 91, 95-96,
    232.
Cummings, Ray, 140.
"Curious Child, The," 239.
CURRENTS OF SPACE, THE, 90.

"Da Capo," 78.
Dahl, Roald, 129, 221.
Daley, John Bernard, 125, 126.
DANDELION WINE, 112-113.
"Dangerous Dimension, The," 37.

DARK CARNIVAL, 112.
DARK DOMINION, 257.
DARKNESS AT NOON, 2, 66, 67, 69.
"Daughters of Earth," 249.
Daughters of the American Revolution,
    95.
Davenport, Basil, x, 4-7.
Davidson, Avram, 122, 127, 284.
"Davy Jones' Ambassador," 71.
"Day of the Boomer Dukes, The," 194.
DAY OF THE TRIFFIDS, THE, 169,
    178, 252.
"De Mortuis," 15.
Dean Machine, the, 34.
"Death Seekers, The," 207.
De Camp, L. Sprague, x, 5, 19, 20,
    43-45, 61, 161, 196, 259.
"Deep Range, The," 189.
DEEP RANGE, THE, 189-190.
Defoe, Daniel, 96, 168.
Del Rey, Evelyn, 267.
Del Rey, Lester, xii, 1, 42-43, 82f, 119,
    121-122, 131, 133, 253, 265, 267.
Democratic Party, the, 29.
DEMOLISHED MAN, THE, 232, 234,
    235, 250.
"Derelict," 133, 177.
Derleth, August, vi, 129-130, 133, 223,
    224.
DESCENT INTO THE MAELSTROM, A,
    27.
"Desertion," 217.
Destiny's Child, 47.
"Devil George and Rosie, The," 14.
"Devil We Know, The," 144.
DEVIL'S ADVOCATE, THE, 29-30.
Dianetics, 35.
Dick, Philip K., 129, 228-234.
Dickens, Charles, 136.
Dickson, Gordon, 196.
"Digging the Weans," 126.
Dikty, T. E., 139.
Dirk Wylie Literary Agency, 193.
DIVIDE AND RULE, 44, 45.
Dockweiler, Harry, 193.
"Doll That Does Everything, The," 239.
DON QUIXOTE, 5.
"Don't Look Now," 129.
"Doomsday Deferred," 221.
DOOR INTO SUMMER, THE, 79-80, 85.
"Doorstop, The," 125, 126.
DOUBLE JEOPARDY, 158.
DOUBLE STAR, 78-79.
Doubleday & Co., 14f, 66, 193.

DRACULA, 63.
"Dream, The," 246.
"Dreaming Is a Private Thing," 122.
Duncan, David, 225, 255-258.
Dunsany, Lord, 146, 191, 225, 226.
"Durna Rangue" series, 276.
DYING EARTH, THE, 158.

"Each an Explorer," 126.
"Early Model," 237.
"Earth, Air, Fire and Water," 237-238
EARTHMAN, COME HOME, 152-155, 241.
"Earth's Holocaust," 129.
Ecclesiastes, 244.
"Eclipse," 78.
Eddison, E. R., 197.
Editors and Other Fungoids, 188.
EDITOR'S CHOICE IN SCIENCE FICTION, 130-133.
"Ego Machine, The," 145.
"Egyptian Hornet, An," 221.
Ehrenhaft, Felix, 34.
Eiseley, Loren, 129.
Eisenhower, Dwight D., 95, 171.
Ellington, Duke, 7.
Elliott, H. Chandler, 69-70.
"Elsewhen," 78.
Elstar, Dow, 73.
EMPIRE OF THE ATOM, 62.
Emshwiller, Carol, 127.
"En la Noche," 111.
ENCHANTED BEGGAR, 20-21.
ENCYCLOPEDIA BRITANNICA, 282.
END OF ETERNITY, THE, 94.
Endersby, Victor, 276.
ENEMY STARS, THE, 135-136.
"Enter the Professor," 61.
"Envoy Extraordinary," 245.
"Escape, The," 8f, 36.
Esquire, 108.
"Ether Vibrates, The," 163.
"Ethicators, The," 123.
"Ex Machina," 139.
"Exit the Professor," 144, 145.
Exodus, 33.
EXPEDITION TO EARTH, 188-189.
EXPLORERS, THE, 148-149.
EYE IN THE SKY, 233-234.

Fadiman, Clifton, 1, 67, 68.
"Fairy Chessmen, The," 140-144.
Falconer, Kenneth, 146.
"Fallen Star," 14.

FALLING TORCH, THE, 202-203.
FALSE NIGHT, 199-200.
Famous Fantastic Mysteries, 131, 187.
FANCIES AND GOODNIGHTS, 13-17.
Fantastic, 131.
Fantasy Amateur Press Association, The, 161, 162.
Fantasy and Science Fiction, see Magazine of Fantasy and Science Fiction.
Fantasy Commentator, vii.
Fantasy Press, 78.
"Far Below," 131.
"Far Centaurus," 85.
"Far Look, The," 124, 125, 126. 267.
FARMER IN THE SKY, 32, 80, 83.
Farmer, Philip José, 4, 8f.
Farnsworth, Mona, 131.
Faulkner, William, 179.
Fawcett, F. Dubrez, 242-243.
"Fear," 38-40, 233.
"Fear in the Night," 238.
Federal Bureau of Investigation, 231.
FINNEGANS WAKE, 272.
Finney, Charles G., 128.
Finney, Jack, 73-75, 118, 123, 225.
"Fire Balloons, The," 111.
"Fire Down Below!," 78.
"First Contact," 192.
FIRST ON MARS, 246.
FIRST TO THE STARS, 246-247.
"Fisherman of Falcon Point, The," 224.
FITTEST, THE, 169.
Fitzgerald, F. Scott, 128.
FLECKER'S MAGIC, 20-21.
Fletcher, George U., 158, 158f.
FLIGHT INTO YESTERDAY, 203-205.
Flint, Homer Eon, 22-25.
Flournoy, Théodore, 216f.
"Flying Machine, The," 245.
"Fondly Fahrenheit," 234.
"For I Am A Jealous People," 122, 253.
Forbidden Planet, 101.
Forester, C. S., 119.
FOUNDATION AND EMPIRE, 90.
"Four in One," 274.
FRANKENSTEIN, 133, 222.
Franklin, H. Bruce, 283.
Freud, Sigmund, 164, 265.
Friend, Oscar J., 131.
"Friend to Man," 148.
FROM CALIGARI TO HITLER, 222.
FROM INDIA TO THE PLANET MARS, 216f.
Front Page, 101.

"Fruits of the Agathon," 205.
"Funeral, The," 239.
Future and *Future combined with Science Fiction Stories* 120, 131, 150, 189.
"Future History" series 76.
FUTURE PERFECT, 283.
Futurian Society, The, 118, 162, 163.

GALACTIC CLUSTER, 156-157.
Galaxy, vii, 115, 131, 189, 194, 195-196, 197, 228, 259, 260, 261.
Galaxy Novels, 189.
GALAXY READER OF SCIENCE FICTION, 96f.
Gale, Floyd C., vi.
Gallun, Raymond Z., 70-73, 133, 177, 274-275.
Garrett, Randall, ix, 126.
GATHER DARKNESS!, 258.
Gault, William Campbell, 132.
Gehman, Richard, 127.
Genesis, 33, 237.
"Gentle Venusian, The," 194.
Gernsback, Hugo, 35, 160, 161, 283, 284.
Gerson, Villiers, vi.
Gibbon, Edward, 223.
Gilpatric, Guy, 175.
GLADIATOR-AT-LAW, 261.
GLADIATORS, THE, 2.
Glasser, Allen 160, 161.
GLORY THAT WAS, THE, 44-45.
Gnome Press, 20, 140, 250.
"God in the Bowl, The," 20.
"God Save the King," 234.
Gold, Horace L., 131, 221, 259-260.
Gold Medal, 64, 280.
"Golden Bird, The," 79.
"Golden Kite, The Silver Wind, The," 111.
Golding, William, 167-169, 245.
"Golem, The," 122, 123.
"Gomez," 148.
GOOD AS GOLD, 254-255.
"Goodly Creatures, The," 148, 149.
Gordon, Rex, 246-247.
Gottesman, S. D., 146, 193.
"Grandmother's Lie Soap," 126.
Graves, Robert, 62, 182, 183.
"Gravy Planet," 95, 146, 194, 232, 260.
Gray, Curme, viii, 181-187.
GREAT MOTHER, THE, 6.
"Great Possibilities," 15.

"Greenface," 129.
Grimm, Jacob and Wilhelm, 79.
Grosset & Dunlap, 82.
"Guardian Angel," 188.
"Gulf," 32, 78.
GULLIVER'S TRAVELS, 2, 8.
Gunn, James E., 123, 258-259.
GUNNER CADE 146.
Gunther, Gotthard, 217-219.

Hadley, Arthur T., 173-174.
Haggard, H. Rider, 251.
Hall, Austin, ix, 22-25, 70.
Hamilton, Edmond, 5, 139.
HAMLET AND OEDIPUS, 265.
"Hands Off," 237.
"Happy Birthday, Dear Jesus," 194.
Harness, Charles L., 203-205.
Harpers, vii(f).
Harper's, 108.
Harper's Bazaar, 2.
Harris, Clare Winger, 177.
Harris, John Beynon, 178.
"Haunted Corpse, The," 194.
HAUNTING OF HILL HOUSE, THE, 226-227.
Hawthorne, Nathaniel, 129.
HEADS OF CERBERUS, THE, 9-11.
Heinlein, Robert A., ix, 1, 4-5, 9, 32, 33, 61, 70, 76-89, 90, 91, 117-121, 132, 189, 232, 258.
"Helen O'Loy," 133, 133f.
"Hell Hath Fury," 226.
HELL'S MY DESTINATION, 234-236.
HELL'S PAVEMENT, viii.
Henderson, Zenna, 123, 124, 126.
Hermitage House, x.
"Hero," 260.
Hibbs, Ben, 170.
"Hide and Seek," 189.
HIGH VACUUM, 98-100.
HIGHWAYS IN HIDING, 84.
"History Lesson," 189.
"Hoka" series, 196.
HOLE IN HEAVEN, 242-243.
"Hole in the Sky," 130.
Holiday, 188.
Holmes, H. H., vi.
Holt, 32.
"Home There's No Returning," 145.
Homer, 82.
"Hoofer, The," 122, 124.
Hornig, Charles, 161.
Hostovsky, Egon, 12.

"Hour of Letdown, The," 129.
HOW NOT TO WRITE A PLAY, 242.
Howard, Allan, 223.
Howard, Robert E., 19-20, 159.
Hubbard, L. Ron, xii, 34, 37-40, 61,
    233, 272.
HUCKSTERS, THE, 91, 232.
Hull, E. Mayne, 61f.
HUMANOIDS, THE, 45-46, 207.
"Hunting Problem," 237.
"Hurricane, The," 267.
"Hurricane Trio," 116.
Huxley, Aldous, 2, 136.
"Hyborian Age, The," 19.

I AM LEGEND, 8, 63-64, 280.
I, CLAUDIUS, 62.
"I, Robot," 133, 133f.
'idiot plot,' 26, 195.
"If I Forget Thee, Oh Earth . . .," 189.
"If This Goes On—," 76, 77, 168, 258.
If: Worlds of Science Fiction, 131.
"I'm Scared," 118.
IMMORTAL STORM, THE, 160-163.
"In the Abyss," 276.
"Incident in Space," 206-207.
INCOMPLETE ENCHANTER, THE, 44.
Independent League for Science Fiction,
    161.
INDEX TO THE SCIENCE FICTION
    MAGAZINES: 1926-1950, 163.
"Indian Serenade," 270.
"Informal Biography of Conan the
    Cimmerian, An," 19.
"Inheritance," 189.
INQUIRY INTO SCIENCE FICTION, x.
Inside, vii.
International Scientific Association, 161.
"Invaders, The," 36.
"Irrelevant, The," 247.
Irving, Washington, 112.
Isherwood, Christopher, 109.
"It," 221, 226.
"It Wasn't Syzygy," 115

"Jabberwocky," 218.
"Jack-in-the-Box," 111.
Jackson, Shirley, 122, 129, 226-227.
Jacobi, Carl, 129, 130.
Jakobsson, Ejler, 131.
James, Henry, 129.
"Jay Score," 119.
Jenkins, Will F., 120.
"Jerry Was A Man," 78.

Jesus Christ, 31, 51, 182.
Johnson, Robert Barbour, 131.
Jones, Ernest, 265.
Jones, Neil R., 153, 276.
"Jon's World," 129.
JOY WAGON, THE, 173-174.
Joyce, James, 150, 272.
Jung, Carl, 272.
"Junior," 123.
"Juvenilia and Early Tales," 224.

"Kaleidoscope," 109, 110.
Karl Rauch Verlag, 217.
Karloff, Boris, 220.
Karp, David, 66-69.
"Keeper of the Dream," 130.
Kemp, Earl, xii, 181f.
Kennicott, Donald, 131.
Kerr, Walter, 124, 242.
"Keyhole," 120.
Khrushchev, N. S., 171.
KIM, 88.
"King and the Oak, The," 19.
"King of the Hill," 156.
KINSMEN OF THE DRAGON, 25-29.
Kipling, Rudyard, 35, 189.
Kirkland, Jack, 131.
Klass, Phil, 266.
Kline, Milton V., 216-217.
Kline, Otis Adelbert, 131.
Kneale, Nigel, 129.
knight, damon, vi-xi, vii (f).
Knight, Damon, ix, x,
Knight, Helen, 266.
"Knights of Arthur, The," 194.
Koestler, Arthur, 2, 30, 66, 67, 69,
    165, 263.
"Kommentar," 219.
Kornbluth, Cyril M., 4, 5-6, 8f, 118,
    119, 125, 126, 146-149, 157, 166,
    193, 196-197, 266, 268f.
Korzybski, Alfred, 55.
Kracauer, Siegfried, 222.
Kubilius, Walter, 118, 119f.
Kurtzman, Harvey, 236.
Kuttner, Catherine [C. L. Moore], 119.
Kuttner, Henry, 78, 84, 119, 122, 129,
    139-145, 151, 219, 249-250.
Kuttner Syndrome, the, 139, 219.

"Lady on the Grey, The," 15.
LaFarge, Oliver, 129.
Lardner, Ring, 195.
Lasser, David, 160.

"Last Day, The," 240.
Lavond, Paul Dennis, 193.
Le Zombie, 119.
"Legal Rites," 221.
Leiber, Fritz, ix, 40-42, 121, 127, 128, 182, 223, 224, 226, 258.
Leinster, Murray, 120, 136-138, 139, 221, 222.
Lemkin, William, 160.
Lenin, V. I., 199.
LEONARDO DA VINCI: A STUDY IN PSYCHOSEXUALITY, 265.
Lesser, Milton, 32.
LEST DARKNESS FALL, 44.
"Let the Ants Try," 194.
LEVEL 7, 170-173.
Lewis, C. S., 226, 259, 267.
"Liberation of Earth," 120.
"Lifeboat Mutiny, The," 238.
LIMBO, 164-165.
"Limits of Walter Horton, The," 129.
"Lion and the Unicorn, The," 250.
Lion Books, 199.
"Little Hercules," 276.
LITTLE LAME PRINCE, 275.
"Little Memento," 15.
"Little Men," 121-122, 176.
Little Monsters of America, The, 154.
Livia [Augusta], 62.
Long, Frank Belknap, 161.
LONG LOUD SILENCE, THE, 179-181.
LONG TOMORROW, THE, 262-264.
"Long View, The," 248.
LONG WAY BACK, THE, 250-252, 253.
Longfellow, Henry Wadsworth, 214.
Longmans, Green, x.
"Loophole," 189.
LORD OF THE FLIES, 167-169.
Lorraine, Lilith, 32.
Los Angeles *Times*, 188.
"Lost Legacy," 78.
"Lotus Eaters, The," 217.
"Lotusesser, Die," 218.
Louis XVI, 91.
"Love in the Dark," 260.
Lovecraft, H. P., 19, 26, 111, 159, 178, 223-224, 225, 226.
"Lovers, The," 4, 8f.
Lowndes, Robert A. W., xii, 118, 119f, 131, 162, 277.
"Luckiest Man in the World, The," 237.
LUCKY JIM, 7.
Lymington, John, 225-226.

MACABRE READER, THE, 220.
McBride, 131.
McCann, Edson, 260-262.
McComas, J. Francis, vi, 131, 158.
MacCreigh, James, 193, 194.
MACH 1, A STORY OF PLANET IONUS, 101-103.
Machen, Arthur, 223.
"Machine, The," 36.
McIlwraith, Dorothy, 131.
McIntosh, J. T., 64-66, 169.
McKenna, Richard M., 127, 128.
McLaughlin, Venard, 126.
MacLean, Katherine, 127.
Mademoiselle, 108.
Magazine of Fantasy and Science Fiction, The, viii, xii, 83, 124, 131, 145, 189, 193.
"Magic, Inc.," 118.
Maine, Charles Eric, 97-100.
"Man of Parts," 260.
MAN WHO JAPED, THE, 231-233.
"Man Who Liked Lions, The," 125, 126.
"Man Who Sold the Moon, The," 76, 189.
"Man Who Vanished, The," 129.
MAN WHO WAS THURSDAY, THE, 60.
"Man With English, The," 260.
"Mapmakers, The," 194.
Marcuse, F. L., 216.
"Margin For Error," 119.
MARS CHILD, 146.
Marsh, Willard, 122.
Marshall, Edison, 276.
"Martian Way, The," 91.
MARTIAN WAY AND OTHER STORIES, THE, 93-94.
Marvel Stories, 139.
Marx, Groucho, 117.
Marx, Karl, 95, 117, 164.
Massachusetts Institute of Technology, 34, 189.
Masters, John, 170.
Matheson, Richard, 8, 63-64, 96, 239-240, 278-283.
Matson, Norman, 20-21.
"Matter of Fact, A," 35.
"Matter of Form, A," 259.
Matthew, 30, 31.
Maugham, W. Somerset, 189.
Mead, Harold, 241-242.
Medici, Lorenzo de', 62.
"Mercy Death," 155.
Meredith, George, 240.

Merliss, R. R., 122.
Merril, Judith, ix, 104-105, 120, 122-128, 146, 249.
Merritt, A., 19, 25, 37, 159.
Merwin, Sam, 155.
MESSIAH, 175-176.
METHUSELAH'S CHILDREN, 32, 78, 86.
Metropolis, 91.
"Midas Plague, The," 195.
"Middle of Nowhere, The," 194.
MIDWICH CUCKOOS, THE, 253-254.
Milford S. F. Writers' Conference, 265.
"Milk Run," 238.
Miller, P. Schuyler, vi, 10, 19.
Miller, R. De Witt, 119.
Miller, Walter M., Jr., 122.
Milton, John, 149.
"Mimsy Were the Borogoves," 217, 219.
"Mindworm, The," 148.
MIRROR FOR OBSERVERS, A, 198-199.
"Misbegotten Missionary," 120.
"Misfit," 76, 78.
"Misogynist, The," 258.
MISSION OF GRAVITY, 177-178.
MR. FOTHERGILL'S PLOT, 248.
"Mixed Men" series, 58.
MODERN SCIENCE FICTION: ITS MEANING AND ITS FUTURE, x, 90.
Mondrian, Piet, 115.
"Monster, The," 119, 217.
MONSTER FROM EARTH'S END, THE, 136-138
MOON IS HELL!, THE, 136.
MOON POOL, THE, 27.
Moore, C. L. [Catherine Kuttner], 4, 122, 144-145.
Moore, Ward, vi.
MORE THAN HUMAN, 114-115, 121.
Morey, Leo, 284.
Morley, Christopher, 112, 274.
Morrison, William, 120-121.
Morton, James F. 224.
Moskowitz, Sam, ix, 12, 25, 33, 91, 128, 130-133, 133f, 160-163, 162f, 284.
"Mother of Necessity, The," 192.
"Mountain Without a Name, The," 237.
Mullen, Stanley, 26-29.
Mulock, Miss [Dinah Maria], 275.
MURDER IN MILLENNIUM VI, viii, 181-187.
MUTANT, 249-250.
MY JOURNEYS WITH ASTARGO, 210-213.
"My Lady Green Sleeves," 196.

MYSTERY WRITERS HANDBOOK, THE, viii(f).
Mystery Writers of America, The, viii(f).

Napoleon [Bonaparte], 276.
Nathan, Robert, 110, 112, 126.
Nero, Lucius Domitius, 236.
NERVES, 42-43.
Neumann, Erich, 6.
"New Accelerator, The," 207.
"New Blood," 258.
NEW MAPS OF HELL, 7-8, 173.
New Yorker, The, 134.
"Next in Line, The," 108.
Nicholas II, 91.
"Night," 133, 193.
"Night He Cried, The," 121.
NIGHT OF THE BIG HEAT, 225-226.
"Nightfall," 90, 217.
NINETEEN EIGHTY-FOUR, 2, 6, 8, 19, 30, 66, 67, 69, 95, 138, 172, 232, 242.
NO BLADE OF GRASS, 169-170.
NO BOUNDARIES, 144-145.
"No Charge For Alterations," 260.
"No Particular Night or Morning," 109.
"No Woman Born," 4, 145.
"Nobody Bothers Gus," 122.
"None But Lucifer," 259.
Norton, Alden H., 131.
NOT THIS AUGUST, 147-148.
"Not With a Bang," viii.
"Note on the Author," 12.
Numbers, 33.
"Nursery Rhyme," 221.

O. HENRY PRIZE STORIES, 108.
OCCAM'S RAZOR, 255-258.
"Oddy and Id," 234.
"Of Missing Persons," 123.
"Of Time and Third Avenue," 234.
"Okie" series, 152-155.
"Old Die Rich, The," 260.
OLD DIE RICH, AND OTHER SCIENCE FICTION STORIES, THE, 259-260.
"Old Faithful," 71, 177, 274-275.
Oliver, Chad, 192-193.
ON THE BEACH, 172.
ONE, 66-69.
ONE IN THREE HUNDRED, 65-66.
"One Ordinary Day, With Peanuts," 122.
ORDEAL BY FIRE, 158.
Orwell, George, 2, 6, 8, 19, 30, 67, 69, 136, 172, 242, 267.

"Other Man, The," 125, 126.
OUT OF THE DEEPS, 178-179, 252, 254.
"Outsider, The," 224.
Oxford University Press, 283.

Padgett, Lewis, 217, 218, 219, 249-250.
Page, Norvell, 37, 279.
Pal, George, 277.
Palmer, Ray, 284.
Pangborn, Edgar, 198-199.
"Paradise Lost," 149.
"Paradise II," 129.
PARADOX MEN, THE, 203-205.
"Pattern For Survival," 240.
Paul, Frank R., 130.
Pauling, Linus, 172.
Peake, Mervyn, 8f, 246.
PEBBLE IN THE SKY, 90.
PELLUCIDAR, 27.
"Pelt," 127.
Pendray, Gawain Edwards, 160.
PEOPLE MINUS X, 70-73.
PERELANDRA, 259.
Permabooks, 269f.
"Peter Rabbit," 120.
PETRIFIED PLANET, THE, 178,
    248-249.
"Phoenix," 129, 130.
"Pictures in the Fire," 15.
PILGRIMAGE TO EARTH, 237-239.
"Pilgrimage to Earth," 238-239.
Piper, H. Beam, 217, 248-249.
"Piper's Son, The," 249.
Planet Stories, 108, 131, 136, 194.
"Plant World, The," 207.
PLAYER PIANO, 166-167, 236.
PLAYERS OF Ā, THE, 52f.
Poe, Edgar Allan, 112, 220.
Pohl, Frederik, 8, 119, 121-122, 146,
    146f, 166, 189, 193-197, 221.
POINT ULTIMATE, 105-107, 147.
"Pond, The," 129.
"Poor Superman," 121.
Popular Publications, 78, 193.
"Population Crisis: 2550," 207.
Post, see Saturday Evening Post.
"Pottage," 123.
Pound, Ezra, 150.
POWER, THE, 278-283.
"Powerhouse," 111.
Pratt, Fletcher, 158-159, 158f, 196,
    225, 248, 249.
PREFERRED RISK, 260-262.
PRELUDE TO SPACE, 189.

Priestley, J. B., 172.
"Prima Belladonna," 126.
"Prize of Peril, The," 127.
"Problem in Murder," 260.
"Protection," 238.
PUPPET MASTERS, THE, 91.
"Put Them All Together, They Spell
    Monster," 126.
"Pythias," 194.

Quaint Quality Quarterly, 228.

"Rafferty's Reasons," 194.
Raginsky, Bernard B., 216, 217.
"Rainmaker," 119.
Rauch, see Karl Rauch Verlag.
RE-BIRTH, 252-253, 264.
RED PLANET, 32, 79, 80.
Reese, John, 119.
Reinsberg, Mark, 78.
Reiss, Malcolm, 131.
"Report on the Barnhouse Effect, The,"
    119.
REPORT ON UNIDENTIFIED FLYING
    OBJECTS, THE, 209-210.
REPRIEVE FROM PARADISE, 69-70.
Republican Party, the, 29.
"Resting Place, The," 129.
Revelation, 244.
REVOLT IN 2100, 76-78.
Reynolds, Mack, 124, 126, 284.
RIDERS TO THE STARS, 100-101.
"Rite of Passage," 192.
Roan, Tom, 37.
Robinson, Frank M., 91, 278-283.
ROBOTS HAVE NO TAILS, 139-140.
"Robots' Return," 133f.
"Rocket of 1955, The," 148.
ROCKET SHIP GALILEO, 80, 82.
Rocklynne, Ross, 90, 129.
Rohmer, Sax, 25.
ROLLING STONES, THE, 80-82.
Roosevelt, Franklin D., 29.
Rosen, Harold, 216.
Roshwald, Mordecai, 170-173.
Rubens, Peter Paul, 115.
"Rulers, The," 61.
Ruppelt, Edward J., 209-210.
Ruppert, Conrad H., 161.
Russell, Bertrand, 172.
Russell, Eric Frank, 119, 178.

"Sack, The," 121.
Salinger, J. D., 112.

"Sam Hall," 95.
"Santa Claus Planet, The," 91.
Santesson, Hans Stefan, vi.
SATELLITE E ONE, 208-209.
"Satellite Passage," 127.
Saturday Evening Post, The, 1, 108, 164.
Saturday Review, The, xi, 277.
"Saucer of Loneliness," 8f, 115, 121.
SCANDALS OF CLOCHEMERLE, 254.
Schachner, Nat, 36-37.
Schmitz, James H., 129.
Schwartz, Julius, 161.
SCIENCE AND SANITY, 55.
Science Fiction Adventures, 1.
"Science Fiction and the Opinion of the Universe," xi(f).
Science Fiction Fan, The 162.
Science Fiction Forum, 265.
SCIENCE-FICTION HANDBOOK, x.
Science Fiction League, 161.
SCIENCE FICTION NOVEL, IMAGI-NATION AND SOCIAL CRITICISM, THE, 4-7.
Science-Fiction Plus, 130, 131.
Science Fiction Quarterly, 119f, 189.
Science Fiction Stories, 277.
Scienceers, The, 160, 161.
"Scientific Method," 192.
SCIENTIFIC REPORT ON "THE SEARCH FOR BRIDEY MURPHY," A, 216-217.
Scribners, 80, 83.
Seabright, Idris, 221.
SEARCH FOR BRIDEY MURPHY, THE, 215-216.
"Second Dawn," 189.
SECOND FOUNDATION, 90.
Second Woman, The, 101.
SEED OF LIGHT, 244-245.
"Seeds of the Dusk," 71.
"Self Portrait," 164-165.
"Sense From Thought Divide," 122.
"Sentinel, The," 189.
"Sex Opposite, The," 115.
S-F, THE YEAR'S GREATEST SCIENCE-FICTION AND FANTASY (1955), 122-124.
SF, THE YEAR'S GREATEST SCIENCE-FICTION AND FANTASY (1956), 124-126.
SF, THE YEAR'S GREATEST SCIENCE-FICTION AND FANTASY (1958), 126-128.
SHADOWS IN THE SUN, 193.

Shakespeare, William, 213.
Shapiro, Arthur, 216, 217.
Sharnik, John Seymour, 129.
Shasta, 35, 76, 78, 182, 183.
Shaw, Artie, 1.
Shaw, Larry, 47, 131.
Sheckley, Robert, 127, 129, 236, 237-239.
Shelley, Percy Bysshe, 14, 219, 270.
SHORES OF SPACE, THE, 239-240.
SHRINKING MAN, THE, 278-283.
"Shuttered Room, The," 223-224.
SHUTTERED ROOM AND OTHER PIECES, THE, 223-224.
Signet Books, 206, 208.
"Silent Brother," 124, 125, 126.
"Silly Season, The," 118.
Simak, Clifford D., 217.
Simon and Schuster, 260.
Siodmak, Curt, 100-101.
SIRENS OF TITAN, THE, 236-237.
"Skeleton," 112, 113.
Skinner, B. F., 174-175.
Skyhook, 115f, 154f.
SKYLARK OF SPACE, THE, 136, 210-211, 212.
SLAN, 60, 254.
Sloane, T. O'Conor, 284.
Smith, Clark Ashton, 129, 130.
Smith, Edward E., vii, 6, 12, 34, 211.
Smith, Evelyn E., 129.
Smith, George O., 84, 284.
Smith, Joseph, 118.
Smith, Robert, 100-101.
Smith, Thorne, 140, 255.
"Smythe Report, The," 37, 42.
Snyder, Mrs. R. J., 223.
Society for Clinical and Experimental Hypnosis, The, 216.
Sohl, Jerry, 96, 105-107.
SOLAR LOTTERY, 228-230, 231.
"Solar Plexus," 271-272.
SOLOMON'S STONE, 43-44.
SOMETIME, NEVER, 245-246.
"Son of Old Faithful," 177.
"Sound Machine, The," 221.
"Sound of His Wings, The," 78.
SPACE CADET, 80.
SPACE FRONTIERS, THE, 206-208.
SPACE LAWYER, 36-37.
SPACE MERCHANTS, THE, 146, 146f, 166, 261.
Space Science Fiction, 131.
"Space-Time For Springers," 128.

"Special Delivery," 15.
Spillane, Mickey, 121, 213, 235, 258.
Stalin, J. V., 199.
Stapledon, Olaf, 151, 199, 245.
"Star Above It, A," 193.
STAR BEAST, THE, 83.
STAR BRIDGE, 258.
STAR SCIENCE FICTION #3, 189.
STAR SHORT NOVELS, 121-122.
"Star That Fell, The," 276.
STARBURST, 234.
"Starcomber, The," 234.
STARMAN JONES, 32, 82-83.
STARS, LIKE DUST . . ., THE, 90.
STARS MY DESTINATION, THE, 6,
  234-236.
STARSHIP THROUGH SPACE, 32-33.
Startling Stories, 4, 189.
"Statement of Randolph Carter, The,"
  223.
"Steel," 240.
"Steel Cat, The," 17.
Steinbeck, John, 127.
Stevens, Francis, 9-11.
Stevens, Lawrence, 284.
Stevenson, Adlai, II, 173.
Stevenson, Robert Louis, 168.
Stirring Science Stories, 146.
"Stolen Centuries," 131.
"Stone Pillow, The," 78.
Stong, Phil, 4.
"Stop Watch, The," 207.
"Story of the Days to Come," 91.
Strand, K. Aa., 178.
"Strange High House in the Mist, The,"
  224.
"Stranger Station," 124, 125, 273, 276f.
Strauss, Richard, 157.
Stuart, Don A., 8f, 34-36.
Studio One, 278.
Sturgeon, Theodore, 8f, 114-116, 121,
  123, 125, 126, 127, 147, 149, 199,
  221, 222, 224, 226.
Sturgeon's Rule, 8, 127.
"Stutterer, The," 123.
"Summer People, The," 129.
Super Science Stories, 131, 150, 153,
  189, 193.
"Superiority," 189.
SURPRISED BY JOY, 267.
"Survival Kit," 194.
"Survival Ship," 120.
Swift, Jonathan, 2, 5-6.
Sykora, Will, 161.

SYNDIC, THE, 147.

Taine, John, 192.
TAKEOFF, 146-147, 148.
TALES FROM THE WHITE HART,
  190-191.
TARZAN, 167.
Ten Story Fantasy, 189.
"Ten-Story Jigsaw," 127.
Tenn, William, 120.
"Test, The," 239-240.
THAT HIDEOUS STRENGTH, 226.
"That Share of Glory," 148.
"They," 118.
"Thirteen O'Clock," 148.
Thirteenth World Science Fiction
  Convention, The, ix.
THIS FORTRESS WORLD, 258-259.
Thomas, Theodore L., 124, 125, 126,
  127, 267.
Thoreau, Henry, 95.
"Three Blind Mice," 250.
"Threshold," 129.
Thrill Book, The, 9.
Thrilling Wonder Stories, 108, 131,
  155, 163, 189.
Tiberius, 62.
TIGER! TIGER!, 234-236.
Tighe, Virginia, 216, 216f.
TIK-TOK OF OZ, 43.
Time, 96, 96f.
"Time and Time Again," 217.
TIME FOR THE STARS, 84-86.
"Time Locker," 140.
TIME MACHINE, THE," 35.
TIME TO COME, 129-130.
Time Traveller, The, 161.
TIMELINER, 97-98.
"To Here and the Easel," 121.
"To See Another Mountain," 194.
"To Serve Man," viii.
"Tomorrow and Tomorrow," 140-141.
TOMORROW PEOPLE, THE, 104-105.
TOMORROW, THE STARS, 117-121.
TOMORROW TIMES SEVEN, 193-194.
TOMORROW'S GIFT, 136-138.
"Tomorrow's Gift," 138.
Toombs, Alfred, 254-255.
Tors, Ivan, 101.
"Touch of Nutmeg Makes It, The," 15.
"Tourist Trade, The," 119.
"Transformer," 193.
TREASURE ISLAND, 82.
"Trespass," 239.

TRITONIAN RING, THE 19.
"Trouble With Water," 260.
Tubb, E. C., 122.
Tucker, Wilson (Bob), 119, 179-181.
TUNNEL IN THE SKY, 84-86.
Twain, Mark, 12, 80.
Twayne, 158, 248.
"Twilight," 35.
"Twink," 123.
*Two Complete Science Adventure
Books*, 153.
"Two-Handed Engine," 145.
"Typewriter in the Sky," 38-40.

ÜBERWINDUNG VON RAUM UND
ZEIT, 217-219.
"Uller Uprising," 248-249.
UNCLE TOM'S CABIN, 5.
UNDER THE TRIPLE SUNS, 12-13.
"Unhuman Sacrifice," 127.
Universal-International, 277.
"Universe," 32, 118, 245.
Unknown 38, 131, 144, 169, 221, 226,
259, 279.
"Unnameable, The," 223.
"Unseen Blushers, The," 6.
UNTOUCHED BY HUMAN HANDS, 237.
Unusual Stories, 161.
"Unwillingly to School," 127.

v. St. Whitelock, Otto, 131-132.
VALLEY BEYOND TIME, 213-215.
Vance, Jack, 139, 158, 197-198, 219.
VANGUARD FROM ALPHA, 243-244.
Vanguard Press, 67.
van Kampen, Karl, 247.
van Vogt, A. E., 2, 47-62, 85, 121, 140,
151, 154, 186, 203, 217, 218, 229,
236, 254.
"Variations on a Theme," 17.
"Veldt, The," 110.
Vernon, Roger Lee, 206-208.
Vidal, Gore, 175-176.
"Vintage Season," 144.
Vonnegut, Kurt, Jr., 119, 166-167,
236-237.
VOR, 155-156.

Wade, James, 223.
Wagner, Richard, 249.
WALDEN TWO, 174-175.
"Waldo," 5, 118.
"Wall of Darkness," 131.
"Wall of Fire, The," 131.

Wandrei, Donald, 224.
"Wapshot's Demon," 195.
WAR OF THE WORLDS, 275.
WAR WITH THE NEWTS, 11-12.
"Warm Dark Places," 221.
Waugh, Evelyn, 136.
"Way Home, A," 116.
"Way in the Middle of the Air," 111.
"Way of Thinking, A," 115.
Wayne, John, 102.
WE, 17-19, 171.
"Weakness of RVOG, The," 155.
"Weapon Shop" series, 58.
"Weapon Shop, The," 60.
"Weeblies, The," 219.
Weinbaum, Stanley G., 217.
Weird Tales, 19, 108, 112, 131, 158.
Weisinger, Mort, 161.
WELL OF THE UNICORN, 158.
Wells, H. G., 8, 35, 72, 91, 178, 179,
207, 252, 253, 276.
"Wer Da?," 218.
Werfel, Franz, 182.
Wessolowski, Hans, 284.
West, Jessamyn, 121-122, 176.
WEST OF THE SUN, 198-199.
Western Printing and Lithographing
Company, 95.
Weyl, Hermann, 76.
"What Thin Partitions," 131.
"What to Do Till the Analyst Comes,"
194.
WHEN WORLDS COLLIDE, 213, 245.
WHERE THE BLUE BEGINS, 274.
"Whirligig World," 178.
White, E. B., 129.
"White Goddess," 221.
"White Pinnacle, The," 130.
Whizzing Star Patrol, 228.
WHO?, 200-202.
WHO GOES THERE?, 35.
"Who Goes There?," 217.
"Why So Much Syzygy?," 115f.
"Wiedererweckung," 218.
Wiener, Norbert, 165.
Wiggins, Olon F., 162, 162f.
Wilkins, Vaughan, 213-215.
Williams, Robert Moore, 133f.
Williamson, Jack, 45-46, 58, 207, 258.
Wilson, Angus, 242.
Winchell, Walter, 277.
WIND IN THE WILLOWS, THE, 82.
Winston, 82.
"Wish, The," 129.

WITCHES THREE, 158.
"With These Hands," 148, 149.
"Wizard of Linn," 62.
Wodehouse, P. G., 191, 214.
WOLFBANE, 196-197.
Wolfe, Bernard, 164-165.
Wollheim, Donald A., 161, 162, 220.
Wonder Stories, 130, 131, 160.
"Word Edgewise," 78.
"Words of Guru, The," 146.
"Work of Art, A," 156, 157.
"World Is Mine, The," 139.
WORLD JONES MADE, THE, 230-231
WORLD OF Ā, THE, 47-58, 203.
"World of van Vogt, The," 47.
WORLD OF WONDER, 225.
Worlds Beyond, ix.

WORM OUROBOROS, THE, 197, 198.
Wylie, Dirk, 193.
Wyndham, John, 119, 147, 169, 178-179, 245-246, 252-254, 264.

"Xenophobia," 207.

YEAR OF CONSENT, 95-96, 232.
YOUR SINS AND MINE, 30-31, 237.

Zamiatin, Eugene, 17-19, 171, 172.
Ziff-Davis, 133f.
Zirul, Arthur, 127.
"Zorome" series, 153.